This book is a very useful milestone addition to our understanding of the evolution and future needs of research on goals, methods, and outcomes of education abroad. It ably directs attention to merging theory and practice which is key to further advances.

**John K. Hudzik**, Professor, Michigan State University, US

This crisp, accessible analysis of existing scholarship in the field of education abroad supports both seasoned education abroad practitioners and emerging scholars who seek rigorous research to inform education abroad programming and practice. With chapters co-authored by two or more authors who represent different geographical regions of the world, the book focuses on the most pressing challenges facing the field today, including curriculum integration, intercultural competency development, and access and opportunity for traditionally under-represented populations. This timely book is certain to benefit education abroad practitioners at all levels and to encourage scholars new to the field to investigate evolving trends and hot topics identified by the authors.

**Melissa Torres**, President, Forum on Education Abroad, US

This book truly encompasses a global treatment of the literature relevant to scholar-practitioners of education abroad around the world. All those interested in this area from beginners to seniors will find as much value and utility in this timely book. Education abroad is flourishing and diversifying but also has plenty of room for improvement. It is a crucial moment to analyze education abroad issues with a collective focus as this book does. This approach makes this book accessible to those scholars and practitioners who are interested in this area of research and are concerned about research to practice.

**Hiroshi Ota**, Professor, Hitotsubashi University, Japan

This book really provides an impressive overview on how organisational support and curricular frameworks can help students experience stimulating study periods abroad. The summary of available research results and discussions addressing a broad range of programmes of various lengths and modes in different regions of the world is valuable both as a basis for further analysis and as guide for practical improvement. Given the varied conditions and the different analytical perspectives underlying available publications, such a comprehensive account is timely.

**Ulrich Teichler**, Professor, University of Kassel, Germany

What will it take to make international a central part of higher education – and for everyone? *Education Abroad* brings home the nature of the challenge today and the complex drivers affecting tomorrow. The authors speak with a truly global perspective and offer lessons for us all.

**Allan Goodman**, President, Institute of International Education, US

This book is a well-put together piece of scholarly work. It collects a great blend of experts who make specific contributions to the emerging and growing field of international student mobility. Whereas it keeps an overview of the core issues that impact the trend, the chapters address the motivators that move individuals, institutions and communities to engage in mobility enhancing different dimensions of teaching, research and service among involved parties. All this is done with the student at the center of the debate. In addition, the co-authors discuss relevant and complex variables that interplay, opening new dimensions for further research with practical implications. Definitely a worth reading book!

**Gustavo Gregorutti**, Professor, Andrews University, US

Student mobility has become a significant feature of higher education throughout the world, including the Asia Pacific Region. Various new types of non-matriculated mobility model beyond traditional student exchange and short-term study programs. This book describes that greater diversification of non-matriculated programs has taken place within recent decades. Readers will learn how institutional strategies play critical roles in assuring success of students' learning.

**Shingo Ashizawa**, Professor, Toyo University, Japan

# Education Abroad

Recent decades have seen unprecedented growth in the number of students travelling abroad for the purpose of short-term academic study. As such, attention is turning to the role that education abroad can have in enhancing student learning and producing global-ready graduates. This volume provides a succinct and accessible analysis of the existing research and scholarship around the world on a range of important areas related to contemporary education abroad, providing practitioners with important implications for programming and practice.

Focusing on fourteen key topics relating to education abroad, this accessible desktop compendium not only synthesizes what is already known, but also indicates which topics need further research and how the existing literature can be applied to daily programming and practice. Extending beyond student learning outcomes to look at essential topics such as institutional outcomes, program models, and host community outcomes, this volume covers major trends in contemporary research as well as an assessment of the methodological and design challenges that are common to education abroad research. The fourteen distinct topics address the broad themes of participation, programming, student outcomes, institutional outcomes and societal outcomes, and include chapters from a broad range of widely acknowledged and respected international experts.

Bridging the gap between scholarship and practice, this accessible guide is essential reading for anyone working in higher education today and involved in shaping and managing education abroad programs. It is useful for all who want to understand and leverage existing research to inform education abroad programming and practice.

**Anthony C. Ogden** is the Associate Vice Provost for Global Engagement at the University of Wyoming, US.

**Bernhard Streitwieser** is an Assistant Professor of International Education and International Affairs, George Washington University Graduate School of Education and Human Development, US.

**Christof Van Mol** is an Assistant Professor of Sociology, Tilburg University, the Netherlands.

## Internationalization in Higher Education Series

*Series Editor*: Elspeth Jones, Emerita Professor, Leeds Beckett University, UK

This series addresses key themes in the development of internationalization within Higher Education. Up to the minute and international in both appeal and scope, books in the series focus on delivering contributions from a wide range of contexts and provide both theoretical perspectives and practical examples. Written by some of the leading experts in the field, they are vital guides that discuss and build upon evidence-based practice and provide a clear evaluation of outcomes.

Titles in the series:

For more information about this series, please visit: https://www.routledge.com/Internationalization-in-Higher-Education-Series/book-series/INTHE

# Education Abroad

Bridging Scholarship and Practice

Edited by
Anthony C. Ogden, Bernhard Streitwieser
and Christof Van Mol

Routledge
Taylor & Francis Group

LONDON AND NEW YORK

First published 2021
by Routledge
2 Park Square, Milton Park, Abingdon, Oxon OX14 4RN

and by Routledge
52 Vanderbilt Avenue, New York, NY 10017

*Routledge is an imprint of the Taylor & Francis Group, an informa business*

*British Library Cataloguing-in-Publication Data*
A catalogue record for this book is available from the British Library

*Library of Congress Cataloging-in-Publication Data*
A catalog record has been requested for this book

ISBN: 978-1-138-36427-1 (hbk)
ISBN: 978-1-138-36428-8 (pbk)
ISBN: 978-0-429-43146-3 (ebk)

Typeset in Galliard
by Taylor & Francis Books

# Contents

# Tables

# About the editors

**Anthony C. Ogden** is the associate vice provost for Global Engagement at the University of Wyoming. Ogden is a senior international educator with over twenty-five years of experience in international higher education. He has held positions related to international education with IES Abroad, The Pennsylvania State University, the University of Kentucky and Michigan State University. Ogden has written widely on topics related to education abroad research and his most recent book is *Education Abroad and the Undergraduate Experience: Critical Perspectives and Approaches to Integration with Student Learning and Development* (Stylus, 2019).

**Bernhard Streitwieser** is an assistant professor of International Education & International Affairs at the George Washington University Graduate School of Education and Human Development. His research looks comparatively at the impact of globalization on the internationalization of higher education with a focus on research on education abroad and international student exchange. He also conducts research on higher education access for underserved populations, focusing on refugees and at-risk migrants in Germany and the United States. Streitwieser's most recent book is *International Education's Scholar-practitioners: Bridging Research and Practice* (Symposium Books, 2016) with Anthony Ogden, and he is the author of more than fifty articles and book chapters. From 2010 to 2014 Streitwieser was a guest professor at the Humboldt University in Berlin, Germany, and before that a researcher and adjunct lecturer at Northwestern University.

**Christof Van Mol** is an assistant professor of Sociology at the Department of Sociology at Tilburg University, the Netherlands. Prior to joining Tilburg in 2017, he worked as a senior researcher at the Netherlands Interdisciplinary Demographic Institute (NIDI, the Netherlands) and the University of Antwerp (Belgium). His research interests are international migration processes, patterns and outcomes, with a specific focus on international student mobility. He has published extensively on international student mobility in leading journals including *Geoforum, Journal of Ethnic and Migration Studies*, and *Population, Space and Place*. His book on intra-European student mobility (Palgrave Macmillan, 2014) received the 2016 Best Book Prize in Sociology of Migration (RC31) of the International Sociological Association.

# About the contributors

**Michelle Barker** is professor of Business Strategy and Innovation, Griffith University. Previously a social worker in international development aid and refugee resettlement, Michelle achieved national recognition for teaching, winning the Australian Award for University Teaching (AAUT) 2005 Individual Teacher Award, and the 2003 Award for integration of the EXCELL Intercultural Skills Program in the curriculum. Michelle co-led the Internationalization at Home project implementing aspects of EXCELL in several Australian universities. Her extensive scholarly research publications are in intercultural skills development, internationalization of the curriculum, and expatriate adjustment.

**Jos Beelen** is a senior policy advisor for internationalization at the Amsterdam School of International Business and senior researcher at The Hague University of Applied Sciences. He is also Honorary Research Fellow at Coventry University and is affiliated to the Center for Higher Education Internationalization (CHEI) at Università Cattolica del Sacro Cuore, Milan. His research focuses on internationalization of learning outcomes in academic programs, particularly on developing the skills of academic staff that enable them to assume ownership of curriculum internationalization.

**Rachel Brooks** is a professor of Higher Education at University College London, and an executive editor of the *British Journal of Sociology of Education*. Her research focuses primarily on the sociology of higher education and she has conducted a wide range of projects in this area on, for example, international student mobility, young graduates and lifelong learning, the experiences of higher education students with dependent children, and the changing nature of students' unions.

**Santiago Castiello-Gutiérrez** is an international student and doctoral candidate at the Center for the Study of Higher Education (CSHE) at the University of Arizona. He is also the Mobility Programs Coordinator for the Consortium for North American Higher Education Collaboration (CONAHEC). His research interests are in internationalization of higher education, intercultural competence development and organization and administration of higher education institutions. He was recently distinguished as a 2019 recipient of the Harold Josephson Award for Professional Promise in International Education by the Association of International Education Administrators (AIEA).

**M. Luz Celaya** is an associate professor in Applied Linguistics in the Department of Modern Languages and Literatures and English Studies at the University of Barcelona (UB). She lectures on Second Language Acquisition, and her research interests include crosslinguistic influence and study abroad, Interlanguage Pragmatics, plurilingual education, and the use of foreign languages in the workplace. She is a member of the GRAL research group and has authored two books and several book chapters and articles published in key journals in the field of SLA.

**Hans de Wit** is Director of the Center for International Higher Education (CIHE) at Boston College. He has been Director of the Center for Higher Education Internationalization (CHEI) at the Università Cattolica del Sacro Cuore and Professor of Internationalization of Higher Education at the Amsterdam University of Applied Sciences. He is the Founding Editor of the *Journal of Studies in International Education* and Consulting Editor of the journal *Policy Reviews in Higher Education*. He is founding member of the European Association for International Education and Chair of the Board of Trustees of World Education Services.

**Neriko Musha Doerr** is an assistant professor at Ramapo College of New Jersey, U.S.A. Her research interests include study abroad experiences with special foci on politics of difference, language, and power, as well as politics of education in Japan, Aotearoa/New Zealand, and the United States. Her publications include *Transforming Study Abroad: A Handbook* (Berghahn, 2018) and *The Global Education Effect and Japan: Constructing New Borders and Identification Practices* (Routledge, 2020), and articles in journals such as *Anthropology and Education Quarterly* and *Identities: Global Studies in Culture*.

**Steve R. Entrich** is acting professor for inclusion and organizational development at the Department of Education, University of Potsdam. His research focuses on social inequality and gender disparities in educational attainment, determinants and effects of out-of-school/supplementary education (esp. private tutoring and study abroad), educational decision-making, education over the life course, and education policy analysis in Germany, Japan, the United States, and in cross-country comparison.

**Chris Glass** is an associate professor of Educational Foundations and Leadership and the Graduate Program Director of the Higher Education program at Old Dominion University in Norfolk, VA. He is the Senior Editor for the *Journal of International Students* and co-Editor of the Routledge Studies in Global Student Mobility book series. He is the recipient of the 2016 NAFSA Innovative Research in International Education award and author of International Student

Engagement (Stylus). His research focuses on social mobility, international students, and senior international officers.

**Nick J. Gozik** is Director of the Office of International Programs and the McGillycuddy-Logue Center for Undergraduate Global Studies at Boston College. Additionally, Gozik has held positions in education abroad at Duke University, New York University, and the University of Richmond. He has served as a visiting professor at New York University, as well as a lecturer at Boston College and Lesley University. Among a wide array of publications, he has most recently co-edited *Promoting Inclusion in Education Abroad: A Handbook of Research and Practice* (Stylus, 2018).

**Wendy Green** is a senior lecturer (adjunct) in the School of Education at the University of Tasmania. She is Executive Editor of the journal *Higher Education Research & Development* and past Convenor of the International Education Association of Australia's Network for Internationalization of the Curriculum. Wendy's research interests cover many aspects of international education, including the global mobility of staff and students, curriculum internationalization, and the experiences of international students.

**John P. Haupt** is a graduate student in the Doctor of Higher Education Program at the University of Arizona. He currently works as research associate responsible for assessing and evaluating UA's micro-campus initiative. His research focuses on issues in comparative and international higher education abroad related to student and faculty mobility, transnational higher education, and international research collaboration.

**Mark Holton** is a lecturer in Human Geography at the University of Plymouth. His research interests address the social and cultural geographies of higher education students and focuses on mobility, belonging and identity. Holton's publications have covered a range of topics, from mobilities and belonging in 21st-century higher education, to youth transitions, international student mobility and traditional or non-traditional student identities. He recently co-authored a book entitled *Everyday Mobile Belonging: Theorising Higher Education Student Mobilities* (Bloomsbury Academic, 2019).

**Martin Howard** is a researcher in Second Language Acquisition and Study Abroad at University College Cork (Ireland). He is founding Editor of the journal *Study Abroad Research in Second Language Acquisition and International Education*, and Chair of the transnational COST Action, "Study Abroad Research in European Perspective" (SAREP). He is President of the Association for French Language Studies and has previously served as Vice President of the European Second Language Association (EuroSLA). Recent publications include *Study Abroad, Second Language Acquisition and Interculturality* (Multilingual Matters, 2019).

**Jeroen Huisman** is professor of Higher Education, Center for Higher Education Governance Ghent, Ghent University, Belgium. His research focuses on higher education governance and policy. He is interested in the themes of quality assurance, internationalization and organizational identity. He is editor of *Higher Education Policy* and co-editor of *Theory and Method in Higher Education* (Emerald) and of the SRHE book series (Routledge). He previously worked at the Center for Higher Education Policy Studies, University of Twente, the Netherlands (1991–2005) and the University of Bath, UK (2005–2013).

**Jane Jackson** is professor of Applied Linguistics in the English Department at the Chinese University of Hong Kong. Her research centers on education abroad, intercultural communication, language and identity, eLearning, and internationalization. Recent books include *Intercultural Interventions in Study Abroad* (Routledge, 2017), *Interculturality in Study Abroad* (Routledge, 2017), *Introducing Language and Intercultural Communication* (Routledge, 2014), and *The Routledge Handbook of Language and Intercultural Communication* (Routledge, 2012). She also wrote *Intercultural Journeys: From Study to Residence Abroad* (Palgrave Macmillan, 2010) and *Language, Identity, and Study Abroad: Sociocultural Perspectives* (Equinox, 2008).

**Uichi Kamiyoshi** is an associate professor at Musashino University in Japan. His research interests include Japanese language learning through critical pedagogy and language policies for immigrants in Japan. He currently serves as the Vice President of The Society for Teaching Japanese as a Foreign Language, as a member of the Japanese Language Educational Issue Subcommittee, the Japanese Language Subdivision of Council for Cultural Affairs (a government agency), and as the advisor for the Start-up Program for Community Japanese Language Education for Council for Cultural Affairs.

**Daniel Klasik** is an assistant professor in the School of Education at the University of North Carolina at Chapel Hill. Klasik has over a decade of experience studying student pathways into and through post-secondary education in the U.S. higher education context. His work can be found in a wide variety of education and policy journals, and in 2016 he was recognized as a NAEd/Spencer Foundation Postdoctoral Fellow for his work trying to better understand students' college application behavior.

**Betty Leask** is an internationally recognized scholar who has researched and published extensively on the internationalization of higher education curricula, teaching and learning, and its facilitation through academic leadership and university strategy. She is Editor-in Chief of the *Journal of Studies in International Education*, the leading journal in the field, visiting professor at the Center for International Higher Education at Boston College, and honorary visiting researcher at the Center for Higher Education Internationalization, Universita Cattolica del Sacre Cuore in Milan.

**John S. Lucas** is President and CEO of International Student Exchange Programs (ISEP). Prior to joining ISEP, Lucas served in several higher education roles, including Provost and Executive Vice President at the School for International Training, and Associate Vice President of Academic Programs at IES Abroad. Lucas worked in Spain for more than ten years as a faculty member and program director for CIEE and Portland State University. Lucas serves on the Board of the Forum on Education Abroad and the President's Advisory Council of World Learning and is active in scholarship on Spanish language, education abroad, and intercultural communication.

**Cheryl Matherly** is Vice President and Vice Provost for International Affairs at Lehigh University, where she has responsibility for the strategic leadership of the university's portfolio of international education programs. Dr. Matherly's research has focused on the impact of education abroad on the development of students' global competencies, especially as related to issues of employability. She has received four National Science Foundation grants to specifically examine the impact of international experiences on learning outcomes for students in STEM fields.

**Joshua S. McKeown** is associate provost for International Education & Programs at SUNY Oswego, and International Education Leadership Fellow at the University at Albany. McKeown authored *The First Time Effect* (SUNY Press, 2009) and has contributed numerous articles and presentations to the field of international education worldwide. He was a Fulbright IEA participant to India, a mentor with the IIE's Connecting with the World Myanmar program, and has served professional organizations including the Forum on Education Abroad.

**Darin Menlove** is Director of Study Abroad at the University of California, Berkeley. Menlove joined UC Berkeley in 2006. With roles in Berkeley Summer Sessions and Berkeley Study Abroad, he oversees advising, the development of summer study abroad programs, and a Summer Sessions partnership program for over one hundred institutions throughout the world. Menlove has more than twenty-five years' experience in international education administration, including eleven years in Russia as resident director of three different study abroad programs.

**Kate Moore** is Vice President of the Academic Internship Council. She also serves on the NAFSA Education Abroad Knowledge Community as Programs & Resources Coordinator, chairs the NAFSA Work, Internship, Volunteering, and Research Abroad (WIVRA) Subcommittee and is content committee co-chair for the Global Internship Conference. Moore has been curriculum dean and served as lead content contributor for the NAFSA Core Education Program Workshop on Internships, Service-Learning, and Research Abroad.

**Nicolai Netz** studied modern languages, cultural science, political science, and economics at the Universities of Bonn, Florence and Maastricht. Since 2008, he has worked at the German Centre for Higher Education Research and Science Studies (DZHW), where he examines the educational and professional careers of students and graduates. He is currently leading a junior research group exploring the determinants and effects of high-skilled mobility. He has extensively worked on various aspects of study abroad.

**Susan Oguro** is an associate professor in International Education in the Faculty of Arts and Sciences at the University of Technology Sydney. She teaches courses and supervises research students in the areas of intercultural communication, languages education and Swiss studies. Oguro's research interests include intercultural education; foreign languages curriculum and policy; and human rights education. Her most recent publication is an edited book *Intercultural Interventions in Study Abroad*, co-edited with Jane Jackson and published in 2018 by Routledge in their Internationalization in Higher Education series.

**Rebecca Pisano** serves as associate dean for international and off-campus study at Stevenson University, where she manages all aspects of study abroad programming, including international and off-campus faculty-directed courses and affiliate programs. Pisano spent extended time in Spain, Poland, Mexico, Paraguay and Ecuador, and has sailed through Southeast Asia and her passion for global learning began with a semester abroad in Seville, Spain as an undergraduate.

**David Puente** is Regional Vice President for Academic Affairs in Granada, Spain for WorldStrides/ISA. He joined ISA in 2003 after completing graduate study in Comparative Literature. Since that time his responsibilities have evolved from leading student groups in Spain to working with resident staff throughout Europe to improve co-curricular programming and maximize student learning abroad. David is a member of several professional organizations and has presented at conferences in Europe and the U.S. on a range of topics.

**John W. Schwieter** is professor of Spanish and Linguistics at Wilfrid Laurier University, Canada, where he is Director of the Language Acquisition, Multilingualism, and Cognition Laboratory. He is Executive Editor of the book series Bilingual Processing and Acquisition and Co-Editor of the hybrid-focus series Cambridge Elements in Second Language Acquisition. His most recent books include *The Cambridge Handbook of Language Learning* (Cambridge University Press, 2019), *The Handbook of the Neuroscience of Multilingualism* (Wiley-Blackwell, 2019), and *Proficiency Predictors in Sequential Bilinguals* (Cambridge University Press, 2019).

**Ravinder Sidhu** is an associate professor at the School of Education, University of Queensland (Australia). Her research interests are in the areas of sociology of higher education and postcolonial studies of globalization with a focus on

Southeast Asia. Prior to joining the academy, she worked in development assistance and as an advisor to international students.

**Martin Tillman** is a respected author and thought leader on employability and education abroad. As President of Global Career Compass, an international consulting practice, his publications focus on the linkage of education abroad experiences to student career development and employability. He is the former Associate Director of Career Services (ret.) at the Johns Hopkins University Paul H. Nitze School of Advanced International Studies in Washington, D.C. In his forty-year career as an international educator, he has held senior leadership positions with pioneering international education programs.

**Adinda van Gaalen** is senior policy officer at Nuffic. Her interests are in the areas of internationalization strategies, policy development, ethics and intercultural competences. Adinda is both an advisor to the board of Nuffic and an advisor to HE institutions in developing internationalization strategies. She also works as a researcher, trainer and auditor. Previously Adinda worked at the Amsterdam UAS. She was a 2014–2016 elected member of the General Council of EAIE.

**Heather H. Ward** joined the University of North Carolina at Chapel Hill in 2019 as associate dean for study abroad and international exchanges. Previously, she was associate director for internationalization and global engagement at the American Council on Education, where she developed programs and resources to support the internationalization of higher education institutions and strengthen global collaboration. Ward has also served as associate director for internationalization and outreach at George Mason University and director of international programs at Mary Baldwin University.

**Johanna Waters** is a reader in Human Geography and Migration Studies at University College London. Previously she taught at the universities of Oxford, Birmingham and Liverpool. She specializes in migration, transnationalism and international education and is focused, largely, on East Asia and on trans-Pacific educational mobilities. Her most recent publications include *Materialities and Mobilities in Education* (Routledge, 2017) and "Education unbound? Enlivening debates with a mobilities perspective on learning," *Progress in Human Geography* (2016). She is co-editor of the journal *Migration and Society*.

**Craig Whitsed** is discipline lead Education and Pedagogy and senior lecturer at Curtin University. He is Co-Executive Editor of the journal *Higher Education Research and Development* (*HERD*). He is also visiting research scholar, School of Management Research Institute, Faculty of Economics and Business, University of Groningen, Netherlands. His research focuses on academic staff engagement in higher education internationalization and internationalization of the curriculum.

**Jannecke Wiers-Jenssen** is an associate professor at the Center for the study of Profession at Oslo Metropolitan University and also has a part-time position at the Nordic Institute for Studies in Innovation, Research and Education (NIFU). Wiers-Jenssen has a long career in higher education research. International student mobility and internationalization, transition from higher education to work and higher education policy are among her fields of interest. These fields have been combined in several studies of labor market effects of higher education, with a particular focus on the Nordic region.

**Christopher Ziguras** is a professor in the School of Global, Urban and Social Studies at the Royal Melbourne Institute of Technology. His research explores varied aspects of the globalization of education, particularly the ways in which regulatory agencies, markets, education providers and other actors shape cross-border provision of higher education. His latest book is *Governing Cross-Border Higher Education* (Routledge, 2015). Ziguras teaches in RMIT's international development and public policy programs and has led the expansion of learning abroad programs in the university's social science programs.

# Foreword to the series
# Internationalization in Higher Education

This series addresses the rapidly changing and highly topical field of internationalization in higher education. Increasingly visible in institutional strategies as well as national, regional and international agendas since the latter part of the twentieth century internationalization has, in all its forms, been informed by diverse disciplines but continues to vary in interpretation. In part its rise can be seen as a response to globalization and growing competition among higher education institutions. Indeed, use of the term "internationalization" itself is not uncontested, particularly when interpreted as neo-liberal, Anglophone or post-colonial in orientation.

There are compelling drivers for university leaders to adopt an integrated approach to internationalization. Intensifying competition for talent, changes in global student flows, international branch campuses and growing complexity in cross-border activity, along with the rising influence of institutional rankings, all provide economic impetus and reputational consequences of success or failure. However, interest in more values-driven rationales is increasingly evident, in part recognizing the need to prepare students for changing local as well as global environments in both personal and professional life.

Student demand for international and intercultural experiences reflects growing employer interest in the knowledge, skills, attitudes and competencies which can result from these experiences. University leadership, academics and support staff must respond accordingly, with programs and activities appropriate to societal change and a complex global landscape. Internationally informed research and collaborative partnerships can support teaching and learning processes which will help develop skills relevant for global contexts but which are equally important for living and working in diverse multicultural societies. Internationalization thus has both global and more local intercultural interests at its heart.

Internationalization as a powerful force for change and the enhancement of quality is an underlying theme of this series. It addresses the complex and varied topics arising as internationalization continues to develop and grow. The series aims to reflect current concerns, with volumes written or edited by leading thinkers and authors from around the world, while giving a voice to emerging researchers. It examines some of the critical contemporary issues in the field of internationalization, and offers theoretical perspectives with practical applications for higher education leaders, academics and practitioners alike.

This volume in the series addresses one of the most common dimensions of internationalization strategies in higher education – for governments as well as providers – education undertaken abroad which contributes to degree requirements at the home institution. In some contexts this is known as "study abroad" or "credit mobility," in contrast to "degree mobility," where the student's whole program takes place in another country.

Increasing numbers of institutions globally are focusing on offering international experiences to enhance students' international and intercultural competencies or to produce "global-ready" graduates. This has led to rising scholarly interest in identifying the true, "objective," value and outcomes of such programs for students and for their future personal and professional lives. It is no longer enough to make assumptions about the benefits of simply participating in education abroad – there is growing demand for appropriate empirical scientific evidence to corroborate these claims.

The increase in student participation has also led to research which may help enhance practice within institutions, in terms of program development and design, to ensure that the potential benefits for students are maximized. Integration of education abroad within curricula, including learning and teaching processes, has been a further focus, along with an emphasis on how students who have not taken part can also benefit.

*Education Abroad: Bridging Scholarship and Practice* pulls together these strands and provides a critical analysis of existing research and scholarship on key topics in education abroad, from experts in different global contexts. It aims to support practitioners and emerging scholars in enhancing all aspects of education abroad design, delivery and evaluation. This timely and important publication will inform future research and be a valuable resource for those who wish to orient themselves in the field or develop their own practice for the benefit of students.

Elspeth Jones, Series Editor
Emerita Professor of the Internationalisation of Higher Education
Leeds Beckett University, UK

# Acknowledgements

For years, we have argued that it is simply not acceptable for international education practitioners to make assertions of the value and benefit of education abroad programming without offering empirical scientific evidence to support such claims. As education abroad programming continues to grow and expand around the world, we believe that it will be ever more important for practitioners to readily challenge untested claims, avoid casual assumptions, and become more adept at utilizing research and scholarship to inform day-to-day practice and decision-making. Fortunately, research and scholarship in this area has become increasingly robust and sophisticated in recent years and today, we know more about the totality of the education abroad experience than ever before. This rapidly expanding body of literature, however, can be overwhelming and confusing to new professionals and emerging scholars. Thus, we determined from the outset of this project to produce a publication that would serve as a much-needed, desk-top reference that could provide readers with a succinct and critical analysis of the existing research and scholarship to date, and also shed light on its implications for contemporary education abroad programming and practice going forward.

Although there are a number of well-received publications focusing on a wide range of education abroad topics, the vast majority are country-specific and offer little in the way of presenting a synthesis of how the current global research and scholarship potentially informs education abroad programming and practice. Thus, to ensure broad reference to the global literature, we sought diverse authorship among well-respected and highly acknowledged experts from around the world. This volume would not have been possible without the knowledge, keen insights and varied experiences of these contributing authors. We are immensely grateful for their hard work, perseverance and infinite patience with us and are indebted and humbled by their dedication to advancing the field and practice of international higher education. Moreover, all chapters have been externally peer-reviewed by international education experts from around the world, themselves all notable scholars whose work focuses on education abroad research. We extend our sincere appreciation to each of the following individuals who expertly served as chapter peer reviewers:

Louis M. Berends, Ph.D., Syracuse University, USA
Elizabeth Brewer, Ph.D., Beloit College, USA
Rajika Bhandari, Ph.D., Institute of International Education, USA
Paige Butler, Ph.D., Middlebury Institute of International Studies at Monterey, USA
Lisa Chieffo, Ph.D., University of Delaware, USA
Lisa Childress, Ph.D., Global Education Consultant, USA
Rahul Choudaha, Ph.D., Study Portals, Netherlands
Giorgio Di Pietro, Ph.D., University of Westminster, United Kingdom
Stephanie Doyle, Ph.D., Victoria University of Wellington, New Zealand
Anita Gopal, Ph.D., George Washington University, USA
Eric Hartman, Ph.D., Haverford College, USA
Atsushi Hasegawa, Ph.D., University of Hawai'i, Mañoa, USA
Margaret Heisel, Ph.D., University of California, Berkeley, USA
Min Hong, Ph.D., University of Queensland, Australia
John Hudzik, Ph.D., Michigan State University, USA
Hilary Kahn, Ph.D., Indiana University, USA
Celeste Kinginger, Ph.D, The Pennsylvania State University, USA
Ross Lewin, Ph.D., University of Maryland, USA
Gregory Light, Ph.D., Northwestern University, USA
John Lucas, Ph.D., International Student Exchange Program, USA
Adriana Medina-López-Portillo, Ph.D., Global Education Consultant, USA
Kelly Carter Merrill, Ph.D., University of Richmond, USA
Nicolai Netz, Ph.D., German Center for Higher Education Research and Science Studies, Germany
Brendan O'Farrell, Ph.D., University of Kentucky, USA
Davina Potts, Ph.D., The University of Melbourne, Australia
Don Rubin, Ph.D., University of Georgia, USA
Manuel Souto-Otero, D.Phil., Cardiff University, United Kingdom
Ulrich Teichler, Ph.D., Universität Kassel, Germany
Leasa Weimar, Ph.D., University of Jyväskylä, Finland
Michal Woolf, Ph.D., CAPA Study Abroad, United Kingdom

We would also like to sincerely thank series editor Professor Elspeth Jones whose leadership, guidance, and encouragement helped to make this edited volume possible. Earlier on, we were gently reminded by Elspeth of the importance of providing a comprehensive treatment of the topic in its global context while striving to retain the simplicity and accessibility necessary for active utilization by practitioners and emerging scholars throughout the world. As knowledgeable and experienced international scholar-practitioners, we were quite confident and yet, as we moved forward with the project, we each realized quickly that our understanding of international higher education has largely been filtered by our own respective national contexts and that we still have much to learn. Education abroad is understood differently around the world and no doubt, editing this volume required continuous discussion and negotiation with our contributing authors around some of the central ideas and concepts we once thought were universally accepted and understood. While we have striven to provide a global "research to practice" orientation with this volume, we also understand that each chapter has been largely framed by the existing research and that the implications we note may not uniformly apply across all national and institutional contexts. This is the nature of the fluid and evolving phenomenon of international education we are studying.

Finally, we would like to acknowledge and express our gratitude to our respective families. Anthony would like to thank his partner Takashi for his patience, support and encouragement. Bernhard would like to thank his wife Mary Beth and his children Max and Lena for their infinite patience and support. Christof would like to thank his wife Ine, and his children Lars, Miró and Kobe for their support, allowing for example Skype calls at inconvenient hours due to the time zone differences between the three editors. Admittedly, writing this book together also involved constructive, pleasant and joyful conversations between the three of us. Lastly, we wish to thank our colleagues, whose unwavering support, encouragement and patience made this project manageable and in the end achievable.

# Glossary

The following is a selection of terms used in specific ways in this edited volume and may deviate from meanings they may denote in specific national or educational contexts. While the definitions reflect the understanding of the editors and are provided as a useful reference, chapter authors may have used these terms in different ways.

**Curriculum integration**. Curriculum integration is conceptualized as a continuum, from "exclusive integration," which maximizes international and intercultural learning of the minority of students undertaking optional education abroad experiences, to "inclusive integration," which integrates mobile students' international experiences and intercultural learning into the curriculum at home for the benefit of all students (see Chapter 11).

**Education abroad**. An encompassing term used to reflect the broad range of experience types associated with outbound educational mobility. It is understood as education that occurs outside a student's home country, and includes study abroad, undergraduate research abroad, international internships, global service-learning, and other program modes as long as these programs are driven to a significant degree by learning goals. This volume focusing specifically on education abroad programming that occurs during post-secondary education whereby students earn credit abroad that is utilized to fulfill home institution degree requirements.

**Faculty-directed program**. An education abroad program, also commonly referred to as "faculty-led" wherein one or more home campus faculty members accompany a cohort of students abroad and generally teach or co-teach home institution courses. These programs are typically discipline-specific and short-term (less than eight weeks), although variations may include semester-length programs and residential courses that embed an international study abroad component.

**Faculty engagement**. Faculty engagement in education abroad is complex and multifaceted with cognitive, emotional and behavioral dimensions. Some forms of engagement will be less apparent than others, but all will be based on a commitment to the learning possibilities education abroad offers to students and faculty (see Chapter 12).

**Internationalization at home**. Efforts to internationalize an institution's home campus so that all students are exposed to international and intercultural learning without leaving the home campus (see Chapter 11).

**Internationalization**. "The intentional process of integrating an international, intercultural or global dimension into the purpose, functions and delivery of post-secondary education, in order to enhance the quality of education and research" (see de Wit, Hunter, Howard & Egron-Polak, 2015).

**Program provider**. An institution or organization that offers education abroad program services to students from a variety of institutions. A program provider may be a college or university, a nonprofit organization, a for-profit business, or a consortium. Providers offer a wide range of education abroad programs, from center-based programming and direct enrollment in a foreign institution to international internships and global service-learning.

**Race and ethnicity**. Race generally refers to shared physical characteristics, nationality and religion of individuals, whereas ethnicity refers to a common cultural identity based on ancestry, language or culture. Social scientists often refer to ethnicity rather than race when discussing a nexus of behaviors shared by a particular group of people (Keister & Southgate, 2012, p. 281), but there is regional variation in the use and meanings of both terms. In line with classical sociological work, and for the purposes of this volume, race/ethnicity is considered a socially constructed concept.

**Scholar-Practitioner**. Practitioners are predominantly viewed as those who work in a profession, while scholars are often viewed as those who work in an academic field conducting research and publishing scholarly reflections. Engaged in both kinds of activity, scholar-practitioners of international higher education engage in the research process and use and disseminate their knowledge and information in the form of concepts, procedures, processes, and skills for the benefit of practitioners. They understand that professional and scholarly success is closely tied to the ability to effectively identify, access, and utilize research and scholarship to inform practice (see Streitwieser & Ogden, 2016).

**Study abroad**. In this volume, study abroad is understood as a distinct subtype of education abroad that results in progress toward an academic degree at a student's home institutions and excludes the pursuit of an academic degree at a foreign institution. Students generally enroll in traditional classroom-based coursework. Academic credit is awarded via the host institution or via the home institution. "Studying abroad" is used as an action verb inclusive of all education abroad experience types.

## References

de Wit, H., Hunter, F., Howard, L., & Egron-Polak, E. (2015). *Internationalisation of higher education*. Brussels: Policy Department B: Structural Cohesion Policies, European Parliament. Retrieved from http://www.europarl.europa.eu/RegData/etudes/STUD/2015/540370/IPOL_STU(2015)540370_EN.pdf

Keister, L. A., & Southgate, D. E. (2012). *Inequality: A contemporary approach to race, class, and gender*. Cambridge and New York: Cambridge University Press.

Streitwieser, B., & Ogden, A. (Eds.) (2016). *International higher education's scholar-practitioners*. Bridging research and practice. Oxford: Symposium Books.

# Framing education abroad within an international context

## A note on terminology

Education abroad has been discussed around the world using numerous terms, including "learning abroad," "study abroad," "mobility," "exchange," and so on. In the U.S., for example, the traditional term "junior year abroad" was long used in reference to those who participate in academic year programs abroad as part of undergraduate education. As education abroad enrollment patterns shifted over time in the U.S., the term "study abroad" emerged but even that term is now gradually being replaced by the more encompassing term, "education abroad." Today, the Forum on Education Abroad – a U.S.-based professional association – defines "education abroad" as "education that occurs outside the participant's home country. Besides study abroad, examples include such international experiences as work, volunteering, non-credit internships, and directed travel, as long as these programs are driven to a significant degree by learning goals" (Forum on Education Abroad, 2019; Peterson et al, 2007). In Australia, the term "learning abroad" is generally used to refer to outbound educational mobility, and like in the U.S., the term refers to "short-term (generally less than one year) international education experiences undertaken as part of an Australian university degree" (Harrison & Potts, 2016, p. 4). However, the terms "exchange" or "study abroad" generally refer to inbound student mobility to Australia. In Europe, where the European Commission's Erasmus+ Programme dominates regional educational mobility, the terms "international student mobility," "international student exchanges," and "study abroad" are most frequently used to refer to temporary learning and/or professional experiences in another country. In Japan, the term "ryugaku" or exchange is generally used to refer to all forms of international educational mobility, degree-seeking or otherwise (see Chapter 8). In the global literature, the term "study abroad" appears to be the most commonly used term. Given these different denominations of temporary stays abroad across the world, it is necessary to clarify our choice of the term for education abroad at the beginning of this volume.

We choose "education abroad" over other terms noted above to reflect the broad range of experience types that are associated with outbound educational mobility across the globe, which include study abroad. In this volume, "study abroad" is therefore understood as a distinct subtype of education abroad that results in progress toward an academic degree at a student's home institution and excludes degree-seeking studies at a foreign institution. Other experience types most commonly referenced in this volume include *undergraduate research abroad, global service-learning*, and *international internships*. Undergraduate research abroad programming, for example, allows students to conduct supervised research abroad in their target disciplines, usually for academic credit. Opposed to stand-alone service or volunteer-focused programming, global service-learning generally offers structured service in international host communities coupled with reflection for academic credit (Hartman & Kiely, 2014; Ogden & Hartman, 2019). International internships have proliferated around the world in response to growing student demand for internationally oriented skills and knowledge that may potentially enhance their effectiveness in navigating a globalizing workforce. Although this volume utilizes the more encompassing term "education abroad," "studying abroad" is used throughout as an action verb that is inclusive of all experience types.

The growth and expansion of education abroad over the years has also led to the diversification of the primary modes of educational mobility. This volume references the most popular modes, namely reciprocal student exchanges, provider programs, and faculty-directed programs, although all modes are not utilized throughout the world (Ogden & Brewer, 2019). Reciprocal student exchange programs have a long history in international higher education, often including both bilateral and multilateral exchanges, where students pay tuition at their home institution (if applicable) but attend an exchange partner institution for a delineated period of time. Over the past decades, there has been a global proliferation of for-profit and non-profit organizations that offer education abroad programs and services to students. Referenced herein as "provider programs," these organizations offer a wide range of education abroad programs, from center-based programming to direct enrollment in a foreign institution. An increasingly popular mode of education abroad, particularly in the U.S. and referenced in this volume, are faculty-directed programs (also commonly referred to as "faculty-led" and in some cases even as "island programs") wherein home-campus faculty and other teaching staff accompany cohorts of students abroad and teach courses that are also offered in the home institution. Although these programs are typically discipline-specific, short-term, and offered during the calendar breaks (Chieffo & Spaeth, 2018), variations are emerging (e.g., semester-length faculty-directed programs, and residential courses that embedded an international travel component).

Finally, due to the differences in national higher education systems, it is important to note that this volume focuses specifically on education abroad programming that takes place during post-secondary education in which students earn credit abroad in fulfillment of home institution degree requirements. When appropriate, distinct chapters draw upon international comparisons of terminology.

## References

Chieffo, L., & Spaeth, K. (Eds.) (2018). *The guide to successful short-term programs abroad.* 3rd Edition. Washington, DC: NAFSA: Association of International Educators.

Forum on Education Abroad (2019). *Education abroad glossary.* Carlisle, PA: The Forum on Education Abroad. Retrieved October 12, 2019 from https://forumea.org/resources/glossary/

Harrison, L., & Potts, D. (2016). Learning abroad at Australian universities: The current environment. International Education Association of Australia. Retrieved October 12, 2019 from www.ieaa.org.au/documents/item/752

Hartman, E. & Kiely, R. (2014). A critical global citizenship. In M. Johnson and P.M. Green (Eds.), *Crossing boundaries: Tension and transformation in international service learning.* Sterling, VA: Stylus Publishing.

Ogden, A. , & Brewer, E. (2019). U.S. education abroad: Historical perspectives, emerging trends, and changing narratives. In E. Brewer & A. Ogden (Eds.), *Critical perspectives on integrating education abroad into undergraduate education.* Sterling, VA: Stylus Publishing.

Ogden, A., & Hartman, E. (2019). To hell and back with good intentions: Global service-learning in the shadow of Ivan Illich. In A. Paczynska & S. Hirsch (Eds.), *Conflict zone, comfort zone: Ethics, pedagogy, and effecting change in field-based courses.* Athens: Ohio University Press.

Peterson, C., Engle, L., Kenney, L., Kreutzer, K., Nolting, W., & Ogden, A. (2007). *Education abroad glossary.* Carlisle, PA: The Forum on Education Abroad.

# Introduction and brief overview of research in education abroad

*Anthony C. Ogden, Bernhard Streitwieser and Christof Van Mol*

Recent decades have seen unprecedented growth in the number of students traveling abroad for the purpose of short-term academic study. In the United States, for example, nearly 333,000 students participated in education abroad programming in 2016–17, allowing them to earn academic credit in fulfillment of home institution degree requirements (IIE, 2018). During that same academic year, approximately 49,000 students from Australian universities studied abroad as part of their degree programs (AUIDF, 2017). Since the establishment of the Erasmus Programme thirty years ago, more than 4 million individuals have gone abroad within the framework of that exchange program within Europe. Asian nations such as Japan, Singapore, Taiwan and Korea have similarly sought to increase education abroad programming through governmental policies and related initiatives (Dall'Alba-Alba & Sidhu, 2015). This edited volume focuses specifically on this type of international student mobility, or non-degree education abroad programming that occurs during post-secondary education whereby students earn credit abroad that is utilized in fulfillment of home institution degree requirements.

Across the world, education abroad is a high priority of governments and higher education institutions' internationalization efforts (Knight, 2012). Consequently, practitioners are interested in the role of education abroad in enhancing, for example, student learning and the production of graduates with global skills (Haupt & Ogden, 2019). Furthermore, this attention has also sparked growing scholarly interest in understanding and documenting the determinants, experiences and outcomes of education abroad. Today, scholars in different disciplines around the world are actively pursuing rigorous research agendas with the aim of providing a better understanding of the totality of the education abroad experience. Similarly, institutional leaders and other stakeholders have grown more insistent in their demands for a vibrant and critical discourse that challenges and scrutinizes long-held claims and assumptions about the value and benefit of education abroad programming. The subsequent expansion of scholarly literature on education abroad in different fields in recent years, although much needed, can be potentially overwhelming and confusing to new professionals and emerging scholars. Thus, the central purpose of this volume is to provide a succinct and accessible analysis of the existing research and scholarship around the world on a range of important areas related to contemporary education abroad. As such, this volume can guide further study in these areas and provide practitioners with important implications for programming and practice drawn from a comprehensive overview of the global literature.

## Orientation to research in international education

As internationalization has become an undeniable force that is impacting the expectations of higher education institutions and educational delivery around the world, scholarly research on international education, broadly defined, has not surprisingly become more central to research agendas. According to Dolby and Rahman (2008), six distinct approaches to research on international education have emerged over time, namely:

1  comparative and international education;
2  globalization of education;
3  international schools;
4  international research on teaching and teacher education;
5  internationalization of K-12 education; and,
6  internationalization of higher education.

It is with the later approach that this volume is primarily concerned. Research on the *internationalization of higher education* itself is broad and may arguably be further subdivided into distinct but reinforcing lines of scholarly inquiry. These lines of research include:

1  internationalization;
2  international higher education;
3  comprehensive internationalization;
4  comparative higher education;
5  disciplinary internationalization; and,
6  international student mobility.

Scholarship on *internationalization* largely examines the conceptual frameworks underpinning the notion of internationalization and analyzes the meaning, definition and rationales associated with it within the context of higher education (Knight, 2004). Similarly, research on *international higher education* focuses primarily on the study of how institutions around the world respond to diverse internationalization forces shaping higher educational delivery and engagement (Altbach & Knight, 2007). The more applied concept of *comprehensive internationalization* has been the focus of considerable discussion among scholar-practitioners of international higher education about both its meaning and application to higher educational contexts (Hudzik, 2014). This line of inquiry has increasingly examined approaches to the internationalization of the curriculum and to internationalization at home (Leask,

2015; see Chapter 11). *Comparative higher education* examines higher educational policies, systems and structures around the world relative to each other (Streit-wieser, Le & Rust, 2012; Streitwieser, 2014) and *disciplinary internationalization* focuses primarily on the internationalization of particular disciplines and their curricula (Green & Whitsed, 2015). Of central focus to this volume is the line of scholarly inquiry focused on *international student mobility*, also sometimes refer-enced as academic mobility. This area of research is primarily concerned with the determinants, experiences and outcomes of global student flows (de Wit, Elmahdy Said, Sehoole & Sirozi, 2008; de Wit, Gacel-Ávila, Jones & Jooste, 2017). Non-degree education abroad programming, the focus of this volume, has emerged as a distinct line of inquiry within the growing body of research focused on interna-tional student mobility.

## Brief overview of education abroad research

In recent years, research on education abroad has increased substantially around the world, although much of the research activity appears to be concentrated in North America, Europe and Australia. There have been several recent publications that have documented the overall growth and expansion of this body of research and most acknowledge that scholarship has become increasingly complex and sophisticated over time (Bedenlier, Kondakci & Zawacki-Richter, 2018; Isabelli-Garcia & Isabelli, 2020; Lewin, 2009; Ogden, 2017; Pisarevskaya, 2019; Velliaris & Coleman-George, 2016). Much of earlier research in this area focused primarily on demonstrating the acquisition of knowledge or skills while abroad. In parti-cular, many of these earlier studies focused on intercultural competence (e.g., Anquetil, 2006; Behrnd & Porzelt, 2012; Deardorff, 2006; Gu et al., 2010) and second language acquisition (e.g., Magnan & Back 2007; Kinginger, 2011; Yager, 1998) and still, there is much research being done in this area (Kinginger, 2009; Isabelli-Garcia & Isabelli, 2020). Over time, areas of inquiry expanded to look at a wider variety of outcomes, including student learning and development labor market outcomes, and so on. Increasingly influential is the emerging research focused on understanding institutional outcomes associated with education abroad programming, such as how participation impacts student retention and persistence, alumni loyalty, employability and so on. This area of research is especially important to institutional leaders and other stakeholders who are seeking compelling evidence to support continued institutional investment in education abroad programming. Still, there have been only few longitudinal studies on the impact of education abroad participation over a lifetime (Dwyer, 2004: Paige, Stallman & Josić, 2008).

Although research on education abroad is developing at fast pace, the field is still regularly undermined by common and often serious methodological and conceptual shortcomings. Much research remains predominantly institution-specific and small scale, in the sense that much research is based on limited sample sizes, qualitative by design, and has limited generalizability. Furthermore, there is widespread utilization of self-reported surveys and few experimental research studies that account for self-selection bias, use control groups effectively or make use of statistical methods that allow determination of causality. Researchers are also challenged by the lack of commonly accepted terminology and the availability of large datasets. Although there are an increasing number of reliable instruments that are being used in education abroad research, there is often a misalignment in the research objectives and the instruments used, thus potentially invalidating research results (Deardorff, 2015). Finally, there is a clear need for more theoretical grounding of empirical research on education abroad. In spite of these longstanding concerns, an increasingly robust and valuable body of research is developing. Much of this research appears to concentrate on seven major themes, most of which is oriented around the areas of student learning and program outcomes (Ogden, 2017).

1   *Academic and professional outcomes.* A substantial theme in education abroad research is concerned with what students learn through education abroad and what happens after graduation in terms of life trajectories. Major research topics language learning, academic development and labor market outcomes.

2   *Student Development.* Student development has long been a focus of higher education research. Regarding education abroad, major research themes focus on student personal growth and identity development, global citizenship development, intercultural learning, and how students make meaning from experiences abroad.

3   *Programming and Development.* A growing area of education abroad research focuses on how design components (e.g., student accommodation, academic programming, co-curricular learning, student services, etc.) impact program outcomes. Similarly, research in this area focuses on how outcomes vary across experience types, such as faculty-directed programming, international internships, undergraduate research and global service-learning.

4   *Student Characteristics and Demographics.* There is considerable research that investigates student characteristics (e.g., language proficiency, previous international experience, etc.) and demographic differences and their relationship to issues such as program choice, student learning and institutional impact. Most commonly, research topics focus on gender, race and ethnicity, and financial background.

5   *Student Choice and Decision-making.* There is growing body of research that focuses on understanding the factors that influence one's intent to study abroad as well as student decision-making while abroad, particularly regarding student behavior, adjustment and conduct.

6   *Discipline-specific Programming.* To a lesser extent, a major theme of research examines education abroad programming within specific disciplines, and much of it is being published in discipline-specific journals that are generally less frequently cited by scholars of international student mobility. Considerable research has focused in fields such as agriculture, nursing, social work and teacher education.

7  *Institutional Strategy*. A growing and increasingly influential research theme focuses on demonstrating how education abroad supports institutional goals, such as increasing student retention and persistence, advancing curriculum internationalization and faculty engagement, fostering alumni loyalty and enhancing graduate employability, etc.

Although scholarly research and attention to education abroad has greatly increased over time and around the world and has expanded to include major themes of relevance and importance to education abroad programming and practice (Bedenlier, Kondakci & Zawacki-Richter, 2018; Brewer & Ogden, 2019; Ogden, 2017; Ogden & Streitwieser, 2016; Roy, Newman, Ellenberger & Pyman, 2019), the existing body of literature is complex, often contradictory, and generally void of explicit applications to practice. Even those education abroad professionals most attuned to major developments in the literature can be overwhelmed and confused. There are seldom definitive implications that span the body of research that professionals can easily understand and apply across national and institutional contexts. Even those seminal publications that have greatly informed programming and practice today become obsolete as philosophies, programming and trends evolve. Coupled with the need to navigate methodological shortcomings in the existing research, professionals can become bewildered as to the implications that can confidently be drawn from the existing literature. Thus, to support and inform new professionals and emerging scholars of international higher education, this volume focuses broadly on fourteen of the most salient and frequently noted areas of needed research (Isabelli-Garcia & Isabelli, 2020; Ogden, & Streitwieser, 2016; Proctor & Rumbley, 2018). The goal is to synthesize what is known and what needs further research in these fourteen areas and to provide professionals with explicit implications for practice. Although the selection of topics is certainly not exhaustive, this volume seeks to provide some answers to the most pressing questions and challenges in education abroad programming and practice today.

1  *Decision-making*. Research on the decision-making processes involved in education abroad have focused on students' intent to study abroad and program selection. Of particular importance for scholars who focus on this topic are key questions such as (a) which macro- (e.g., economic, educational and political context), meso- (institutional context) and micro-level factors (e.g., social networks) influence the likelihood of participating in education abroad; (b) what role does (social) selectivity play in education abroad decision-making processes; (c) what are the similarities and differences in the decision-making processes of those who participate in education abroad and those who aim for a full degree abroad; and (d) to what extent does program value, as opposed to program cost, factor into the program selection process?

2  *Socio-Demographics*. It is important that education abroad professionals not only understand national enrollment trends, but also understand the enrollment trends within their own education abroad populations. Failure to understand who is underrepresented and strategize accordingly can potentially lead to missed opportunities for certain populations. While there is considerable professional reporting on participation trends, there is less research focused on the outcomes associated with their participation. Of importance to this topic are key questions, such as (a) what is the current profile of participants and how does that profile compare across national systems; (b) how does the student profile (e.g., gender, socioeconomic background) vary by program mode or program experience type; and (c) to what extent have efforts to diversify participation been effective?

3  *Program Types*. A variety of program modalities have emerged over time, with the most common including bilateral and multilateral student exchanges, faculty-directed programs, consortia programming, and provider organizations. Much of the existing research does not distinguish between program modality. Similarly, much of the existing research has focused primarily on study abroad and there has been relatively little research on other experience types, such as undergraduate research abroad, international internships and global service-learning abroad. Of importance to this topic are key questions, such as (a) how does educational value vary by experience type and (b) how does educational value vary by education abroad program modality?

4  *Program Components*. Research on the traditional programmatic components of education abroad programming, namely student accommodation, academic programming, co-curricular learning, and student services, generally does not support the many long-held assumptions of the value of these design choices. Of importance to this topic are key questions, such as (a) how do student learning outcomes differ based on housing type (e.g., homestay, apartment, dormitory, etc.); (b) how do student learning outcomes differ based on the mode of instruction (e.g., faculty-directed, direct enrollment, island programming, etc.); (c) how do student services enhance student learning outcomes (e.g., field trips and excursions, language exchanges, ongoing orientation programming, co-curricular and extracurricular activities, etc.); and (d) how are language proficiency gains influenced by the manipulation of programmatic components?

5  *Academic Development*. Although widely considered a high-impact educational practice, there is little research that demonstrates how students develop academically and intellectually over time as a result of having studied abroad. Similarly, few studies have investigated how education abroad participation impacts interdisciplinary learning outcomes. Of importance to this topic are key questions, such as (a) to what extent does participation in education abroad enhance academic development; and (b) to what extent does participation in education abroad influence academic decision-making?

6  *Language Proficiency*. Developing proficiency in a foreign language has long been considered a central and viable rationale for developing and promoting

education abroad. Although there has been considerable research over the decades in this area, of importance to this topic today are key questions, such as (a) what education abroad program elements (i.e., housing, student services, etc.) mediate language learning proficiency gains; b) to what extent can education abroad programming of less than eight weeks be used strategically to retain students in advanced level coursework; and (c) how does social media used in an education abroad context impact language proficiency gains?

7 *Student Development.* Research has focused broadly on the extent to which students change or develop personally as a result of participation in education abroad. How education abroad participation affects students and what components of an education abroad experience lead to significant gains in student development are of interest to education abroad professionals and institutional leaders alike. Of importance to this topic are key questions, such as (a) to what extent does education abroad participation enhance student development (i.e., psychosocial, cognitive, identity, etc.); and (b) to what extent can education abroad programming be leveraged to propel student development?

8 *Global Citizenship, Identity, & Intercultural Competence.* Intercultural competency, identity development and global citizenship have emerged as key reasons for developing and promoting education abroad. Although there has been significant research in this area, still of importance are key questions, such as (a) to what extent does participation in education abroad programming lead to changes in students' identification and identity processes; (b) how does education abroad participation impact one's sense of social responsibility; (c) to what extent does education abroad participation impact intercultural competency development; and (d) to what extent are intercultural competency gains retained after returning from abroad?

9 *Employability.* While leveraging education abroad for employability is not new, the research in this area is only emerging. What research that does exist has primarily been focused on long-term career impact and heavily relied on self-reports. Of importance to this topic are key questions, such as (a) how does education abroad participation increase employability and shape career development; (b) how does education abroad participation prepare students for graduate or professional school; and (c) how do prospective employers view education abroad?

10 *Institutional Impact.* To be sure, international educators around the world share similar challenges with respect to effectively collecting and utilizing data for strategic institutional planning and advocacy. Education abroad professionals are increasingly being asked to provide evidence of the extent to which internationalization efforts potentially enhance and extend institutional missions, values and priorities. Research that advances and supports this growing demand is essential. Of importance to this topic are key questions, such as (a) does education abroad participation impact alumni loyalty, giving and development; (b) to what extent does education abroad participation affect institutional reputations and global standings; (c) how do institutional policies (e.g., financial

aid, credit transfer, fee structures) impact education abroad enrollment; (d) to what extent is education abroad a high-impact experience supporting student success (i.e., retention and persistence); and (e) to what extent are first-year education abroad program participants retained into the second year and persist to graduation?

11  *Curriculum Integration.* As education abroad programming becomes strategically aligned with the curriculum and leveraged in support of intended outcomes, research is needed that assesses the efficacy of these efforts. Of importance to this topic are key questions, such as (a) to what extent are curriculum integration efforts influential in the program selection process; (b) how is the home campus culture impacted when students return; and c) to what extent are curriculum integration efforts internationalizing the home school curriculum and the student learning experience?

12  *Faculty Engagement.* Greater attention is being placed on understanding how faculty members benefit from engaging in education abroad programming and how campus-based curricula are enhanced when faculty are more internationally engaged. Of importance to this topic are key questions, such as (a) how does comprehensive internationalization efforts impact faculty teaching, research and service; (b) how does faculty engagement in education abroad programming impact curriculum internationalization on the home campus; (c) how does consistent and sustained contact with faculty through cohort programming abroad create conditions that foster student success; and (d) to what extent does recognition of international programming in the promotion and tenure process, if applicable, drive faculty engagement?

13  *National Policies on Education Abroad Outcomes.* National policies on education abroad are widely present throughout the world, although most are oriented around quantitative goals and metrics. Very little scholarly attention has been given to documenting and analyzing the efficacy of such policies and related national initiatives. Of importance to this topic are key questions, such as (a) what are the societal implications of national policy initiatives to advance international education programming; (b) what student-level barriers explain cross-country variation in participation rates; (c) what components of national policy initiatives are most effective to generate mobility?

14  *Host Community Impact.* The extent to which host communities are impacted by the presence of visitors has long been the focus of both anthropologists and tourism scholars but this question has only recently been asked in relation to education abroad programming. There has been little research that has specifically examined how the prolonged and recurring presence of students impacts local communities over time. Of importance to this topic are key questions, such as (a) what are the economic effects on local communities that host education abroad programs; (b) how are local communities impacted culturally by the prolonged presence of international students; and (c) how do host communities react (i.e., socially, politically, etc.) to the presence of international students?

## Volume overview and structure

This volume seeks to provide a succinct and critical analysis of existing global research and scholarship on the aforementioned fourteen topics with the goal of synthesizing what is known and what needs further research and drawing from that analysis key implications for professional practice. As such, the volume is intended to be an accessible desktop compendium of essential research on contemporary issues in education abroad programming that occurs as a distinct component of a post-secondary degree. The volume may be most useful to international education practitioners and emerging scholars who are new to the field, higher education administrators, researchers, faculty members, policy makers, graduate students and others who want to understand and leverage existing research to inform daily education abroad programming and practice.

The volume offers fourteen distinct chapters organized in five parts, with each part introduced by the editors. The five parts address the broad themes of (I) Participation, (II) Programming, (III) Student outcomes, (IV) Institutional outcomes, and (V) Societal outcomes. Authored by well-regarded and widely acknowledged education abroad experts, each chapter provides a succinct synthesize of the existing literature to make recommendations for future study and draw implications to inform professional practice. Each chapter, to the extent practical, is of similar length and follows a similar orientation, structure and style.

To further support user accessibility, each chapter includes an introductory section highlighting the chapter's key points. Also, a concluding section to each chapter offers 3–5 suggestions for further in-depth reading on the specific topics addressed.

While this volume strives to provide a global treatment of the existing literature, we acknowledge that each chapter has largely been framed by the existing research filtered by the knowledge and experiences of the chapter authors and that the implications noted may not apply across all national and institutional contexts. Moreover, given the ever-changing nature and orientation of research, we wish to remind the reader to consider the content herein but a mere snapshot in time. No research is ever quite complete. Yet, we hope that this volume reinforces a pathway for international education professionals and emerging scholars to a world where research informs practice and practice guides and shapes the direction of future research.

## References

Altbach, P., & Knight, J. (2007). "The internationalization of higher education: Motivations and realities." *Journal of Studies in International Education*, 11, 290–305.

Anquetil, M. (2006). *Mobilité Erasmus et communication interculturelle. Une recherche-action pour un parcours de formation*, Bern: Peter Lang.

Australian Universities International Directors Forum (AUIDF) (2015). *Learning abroad report 2017*. Newcastle, Australia. Retrieved from https://internationaleducation.gov.au/research/research-snapshots

Bedenlier, S., Kondakci, Y., & Zawacki-Richter, O. (2018). "Two decades of research into the internationalization of higher education: Major themes in the Journal of Studies in International Education (1997–2016)." *Journal of Studies in International Education*, 22 (2), 108–135.

Behrnd, V., and Porzelt, S. (2012). "Intercultural competence and training outcomes of students with experiences abroad." *International Journal of Intercultural Relations*, 36 (2), 213–223.

Brewer, E., & Ogden, A. (Eds.) (2019). *Critical perspectives on integrating education abroad into undergraduate education.* Sterling, VA:Stylus Publishing, LLC.

Dall'Alba, G. and Sidhu, R. (2015) "Australian undergraduate students on the move: Experiencing outbound mobility." *Studies in Higher Education*, 40(4), 721–744.

Deardorff, D. K. (2006). "Identification and assessment of intercultural competence as a student outcome of internationalization." *Journal of Studies in International Education*, 10(3), 241–266.

Deardorff, D. K. (2015). *Demystifying outcomes assessment in education abroad programs.* Sterling, VA: Stylus Publishing.

de Wit, H., Agarwal, P., Elmahdy Said, M., Sehoole, M., & Sirozi, M. (Eds.) (2008). *The dynamics of international student circulation in a global context.* Netherlands: Sense Publishers.

de Wit, H., Gacel-Avila, J., Jones, E., & Jooste, N. (Eds.) (2017). *The globalization of internationalization: Emerging voices and perspectives.* Oxford: Routledge.

Dolby, N., & Rahman, A. (2008). "Research in international education." *Review of Educational Research*, 78(3), 676–726.

Dwyer, M. (2004). "Charting the impact of studying abroad." *International Educator*, 13 (1), 14–20.

Green, W., & Whitsed, C. (Eds.) (2015). *Critical perspectives on internationalizing the curriculum in disciplines.* Netherlands: Sense Publishers.

Gu, Q., Schweisfurth, M., & Day, C. (2010). "Learning and growing in a 'foreign' context: intercultural experiences of international students." *Compare: A Journal of Comparative and International Education*, 40(1), 7–23.

Haupt, J., & Ogden, A. (2019). Education abroad as a high impact practice: Linking research and practice to the educational continuum. In E. Brewer & A. Ogden (Eds.), *Critical perspectives on integrating education abroad into undergraduate education.* Sterling, VA: Stylus Publishing, LLC.

Hudzik, J. (2014). *Comprehensive internationalization: Institutional pathways to success.* New York, NY: Routledge.

Institute of International Education (2018). *Open Doors report on international education exchange.* Retrieved from IIE: www.iie.org/opendoors

Isabelli-Garcia, C., & Isabelli, C. (2020). *Research second language acquisition in the study abroad learning environment: An introduction for student researchers.* Basingstoke: Palgrave Macmillan.

Kinginger, C. (2009). *Language learning and study abroad: A critical reading of research.* New York: Palgrave Macmillan.

Kinginger, C. (2011). "Enhancing language learning in study abroad." *Annual Review of Applied Linguistics*, 31, 58–73.

Knight, J. (2004). "Internationalization remodeled: Definitions, approaches, and rationales." *Journal of Studies in International Education*, 8, 5–31.

Knight, J. (2012). "Student Mobility and Internationalization: trends and tribulations." *Research in Comparative and International Education*, 7(1), 20–33.

Leask, B. (2015). *Internationalizing the curriculum*. Abingdon: Routledge.

Lewin, R. (2009). *The handbook of practice and research in study abroad: Higher education and the quest for global citizenship*. New York: Routledge.

Magnan, S. S., & Back, M. (2007). "Social interaction and linguistic gain during study abroad." *Foreign Language Annals*, 40(1), 43–61.

Ogden, A. (2017). What we know and need to know about short-term, education abroad: A concise review of the literature. In L. Chieffo & C. Spaeth (Eds.), *NAFSA's guide to successful short-term programs abroad*, 3rd Edition. Washington, DC: NAFSA: Association of International Educators.

Ogden, A., & Streitwieser, B. (2016). An overview of research on US education abroad. In D. Velliaris & D. Coleman-George (Eds.), *Handbook of research on study abroad programs and outbound mobility*, IGI Global Press, Adelaide, Australia.

Paige, M., Stallman, E., & Josić, J. (2008). "*Study abroad for global engagement: A preliminary report on the study abroad global engagement (SAGE) research project*." Presentation at the SAGE Annual Conference, Washington, DC, May.

Pisarevskaya, A., Levy, N., Scholten, P., & Jansen, J. (2019). "Mapping migration studies. An empirical analysis of the coming of age of a research field." *Migration Studies*. doi:10.1093/migration/mnz031

Proctor, D., & Rumbley, R. (2018). *The future agenda for internationalization in higher education: Next generation insights into research, policy, and practice*. Oxford: Routledge.

Roy, A, Newman, A., Ellenberger, T., & Pyman, A. (2019). "Outcomes of international student mobility programs: A systematic review and agenda for future research." *Studies in Higher Education*, 44(9), 1630–1644.

Streitwieser, B., Le, E., & Rust, V. (2012). "Research on study abroad, mobility, and student exchange in comparative education scholarship." *Research in International and Comparative Education*, 7(1), 5–19.

Streitwieser, B. (Ed.) (2014). *Internationalization of higher education and global mobility*. Oxford Studies in Comparative Education. Oxford: Symposium Books.

Velliaris, D., & Coleman-George, D. (Eds.) (2016). *Handbook of research on study abroad programs and outbound mobility*. Australia: IGI Global Press.

Yager, K. (1998). "Learning Spanish in Mexico: The effect of informal contact and student attitudes on language gain." *Hispania*, 81(4), 898–913.

# Part 1

# Participation

Globally, there is a dominant discourse among policy makers and in international offices focusing on an increase in the absolute numbers of students who participate in education abroad. Such discourses are often informed by ideas that education abroad provides higher education students with skills and competences that are necessary to be competitive in global knowledge economies. As a consequence, across the world ambitious benchmarks are put forward, at the supranational level (e.g., the European Union, which has a benchmark of 20% of all graduates in EU countries to have experienced short-term or full-degree mobility by 2020 (Council of the European Union, 2011)), the national and regional level (e.g., Flanders in Belgium, with a 33% benchmark of all graduates by 2020 (Vlaamse Regering, 2013)) and the institutional level (e.g., 50% of all graduates at the University of Sydney). However, if these benchmarks are to be met, a first and essential step is to get insight into why higher education students move abroad and what makes them decide to do so.

Similarly, there is increasing attention among policymakers to the inclusion of students from disadvantaged groups in education abroad. Examples include Proyecta 100,000 in Mexico and Generation Study Abroad in the United States, as well as recent discussions about promoting the participation of students from disadvantaged groups in the Erasmus+ Programme in Europe. Indeed, many studies across the world indicate how education abroad is a selective process, which might increase or sustain existing social inequalities (e.g., Netz and Finger, 2016, Salisbury et al., 2009). As such, besides gaining a better insight into the education abroad decision-making process, it is also essential to grasp how social markers influence the mobility process. The two chapters in this section of the volume specifically address these two issues.

In Chapter 1, Rachel Brooks and Johanna Waters focus on the decision-making process and how this process is embedded within micro-, meso- and macro-level structures, including students' individual characteristics, attitudes, dispositions and interests, higher education institutions and the wider economic and political contexts in which higher education students are situated. Importantly, the chapter underlines that although education abroad is often conceptualized as a "free" choice for students, the individual agency of students is significantly constrained and enabled by their surrounding environments. Depending on the specific contexts in which higher education students are situated, participation in education abroad may or may not be available as an option.

The second chapter then dives deeper into different axes of inequality in education abroad programs. Nicolai Netz, Daniel Klasik, Steve R. Entrich, and Michelle Barker clearly show that – across the world – students who participate in education abroad are most likely young, female, from the ethnic majority population and from higher socio-economic backgrounds. As such, they point to the role that selectivity plays in education abroad, an issue that is also important when assessing the outcomes of education abroad (see Part III of this volume). Their chapter clearly highlights the need to establish policies that address these inequalities in participation, since the current situation tends to increase or at least reproduce existing inequalities.

Together, both chapters highlight the need for research and practice to go beyond individual motivations when analyzing the determinants of education abroad or designing education abroad programs. They clearly indicate that we cannot fully understand education abroad, or adequately design education abroad programs, without taking into account the embeddedness of education abroad decisions within wider contexts or existing social inequalities.

## References

Council of the European Union (2011). "Council conclusions on a benchmark for learning mobility." *Official Journal of the European Union*, 2011/C 372/08.

Netz, N., & Finger, C. (2016). "New horizontal inequalities in German higher education? Social selectivity of studying abroad between 1991 and 2012." *Sociology of Education*, 89 (2), 79–98. doi:10.1177/0038040715627196

Salisbury, M. H., Umbach, P. D., Paulsen, M. B., & Pascarella, E. T. (2009). "Going global: Understanding the choice process of the intent to study abroad." *Research in Higher Education*, 50(2), 119–143.

Vlaamse Regering (2013). *Brains on the Move. actieplan mobiliteit.* Brussels: Departement Onderwijs en Vorming.

# Chapter 1

# Decision-making

## Spatio-temporal contexts of decision-making in education abroad

*Rachel Brooks and Johanna Waters*

### Highlights:

- A decision to study abroad is rarely an individual one; instead it is usually strongly influenced by the surrounding social context.
- Decisions are typically influenced by students' social characteristics, particularly their social class.
- The institutional setting and wider economic and political context can also often have an important bearing on decisions whether to study abroad at all and, for those who do go, their destination.

### 1.0 Introduction and chapter overview

On University College London's education abroad pages, students and staff are able to view the 'vlogs' of those who have returned from a short period (a term to a year) overseas, as part of their 'British' undergraduate degree programme. From Japan to Sweden, Singapore to Australia, a range of destination countries and 'equivalent' institutions are available to students wanting to experience some time living and studying in another country. The institution is able to convert, on students' return, the courses they took overseas into 'credit' for their British degree course. The students are effusive in their tales of excitement, fun, love and culture shock, captured in the vlogs. When difficulties arose, they were overcome, and the students emerged stronger and better able to cope with the world as a result. And yet, under a third of the college's total undergraduate student body (29.3% for 2017/2018) actually take this opportunity (open to all students with the necessary academic grades). This specific vignette leads us to ponder some interesting questions about the decision-making process underpinning education abroad.[1]

An increasing number of students within the European Union and more widely are being given the opportunity, as part of a higher education degree programme, to study for a period (usually between one term and one year) abroad (Seal, 2018; Sidhu and Dall'Alba, 2017). These programmes include Erasmus, summer schools, 'study China' programmes and international volunteering partnerships arranged through home universities. These trends necessarily prompt various intellectually driven questions about the decision for education abroad, and how it is realised. From the perspective of some students, in many ways, the decision may seem like no decision at all – the opportunity to spend some time overseas in an institution of roughly equal global standing, with often subsidised fees and living costs, seems too good to be true. However, it is clear that this ostensibly individual, individualised 'decision' represents, *inter-alia*, a longer (socialisation) process and a wider (social, political and institutional) context than the individual student (Brooks and Waters, 2011). As reflected upon by McCormack and Schwanen (2011):

> Despite the ease with which decisive moments can be identified and accounted for retrospectively, the decision remains a spectral event, difficult to pin down or isolate as a bounded moment. Equally, while often assumed to be taken by an individual, the decision is not so easily located within the limits of a self-contained, sovereign subject, emerging instead as a distributed, relational process ... In this context it becomes all the more important to address the question of where, when, and how decision-making takes place and the practices and techniques that aim to facilitate this process towards different political and ethical ends. Equally importantly, it becomes imperative to examine how practices of decision-making are implicated in space-times–that is, to examine how decision-making takes place in particular spatio-temporal contexts ... (McCormack and Schwanen, 2011, pp. 2801–2802)

This chapter focuses on the particular spatio-temporal contexts of decision-making around education abroad. It considers decisions students make about whether or not to engage in short-term international mobility and also, for those who *do* decide to study abroad, how they choose a country and institution. Reflecting the biases inherent in wider literature on which it draws,[2] the chapter focuses largely, although not exclusively, on migration to the Global North and to Anglophone nations in particular.

## 2. Key questions to be addressed

There are many theories of decision-making that have informed work on international student mobility, such as: 'rational choice theory' (e.g. Lörz, Netz and Quast, 2016), 'expectancy theory' (Sánchez, Fornerino & Zhang, 2006), and the 'theory of planned behaviour' (e.g. Presley, Damron-Martinez and Zhang, 2010). These studies show that decision-making is not an unfettered process – an exercise in free will and agency – but, rather, it is embedded within pre-existing societal structures underpinned by fundamental inequalities (Brooks and Waters, 2011). In other words, the importance of the *socio-economic context* is highlighted in all of these studies. It is this *context* to decision-making in international student mobility that shall be the focus here, drawing in particular upon Bourdieu's theories of capital, which encompasses the notion of 'habitus' (a form of socialisation) – a fundamental determinant of decision-making amongst young people.

Students are shaped by their social class and family background and gender, amongst other factors (Brooks and Waters, 2011). Students' attitudes towards education and travel clearly influence the decision to study abroad, but these attitudes are themselves the product of a familial habitus and a particular *milieu*. Furthermore, higher education institutions (HEIs) both direct and enable education abroad to a large extent, marketing particular destinations, and providing practical support (necessary 'support structures') to students. And then there is the essential wider economic and political context to study, including the role played by national and supranational organisations. Consequently, this chapter draws upon the extant academic literature and debates around student mobilities and higher education internationalisation to discuss 'decision-making' relating to education abroad in the fullest possible way. The following key questions are posed and at least partially answered:

- How do students' social characteristics impact decision-making relating to education abroad?
- How are students' attitudes towards education abroad formed?
- What is the role played by HEIs in enabling and directing education abroad?
- How does the wider economic and political context direct decision-making around short-term educational mobilities?

These questions provide a frame through which to understand that decision-making is rarely an individualised process and is, instead, often strongly influenced by the particular social contexts. The next section of the chapter provides a synthesis of the global literature on education abroad decision-making.

## 3. Review of the literature

### 3.1 Students' social characteristics

Extant research has provided clear evidence of the significant impact a student's social class and family background can have on a decision to move abroad for part of a degree programme. Within Europe, for example, this has been noted with respect to the 'Erasmus' scheme, in which students from more affluent backgrounds have tended to be over-represented (Findlay et al., 2006; Lörz et al., 2016; Bahna, 2018). Studies of short-term mobility among Chinese students have also emphasised the importance of family background. Those interviewed as part of Hansen's (2015) research in Denmark were all middle class and reliant on financial support from their families. Many have theorised such influences in terms of Bourdieu's 'capitals', noting the influence exerted by economic capital (e.g., through having enough money to be able to afford flights to and from the destination country, for example, or expensive accommodation), cultural capital (e.g. a familiarity with other cultures and previous experience of international travel that can help reduce the anxiety of studying abroad), and social capital (such as links to others, particularly friends and peers, who have spent time abroad, who can offer advice and also reduce the 'fear of the unknown') (see, for example, Bahna, 2018). Research from the US has also highlighted the impact of students' social networks on a decision to embark on education abroad schemes (Luo and Jamieson-Drake, 2015). Moreover, scholars have argued that the deployment of these capitals is linked to a broader process of social reproduction, whereby more privileged groups in society use their advantages (the capitals outlined above) to access education abroad opportunities, in the belief that they will help to secure 'distinction' post-graduation, particularly when students are entering the labour market (Murphy-Lejeune, 2003; Bahna, 2018; King, 2018). Here, there are strong similarities with studies that have shown how 'diploma mobility' (i.e. moving abroad for the whole of a degree) is often motivated by an equivalent desire to secure distinction (Prazeres et al., 2017).

However, the literature also provides examples of how these patterns can, in some cases, be disrupted. For example, practical and emotional support and encouragement offered by families can have a significant influence on decisions, but is not always obviously related to the possession of particular capitals (Seal, 2018). It also suggests that some decisions are not 'strategic' in this way, and prioritise travel, enjoyment and new experiences instead (Seal, 2018). Seal's (2018) work shows how educational institutions can increase participation in mobility schemes among traditionally under-represented groups – by, for example, giving them easy access to peers who have successfully completed a period overseas previously, and providing extensive information and support to those who show an initial interest. Moreover, Deakin (2014) has argued that the introduction of paid work placements as part of the Erasmus mobility scheme had a notable effect in widening access, particularly among those from low income families. The clear implication of this analysis is that students from less affluent families are not necessarily deterred by the idea of living abroad per se, but by the anticipated financial outlay of such a move. The literature provides examples of a small number of cases where institutions have sought to address some of the financial barriers experienced by students. At the University of Queensland, Australia, staff from the School of Nursing assisted students to raise funds for a group-based learning trip to Cambodia and work in a local health clinic. Here, the funds raised by students were matched by the School, reducing the financial barriers to overseas study (Sidhu and Daell'Alba, 2017).

While the majority of studies that have considered the impact of students' social characteristics have tended to focus on social class and family background, some research has illustrated the role played by other variables such as age, ethnicity and gender, as illustrated in the next chapter of this volume. Subject of study can also impact education abroad decisions, with arts and humanities students more likely to avail themselves of opportunities to move abroad than their peers in other disciplines (e.g. Amendola and Restaino, 2017; Stroud, 2010). Furthermore, American research has suggested that studying at a university further away from the parental home is positively correlated with propensity to engage in education abroad (Stroud, 2010).

### 3.2 Students' attitudes, dispositions and interests

Alongside research on the social characteristics of students, and how they impact on decisions whether or not to engage in short-term mobility programmes, studies have examined the importance of students' attitudes[3] and/or dispositions. (It is important to note, however, that attitudes are often closely linked with social characteristics, and particularly social class.) Firstly, research has highlighted the influence of a desire for travel, and personal and professional development (see, for example, Lai's (2015) study of Chinese students in Japan). In Dall'Alba and Sidhu's (2015) Australian study the most common reasons given by the research participants for studying abroad related to gaining life experience, such as travel, meeting new people and experiencing new cultures. Bartram (2013) has argued that there is sometimes a significant disconnect between students' positive attitudes towards *being* abroad and their less positive attitudes to *studying* abroad. In his UK-based study, respondents felt relatively under-prepared for the academic component of their education abroad, largely because their primary motivation had been to spend time abroad rather than study their degree subject in an overseas institution. Similarly, Polish research has highlighted the significance to students of what Bótas and Huisman (2013) call 'Erasmus tourism'. An interest in other cultures has also been shown to be positively correlated with intent to study abroad as part of a degree programme (Stroud, 2010). Thus, on the whole, research on education abroad has suggested that students are perhaps less motivated by the intention to secure 'distinction' from other students (see discussion above) than those who embark on whole-degree mobility. Indeed, students are often motivated by a desire to have fun and gain new experiences rather than anything more 'strategic' (see also Waters and Brooks, 2011).

Research has, however, highlighted that education abroad can be seen as a valuable opportunity to gain new skills and competencies, which may advantage students when they enter the labour market at the end of their higher education. On the basis of their analysis of the decisions of Erasmus students from 26 nations, Lesjak et al. (2015) argue that both professional and personal motivations are significant. The former include a desire to learn or improve a foreign language, develop new contacts and improve employment opportunities. In general, however, these were viewed by students as less important than more intrinsic motivations such as experiencing something new, personal growth, and learning about different cultures. Research conducted with Italian students also suggests that both personal and professional motivations are important; in this case, however, relatively greater emphasis was placed on the latter (Amendola and Restaino, 2017; see also Van Mol and Timmerman, 2014).

### 3.3 Higher education institutions

Students' decisions are also influenced by the institutional context in which they are located (Beerkens et al. 2016). At the most fundamental level, this relates to the extent to which opportunities for mobility are provided and/or integrated into the curriculum at their home higher education institution. Research has highlighted that there are important disparities here. Although HEIs may feel an increasing pressure to make such opportunities available to their students, in many nations, education abroad tends to be better supported and promoted within prestigious and higher status institutions (that are perhaps under more pressure to demonstrate their international credentials; see discussion below). Hansen's (2015) study of Chinese exchange students in Denmark notes, for example, that all participants come only from high-status institutions. The promotion of education abroad opportunities often falls to specific individuals within higher education institutions, typically located in international units or their equivalent. Research conducted in Poland by Bótas and Huisman (2013) demonstrates the ways in which these various institutional actors attempt to influence students' mobility decisions – in this case, in relation to the Erasmus programme. They argue that, in their interactions with students, local international officers and Erasmus co-ordinators emphasise primarily the positive impact participation is likely to have on the students' human capital and their 'market value'. The framing of the mobility experience is thus, in Poland, mainly about the development of professional advantage rather than the 'fun' alluded to above.

Another example of how education abroad opportunities are marketed to students by their institutions is provided by Sidhu and Dall'Alba (2017) with respect to the University of Queensland in Australia. Reflecting some of the themes that are touched upon in the Polish study, Sidhu and Dall'Alba argue that studying abroad is promoted largely as what they call a 'strategy of distinction'. They note that the materials accessed by students about education abroad opportunities tend to be characterised by unclear academic objectives and competing institutional priorities, arguing that this ambivalence is shaped by the particular Australian context 'in which international study has been regarded, on the one hand, as a revenue source or, alternatively, as an elite project of self-improvement' (p. 481). Despite this ambivalence, they contend that mobility is closely related to the labour market, and that more progressive outcomes (such as learning from those from the Global South, and rethinking one's own cultural habitus) are thus not explored. They contend that the strategies for outward mobility in place at the University of Queensland are typical of those in numerous other national contexts, which 'have focused on training for global entrepreneurs through a series of instrumentalist, disembodied pedagogies' which, at best 'produces banal cosmopolitanism in students; at worse, it creates the conditions for cultural misrepresentations and exploitative relations with the planet and its people' (p. 481).

While these wider discourses are important in framing the way in which educational mobility is discussed and understood, research has also highlighted the impact of more practical interventions made by HEIs. Local support structures, for example, can be important to students – both while they are making a decision about whether or not to study abroad, and then once they are in their destination country. Bartram's (2013) survey of UK students, based at a range of different higher education institutions, engaged in education abroad, indicated that only about two-thirds believed that their academic, practical and socio-cultural needs had been met. Moreover, the majority of students reported trying to meet their needs themselves, rather than drawing on systems in their institution (or even the resources available in their social networks) (ibid.). More work appears necessary here to ensure that students are supported in their mobility decisions. As noted above, local financial aid can also facilitate mobility and open up opportunities to traditionally under-represented groups, whether this be at a regional level (in the example of the paid work placements introduced as part of the Erasmus scheme (Deakin, 2014)), or local schemes targeted at specific course groups (in the example of the nursing students at the University of Queensland: Dall'Alba and Sidhu, 2015). Curriculum innovations can also facilitate short-term mobility, including the development of joint master's programmes, where students are required to spend part of their programme at one or more partner institutions (see Papatsiba 2014 for an examination of joint master's programmes within Europe).

### 3.4 Wider economic and political context

Decisions about whether or not to move abroad for part of a higher education programme are also informed by the wider economic and political context in which both institutions and individuals are situated (Rodríguez González et al., 2011). The increasingly globalised market for higher education has put pressure on HEIs to indicate their international credentials, promote a global image and engage in student mobility programmes (Brooks and Waters, 2011; Rizvi and Lingard, 2010). Demonstrating an 'international profile' is deemed important, within this context, as a means of attracting both home and international students and signalling the status of the institution (Dall'Alba and Sidhu, 2015). This can then have a material impact on the decision-making processes of students. Moreover, as many graduate employers are now recruiting from universities across the world, rather than from national markets – what Brown et al. (2011) have called the 'global war for talent' – higher education leaders feel increasing pressure to prepare their students to work in companies based outside their own nation-state and to compete with graduates from universities worldwide. Spending a period abroad, as part of a degree programme, can be seen as an effective means of developing the inter-cultural competencies believed to be required by such graduate recruiters.

Both national and regional governments, and supranational organisations have encouraged movement in this direction. For example, the European Union has currently a target in place that, by 2020, 20% of higher education students within Europe will have spent a period studying or training abroad, and various national governments in the region have incorporated this target into their own national plans. Similarly, wealthier Asian nations such as Japan, Singapore, Taiwan and Korea have recently sought to increase participation in short-term mobility programmes, while Japan, Korea and China have worked together to develop a framework for standardising assessment of student work and certifying credits to help facilitate student mobility within the region (Dall'Alba and Sidhu, 2015). The US also implemented a short-term mobility target in the early years of the 21st century (to have 1 million American undergraduate outward mobility participants by 2017) although this was subsequently adversely affected by domestic financial problems (ibid.).

Similarly, the national and/or international economic context – in which many graduates fail to secure 'graduate-level' jobs, and top companies engage in an internationally focused 'war for talent' (Brown et al., 2011) – can impress upon students themselves that they need to do all they can to improve their economic position. From this perspective, education abroad can be seen as a means of differentiating oneself from other graduates, and developing inter-cultural skills and competences thought to be valued within the workplace. Van Mol and Timmerman (2014) also argue, on the basis of their research with participants in intra-European mobility programmes, that students' motivations are influenced by economic factors and, specifically, the comparisons they draw between the macro-economic situation in their own country and that in the possible destination countries. For example, in countries where employment is precarious for many graduates, spending a period abroad can be viewed as a strategy to minimise future labour market risk (ibid.; see also Cairns, 2014 in relation to the educational mobility decisions of young people from 'economically peripheral' countries within Europe). As noted in the previous discussion, this perception that education abroad will enhance one's employability is commonly reinforced by those individuals (from international offices, for example) promoting such experiences (Bótas and Huisman, 2013) as well as often being engrained within the institutional discourse. There is less clarity, however, on the actual impact on employment of a period spent studying abroad (see Wiers-Jenssen et al., this volume, Chapter 9).

### 3.5 Where to go and what to study

The final part of this section turns to decisions about institution and host country. Although many short-term mobility schemes within higher education institutions emphasise the wide variety of possible destinations, scholarship in this area has consistently pointed to the very circumscribed geographies of education abroad (see, for example, Rodríguez González et al., 2011). Students tend to choose between a limited range of countries, frequently privileging those that are larger, richer and Anglophone. In many cases, they are also restricted to the countries with which their institution has a prior agreement. In relation to intra-European mobility, for example, research has shown how students typically move from countries that have a more marginal position within Europe – both economically and politically – to nations that have long been part of the European project and which tend to exert more political power. Thus, the most popular destination countries within Europe are Germany, the UK, Italy, France and

Spain, whereas the countries that send the largest proportion of their student population abroad include Latvia, Lithuania, Luxembourg and Lichtenstein (European Commission, 2015). Recent research by Baláž et al. (2017) has shown, further, how 'connectivity factors', such as language, spatial proximity and established flows of labour, trade and knowledge underpin dominant patterns of intra-European mobility.

Caruso and de Wit's (2015) analysis of patterns of short-term mobility within Europe for the period 1998–2009 has suggested that country choice is affected, primarily, by the amount spent on higher education students (i.e. students are likely to choose countries where higher education services are adequately funded). Secondary influences include the perceived level of safety within the destination country, its degree of openness and its Gross Domestic Product (Caruso and de Wit, 2015; Lesjak et al., 2015). There are clear links here to the points made previously about the impact of the wider macro-economic context. Studies have indicated that the culture of the destination country can also be influential. Indeed, Lesjak et al.'s (2015) analysis of the motivations of Erasmus students suggests that some of the key reasons given by their respondents for choosing particular countries for education abroad included the perceived richness in cultural attractions and sights, an interesting history, and the variety of public events on offer. The destinations of students beyond Europe are also limited. Despite some growth in regional credit mobility with Asia (discussed above), the international literature indicates that students still tend to prefer moving to nations in the Global North, while patterns of movement often continue to be shaped by previous colonial relationships (Brooks and Waters, 2011; Börjesson, 2017; Franca et al., 2018; Sidhu and Dell'Alba, 2017). It should also be noted that students' choices are very often constrained by the prior arrangements for exchanges developed by their particular HEI and they cannot simply 'choose' a destination. Educational mobility thus remains far from worldwide in its geographical scope.

## 4. Implications for practice

Given the close relationship between education abroad and social-class status, the findings with respect to possibilities for *widening access* to education abroad opportunities are important. They relate to questions about how educational systems can be transformative (enabling students to *improve* their social positioning/class standing), not merely reproductive and, consequently, regressive (cf. Bourdieu, 1984). The Erasmus scheme has been notable in the financial incentives and support it provides (potentially) to less wealthy students (and, as noted above, the extension of Erasmus funding to work placement schemes has had a positive impact on the participation of students from lower socio-economic groups (Deakin, 2014)). However, it is also necessary to recognise that the type of higher education institutions (more elite) supporting education abroad programmes themselves tend to be accessed by already more privileged students. There are limits to the kinds of social transformation mobility schemes can effect when they tend to be offered within already 'elite' institutions with circumscribed student intakes.

Nevertheless, the goal of governments and institutions should be to try to widen access along class lines to short-term mobility schemes, not least for the cultural and social capital that such mobility would seem (overwhelmingly, according to the literature) to provide. The literature would also suggest that mobility begets mobility (Weichbrodt, 2014) – young people undertaking short-term mobility programmes were far more likely to engage in future mobility for study or work. Short-term mobility, and the opportunities it provides, is almost always advantageous for young people. Offering support for students, therefore, is crucial: whether that is financial support (through scholarships and bursaries), logistical support (with arranging flights, finding accommodation and providing insurance) or more general institutional support with the whole process of applying for and securing overseas placements. The literature suggests that students are often having to rely on their own social networks and this can only result in disadvantaging less privileged individuals. Support for outward mobility can also involve curriculum innovation (such as joint degree programmes) to facilitate exchanges, and policy intervention to ensure that institutions more usually accessed by less privileged students are themselves set up to support outward mobility. Moreover, it is important to note that supporting students in this way is rather different from the marketing-led approach to education abroad often seen at governmental- and institutional-level. The marketing of the (sometimes only assumed) benefits of studying abroad is clearly not the same as actually supporting students in taking an informed decision about whether and, if so, where to study abroad.

## 5. Directions for future research

This review of work on decision-making to education abroad has drawn our attention to the fact that further research is needed on the particular socio-temporal contexts within which decisions to study (or not to study) abroad are made. These contexts have a decisive influence in determining who goes abroad and the social inequalities that may result. Other questions also arise about the amount of time spent abroad during their mobility experience and whether this is, in fact, important in students' experiences and subsequent outcomes. How does the period spent abroad impact upon the *value* of that experience? Ackers (2010), for example, has considered short-term mobility (as opposed to longer stays abroad) and how it influences the academic careers of scientists, with a particular focus on gender (there is an often held assumption that women, as primary carers of children, find it more difficult than their male counterparts to undertake longer periods of academic work overseas). She argues that there was, in fact, great value to be had in shorter stays, contrary to the expectation that only longer stays were of any benefit. Consequently, in the context of a wider academic literature on programme or longer-term mobility, short-term mobility should not be dismissed as insignificant or somehow less important. It might be easier for some students (those with fewer resources, caring responsibilities etc.) to undertake shorter periods of study overseas than studying for a whole degree, and yet the benefits might be equivalent.

Other areas that would benefit from further research include diversifying the focus on age and source/destination countries. A small amount of emerging research on younger students participating in short-term mobility programmes (e.g. Weichbrodt, 2014, on high-school exchanges in the US) suggests that more research is needed on the mobility of both younger students (pre-higher education) and more mature students (about whom little is known when it comes to short-term mobility experiences). A more explicit focus on emergent south–south educational exchanges (see Waters and Leung, 2019) and, with that, an attempt to diversify geographically the academic literature on student mobilities (e.g. Jazeel, 2018), would also be hugely welcomed.

## Notes

1 The authors chose to begin this chapter with an example from a UK higher education institution because, over the past few decades, short-term international mobility has become an increasingly important priority for individual UK universities as well as the UK government more generally. The UK clearly has a long history of encouraging inward diploma mobility but, since the early 2000s, has also emphasised the importance of short-term outward mobility of UK students.
2 See Jazeel's (2018) piece on 'decolonizing geographical knowledge' for reflections on the biases in academic literature and citation practices.
3 Here, the authors are using 'attitudes' in a broad sense, and not in the narrower way it may be used in social psychology or political science, for example.

## Further reading

Beerkens, M., Souto-Otero, M., de Wit, H. and Huisman, J. (2016). Similar students and different countries? An analysis of the barriers and drivers for Erasmus participation in seven countries, *Journal of Studies in International Education*, 20, 2, 184–204.
Deakin, H. (2014). *The drivers to Erasmus work placement mobility for UK students Children's Geographies*, 21, 1, 25–39.
Sidhu, R. and Dall'Alba, G. (2017). 'A strategy of distinction' unfolds: unsettling the undergraduate outbound mobility experience, *British Journal of Sociology of Education*, 38, 4, 468–484.

## References

Ackers, L. (2010). Internationalisation and equality: The contribution of short stay mobility to progression in science careers. *Recherches sociologiques et anthropologiques*, 41, 83–103.
Amendola, A. and Restaino, M. (2017). An evaluation study on students' international mobility experience. *Quality and Quantity*, 51, 525–544.
Baláž, V., Williams, A. and Chrančoková, M. (2017). Connectivity as the facilitator of intra-European student migration. *Population, Space and Place*, 24, 3, 1–15.
Bartram, B. (2013). 'Brits abroad': The perceived support needs of UK learners studying in higher education overseas. *Journal of Studies in International Education*, 17, 1, 5–18.

Beerkens, M., Souto-Otero, M., de Wit, H. and Huisman, J. (2016). Similar students and different countries? An analysis of the barriers and drivers for Erasmus participation in seven countries. *Journal of Studies in International Education*, 20, 2, 184–204.

Bótas, P. and Huisman, J. (2013). A Bourdieusian analysis of the participation of Polish students in the Erasmus programme: Cultural and social capital perspectives. *Higher Education*, 66, 741–754.

Börjesson, M. (2017). The global space of international students in 2010. *Journal of Ethnic and Migration Studies*, 43, 8, 1256–1275.

Bourdieu, P. (1984). *Distinction: A Social Critique of the Judgement of Taste*. Cambridge, MA: Harvard University Press.

Bahna, M. (2018). Study choices and returns of international students: On the role of cultural and economic capital of the family. *Population, Space and Place*, 24, 2, 1–10.

Brooks, R. and Waters, J. (2011). *Student Mobilities, Migration and the Internationalization of Higher Education*. Basingstoke: Palgrave Macmillan.

Brown, P., Lauder, H. and Ashton, D. (2011). *The Global Auction: The Broken Promises of Education, Jobs, and Incomes*. New York: Oxford University Press.

Cairns, D. (2014). *Youth Transitions, International Student Mobility and Spatial Reflexivity. Being Mobile?* Basingstoke: Palgrave Macmillan.

Cairns, D. and Smyth, J. (2011). I wouldn't mind moving actually: Exploring student mobility in Northern Ireland. *International Migration*, 49, 2, 135–161.

Caruso, R. and de Wit, H. (2015). Determinants of mobility of students in Europe: Empirical evidence for the period 1998–2009. *Journal of Studies in International Education*, 19, 3, 265–282.

Dall'Alba, G. and Sidhu, R. (2015). Australian undergraduate students on the move: Experiencing outbound mobility. *Studies in Higher Education*, 40, 4, 721–744.

Deakin, H. (2014). The drivers to Erasmus work placement mobility for UK students. *Children's Geographies*, 21, 1, 25–39.

European Commission (2015). Erasmus. Facts, figures and trends. Available online at: http://ec.europa.eu/dgs/education_culture/repository/education/library/statistics/erasmus-plus-facts-figures_en.pdf (Accessed 10/9/19).

Findlay, A., King, R., Stam, A. and Ruiz-Gelices, E. (2006). Ever reluctant Europeans: The changing geographies of UK students studying and working abroad. *European Urban and Regional Studies*, 13, 4, 291–318.

Franca, T., Alves, E. and Padilla, B. (2018). Portuguese policies fostering international student mobility: A colonial legacy or a new strategy? *Globalisation, Societies and Education*, 16, 3, 325–338.

Hansen, A. S. (2015). The temporal experience of Chinese students abroad and the present human condition. *Journal of Current Chinese Affairs*, 44, 3, 49–77.

Jazeel, T. (2018). Singularity. A manifesto for incomparable geographies. *Singapore Journal of Tropical Geography* (online early) doi:10.1111/sjtg.12265

King, R. (2018). Theorising new European youth mobilities. *Population, Space and Place*, 24, 1, e2117.

Lai, H. (2015). The Pragmatic Cosmopolitan: The 'Serving China' Discourse, Career Plans, and Cosmopolitan Dispositions of Chinese Students in Japan, in F. Dervin (ed.), *Chinese Educational Migration and Student-Teacher Mobilities: Experiencing Otherness*. Basingstoke: Palgrave.

Lesjak, M., Ineson, E., Yap, M. and Axelsson, E. (2015). Erasmus student motivation: Why and where to go? *Higher Education*, 70, 845–865.

Lörz, M., Netz, N. and Quast, H. (2016). Why do students from underprivileged families less often intend to study abroad? *Higher Education*, 72, 2, 153–174.

Luo, J. and Jamieson-Drake, D. (2015). Predictors of study abroad intent, participation, and college outcomes. *Research in Higher Education*, 56, 29–56.

McCormack, D. P. and Schwanen, T. (2011). Guest editorial: The space—times of decision making. *Environment and Planning A*, 40, 12, 2801–2818.

Murphy-Lejeune, E. (2003). *Student Mobility and Narrative in Europe: The New Strangers*. London and New York: Routledge.

Papatsiba, V. (2014). Policy goals of European integration and competitiveness in academic collaborations: An examination of joint master's and Erasmus Mundus programmes. *Higher Education Policy*, 27, 43–64.

Prazeres, L., Findlay, A., McCollum, D., Sander, N., Musil, E., Krisjane, Z. and Apsite-Berina, E. (2017). Distinctive and comparative places: Alternative narratives of distinction within international student mobility. *Geoforum*, 80, 114–122.

Presley, A., Damron-Martinez, D. and Zhang, L. (2010). A study of business student choice to study abroad: A test of the theory of planned behavior. *Journal of Teaching in International Business*, 21, 4, 227–247.

Rizvi, F. and Lingard, B. (2010). *Globalizing Education Policy*. London: Routledge.

Rodríguez González, C., Bustillo Mesanza, R., and Mariel, P. (2011). The determinants of international student mobility flows: An empirical study on the Erasmus programme. *Higher Education*, 62, 4, 413–430.

Sánchez, C., Fornerino, M. and Zhang, M. (2006). Motivations and the intent to study abroad among U.S., French, and Chinese students. *Journal of Teaching in International Business*, 18, 1, 27–52.

Seal, A. (2018). The motivations, experiences, and aspirations of UK students on short-term international mobility programmes. Doctoral thesis, University of Surrey.

Sidhu, R. and Dall'Alba, G. (2017). 'A strategy of distinction' unfolds: Unsettling the undergraduate outbound mobility experience.

Stroud, A. (2010). Who plans (not) to study abroad? An examination of US student intent. *Journal of Studies in International Education*, 14, 5, 491–507.

Van Mol, C. and Timmerman, C. (2014). Should I stay or should I go? An analysis of the determinants of intra-European student mobility. *Population, Space and Place*, 20, 465–479.

Waters, J., Brooks, R. and Pimlott-Wilson, H. (2011). Youthful escapes? British students, overseas education and the pursuit of happiness. *Social and Cultural Geography*, 12, 5, 455–469.

Waters, J. and Leung. M. (2019). South-South Cooperation through Education? The Example of China with/in Africa, in E. Fiddian-Qasmiyeh and P. Daley (eds), *The Handbook of South-South Relations*. Abingdon: Routledge.

Weichbrodt, M. (2014). Learning mobility: High-school exchange programs as a part of transnational mobility. *Children's Geographies*, 12, 1, 9–24.

# Chapter 2

# Socio-demographics

## A global overview of inequalities in education abroad participation

*Nicolai Netz, Daniel Klasik, Steve R. Entrich and Michelle Barker*

**Highlights:**

- Despite variations across countries, students who are young, female, from ethnic majority and higher socio-economic backgrounds tend to be more likely to study abroad.
- Most parts of the world lack policies that address these socio-demographic inequalities, making education abroad a possible channel for the reproduction of social inequalities.
- Support from policymakers to generate high-quality, longitudinal, and internationally comparable data would facilitate research that reveals the reasons for socio-demographic inequalities in education abroad participation and evaluates the impact of policies to reduce them.

## 1. Introduction: Policy context

Scholars examining inequalities in higher education seek to understand who reaps the benefits of studying abroad. There is also intense political interest in the topic, as policymakers across the globe have promoted initiatives to increase education abroad participation, some of which address socio-demographic inequalities in access to education abroad.

During the Bologna Process, European education ministers agreed to improve the so-called social dimension of higher education. While originally envisaging student bodies that reflect the diversity of national populations, they later promised to "give extra attention and opportunities to under-represented groups to be mobile" (EHEA Ministerial Conference, 2012, p. 3). This goal has been concretized by national-level mobility strategies. In Germany, for instance, reforms of the major student assistance scheme (*Bundesausbildungsförderungsgesetz*, BAföG) have allowed students from lower socio-economic backgrounds to receive financial support whilst abroad. Further measures to reduce inequalities in education abroad participation have been announced by the German Academic Exchange Service, which administers merit-based scholarships (DAAD, 2013).

In North America, many efforts to encourage education abroad come from non-profit organizations like the Institute of International Education (e.g. Generation Study Abroad), partnerships between non-profit organizations and the U.S. Department of State, or consortia promoting education abroad between member institutions (e.g. the Consortium for North American Higher Education Collaboration, CONAHEC). These partnerships typically support education abroad in particular parts of the world, such as the 100,000 Strong programs for U.S. students studying in China, North, Central, or South America. Although these initiatives do not aim to reduce inequalities in education abroad participation, they make studying abroad more accessible for students from lower socio-economic backgrounds. Some institutions designed specific programs to create education abroad opportunities for first-generation college students (Martinez et al., 2010).

In some Central and South American countries, government-based support for education abroad encourages students to pursue graduate degrees abroad, or aims to dispose students who graduated abroad back to their home countries. Although government scholarships can make education abroad more affordable for students from lower socio-economic backgrounds, these students often do not have access to higher education in South America, and scholarship allocation does not seem to be needs-based (de Wit et al., 2005).

Australian policies have also traditionally focused on increasing the overall education abroad participation (Adams et al., 2011). Australian government-funded initiatives such as UMAP (University Mobility for the Asia Pacific), AsiaBound awards, and the New Colombo Plan (NCP) promote education abroad in Indo-Pacific countries. The 1988 Bradley Review of Australian Higher Education and the recent removal of a 20% loan scheme fee in the Overseas Higher Education Loan Program (OS-HELP) have made studying abroad more accessible for socially disadvantaged students (Dall'Alba & Sidhu, 2015).

In Asia, several countries have adopted plans to promote education abroad based on merit and academic performance (e.g. China: National Program for Medium and Long-term Educational Reform and Development; Japan: Study Abroad Japan!; Singapore: Young Talent Program, see Ziguras & McBurnie, 2011). These policies were not designed to reduce socio-demographic inequalities in education abroad participation. In Hong Kong, however, the local government supports socio-economically disadvantaged students from China (Li & Bray, 2007).

In Africa, education abroad policies mainly promote economic development by supporting students to complete degrees in economically developed countries, while ensuring that they return after graduation (Teferra & Knight, 2008).

Overall, few countries have developed policies with the explicit goal of reducing inequalities in education abroad participation. However, Europe and the Anglo-Saxon countries have come to view participation in education abroad as an important facet of higher education in internationalized societies, which should not depend on immutable socio-demographic features like gender, age, socio-economic background, and ethnicity.

## 2. Key questions to be addressed and definitions

Within this policy context, this chapter reviews empirical studies addressing the following questions:

- How do students' gender, age, socio-economic background, and ethnicity influence the likelihood of studying abroad?
- How can the observed patterns be explained?
- To what extent have socio-demographic inequalities in education abroad participation changed over time?

*Education abroad* – used synonymously with the term study abroad – is understood as stays in countries other than where students have previously been enrolled in higher education. Common types of education abroad are temporary enrollment, internships, language courses, and study-related stays such as summer schools, excursions, and field work. This chapter focuses on education abroad, but also considers some theoretically relevant studies on international degree mobility.

*Socio-economic background* reflects the socialization that students have experienced during childhood, and their economic, social, and cultural capital. The reviewed studies capture socio-economic background based on the highest educational degree of students' parents, parents' income and financial assets, or the prestige of parents' occupation.

*Ethnicity* captures the idea that people identify with and are perceived as being part of societal groups because of a shared history, culture, language, religion, and/or citizenship. The broad concept of ethnicity is used in education abroad research globally. The related, but more specific concept of race, which emphasizes socially recognized physical distinctions between groups of people, is primarily used in North America. Migration background is another more specific concept, which is primarily used in Asian, Australian, and European research. According to a common definition, students with a migration background were either born abroad themselves (first-generation immigrants), or have at least one parent who was born abroad (second-generation immigrants). Additionally, there are national idiosyncrasies in education abroad research. For instance, Chinese research distinguishes between mainland Chinese students and those from special administrative regions (Hong Kong, Macau, Taiwan). Ethnicity is used as an umbrella term in this chapter, and where possible, the respective authors' terminology is used when summarizing empirical studies.

## 3. Review of the literature

### 3.1 Gender

With some exceptions (e.g. Salisbury et al., 2010; Shirley, 2006; Tompkins et al., 2017), existing studies do not focus on describing and explaining gender differences in education abroad participation, but treat gender as a control variable or ancillary influencing factor. Most studies use the classic binary distinction of female versus male students (for a first study using a broader conception of students' sexual orientation and gender identity see Bryant & Soria, 2015).

Women tend to be over-represented in the education abroad population in Australia (Daly & Barker, 2005; Nerlich, 2015) and the USA (Bryant & Soria, 2015; Luo & Jamieson-Drake, 2015; Naffziger et al., 2008; Salisbury et al., 2009, 2010; Stroud, 2010; Whatley, 2017). They are also slightly over-represented in the education abroad populations of many European countries (Böttcher et al., 2016). This over-representation is most evident in temporary enrollments and language courses, and less so in internships abroad (Hauschildt et al., 2015, 2018). Multivariate studies suggest that, after controlling for confounding factors, the influence of being female on the likelihood of studying abroad is positive in the USA (Bryant & Soria, 2015; Luo & Jamieson-Drake, 2015; Salisbury et al., 2009; Stroud, 2010; Whatley, 2017), Italy (Di Pietro & Page, 2008), Austria, Germany, and the Netherlands (Netz, 2015), slightly positive but not significant in Switzerland (Messer & Wolter, 2007; Netz, 2015), and negative in France concerning stays abroad outside of the Erasmus program (Di Pietro & Page, 2008). Robust evidence on gender-specific education abroad participation in African and Asian countries is not known – apart from an experimental study on students at a Japanese university who had already completed a short-term stay abroad, which finds no gender differences (Kato & Suzuki, 2019).

Gender differences in education abroad participation may arise for various reasons, mostly driven by socially constructed gender roles. First, participation in education abroad mirrors other gender differences in educational decision-making: Women tend to choose fields of study in which it is more common and advisable, as regards the subject matter, to study abroad. These fields, such as the humanities, cultural, or social sciences, also tend to have more flexible curricula, which allow for stays abroad without prolonging the time to graduation. Accordingly, studies in Australia (Daly, 2011; Nerlich, 2015), the USA (Bandyopadhyay & Bandyopadhyay, 2015; Naffziger et al., 2008; Salisbury et al., 2010), and Continental European countries (Netz, 2015) find that field-of-study choice partly explains gender differences in education abroad participation.

According to Tompkins et al. (2017), these patterns reflect broader gender roles-related differences regarding students' interest in broadening their intercultural and global horizons. They find women to be more interested in learning about new cultures, and men to be more focused on fulfilling (perceived) expectations to become successful breadwinners. Correspondingly, men seek a speedy labor market entry, instead of potentially prolonging their studies through studying abroad. These interest profiles are likely shaped by students' familial environments: Shirley (2006) suggests that women receive more support from their family members in their decision to study abroad. However, stronger parental support for female students may be restricted to highly educated families (Salisbury et al., 2010).

Authors examining the degree mobility of students from Central and South Asia to Anglo-Saxon countries highlight that gender-specific mobility patterns result from cultural norms that influence the position of females and males in their local social hierarchy. In Kazakhstan, women sometimes refrain from studying abroad because they fear to appear as over-qualified relative to potential spouses (Holloway et al., 2012). Anticipated gender discrimination in the labor market also seems to play a role. On the one hand, it can make women in countries with more traditional gender roles skeptical that international mobility pays off. On the other hand, it can position mobility as a strategy to enable access to less gender-discriminatory labor markets (Sondhi & King, 2017).

Finally, women are more strongly deterred from studying abroad in specific countries because of safety concerns (Lee, 2014). The authors are not aware of research examining how gender differences in education abroad participation may have changed over time, or assessing the impact of policies on such inequalities.

### 3.2 Age

Few studies examine the relationship between students' age and studying abroad. One explanation is that many students enroll in higher education shortly after completing secondary education, so that the option to study abroad occurs within a narrowly defined age range during young adulthood. In this respect, national framework conditions matter: in the USA and Australia, the modal student goes abroad in the third year of undergraduate studies (Daly & Barker, 2005). Students in Japan prefer to complete their last year of undergraduate education at home to compete for jobs in the domestic labor market (Asaoka & Yano, 2009). Students in China (Li & Bray, 2007) and Thailand (Pimpa, 2003) prefer education abroad at postgraduate level. In Chile, the government supports education abroad for graduate students only (Trines, 2017).

Age is arguably more clearly related to studying abroad where students do not enroll in higher education immediately after secondary education, or where studying abroad does not require the prior completion of specific coursework, as in (post)graduate education and countries offering lengthy degrees with flexible curricula (e.g. Austria, France, and Italy: Hauschildt et al., 2018). Additionally, it may apply to countries with traditions of lifelong learning in higher education institutions, leading to enrollments by students of all ages (e.g. Scandinavia and Ireland: Hauschildt et al., 2018).

The few multivariate studies that include students' age as a control variable reach different conclusions: Di Pietro and Page (2008) find no significant age effect among students in Italy, but a higher propensity to study abroad among older students in France. However, they do not consider that older students have usually spent more time in higher education, and thus had more opportunities to complete stays abroad. In fact, age is negatively associated with studying abroad when the number of semesters is controlled for, as Messer and Wolter (2007) show for Switzerland.

Age is linked to factors both conducive and detrimental to studying abroad. Older students tend to be less dependent on their parents to finance stays abroad (Di Pietro & Page, 2008; Pimpa, 2003). However, older students' higher income may also constitute opportunity costs of studying abroad. Moreover, older students are more likely to have children and other social responsibilities, which may deter them from studying abroad. On balance, Netz (2015) finds that age is negatively related to study abroad intent among students in Austria, Germany, Switzerland, and the Netherlands, even controlling for factors like students' self-earned income, living situation (with family members versus alone), responsibility for children, and the number of semesters. This lends support to the prediction of the human capital model of migration that individuals will only become mobile if they believe they will benefit from it over a longer time, which is more probable among younger individuals.

The authors are not aware of studies examining either how age selectivity in access to education abroad opportunities has developed over time, or how policies – such as scholarships to support education abroad for students with young children – may have influenced age selectivity.

### 3.3 Socio-economic background

Scholars concerned with both the determinants of education abroad and with social inequality in higher education have studied the relationship between socio-economic background and education abroad participation. For all regions except Africa and South America, there is evidence on the relationship between socio-economic background and education abroad participation. Generally, students from high socio-economic backgrounds are more likely to study abroad than students from low socio-economic backgrounds. This pattern is visible in North America (USA: e.g. Salisbury et al., 2009, 2010; Simon & Ainsworth, 2012), Australia (Dall'Alba & Sidhu, 2015; Daly, 2011; Nerlich, 2015), some Asian countries (Kazakhstan: Holloway et al., 2012; Korea: Park, 2018), and various European countries (Allinson, 2017; Brooks & Waters, 2010; Hauschildt et al., 2018; Saarikallio-Torp & Wiers-Jenssen, 2010).

Even after controlling for confounding factors, students from high socio-economic backgrounds are more likely to study abroad in Austria and the Netherlands (Netz, 2015), Belgium (Van Mol & Timmerman, 2014), Germany (e.g. Lörz & Krawietz, 2011; Lörz et al., 2016; Neumeyer & Pietrzyk, 2016), Italy (Di Pietro & Page, 2008), Switzerland (Messer & Wolter, 2007; Netz, 2015), Estonia (Pungas et al., 2015), and the USA (Salisbury et al., 2009, 2010; Simon & Ainsworth, 2012). Additionally, students from high socio-economic backgrounds tend to receive more prestigious scholarships and complete longer stays (Netz & Finger, 2016) at more prestigious institutions abroad (Cebolla-Boado et al., 2018). In many European countries, social selectivity – that is, the over-representation of students from high socio-economic backgrounds compared to those from low socio-economic backgrounds – is stronger concerning temporary enrollment abroad than concerning internships abroad (Hauschildt et al., 2015, 2018).

Theories of cultural reproduction and of rational choice offer explanations for the social selectivity of education abroad. While the former tend to consider differences in students' group-specific habitus and endowment with economic, social, and cultural capital (e.g. Brooks & Waters, 2010; Bótas & Huisman, 2013), the latter accentuate differences in group-specific assessments of costs, benefits, and the probability of successfully completing stays abroad (e.g. Lörz et al., 2016).

Empirical studies align closely with both theoretical approaches. Compared to students from high socio-economic backgrounds, students from low socio-economic backgrounds are more strongly deterred by the costs of studying abroad: They are less likely to receive scholarships and financial support from their parents for studying abroad, and therefore, more reliant on gainful employment (Hauschildt et al., 2015; Li & Bray, 2007; Netz & Finger, 2016; Whatley, 2017). Related to their greater income dependency, average age, and familial responsibilities, they are also more worried about delaying their study progress, and about being separated from family and friends. Simultaneously, they consider stays abroad less beneficial for their personal and career development (Lörz et al., 2016). Furthermore, they tend to be less well-embedded in kinship, academic, and peer networks that value stays abroad and provide useful information and assistance (Brooks & Waters, 2010; Van Mol & Timmerman, 2014). Accordingly, they seem to be less well-informed about financial support (Nerlich, 2015). Another crucial explanation is that they develop less mobility-relevant cultural capital because they are less likely to travel internationally with their family, complete first stays abroad in secondary school, and develop the competences for studying abroad through early foreign language learning, the latter being related to their preference for nationally-oriented vocational, instead of internationally oriented academic schools (Brooks & Waters, 2010; Lörz et al., 2016; Salisbury et al., 2009). Relatedly, they are also under-represented at internationally oriented higher education institutions (Lörz & Krawietz, 2011).

Some studies examine the social selectivity of education abroad opportunities over time. Among UK students, the socio-economic background gap in education abroad participation did not change between 2013–2014 and 2015–2016 (Allinson, 2017). In Germany, the social selectivity of education abroad increased across school-leaver cohorts between 1990 and 2002 (Lörz & Krawietz, 2011). There is similar evidence that this social selectivity increased across German student populations between 1991 and 2003, and stagnated between 2003 and 2012 (Netz & Finger, 2016). The increase in inequality may have resulted from students from educationally advantaged families using education abroad to distinguish themselves from others who pursue higher education degrees. Students from educationally advantaged families were substantially more likely to profit from the provision of merit-based mobility scholarships during the Bologna Process. The stabilization after 2003 may have occurred either because of an equalizing effect of the BAföG reforms, or because educationally advantaged students became increasingly likely to complete entire degrees abroad, which would not be captured in the data (Netz & Finger, 2016).

One recent analysis of how public funding may influence socio-economic inequalities in education abroad participation (Kramer & Wu, 2019) examines how a state-funded merit-based financial aid policy in Tennessee, USA, influenced the share of students participating in education abroad. They conclude that "on average, the adoption of broad-based merit-aid policies increases participation in study abroad programs. However ... increases in merit-aid-induced study abroad participation may be concentrated in more selective institutions of higher education and in institutions with students from more affluent families" (p. 22).

### 3.4 Ethnicity

In most countries, the respective ethnic majority population has the highest rate of participation in education abroad. In the USA, Asian, African, and Indian Americans tend to be less likely to study abroad than Whites and Hispanics (Luo & Jamieson-Drake, 2015; Whatley, 2017). In the 1990s, Asian Americans were almost as likely to study abroad as Whites (Simon & Ainsworth, 2012). Among Asian Americans, Filipino and Vietnamese students are less likely to study abroad than Chinese, Korean, and Taiwanese students (Van Der Meid, 2003). Although there is some evidence that Asian Americans (Luo & Jamieson-Drake, 2015; Salisbury et al., 2009) and African Americans (Salisbury et al., 2011) are somewhat less likely to study abroad, race and ethnicity seem to be less influential regarding education abroad *intent* among U.S. students (Stroud, 2010). In Australia, students from culturally and linguistically diverse backgrounds seem to be under-represented in the education abroad population (Daly, 2011). In the UK, British Indian and Chinese students participate in education abroad at comparable rates to the overall population, while British Black, Bangladeshi, and Pakistani students participate at much lower rates (Allinson, 2017). In Germany, first-generation immigrants seem to be slightly under-represented in the education abroad population, but second-generation immigrants – especially those with dual citizenship – seem to be over-represented (Middendorff et al., 2013). Among Estonian high school graduates, the Russian-speaking minorities are substantially more likely to intend to study at universities abroad than the Estonian majority population (Pungas et al., 2015).

Scholars have suggested different explanations for ethnic differences in education abroad participation. First, theories explaining the educational and professional pathways of students as functions of their economic, social, and cultural capital help understand ethno-specific educational choices (Pungas et al., 2015). This perspective, which highlights that some ethnic groups are more likely to face economic hardships and less likely to access high-ranked institutions offering good education abroad opportunities, notably explains ethnic and racial differences in education abroad intent and participation among U.S. students (Salisbury et al., 2011; Simon & Ainsworth, 2012).

Furthermore, participation in education abroad may depend on the values and beliefs that particular racial and ethnic groups hold. For example, parents of Asian-American and Black students sometimes do not encourage education abroad because they consider it outside their goals for higher education (Brux & Fry, 2010; Salisbury et al., 2011).

Moreover, there is evidence that Black students may avoid education abroad because they fear to experience stereotype threat and racism whilst abroad. However, students from minority groups also consider education abroad appealing, particularly if they can explore the countries of their cultural heritage (Brux & Fry, 2010; Salisbury et al., 2011).

Pungas et al. (2015) suggest that ethnic minorities' lower attachment to Estonia and their stronger sensibility to intra-European opportunity differentials are more important in explaining ethnic gaps in education abroad participation than factors that are well-known to influence education abroad participation, such as socio-demographic characteristics and personality traits. They highlight that ethnic differences in education abroad participation are highly dependent on students' political, economic, and social context conditions.

The authors are not aware of studies examining ethnic inequalities over time, or possible effects of policies intending to reduce ethnic inequalities.

## 4. Implications for practice

An increasing body of evidence suggests that studying abroad can have positive effects on students (Part III of this volume). If students from different socio-demographic backgrounds profit to similar extents from it, the differing likelihood of studying abroad across socio-demographic groups is likely to result in social inequalities. It is understandable, therefore, that policymakers have called for equal opportunities to participate in education abroad.

At present, education abroad policies are designed primarily to increase the overall numbers of students studying abroad, often with a view to promoting national development and fostering diplomatic ties with other countries. With the exception of some European initiatives, few policies address equality of opportunity in education abroad participation. Such policies may be particularly important, as broad-based policies to increase college enrollment may inadvertently generate further inequalities in education abroad participation (Kramer & Wu, 2019).

Where possible, national governments, non-governmental organizations, and higher education institutions could provide further support targeted at the needs of disadvantaged socio-demographic groups. Such efforts could include tailored advertising and information campaigns, customized advising practices, and ongoing organizational and moral support to enhance students' understanding of the benefits of studying abroad. Besides the involvement of students' family members and education abroad alumni, the provision of additional financial support, the design of shorter or integrated mobility programs that do not delay graduation (Martinez et al., 2010), and a loosening of visa restrictions to allow students to work part-time whilst abroad, could be beneficial (Ziguras & McBurnie, 2011).

Additional measures may be needed to reduce socio-demographic inequalities not only within countries but also to counteract the widening divide between more- and less-affluent countries, so that students from many countries of the world can reap the benefits of studying abroad.

With regard to socio-demographic gaps in education abroad participation, researchers and practitioners could devote more attention to determining how gaps result from differences in prior academic performance, as opposed to differences in resources, cultural norms, discrimination, and parental values. Students fulfilling the academic requirements for studying abroad, but refraining from it for other reasons, are a particularly important group to target with affirmative action policies. Thus, a better understanding of the reasons why these students do not study abroad would allow policymakers and practitioners to address socio-demographic gaps in education abroad participation more effectively and efficiently.

The literature overeview also has implications for data collection: research would benefit from internationally comparative and nationally representative surveys that explore education abroad intent and behavior, socio-demographics, and variables addressing possible explanatory mechanisms. Ideally, the sampling designs of such surveys would capture various ethnic minorities representatively.

Clearly, policymakers have a role to play in addressing blind spots in knowledge about inequalities in education abroad participation. Tackling the research gaps sketched below will hardly be possible without political commitment and longer-term financial support to collect data through sophisticated longitudinal and internationally comparative designs.

## 5. Directions for future research

This chapter identified a number of studies examining how students are represented in education abroad populations depending on their socio-demographics. However, the sophistication of this research varies across regions of the world and the relative popularity of education abroad. Knowledge about socio-demographic differences in education abroad participation is most developed in Europe and North America, and scarce in regions where overall education abroad rates are low, as in Africa and South America. Here, we are left to assume that education abroad participation is likely restricted to student groups who can afford the costs.

This literature review found few studies providing explanations for socio-demographic inequalities in education abroad. Research has tended to focus on the overall likelihood of participation and host country choice, rather than on factors that explain socio-demographic differences in the likelihood of studying abroad. Particularly in countries with high support for education abroad, it is not yet entirely clear why specific socio-demographic groups do not take advantage of these opportunities.

Because group-specific participation rates and explanatory factors vary across national contexts, national idiosyncrasies need to be considered when examining socio-demographic inequalities in education abroad participation. It is likely that country differences in institutional support, and the value attached to education abroad, determine which students study abroad. By conducting internationally comparative research, this variation could be exploited to identify the influence of specific country-level framework conditions.

Few studies examine changes in socio-demographic inequalities in education abroad participation over time. Thus, there is also scant research on the impacts of policies to increase education abroad participation and to reduce inequalities in access to it. Knowledge about the relationship between education abroad participation and country-level as well as institutional-level characteristics is primarily derived from cross-sectional data. Thus, more impact assessments – such as the longitudinal study by Kramer and Wu (2019) – are needed. Kramer and Wu's (2019) use of institution-level rather than student-level data limits conclusions about whether inequality has changed, but their work provides an example of how researchers can study the effects of policies on socio-demographic inequalities in education abroad participation.

Additionally, more research could adopt an intersectional perspective and examine interactions of socio-demographic variables, as did Park (2018), Salisbury et al. (2011), and Sondhi and King (2017). One may ask whether and why the influence of age on the likelihood of studying abroad differs by gender, or how the influence of ethnicity differs depending on students' socio-economic background. Besides studying such multiple (dis)advantages and compensating mechanisms, scholars could examine the sensitivity of different socio-demographic groups to specific policy interventions.

Future research could also examine how inequalities arise due to group-specific patterns of engaging with international and local students, and the ways and extent to which students acquire soft and scientific skills whilst abroad.

Finally, future research could better examine the extent to which effects of studying abroad – both positive and negative – vary across socio-demographic groups. Only by addressing this question can scholars determine whether socio-demographic inequalities in access to and during stays abroad will eventually translate into an unequal distribution of the benefits of studying abroad.

## Acknowledgements

The authors wish to thank Fine Cordua, Luisa Klee, Christopher McCarthy, and Jalaluddin Schekeb for supporting their literature search.

## Further reading

Netz, N., & Finger, C. (2016). New horizontal inequalities in German higher education? Social selectivity of studying abroad between 1991 and 2012. *Sociology of Education*, 89 (2), 79–98.

Salisbury, M., Paulsen, M., & Pascarella, E. (2010). To see the world or stay at home: Applying an integrated student choice model to explore the gender gap in the intent to study abroad. *Research in Higher Education*, 51(7), 615–640.

Simon, J., & Ainsworth, J. (2012). Race and socioeconomic status differences in study abroad participation: The role of habitus, social networks, and cultural capital. *ISRN Education, Article ID 413896*, 21. www.hindawi.com/journals/isrn/2012/413896/

## References

Adams, T., Banks, M., & Olsen, A. (2011). International education in Australia: From aid to trade to internationalization. In R. Bhandari & P. Blumenthal (Eds.), *International students and global mobility in higher education* (pp. 107–128). New York: Palgrave Macmillan.

Allinson, K. (2017). *Widening participation in UK outward student mobility: A picture of participation*. London: Universities UK International.

Asaoka, T., & Yano, J. (2009). The contribution of 'study abroad' programs to Japanese internationalization. *Journal of Studies in International Education*, 13(2), 174–188.

Bandyopadhyay, S., & Bandyopadhyay, K. (2015). Factors influencing student participation in college study abroad programs. *Journal of International Education Research*, 11(2), 87–94.

Bótas, P., & Huisman, J. (2013). A Bourdieusian analysis of the participation of Polish students in the ERASMUS programme: Cultural and social capital perspectives. *Higher Education*, 66(6), 741–754.

Böttcher, L., Araújo, N., Nagler, J., Mendes, J., Helbing, D., & Herrmann, H. (2016). Gender gap in the ERASMUS mobility program. *PLOS ONE*, 11(2), e0149514.

Brooks, R., & Waters, J. (2010). Social networks and educational mobility: The experiences of UK students. *Globalisation, Societies and Education*, 8(1), 143–157.

Brux, J., & Fry, B. (2010). Multicultural students in study abroad: Their interests, their issues, and their constraints. *Journal of Studies in International Education*, 14(5), 508–527.

Bryant, K., & Soria, K. (2015). College students' sexual orientation, gender identity, and participation in study abroad. *Frontiers: The Interdisciplinary Journal of Study Abroad*, 25, 91–106.

Cebolla-Boado, H., Hu, Y., & Soysal, Y. (2018). Why study abroad? Sorting of Chinese students across British universities. *British Journal of Sociology of Education*, 39(3), 365–380.

DAAD. (2013). *Strategie DAAD 2020*. Bonn: DAAD.

Dall'Alba, G., & Sidhu, R. (2015). Australian undergraduate students on the move: Experiencing outbound mobility. *Studies in Higher Education*, 40(4), 721–744.

Daly, A. (2011). Determinants of participating in Australian university student exchange programs. *Journal of Research in International Education*, 10(1), 58–70.

Daly, A., & Barker, M. (2005). Australian and New Zealand university students' participation in international exchange programs. *Journal of Studies in International Education*, 9(1), 26–41.

de Wit, H., Jaramillo, I., Gacel-Avila, J., & Knight, J. (Eds.). (2005). *Higher education in Latin America: The international dimension.* Washington, D.C.: World Bank.

Di Pietro, G., & Page, L. (2008). Who studies abroad? Evidence from France and Italy. *European Journal of Education,* 43(3), 389–398.

EHEA Ministerial Conference. (2012). *Mobility for better learning: Mobility strategy 2020 for the European Higher Education Area.* www.cmepius.si/wp-content/uploads/2014/02/2012-EHEA-Mobility-Strategy.pdf.

Hauschildt, K., Gwosć, C., Netz, N., & Mishra, S. (2015). *Social and economic conditions of student life in Europe. EUROSTUDENT V 2012–2015.* Bielefeld: W. Bertelsmann Verlag.

Hauschildt, K., Vögtle, E., & Gwosć, C. (2018). *Social and economic conditions of student life in Europe. EUROSTUDENT VI 2016–2018.* Bielefeld: W. Bertelsmann Verlag.

Holloway, S., O'Hara, S., & Pimlott-Wilson, H. (2012). Educational mobility and the gendered geography of cultural capital: The case of international student flows between Central Asia and the UK. *Environment and Planning A,* 44(9), 2278–2294.

Kato, M., & Suzuki, K. (2019). Effective or self-selective: Random assignment demonstrates short-term study abroad effectively encourages further study abroad. *Journal of Studies in International Education,* 23(4), 411–428.

Kramer, D., & Wu, J. (2019). A HOPE for study abroad: Evidence from Tennessee on the impact of merit-aid policy adoption on study abroad participation. *Educational Policy,* 1–30. doi:doi:10.1177/0895904818823752

Lee, C.-F. (2014). An investigation of factors determining the study abroad destination choice: A case study of Taiwan. *Journal of Studies in International Education,* 18(4), 362–381.

Li, M., & Bray, M. (2007). Cross-border flows of students for higher education: Push—pull factors and motivations of mainland Chinese students in Hong Kong and Macau. *Higher Education,* 53(6), 791–818.

Lörz, M., & Krawietz, M. (2011). Internationale Mobilität und soziale Selektivität: Ausmaß, Mechanismen und Entwicklung herkunftsspezifischer Unterschiede zwischen 1990 und 2005. *Kölner Zeitschrift für Soziologie und Sozialpsychologie,* 63(2), 185–205.

Lörz, M., Netz, N., & Quast, H. (2016). Why do students from underprivileged families less often intend to study abroad? *Higher Education,* 72(2), 153–174.

Luo, J., & Jamieson-Drake, D. (2015). Predictors of study abroad intent, participation, and college outcomes. *Research in Higher Education,* 56(1), 29–56.

Martinez, M., Ranjeet, B., & Marx, H. (2010). Creating study abroad opportunities for first-generation college students. In R. Lewin (Ed.), *The handbook of practice and research in study abroad* (pp. 527–542). New York: Routledge.

Messer, D., & Wolter, S. (2007). Are student exchange programs worth it? *Higher Education,* 54(5), 647–663.

Middendorff, E., Apolinarski, B., Poskowsky, J., Kandulla, M., & Netz, N. (2013). *Die wirtschaftliche und soziale Lage der Studierenden in Deutschland 2012.* Berlin: BMBF.

Naffziger, D., Bott, J., & Mueller, C. (2008). Factors influencing study abroad decisions among college of business students. *International Business: Research, Teaching and Practice,* 2(1), 40–52.

Nerlich, S. (2015). Students from Australian universities studying abroad: A demographic profile. *Australian Universities' Review,* 57(1), 52–59.

Netz, N. (2015). What deters students from studying abroad? Evidence from four European countries and its implications for higher education policy. *Higher Education Policy,* 28(2), 151–174.

Netz, N., & Finger, C. (2016). New horizontal inequalities in German higher education? Social selectivity of studying abroad between 1991 and 2012. *Sociology of Education*, 89 (2), 79–98.

Neumeyer, S., & Pietrzyk, I. (2016). Auslandsmobilität im Masterstudium: Hat die Bildungsherkunft einen Einfluss auf die Dauer und die Art der Auslandsmobilität und falls ja, warum? *Beiträge zur Hochschulforschung*, 38(4), 108–126.

Park, J. (2018). Public fathering, private mothering: Gendered transnational parenting and class reproduction among elite Korean students. *Gender & Society*, 32(4), 563–586.

Pimpa, N. (2003). The influence of family on Thai students' choices of international education. *International Journal of Educational Management*, 17(5), 211–219.

Pungas, E., Täht, K., Realo, A., & Tammaru, T. (2015). Does ethnicity matter in intentions to study abroad? Analysis of high school students in Estonia. *Journal of Ethnic and Migration Studies*, 41(14), 2376–2395.

Saarikallio-Torp, M., & Wiers-Jenssen, J. (Eds.). (2010). *Nordic students abroad: Student mobility patterns, student support systems and labour market outcomes*. Helsinki: Kela.

Salisbury, M., Paulsen, M., & Pascarella, E. (2010). To see the world or stay at home: Applying an integrated student choice model to explore the gender gap in the intent to study abroad. *Research in Higher Education*, 51(7), 615–640.

Salisbury, M., Paulsen, M., & Pascarella, E. (2011). Why do all study abroad students look alike? Applying an integrated student choice model to explore differences in the factors that influence white and minority students' intent to study abroad. *Research in Higher Education*, 52(2), 123–150.

Salisbury, M., Umbach, P., Paulsen, M., & Pascarella, E. (2009). Going global: Understanding the choice process of the intent to study abroad. *Research in Higher Education*, 50(2), 119–143.

Shirley, S. (2006). *The gender gap in post-secondary study abroad: Understanding and marketing to male students*. Grand Forks: University of North Dakota.

Simon, J., & Ainsworth, J. (2012). Race and socioeconomic status differences in study abroad participation: The role of habitus, social networks, and cultural capital. *ISRN Education, Article ID-413896*, 21. www.hindawi.com/journals/isrn/2012/413896/.

Sondhi, G., & King, R. (2017). Gendering international student migration: An Indian case-study. *Journal of Ethnic and Migration Studies*, 43(8), 1308–1324.

Stroud, A. (2010). Who plans (not) to study abroad? An examination of U.S. student intent. *Journal of Studies in International Education*, 14(5), 491–507.

Teferra, D., & Knight, J. (Eds.). (2008). *Higher education in Africa: The international dimension*. Chestnut Hill, MA: CIHE.

Tompkins, A., Cook, T., Miller, E., & LePeau, L. (2017). Gender influences on students' study abroad participation and intercultural competence. *Journal of Student Affairs Research and Practice*, 54(2), 204–216.

Trines, S. (2017, September 18). Going north: The student mobility outlook from Brazil, Colombia, Mexico, and Venezuela. Retrieved from https://wenr.wes.org/2017/09/going-north-the-student-mobility-outlook-from-latin-america

Van Der Meid, S. (2003). Asian Americans: Factors influencing the decision to study abroad. *Frontiers: The Interdisciplinary Journal of Study Abroad*, 9, 71–110.

Van Mol, C., & Timmerman, C. (2014). Should I stay or should I go? An analysis of the determinants of intra-European student mobility. *Population, Space and Place*, 20(5), 465–479.

Whatley, M. (2017). Financing study abroad: An exploration of the influence of financial factors on student study abroad patterns. *Journal of Studies in International Education*, 21(5), 431–449.

Ziguras, C., & McBurnie, G. (2011). International student mobility in the Asia-Pacific: From globalization to regional integration? In S. Marginson, S. Kaur, & E. Sawir (Eds.), *Higher education in the Asia-Pacific: Strategic responses to globalization* (pp. 123–140). Dordrecht: Springer.

# Part 2

# Programming

For a long time, empirical scholars focusing on education abroad primarily investigated single education abroad programs. However, in recent years scholars have increasingly turned their attention towards a comparison of program types and individual program components in order to investigate how these differences influence the outcomes of education abroad (Roy et al., 2019). This is a useful effort, as different programs have been shown to lead to different outcomes (see e. g., Van Mol, 2017 on the differential value employers attach to study abroad and international internships). Furthermore, individual program components likely also have an impact on the outcomes of education abroad. In this regard, program duration, accommodation type, language of instruction, social interaction patterns during education abroad, study major and host country are themes that are commonly assessed (Moore et al. this volume, Chapter 3; Roy et al., 2019). Existing research shows, for example, that the longer the program's duration the stronger its positive influence on intercultural development (Behrnd & Porzelt, 2012), international perspectives, personal development (Zorn, 1996), and intellectual development (Varela & Gatlin-Watts, 2014, cited in Roy et al., 2019; Zorn, 1996). Chapters 3 and 4 in this section aim to provide a global overview of what is currently known about the relationship between different programs, program components and educational outcomes.

In Chapter 3, Kate Moore, Darin Menlove and Rebecca Pisano provide a matrix of program types and modalities in relation to their educational value. Their analysis clearly indicates the importance of program design, whereby different types and modalities are considered to enhance students' learning, depending on the specific learning goals that need to be addressed. At the same time, the authors draw attention to the importance of taking the specific institutional context (e.g., resources, institutional capacity) into account when designing education abroad programs, as there is no one-size-fits-it-all approach.

In Chapter 4, Nick Gozik and Susan Oguro review the role of individual program components, namely modes of instruction, housing, extra- and co-curricular activities, experiential learning, and support services in achieving desired learning outcomes. Similarly to Chapter 3, the authors highlight that scholars and practitioners need to carefully consider how individual program components impact students, with particular attention to the need to identify first what students are expected to learn. They indicate, for example, how very often assumptions are taken for granted in the design of individual education abroad programs such as housing, without considering the available evidence. Nevertheless, if students have to attain the expected outcomes, it is essential to evaluate the success of individual program components through data collection and analysis.

Together, both chapters indicate the need to empirically analyze education abroad beyond the individual program level. Comparisons of programs and individual program components can provide useful insights into what works in terms of achieving desired outcomes and can assist practitioners in (improving) the design of education abroad programs and individual program components.

## References

Behrnd, V., & Porzelt, S. (2012). "Intercultural competence and training outcomes of students with experiences abroad." *International Journal of Intercultural Relations*, 36 (2), 213–223.

Roy, A., Newman, A., Ellenberger, T., & Pyman, A. (2019). "Outcomes of international student mobility programs: A systematic review and agenda for future research." *Studies in Higher Education*, 44(9), 1630–1644.

Van Mol, C. (2017). "Do employers value international study and internships? A comparative analysis of 31 countries." *Geoforum*, 78(1), 52–60.

Varela, O. E., & Gatlin-Watts, R. (2014). "The development of the global manager: An empirical study on the role of academic international sojourns." *Academy of Management Learning & Education*, 13(2), 187–207.

Zorn, C. R. (1996). "The long-term impact on nursing students of participating in international education." *Journal of Professional Nursing*, 12(2), 106–110.

# Chapter 3

# Program types

## A matrix for cross-sectional analysis

*Kate Moore, Darin Menlove and Rebecca Pisano*

### Highlights:

- Transformative learning outside a student's comfort zone is enhanced by intentional program design and delivery
- An understanding of student learning goals helps administrators determine which program type fits best with student motivations and institutional strategy
- Institutional context varies and there is no one size fits all model for program delivery

### 1. Introduction and chapter overview

As the number and variety of outbound educational opportunities expands worldwide, higher education institutions face a growing range of opportunities and challenges. Researchers and administrators within education abroad particularly face an increased demand for the demonstration of proven outcomes as an integral part of the educational venture. Shared program models are helpful to describe, compare, select, and review program types and delivery modalities.

With the acknowledgement that institutional context and regional or local environment can vary dramatically, this chapter synthesizes academic literature to classify program types and codify program modalities, creating a matrix to assist with a cross-sectional analysis of educational value for a range of programs.

### 2. Key questions to be addressed

- Based on the relationship between level of host country immersion and amount of classroom activity, how does the literature currently classify program types ranging from study abroad to international internships to global research?
- As delivery modalities expand and evolve beyond student exchanges to range from faculty-directed initiatives to third-party provider organizations, how do researchers and administrators codify modes of program delivery for education abroad?

- After merging the classification of program types and codification for modes of program delivery to create a matrix, what can be garnered from cross-sectional analysis of educational value?

## 3. Review of the literature

Established research on program types and modalities has thus far focused on specific descriptors or subsets of data without extensive cross-sectional analysis. On the one hand, descriptors for research include program duration, accommodation type or language of instruction (Engle and Engle, 2003). On the other hand, as organizations around the world capture education abroad numbers to monitor trends and develop policies, existing data includes destination country, area of study, type of home institution, participant diversity, or program duration (AUIDF, 2015; CBIE, 2016; Institute of International Education, 2018). Much of the research exploring outcomes of education abroad programs focused on program duration, in part to evaluate the relative impact of shorter-term programs as the fastest growing segment of education abroad (Szekely and Krane, 1997).

### 3.1 Classification of program types and codification for modes of program delivery

As a foundation to develop a matrix for cross-sectional analysis, this chapter first classifies program types and then codifies modes of program delivery.

A classification of education abroad program types is provided in Table 3.1. This classification groups program types through *primary* activity and then classifies each type based on degree of immersion in the classroom *relative* to the degree of immersion in the host community, with primarily classroom only listed first and primarily community only listed last. This reflects education abroad program types including a range of learning within and beyond the classroom. For the purposes of this chapter, classroom may be on a local campus, at a study center, or an extension of the home university. The term community encompasses the local environment for learning outside the classroom and examples may include an agency for volunteering, city for exploring or company for interning. For each program type, definitions and alternate terminologies are included to allow for global application of the program type classification (NSEE, 2010; Filson, 2010; The Forum on Education Abroad, 2011; Hernandez et al., 2014; State University of New York, 2018).

These classifications are intended to provide a shared foundation to assist with the description, review and assessment by grouping specific program models into broad categories of program type (Paterson et al., 2007). Again, it is the *primary* activity and the degree to which a program is classroom-based *relative* to community-based that has determined the program type classification for this chapter.

A codification for modes of program delivery is provided in Table 3.2. This codification groups programs based on the *primary* party delivering the program

Table 3.1 Classification of education abroad program types

| Program Type | Definition | Alternate Terminology | Classroom to Community |
|---|---|---|---|
| Study Abroad | Classroom-based education abroad primarily taking place on a campus or study center | Includes exchange, direct enrollment, classroom study, language instruction, center-based | Primarily classroom-based |
| Research Abroad | Faculty-supervised research projects within classroom and/or incorporating community setting | Includes field work, laboratory work, data collection, first person interviewing, observational study, guided research project, independent project, capstone | Either classroom-based, or community-based |
| Global Service-Learning | Community-based volunteer projects with structured reflection exercises often with classroom component | Includes community service, civic engagement, volunteerism, community-engaged learning | More community-based than classroom-based |
| International Internships | Individual community-based professional placements that may include academic component, often faculty-directed or via online learning | Includes co-op, clinical placements, practicum, stage, work-integrated learning, practical training | Primarily community-based |

Table 3.2 Codification for modes of education abroad program delivery

| Program Modality | Definition | Alternate Terminology | Affiliation with Home Institution |
|---|---|---|---|
| Home Institution Program | Overseas study arranged by a home university or college where student is matriculated | Includes departmental program, university program | Completely affiliated to home institution |
| Faculty-Directed Program | Study directed by faculty member from home campus, who typically accompanies the program | Includes faculty-led, study tour | Closely affiliated to home institution |
| Host Institution Program | Study in overseas university or college | Includes student exchange, direct enrollment | Weakly affiliated to home institution |
| Third-Party Provider Program | Overseas study arranged by institution or organization that offers programs to students from variety of institutions | Includes independent program provider, program provider | Not affiliated to home institution |

and then describes each modality based on the *extent* to which the program is affiliated with – or controlled by – the home institution, listed from most to least. For each program modality, definitions and alternate terminologies are included to allow for global application of the description for modes of program delivery (The Forum on Education Abroad, 2011; Filson, 2010; Hernandez et al., 2014).

Clarity about *primary* party delivering the program needs to be articulated based on situation or audience. For example, even within consortia studies there remains a primary focus on either exchange or third-party provider programs within a portfolio of offerings (Korbel, 2007). A home university program might also be provided to other universities or to direct enroll students, thereby making the university a third-party provider. A third-party provider might customize services to create a home institution program, with the institution's academic credit and to their specifications. There are certainly delivery modes that incorporate multiple approaches, such as a facilitated direct enrollment through a third-party provider (Mills et al., 2010; Norris and Dwyer, 2009). Again, it is *primary* party delivering the program and the *extent* to which the program is affiliated with the home university that has determined the program delivery codification for this chapter.

### 3.2 Introduction to the matrix for cross-sectional analysis and research synthesis by segment

The classification of program types is combined with the codification for modes of program delivery to create the matrix for cross-sectional analysis presented in Table 3.3. Program type classifications are in rows, or the y axis, reflecting the *primary* activity and the degree of to which a program is classroom-based *relative* to community-based. The greater degree of classroom activity is at the top and the greater degree of community activity is at the bottom. Program modality codifications are in columns, or the x axis, reflecting the *primary* party delivering the program and the *extent* to which a program is affiliated with the home institution.

*Table 3.3* Matrix for cross-sectional analysis

|  |  | *Modes of Program Delivery* | | | |
|---|---|---|---|---|---|
|  |  | Home Institution | Faculty-Directed | Host Institution | Third-Party Provider |
| **Program Types** | Study Abroad | *Segment 1* | *Segment 2* | *Segment 3* | *Segment 4* |
|  | Research Abroad | *Segment 5* | *Segment 6* | *Segment 7* | *Segment 8* |
|  | Global Service-Learning | *Segment 9* | *Segment 10* | *Segment 11* | *Segment 12* |
|  | International Internships | *Segment 13* | *Segment 14* | *Segment 15* | *Segment 16* |

Those most affiliated to the home institution are to the left while those least affiliated with the home institution are to the right. As can be observed, there are sixteen segments labeled within the matrix that each combine one program type with one mode of program delivery.

### 3.2 Research synthesis by segment, focused on the cross-sectional analysis of educational value

Research related to the educational value of study abroad through a home institution (Segment 1) is most closely aligned to the literature on general study abroad and includes the extent to which a university's own programming may have an increased connection to the home curriculum content or enhanced pre- and post-program mentoring (Calhoon et al., 2003). Research related to the educational value of faculty-directed study abroad (Segment Two) extrapolates from the literature about short-term study abroad regarding gains in cross-cultural understanding, increased access for diverse student populations, and the opportunity to build community within student cohorts (Gaia, 2015; Sachau, Brasher, and Fee, 2009; Bradshaw, 2013; Peppas, 2005). Research related to the educational value of study abroad through a host institution (Segment Three) includes positive impact of the local learning context and recommendations to support varying degrees of student services (Norris and Dwyer, 2005).

No known study exists that focuses on the educational value of study abroad through third-party provider (Segment Four) or research abroad through a home institution (Segment Five).

Research related to the educational value of faculty-directed research abroad (Segment Six) indicates enhanced learning outcomes in the areas of collaboration with others, critical thinking, problem solving, and informed decision making (Lewis and Niesenbaum, 2005; McLaughlin and Johnson, 2006). Additional benefits include expanded worldview, stronger student-faculty relationships, and incorporating the experience into future research or presentations (Barkin, 2016; Ruth et al., 2018; Shostya and Morreale, 2017).

The literature related to the educational value of research abroad through a host institution (Segment Seven) indicates students gain a unique perspective on their field of research, experience with international research practices, refinement of personal and educational goals, potential joint publications, and invigoration toward further study (Mohunlol et al., 2014). Studies related to the educational value of research abroad with a third-party provider (Segment Eight) are limited to those that highlight a unique opportunity to explore individual connections to career goals or consider the long-term impacts on local communities (School for Field Studies, 2017; SIT, 2018).

Further study is needed related to the educational value of global service-learning through a home institution (Segment Nine) and international internships through a home institution (Segment Thirteen). When reviewed as a part of overall student engagement in either a local or global context, service-learning and internships demonstrate a greater level of deep learning and are cited as high-impact practices that increase self-directed or lifelong learning (Kuh and O'Donell, 2013; Kilgo, Ezell Sheets, and Pascarella, 2015; Jiusto and DiBiasio, 2006; Montrose, 2015).

The literature related to the educational value of faculty-directed global service learning indicates increased connectedness to the world and expanded engagement with lifelong volunteerism (Parker and Altman Dautoff, 2007; Kuh, 2008; Lewis and Niesenbaum, 2005; Horn and Fry, 2013). While these benefits are consistent with domestic service-learning and are seen across all modes of delivery, they are highlighted here because of the expectation for reflective exercises enhancing the learning as part of faculty-directed programs.

Particularly striking is the research related to education abroad in environments least consistent with the home campus experience. The literature finds these experiences provide the most significant increases in resiliency, ability to make connections across global contexts, enhancements in comparative or critical thinking, and other aspects of transformative learning (Engle and Engle 2003; Lilley et al., 2014; McLeod et al., 2015; Strange and Gibson, 2017). These studies are relevant to global service learning through a host institution (Segment Eleven), global service-learning with a third-party provider (Segment Twelve), international internships through a host institution (Segment Fifteen), and international internships with a third-party provider (Segment Sixteen).

Research related to the educational value of faculty-directed international internships (Segment Fourteen) indicates internships help participants understand the global workforce, enhance technical knowledge, and increase employability (Steinberg, 2015; Gates, 2014; Knouse and Fontenot, 2011; Nohara, Norton, Saijo, and Kusakabe, 2008). While these benefits are seen across modes of delivery, they are highlighted here because of the expectation for reflective exercises enhancing the learning as part of faculty-directed programs.

When compared to travel abroad for recreation, education abroad programs show improvements in understanding the complexities of global issues and applying disciplinary knowledge to a global context (Stebleton, Soria, and Cherney, 2013). When compared to control groups back on campus, general benefits to education and career trajectories were affirmed across a range of program types (Chieffo and Griffiths, 2004; Dwyer, 2004; Anderson and Lawton, 2011).

## 4. Implications for practice

Even as program types and modalities continue to emerge and evolve, the underlying implication is that *some* education abroad is better than none to achieve significant impact in the areas of language acquisition, intercultural development, and academic attainment measures. Further, a *well-designed* program can have lasting impacts on student learning regardless of duration (Dwyer, 2004; Shiveley and Misco, 2015).

Program design should balance a structure and support system that prepares students for different learning environments while also providing authentic experiences which may include a level of ambiguity that can stretch participants to a place of transformative learning (Strange and Gibson, 2017; Mills, Deviney, and Ball, 2010; Scally, 2015; Tarrant, 2010). Well-designed programs apply classroom study to "real world" challenges through direct engagement with local communities and incorporate local issues while providing cultural mentors that amplify linkages (Stebleton, Soria, and Cherney, 2013; AAC&U, 2007; Stansbie, Nash, and Chang, 2016; Paige and Vende Berg, 2012).

Administrators are advised to create holistic programming that incorporates the host community and considers impact on local stakeholders (Boni et al., 2015; Sherraden et al. 2008; Wessel, 2007). Indeed, regardless of mode of delivery or program type greater engagement with community members was found to have a significant impact on student learning (Niehuas and Kavaliauskas Crain, 2013).

The recurring themes of engagement with local community and transformative learning outside a student's comfort zone are enhanced through intentional program design and delivery. These are intended as considerations instead of absolutes, particularly when examining how best to apply the matrix for cross-sectional analysis of educational value.

Faculty-directed programs found students reporting greater learning than other program modality through instructor guidance, in part because reflection with an instructor was built into their study abroad curriculum (Graham and Crawford, 2012; Ritz, 2011; Smith-Pariola and Goke-Pariola, 2006). Regardless of instructor-led or individually driven, structured reflections are important across all programming to help students articulate their experiences (Gardner, Gross, and Steglitz, 2008).

Particularly given the changing student population and diversification of participation in education abroad, an understanding of student goals will help administrators determine which program types or modes of delivery correlate most closely with current and future student motivations (Yang et al., 2011). As one example, future participants may be seeking very pragmatic outcomes such as a direct link to future employability (Mills, Deviney, and Ball, 2010; Toncar, Reid, and Anderson, 2008).

Just as individual students differ, so does the institutional context and there is no *one size fits all* model. Administrators should consider the level of resources on campus and extent of capacity in a country when arriving at their ideal program types and modes of delivery as well as considering how best to incorporate research into practice (Nolting, Donohue, Matherly, and Tillman, 2013; Tarrant, 2010; Wolf-Wendel and Ward, 2009).

## 5. Directions for future research

Research regarding education abroad has largely focused on the benefits that studying abroad generally has in terms of interculturality, learning outcomes, employment impact, and identities rather than exploring the comparative impacts of program types or program modalities (Vande Berg, Connor-Linton, and Paige,

2009; Sutton and Rubin, 2004; Braskamp, Braskamp, and Merrill, 2009). The variable most often studied for comparative impact is program duration (Llanes and Munoz, 2009; Kehl and Morris, 2008; Medina-Lopez-Portillo, 2004; Chieffo and Griffiths, 2004). Other variables studied for impact, albeit to a lesser degree, are specific program components such as homestay accommodations (Tucker et al., 2011; Wilkinson, 1998; see also Chapter 4, this volume).

Future research might expand upon cross-sectional analysis of educational value, comparing program types and modes of delivery at single institutions or organizations or expanding study across multiple institutions and organizations.

When designing future research, best practices incorporate longitudinal studies with large numbers and global engagement (Dwyer, 2004; Paige et al., 2009; Parey and Waldinger, 2011). Studies could move more quickly from correlation to causation by minimizing reliance upon self-reporting, utilizing control groups, and bridging large-scale studies with shared research parameters drawing from existing metrics such as those from the Association of American Colleges & Universities (Norris and Gillespie, 2009; Twombly, Salisbury, Tumanut, and Klute, 2012, AAC&U, 2007).

Existing measurements could be refined for specific program types. For internships, employability gains or perceived career benefits have been surveyed as related to education abroad and this research could be foundational for future study (Potts, 2015; Trooboff, Vande Berg, and Rayman, 2008). With service-learning, the incorporation of existing research from a domestic context is a natural extension (Eyler, 2012). Further examination of undergraduate research outcomes might include best practices for training faculty and staff to deliver this type of programming as the need for training has been noted, but not the formula for best doing so (The Forum on Education Abroad, 2013; Streitwieser, 2010).

As the evolution and emergence of new program types and program modalities continue, research will need to be responsive to new approaches to education abroad such as online coursework and globally distributed team projects (Bartel-Radic et al., 2015). With students undertaking more than one education abroad experience, the implications of multiple contexts and impact on their combined experiences back on campus will be another area of potential inquiry (Dolby, 2008; Keen and Hall, 2009; Xu et al., 2013). In addition, more comprehensive studies could incorporate outcomes that demonstrate both short-term learning or medium-term action during university as well as long-term impacts on professional and personal life (Deardorff, Pysarchik, and Yun, 2009; Potts, 2016).

## Further reading

Engle, L., & Engle, J. (2003). Study Abroad Levels: Towards a Classification of Program Types. *Frontiers: The Interdisciplinary Journal of Study Abroad.* https://aucp.fr/wp-content/uploads/2014/04/Study-Abroad-Levels-Toward-a-Classification-of-Program-Types.pdf

Filson, C. (2010). *Abroad by Design: Key Strategies.* Washington, DC: NAFSA: Association of International Educators.

Kuh, G. D. (2008). *High-Impact Educational Practices: What They Are, Who Has Access to Them, and Why They Matter.* Washington, DC: Association of American Colleges and Universities.

Norris, E., & Dwyer, M. (2005). Testing Assumptions: The Impact of Two Study Abroad Program Models. *Frontiers: The Interdisciplinary Journal of Study Abroad,* pp. 121–142.

## References

Anderson, P. H., & Lawton, L. (2011, Fall). Intercultural Development: Study Abroad vs. On-Campus Study. *Frontiers: The Interdisciplinary Journal of Study Abroad,* pp. 86–108.

Association of American Colleges and Universities. (2007). *Global Learning VALUE Rubric.* Washington, DC: AAC&U. Retrieved from www.aacu.org/value/rubrics/global.

AUIDF. (2015). Learning Abroad 2015: Australian Universities International Directors' Forum. *i-graduate International Insight.* Retrieved from https://www.ieaa.org.au/blog/leading-the-way-for-learning-abroad

Barkin, G. (2016). Undergraduate Research on Short-term, Faculty-led Study Abroad. *Council on Undergraduate Research Quarterly,* pp. 26–32.

Bartel-Radic, A., Moos, J. C., & Long, S. K. (2015). Cross-cultural Management Learning through Innovative Pedagogy: An Exploratory Study of Globally Distributed Student Teams. *Decision Sciences: Journal of Innovative Education,* pp. 539–562.

Boni, A., Sastre, J.J., & Calabuig, C. (2015, November 28). Educating Engineers for the Public Good through International Internships: Evidence from a Case Study at Universitat Politecnica de Valencia. *Science and Engineering Ethics,* pp. 1–17.

Bradshaw, G. W. (2013). Internationalization and Faculty-led Service Learning. In T. Treat, & L. Serra Hagedorn (eds.), *The Community College in a Global Context.* New Directions for Community Colleges, 161 (pp. 40–56). Hoboken, NJ: John Wiley & Sons.

Braskamp, L. A., Braskamp, D. C., & Merrill, K. (2009, Fall). Assessing Progress in Global Learning and Development of Students with Education Abroad Experiences. *Frontiers: The Interdisciplinary Journal of Study Abroad,* pp. 101–118.

Calhoon, J. A., Wildcat, D., Annett, C., Pierotti, R., & Griswold, W. (2003). Creating Meaningful Study Abroad Programs for American Indian Postsecondary Students. *Journal of American Indian Education,* pp. 46–57.

CBIE. (2016). *A World of Learning: Canada's Performance and Potential in International Education 2016.* Ottawa: Canadian Bureau for International Education.

Chieffo, L., & Griffiths, L. (2004, Fall). Large-Scale Assessment of Student Attitudes after a Short-Term Study Abroad Program. *Frontiers: The Interdisciplinary Journal of Study Abroad,* pp. 165–177.

Deardorff, D., Pysarchik, D. T., & Yun, Z.-S. (2009). Towards Effective International Learning Assessments: Principles, Design, and Implementation. In H. de Wit, *Measuring Success in the Internationalisation of Higher Education: EAIE Occasional Paper 22* (pp. 23–37). Amsterdam: European Association for International Education.

Dolby, N. (2008). Global Citizenship and Study Abroad: A Comparative Study of American and Australian Undergraduates . *Frontiers: The Interdisciplinary Journal of Study Abroad,* pp. 51–67.

Dwyer, M. M. (2004, Fall). More Is Better: The Impact of Study Abroad Program Duration. *Frontiers: The Interdisciplinary Journal of Study Abroad,* pp. 151–163.

Engle, L., & Engle, J. (2003). Study Abroad Levels: Towards a Classification of Program Types. *Frontiers: The Interdisciplinary Journal of Study Abroad*. https://aucp.fr/wp-content/uploads/2014/04/Study-Abroad-Levels-Toward-a-Classification-of-Program-Types.pdf

Eyler, J. (2012). What International Service Learning Research can Learn from Research on Service Learning. In R. Bringle, J. Hatcher, & S. Jones (Eds.), *International Service Learning: Conceptual Frameworks and Research* (pp. 225–242). Sterling, VA: Stylus.

Filson, C. (2010). *Abroad by Design: Key Strategies*. Washington, DC: NAFSA: Association of International Educators.

Gaia, A. C. (2015). Short-term Faculty-led Study Abroad Programs Enhance Cultural Exchange and Self-Awareness. *The International Education Journal: Comparative Perspectives*, pp. 21–31.

Gardner, P., Gross, L., & Steglitz, I. (2008). *Unpacking your Study Abroad Experience: Critical Reflections for Workplace Competencies*. East Lansing: Collegiate Employment Research Institute.

Gates, L. (2014, June 2). The Impact of International Internships and Short-Term Immersion Programs. *Undergraduate Global Education: Issues for Faculty, Staff, and Students*, pp. 33–40.

Graham, N., & Crawford, P. (2012). Instructor-Led Engagement and Immersion Programs: Transformative Experiences of Study Abroad. *Journal of Higher Education Outreach and Engagement*, pp. 107–109.

Hernandez, M., Wiedenhoeft, M., & Wick, D. (2014). *NAFSA's Guide to Education Abroad for Advisers and Administrators: Fourth Edition*. Washington, DC: NAFSA: Association of International Educators.

Horn, A., & Fry, G. (2013, December). Promoting Global Citizenship through Study Abroad: The Influence of Program Destination, Type, and Duration on the Propensity for Development Volunteerism. *VOLUNTAS: International Journal of Voluntary and Nonprofit Organizations*, pp. 1159–1179.

Institute of International Education. (2018, June 18). Open Doors Report on International Education Exchange. Retrieved from IIE: www.iie.org/opendoors.

Jiusto, S., & DiBiasio, D. (2006, July). Experiential Learning Environments: Do They Prepare our Students to be Self-Directed, Life-Long Learners? *Journal of Engineering Education*, pp. 195–204.

Keen, C., & Hall, K. (2009). Engaging with Difference Matters: Longitudinal Student Outcomes of Co-Curricular Service Learning Programs. *The Journal of Higher Education*, pp. 59–79.

Kehl, K., & Morris, J. (2008, Winter). Differences in Global-Mindedness between Short-Term and Semester-Long Study Abroad Participants at Selected Private Universities. *Frontiers: The Interdisciplinary Journal of Study Abroad*, pp. 67–79.

Kilgo, C. A., Ezell Sheets, J. K., & Pascarella, E. T. (2015, April). The Link between High-Impact Practices and Student Learning: Some Longitudinal Evidence. *Higher Education: The International Journal of Higher Education and Educational Planning*, pp. 509–525.

Knouse, S. B., & Fontenot, G. (2011, December 23). Benefits of the Business College Internship: A Research Review. *Journal of Employment Counseling*, pp. 61–66.

Korbel, L. A. (2007, June 19). In Union there is Strength: The Role of State Global Education Consortia in Expanding Community College Involvement in Global Education. In *New Directions for Community Colleges*. San Francisco, CA: Jossey-Bass.

Kuh, G. D. (2008). *High-Impact Educational Practices: What They Are, Who Has Access to Them, and Why They Matter.* Washington, DC: Association of American Colleges and Universities.

Kuh, G. D., & O'Donell, K. (2013). *Ensuring Quality & Taking High-Impact Practices to Scale.* Washington, DC: Association of American Colleges and Universities.

Lewis, T. L., & Niesenbaum, R. A. (2005, September 1). Enhancing the Stay: Using Community-Based Research and Service Learning to Enhance Short-Term Study Abroad. *Journal of Studies in International Education*, pp. 251–264.

Lilley, K., Barker, M., & Harris, N. (2014, September 11). Exploring the Process of Global Citizen Learning and the Student Mind-Set. *Journal of Studies in International Education*, pp. 225–245.

Llanes, A., & Munoz, C. (2009, September). A Short Stay Abroad: Does it Make a Difference? *System*, pp. 353–365.

McLaughlin, J. S., & Johnson, D. K. (2006). Assessing the Field Course Experiential Learning Model: Transforming Collegiate Short-Term Study Abroad Experiences into Rich Learning Environments. *Frontiers: The Interdisciplinary Journal of Study Abroad*, pp. 65–85.

McLeod, M., Carter, V., Nowicki, S., Tottenham, D., Wainwright, P., & Wyner, D. (2015, Fall). Evaluating the Study Abroad Experience using the Framework of Rotter's Social Learning Theory. *Frontiers: The Interdisciplinary Journal of Education Abroad*, pp. 30–38.

Medina-Lopez-Portillo, A. (2004, Fall). Intercultural Learning Assessment: The Link Between Program Duration and the Development of Intercultural Sensitivity. *Frontiers: The Interdisciplinary Journal of Study Abroad*, pp. 179–199.

Mills, V., Deviney, D., & Ball, B. (2010). Short-Term Study Abroad Programmes: A Diversity of Options. *The Journal of Human Resources and Adult Learning*, pp. 1–13.

Montrose, L. (2015). International Study and Experiential Learning: The Academic Context. *Frontiers: The Interdisciplinary Journal of Study Abroad*, pp. 1–15.

Mohunlol, U., Banks, C., Beaudoin, L., Gallagher, J., & de Bok, C. (2014). Undergraduate Research in Study Abroad. In M. Green*et al.* (Eds.), *Internationalisation of Higher Education*, Vol. 2 (pp. 59–84). Berlin: DUZ Academic Publishers.

Niehuas, E., & Kavaliauskas Crain, L. (2013, Fall). Act Local or Global? Comparing Student Experiences in Domestic and International Service-Learning Programs. *Michigan Journal of Community Service Learning*, pp. 31–40.

Nohara, K., Norton, M., Saijo, M., & Kusakabe, O. (2008, March). Overseas Internships as a Vehicle for Developing Meta-Level Awareness Regarding Science Communication. *Journal of Science Communication*, pp. 1–12.

Nolting, W., Donohue, D., Matherly, C., & Tillman, M. (2013). *Internships, Service Learning, & Volunteering Abroad: Successful Models and Best Practices.* Washington, DC: NAFSA: Association of International Educators.

Norris, E. M., & Gillespie, J. (2009). How Study Abroad Shapes Global Careers: Evidence from the United States. *Journal of Studies in International Education*, pp. 382–397.

Norris, E., & Dwyer, M. (2005). Testing Assumptions: The Impact of Two Study Abroad Program Models. *Frontiers: The Interdisciplinary Journal of Study Abroad*, pp. 121–142.

NSEE. (2010). *Experiential Education Academy Curriculum.* Mt. Royal, NJ: National Society of Experiential Education.

Paige, R. M., & Vande Berg, M. (2012). Why Students Are and Are Not Learning Abroad: A Review of Recent Research. In M. Vande Berg, R. M. Paige, & K. Hemming Lou

(Eds.), *Student Learning Abroad: What Our Students Are Learning, What They're Not, and What We Can Do About It* (pp. 29–60). Sterling, Virginia: Stylus.

Paige, R., Fry, G., Stallman, E., Josi, J., & Jon, J. (2009). Study Abroad for Global Engagement: The Long-Term Impact of Mobility Experiences. *Intercultural Education*, pp. 29–44.

Parey, M., & Waldinger, F. (2011, March 1). Studying Abroad and the Effect on International Labour Market Mobility: Evidence from the Introduction of ERASMUS. *The Economic Journal*, pp. 194–222.

Parker, B., & Altman Dautoff, D. (2007). Service-Learning and Study Abroad: Synergistic Learning Opportunities. *Michigan Journal of Community Service Learning*, pp. 40–53.

Paterson, C., Engle, L., Kenney, L., Kreutzer, K., Nolting, W., & Ogden, A. (2007). Defining Terms for Use in Designing Outcomes Projects. In M. C. Bolen (Ed.), *A Guide to Outcomes Assessment in Education Abroad* (pp. 163–203). Carlisle, PA: The Forum on Education Abroad.

Peppas, S. C. (2005, August). Business Study Abroad Tours for Non-Traditional Students: An Outcomes Assessment. *Frontiers: The Interdisciplinary Journal of Study Abroad*, pp. 143–163.

Potts, D. (2015, November 1). Understanding the Early Career Benefits of Learning Abroad Programs. *Journal of Studies in International Education*, pp. 441–459.

Potts, D. (2016). *Outcomes of Learning Abroad Programs*. Melbourne: Universities Australia.

Ritz, A. (2011, May 25). The Educational Value of Short-Term Study Abroad Programs as Course Components. *Journal of Teaching in Travel & Tourism*, pp. 164–178.

Ruth, A., Brewis, A., Blasco, D. & Wutich, A. (2018). Long-Term Benefits of Short Term Research-Integrated Study Abroad. *Journal of Studies in International Education*, 1–16.

Sachau, D., Brasher, N., & Fee, S. (2009, July 6). Three Models for Short-Term Study Abroad. *Journal of Management Education*, pp. 645–670.

Scally, J. (2015). Intercultural Competence Development in Three Different Study Abroad Program Types. *Intercultural Communication Studies*, pp. 35–70.

School for Field Studies. (2017). The School for Field Studies Research Philosophy. Retrieved from https://fieldstudies.org/wp-content/uploads/2017/08/SFS-Research-Philosophy-GENERAL.pdf.

Sherraden, M., Lough, B., & Moore McBride, A. (2008, December 7). Effects of International Volunteering and Service: Individual and Institutional Predictors. *VOLUNTAS: International Journal of Voluntary and Nonprofit Organizations*, pp. 395–421.

Shiveley, J., & Misco, T. (2015, Fall). Long-Term Impacts of Short-Term Study Abroad: Teacher Perceptions of Preservice Study Abroad Experiences. *Frontiers: The Interdisciplinary Journal of Study Abroad*, pp. 107–120.

Shostya, A., & Morreale, J. (2017). Fostering Undergraduate Research through a Faculty-Led Study Abroad Experience. *International Journal of Teaching and Learning in Higher Education*, 300–308.

SIT. (2018, October 24). Why SIT. Retrieved from https://studyabroad.sit.edu/why-sit/

Smith-Pariola, J., & Goke-Pariola, A. (2006, March 1). Expanding the Parameters of Service Learning: A Case Study. *Journal of Studies in International Education*, pp. 71–86.

Stansbie, P., Nash, R., & Chang, S. (2016, November). Linking Internships and Classroom Learning: A Case Study in Examination of Hospitality and Tourism Management Students. *Journal of Hospitality, Leisure, Sport & Tourism Education*, pp. 19–29.

State University of New York. (2018, October 25). Applied Learning at SUNY. Retrieved from www.suny.edu/applied-learning/

Stebleton, M., Soria, K., & Cherney, B. (2013, Winter). The High Impact of Education Abroad: College Students' Engagement in International Experiences and the Development of Intercultural Competencies. *Frontiers: The Interdisciplinary Journal of Study Abroad*, pp. 1–24.

Steinberg, M. (2015). "Involve Me and I Will Understand": Academic Quality in Experiential Programs Abroad. *Frontiers: The Interdisciplinary Journal of Study Abroad*, pp. 207–229.

Strange, H., & Gibson, H. (2017, April). An Investigation of Experiential and Transformative Learning in Study Abroad Programs. *Frontiers: The Interdisciplinary Journal of Study Abroad*, pp. 85–100.

Streitwieser, B. (2010). Undergraduate Research during Study Abroad: Scope, Meaning, and Potential. In R. Lewin (Ed.), *The Handbook of Practice and Research in Study Abroad: Higher Education and the Quest for Global Citizenship* (pp. 399–419). London: Routledge.

Sutton, R. C., & Rubin, D. L. (2004, Fall). The GLOSSARI Project: Initial Findings from a System-Wide Research Initiative on Study Abroad Learning Outcomes. *Frontiers: The Interdisciplinary Journal of Study Abroad*, pp. 65–82.

Szekely, B. B., & Krane, M. (1997). The Current Demographics of Education Abroad. In W. Hoffa, & J. Pearson (Eds.), *NAFSA's Guide to Education Abroad for Advisors and Administrators, Second Edition*. Washington, DC: NAFSA: Association of International Educators.

Tarrant, M. (2010). A Conceptual Framework for Exploring the Role of Studies Abroad in Nurturing Global Citizenship. *Journal of Studies in International Education*, pp. 433–451.

The Forum on Education Abroad. (2011). *Education Abroad Glossary*. Carlisle, PA: The Forum on Education Abroad.

The Forum on Education Abroad. (2013). *Forum Guidelines for Undergraduate Research Abroad*. Carlisle, PA: The Forum on Education Abroad.

Toncar, M. F., Reid, J. S., & Anderson, C. E. (2008, September 23). Perceptions and Preferences of Study Abroad: Do Business Students Have Different Needs? *Journal of Teaching International Business*, pp. 61–80.

Trooboff, S., Vande Berg, M., & Rayman, J. (2008, Winter). Employer Attitudes towards Study Abroad. *Frontiers: The Interdisciplinary Journal of Study Abroad*, pp. 17–33.

Tucker, M. L., Gullekson, N. L., & McCambridge, J. (2011, December). Assurance of Learning in Short-Term Study Abroad Programs. *Research in Higher Education Journal*. https://pdfs.semanticscholar.org/1d19/a2eea4cffce1a65048f.5b1e1c80f.036d7a71.pdf

Twombly, S., Salisbury, M. H., Tumanut, S. D., & Klute, P. (2012). *Study Abroad in a New Global Century: Renewing the Promise, Refining the Purpose: ASHE Higher Education Report*. Hoboken, NJ: John Wiley & Sons.

Vande Berg, M. (2009). Intervening in Student Learning Abroad: A Research-Based Inquiry. *Intercultural Education*, pp. S15–S27.

Vande Berg, M., Connor-Linton, J., & Paige, R. M. (2009, Fall). The Georgetown Consortium Project: Interventions for Student Learning Abroad. *Frontiers: The Interdisciplinary Journal of Study Abroad*, pp. 1–75.

Wessel, N. (2007, March 1). Integrating Service Learning Into the Study Abroad Program: U.S. Sociology Students in Mexico. *Journal of Studies in International Education*, pp. 73–89.

Wilkinson, S. (1998, Fall). On the Nature of Immersion during Study Abroad: Some Participant Perspectives. *Frontiers: The Interdisciplinary Journal of Study Abroad*, pp. 121–138.

Wolf-Wendel, L., & Ward, K. K. (2009, July/August). A Tangled Web of Terms: The Overlap and Unique Contribution of Involvement, Engagement, and Integration to Understanding College Student Success. *Journal of College Student Development*, pp. 407–428.

Xu, M., de Silva, C. R., Neufeldt, E., & Dane, J. H. (2013, Fall). The Impact of Study Abroad on Academic Success: An Analysis of First-Time Students Entering Old Dominion University, Virginia, 2000–2004. *Frontiers: The Interdisciplinary Journal of Study Abroad*, pp. 90–103.

Yang, M., Webster, B., & Prosser, M. (2011, January). Travelling a Thousand Miles: Hong Kong Chinese Students' Study Abroad Experience. *International Journal of Intercultural Relations*, pp. 69–78.

# Chapter 4

# Program components

## (Re)considering the role of individual areas of programming in education abroad

*Nick J. Gozik and Susan Oguro*

---

### Highlights:

- Current research on education abroad in higher education has mostly analyzed education abroad programs without isolating individual program components, making it difficult for scholars and practitioners to determine which specific aspects of a program are most effective in helping students achieve stated learning outcomes.
- Existing research has been disproportionately conducted by scholars in a handful of countries, including the U.S.
- This chapter explores five areas of programming often associated with education abroad: modes of instruction, housing, extra- and co-curricular activities, experiential learning, and student support services.

### 1. Introduction and chapter overview

Over the past decades, a growing body of scholarship has sought to assess the extent to which education abroad programs deliver on intended outcomes for students. Scholars and practitioners share a common interest in moving beyond the assumption that education abroad is automatically and necessarily a transformational process, to find evidence of the ways that students may (or may not) develop as part of their time abroad (Gozik, 2014). While much has been examined regarding the success of *programs* in maximizing student learning (see e.g. Chapter 3, this volume), this chapter explores an area in the research literature that has received far less attention, namely the role that *individual program components* have in contributing to student learning.

Reviewing the existing literature, this chapter explores five areas of programming often associated with education abroad: modes of instruction, housing, extra- and co-curricular activities, experiential learning, and student support services. These align with the categorization of "meeting grounds" for intercultural learning, as developed by Ogden, Streitwieser, and Crawford (2014). "Academic programming" has been further split out into "modes of instruction" and "extra and co-curricular learning," given the great expansion of both areas.

Instead of viewing a particular element or a combination of practices as the "gold standard," it is argued that scholars and practitioners need to be aware of how all individual program components impact students (Strange & Gibson, 2017; Tarrant, Ruben & Stoner, 2014). A critical stance is essential to ensure the combination of components of any education abroad program is understood for their value in facilitating students' achievement of desired outcomes.

## 2. Key Questions to be addressed

- What components of education abroad programs should practitioners consider when designing or evaluating programs?
- What research evidence is there for assumptions about the effectiveness of individual program components?
- What future research is needed to fill the gaps on what is known about the effectiveness of individual program components?

## 3. Review of the literature

The review of the global research literature here builds on a previous chapter by Ogden et al. (2014), one of the few scholarly works to consider a range of program components in education abroad. In addition to providing an updated review of the literature, this chapter covers areas that were not explored as extensively in the earlier publication, including the role of technology, the extent to which program components have been explored outside of U.S.-based programs, and the implications of current and future research findings for practitioners.

### 3.1 Modes of instruction

Before determining which sort of classroom environment will be most appropriate on a given program, it is necessary to identify what students are expected to learn. Is the goal for students to become more interculturally competent, adaptable to new situations, linguistically proficient, knowledgeable of disciplinary theories/practices, or something else? Based on the answer to this question, students may be given the choice of enrolling directly in courses offered by the host university alongside local students, taking classes designed by the host university for international students, taking classes offered through a program provider and/or onsite staff, or a combination of two or more of these options. Among the many models that exist, it has been difficult for practitioners to make informed choices because, as Ogden et al. (2014) argue, "research has yet to thoroughly and systematically examine variations in modes of academic delivery in education abroad" (p. 238).

One study that sought to examine the relevance of particular courses of study and the composition of classes in education abroad programs is the consortium project led by Georgetown University (Vande Berg, Connor-Linton, & Paige, 2009), with a research sample of 1,297 students from four U.S. institutions and several providers. Surprisingly, the researchers found greater gains in terms of intercultural development among students taking classes alongside other U.S. students compared to those enrolled directly with local students (See also Norris & Dwyer, 2005). While this study relied primarily on student self-reporting, an inherent weakness, it nonetheless raises an important question of whether direct enrollment is necessarily more effective in allowing students to adapt to new educational systems or in gaining new, culturally informed perspectives on their academic subjects. The results point further to the absence of meaningful interactions between local and international students required for the development of intercultural competency (Leask, 2009; Montgomery, 2010).

In responding to market demands, a growing number of courses offered for international students are delivered by teaching staff of the home university, such as within the context of short-term, faculty-directed programs. These offerings are designed to meet the needs of an increasingly diverse group of students, who may not be able to study abroad for longer periods of time (Redden, 2018). Institutions may too appreciate the ability to put more quality controls in place, with greater oversight over faculty hiring and curricular choices. Coleman notes that these courses can limit students' exposure to alternative teaching styles and approaches and may prevent students from developing cultural awareness and intercultural competency (2009, p. 192). Thus, extra measures are needed to overcome such shortcomings, e.g. opening up the courses to local students and/or incorporating other forms of immersion to complement the coursework.

While more evidence is needed, the above examples disrupt the long-held conviction that direct enrollment in a host institution is automatically the best means for helping students to achieve learning outcomes. They also show it is all that more necessary to monitor students' progress in various learning environments, leading to program changes based on what works in a given location and for a given set of students.

### 3.2 Student accommodation

If academic coursework is at the core of an education abroad experience, other factors like housing are instrumental in facilitating students' ability to attain learning outcomes. Studies have long explored the role of a student's homestay experience on their language learning and to some extent cultural awareness development. Challenging the logic that living with a family inevitably promotes better language skills, scholars have observed that such gains are not always guaranteed (Frank, 1997; Rivers, 1998; Wilkinson, 2002; Segalowitz & Freed, 2004; Schmidt-Rinehart & Knight, 2004; DuFon & Churchill, 2006). In comparing students living with Russian host families with those living in a residence hall, Rivers (1998) was one of the first to conclude that homestays may be at times a negative predictor for second language gains in speaking skills and have no effect on listening skills (see also Engle & Engle, 2012).

Helping to explain the findings of Rivers and others, scholars note that home-stays are not pure immersive environments. In a study of homestay meal practices in Japan, Iino (2006) noticed for instance that Japanese families tended to be overly accommodating and nice, while using "foreigner talk" and speaking in a more stilted, formal Japanese with students. Some students reported that they were being treated as "pets" (see also Pelligrino 2005) or expected to play the part of a non-threatening and clownish *gaijin* (foreigner), making it difficult for them to be accepted as full members of the family. In another mealtime study in China, Lee, Wu, Di, and Kinginger (2017) observed that one student's table etiquette was viewed as so unfitting that the host mother separated his meals from the rest of the family.

To maximize a student's success in a homestay, it is recommended that pro-gram leaders set clear expectations for students so that they know what to antici-pate once they reach a homestay (Schmidt-Rinehart & Knight 2004, p. 257). It may help to provide knowledge about the various models of the education abroad adjustment process (Storti, 1990), as well as training in strategies for intercultural communication. Efforts can also be made to reach out to families, so that they too understand their role in facilitating students' learning (Lee et al., 2017).

While much has been written on homestays, little has been researched and written on other types of housing like residence halls and private apartments. A few notable exceptions include inquiries evaluating language learning in homestays versus residence halls (Rivers, 1998), friendship patterns among international and domestic students (Nesdale & Todd, 2000; Kudo, Volet, & Whitsed, 2018), overseas students' psychological and sociocultural adjustment (Ward, Okura, Kennedy, & Kojima, 1998), and students' social networks abroad (Van Mol & Michielsen, 2015). While the findings vary greatly, these studies as a whole highlight the complexity of social relationships, the fact that language proficiency does not necessarily increase with one form of housing or another, and that much comes down to an individual student's psychological disposition.

### 3.3 Extra- and co-curricular learning

Along with housing, activities that may be classified as "co-curricular" – including visits to museums, historical and cultural sites; concerts and theatre performances; meals and food tastings; and visits to local organizations and companies – are expected to enhance the learning that takes place in a classroom. There is a sense that if program participants, "can see, taste, feel, hear, and touch the objects or items in the study tour environment, then learning will have a greater and deeper meaning for [them]" (Gomez-Lanier 2017, p. 140). Within co-curricular offer-ings, instructors may opt to combine teaching with an excursion, e.g. an art his-tory lecture delivered at a museum, while in other cases extracurricular activities may be entirely outside of teaching, designed to introduce students to the culture and history of a location.

A handful of scholarly works note the merits of supplemental activities, particularly in programs that have a specific disciplinary or pre-professional focus. Bai, Larimer, and Riner, for instance, describe the usefulness of visits to hospitals for a social work program set in Beijing (2016, p. 77). Similarly, Duke points out the relevance of tours to companies for marketing students that highlight both good and bad marketing practices, connecting onsite observations to what students have learned in the classroom (2000, p. 159). Gomez-Lanier (2017) goes a step further in examining student development in two interior design study tours, one in New York City and the other in China, with the finding that students learned in both places yet perceived their learning experiences as more meaningful and positive in China due to greater cultural differences (p. 140).

While progress has been made, few studies isolate activities from the rest of the program components in their research design or analysis, leading to questions of what students gain from participating. Admittedly, such isolation is challenging because it potentially takes away expected services from one group of students. Nonetheless, it is imperative to understand which curricular and extracurricular activities complement classroom learning, to ensure that all program components are meaningful and worthy of an investment.

### 3.4 Experiential learning

In addition to extra-and co-curricular activities, a number of programs offer service-learning, international internships, and research opportunities, which are intended to help students hone their academic and professional skills while also becoming more immersed in a local culture. There has been an increasing drive to offer options that are aligned to industry needs, incorporating practice-based learning and authentic types of assessment linked to professional fields (Marijuan & Sanz, 2018). While such opportunities may be offered on their own, as a stand-alone option, others are being woven into more traditional education abroad programs alongside coursework.

*Service-Learning*: Service as a component of education abroad has been explored for its potential to contribute to students' learning and a host community's well-being and development (McBride & Mlyn, 2011). Numerous studies have found evidence that overseas service-learning contributes to students' linguistic skills (Curtin, Martins, Schwartz-Barcott, DiMaria, & Ogando, 2013; Sherraden, Lough, & Bopp, 2013), as well as intercultural sensitivity and tolerance (Paige & Vande Berg, 2012). Spenader and Retka's (2015) investigation across different education abroad groups reveals, for example, that the students who made the greatest gains in intercultural competence were those who had completed a service activity as part of their education abroad program. The language environment and housing arrangements were also factors yet not predictors of significant growth.

In addition to what students gain, a few authors remind us of the importance of setting up service-learning experiences that benefit those being served (Jacoby, 2015). Doing so involves carefully considering, "the complex intended and unintended consequences of our work with and in host communities" (Crabtree, 2013, p. 61), as in the drain on local community resources (Lough, McBride, Sherraden, & O'Hara, 2011). By not following recommendations from these and other related studies, there is a very real concern that service-learning activities might be reinforcing bad practices, doing more harm than good (Hartman, 2016).

*International Internships:* An unprecedented range of opportunities now exists for students to engage in international internships as part of their university studies, both as a way of giving students additional international experiences, yet also in setting students on a path towards employment (Deakin, 2013). As with domestic pre-professional opportunities, students interning abroad have been found to display increased disciplinary knowledge, a deeper understanding of particular professional fields and prospects for future career pathways (He & Qin, 2017; Wu, 2017), a greater understanding of the importance of global issues for their academic trajectories and future careers (Gates, 2014), and a positive effect on students' language skills and intercultural development (Marijuan & Sanz, 2018).

Despite the apparent gains, Van Mol (2017) notes in a wide-ranging study of European employers that not all employers necessarily value study abroad or international internships in the hiring process, with great variations by country and type of skills sought. This finding suggests that international educators need to do a better job of helping students articulate the skills that they gain while abroad for employers, as well as to ensure that internships are organized in ways that lead to maximum student outcomes. Moreover, success largely depends on the extent to which an international work experience is integrated within a student's academic degree and involves considerations of whether and how academic credit is awarded, the level of home university support and mentoring, and the role in which university partners and internship supervisors play in student development (Gates, 2014; Bullock, Gould, Hejmadi, & Lock, 2009).

*Research:* With more institutions of higher education wanting to prepare students for post-graduate studies and in providing a pre-professional experience, overseas research opportunities have become increasingly popular. In addition to more general education abroad-related outcomes, students conducting research abroad are expected to gain disciplinary knowledge and diagnostic skills.

To test these expectations, a recent study set on a short-term, faculty-directed program in China found that research activities did permit economics students to gain critical analytical and data collection expertise, along with closer connections with mentors and a greater awareness of international affairs (Shostya & Morreale, 2017). Barkin (2016) adds that a research component within an education abroad experience can improve program quality, by overcoming the limitations that come with reduced immersion on a faculty-directed program. Other studies find that undergraduate research helps students cultivate a notion of global citizenship, by developing learning tied to civic engagement (Streitwieser, 2009), provided that they receive the needed support and oversight to conduct well designed and responsible research that goes through the proper regulatory channels. To this end, students should be encouraged to share results with locals, for feedback on their findings as well as to ensure that their work benefits the host society.

Further investigation needs to be undertaken to gauge which models are most effective, as with comparative studies examining the length of internship abroad, type of support, effectiveness of an associated academic component, and requirements around language for participants. Even in chapters that describe the positive aspects of in-country fieldwork activities (Oguro, 2016), additional testing will help to back up assumptions.

### 3.5 Student support services

In addition to the other program components outlined above are the program features designed not only to provide needed student support yet also to aid in the attainment of learning outcomes. These services begin before students leave their home country, with advising and pre-departure orientations, and continue through the sojourn until students return home with reentry activities.

Threaded throughout these activities is a sense that students gain more through mentorship and a series of interventions before, during, and after their sojourn rather than by only completing a program abroad. It has long been argued that students will automatically become more interculturally competent simply by being in a new culture (e.g. Brown, 2009; Vande Berg et al., 2009; Volet & Ang, 1998). A range of interventions is possible to maximize the learning afforded by education abroad programs. The extent to which this occurs varies extensively on the degree to which a given program is embedded within the student's course of study. While it has been raised in the literature focused on students' intercultural development outcomes (Bathurst & La Brack, 2012; Jackson & Oguro, 2018), existing research remains mostly in the form of case studies rather than large-scale comparisons between intervention types. Developments in online technologies have more recently opened up opportunities for further options for education abroad (Giovanangeli, Oguro, & Harbon, 2018; Lee, 2018), however the field still needs to interrogate these interventions extensively to determine connections to specific student learning outcomes. It is also important to note that while all students may benefit from mentoring programs, Yao and Mwangi (2017) add that a support system is expressly critical for those who have traditionally been underrepresented in education abroad and may feel out of place overseas, including students of color and first-generation students (See also Barclay-Hamir & Gozik (2018) for an overview of diversity and inclusion efforts over the past several decades).

Much of the work on support services has focused on packaged programming targeted primarily at U.S. students, which includes coursework, housing, activities, and support services. In other countries, students have been expected to be more independent, without the same level of assistance. That said, more research in this area is being undertaken in other regions, as in Europe with the recently completed Erasmus+ higher education impact study (European Commission, 2019), as well as the work of Perez-Encinas and Rodriguez-Pomeda (2018), both of which argue for improved student services. Less attention in these studies is paid to mentorship and interventions, and instead there is an interest in improving support around admissions, living costs, housing, technology, and banking matters. A few recent studies in European institutions (e.g. Ballo, Mathies, & Weimer, 2020; Nilsson, 2020), complement this work by examining international student integration theory and practices.

## 4. Implications for practice

This literature review illustrates how important it is for those developing education abroad programs to think intentionally about what students should be expected to gain from a given experience and, in turn, to determine which program components will most effectively aid students in achieving stated goals and learning outcomes, based on evidence from data collection and research.

### 4.1 Applying research to practice

To apply the existing research to practice, it is important to consider that not all studies may be generalizable, and conditions will change over time. However, the research points to the need for educators developing learning abroad programs to be aware of the assumptions made in the decisions to incorporate specific program components, which sometimes can be taken for granted. Most importantly, the application of findings requires practitioners to be open to evidence that may not support their own observations, derived from first-hand experience and expertise. While adapting programs based on lessons learned from research may feel like a leap of faith at first, the risk of not doing so is greater; there is a real chance that students may not attain expected outcomes and that limited resources will be squandered in the process.

### 4.2 Continuous evaluation and experimentation

In addition to research findings, it becomes incumbent upon practitioners to evaluate the success of program components through their own data collection and analysis. If intercultural competency is the goal, students' proficiency should be tested over time, using a mix of methods. Doing so might determine whether students enrolled in courses designed specifically for international students have greater gains than those who are directly enrolled with local students. If not, it is necessary to be open to the finding and understand what may cause the result. It takes time and ongoing experimentation to fine tune a program, and even then the outcomes should be continuously monitored, as programs and students do not exist in a vacuum; circumstances change and programs require continual modifications (Gozik, 2014).

## 5. Directions for future research

In addition to recommendations for practice offered above, this chapter offers a few observations on gaps that remain in the research, as well as other issues that must be taken into account in charting a path forward in the field of education abroad.

### 5.1 Technology

Within a few decades, access to media and the Internet has expanded exponentially, permitting students abroad to stay in much closer touch with family and friends, without ever fully leaving home. This poses a challenge to immersion programs, with a recognition that it is impossible to limit access to the Internet in most parts of the world, even if one wanted to try doing so. Given this reality, specific aspects of technology in education abroad are now being explored in the research literature, including the implications for language learning (Godwin-Jones, 2016) and intercultural mentoring (Jackson, 2018; Lee, 2018).

Some see strong advantages afforded by technology, noting for instance that online communication can be used for mentoring students, adding to (or substituting for) support provided by onsite staff (Hampton, 2015). At Boston College, for example, an online course entitled "Reflections on *Being* Abroad" helps students to be more intentional about their experiences overseas (Smith, 2016). Likewise, Godwin-Jones (2016) notes that, with video and audio recording capabilities, smartphones and tablets can permit students to gather data for fieldwork as part of course-based exercises. More research can and needs to be done to collect examples of how technology is being employed effectively within overseas programs.

### 5.2 Expanding the breadth of case studies

If not exclusively, a significant amount of research on program components has come from U.S. scholars and practitioners, as evidenced throughout this chapter. While beneficial, studies from the U.S. are limited in their applicability to other cultural contexts. The packaged aspect of programs, expected to replicate what is available on U.S. campuses overseas, does not exist in other countries, where students are expected to operate more independently, with limited support. In addition to the examples provided in this chapter, readers are encouraged to also consider cases of education abroad programming and activities from around the world as explored elsewhere in this volume.

### 5.3 Bridging research and practice

Lastly, while recognizing the pressures for institutions of higher education to maintain healthy enrollments and budgets, it is difficult to find international educators who are not fully committed to helping students maximize their overseas experiences. Similarly, scholars contributing to the literature on education abroad hope that their research will aid practitioners in delivering more impactful programming. The snag can be in ensuring that program developers have access to and are able to find ways of implementing practical takeaways from the scholarship.

To ensure that scholarly findings are widely accessible, it is necessary to foster other avenues for distribution, including more frequent scholarly presentations at practitioner-oriented conferences, abridged versions of longer books, articles in trade publications, and more spaces in which scholars and practitioners can share perspectives. All of this already happens on some level, fostered by those who identify as "scholar-practitioners" (Streitwieser & Ogden, 2016), though more is needed. Otherwise, we risk maintaining our assumptions that certain components are the "gold standard" of education abroad, even when they are not supported by the research – something that will prevent us from maximizing limited resources to serve students best.

## Further reading

Bathurst, L., & La Brack, B. (2012). Intervening prior to and after student experiences abroad. In M. Vande Berg, M. Paige, & H. K. Lou (Eds.), *Student learning abroad: What our students are learning, what they're not, and what we can do about it* (pp. 261–283). Sterling: Stylus.

McKee, R. (2016). International service-learning: Common goals and issues among programs across disciplines. *Journal of Service-Learning in Higher Education*, 5, 28–40.

Ogden, A. C., Streitwieser, B., & Crawford, E. C. (2014). Empty meeting grounds: Situating intercultural learning in US education abroad. In B. Streitwieser (Ed.), *Internationalisation of Higher Education and Global Mobility* (pp. 229–258). Oxford: Symposium.

Strange, H., & Gibson, H. J. (2017). An investigation of experiential and transformative learning in study abroad programs. *Frontiers: The Interdisciplinary Journal of Study Abroad*, 29(1), 85–100.

Vande Berg, M., Connor-Linton, J., & Paige, R. M. (2009). The Georgetown Consortium Project: Interventions for student learning abroad. *Frontiers: The Interdisciplinary Journal of Study Abroad*, 17, 1–75.

## References

Allen, D., & Young, M. (1997). From tour guide to teacher: Deepening cross-cultural competence through international experience-based education. *Journal of Management Education*, 21(2), 168–189.

Bai, J., Larimer, S., & Riner, M. (2016). Cross-cultural pedagogy: Practical strategies for a successful interprofessional study abroad course. *Journal of the Scholarship of Teaching and Learning*, 16(3), 72–81.

Balloa, A., Mathiesb, C., & Weimer, L. (2020). Applying student development theories: Enhancing international student academic success and integration. *Journal of Comparative and International Higher Education*.

Barclay-Hamir, H., & Gozik, N. (2018). In H. Barclay-Hamir & N. Gozik (Eds.), *Promoting inclusive excellence in education abroad: A handbook of research and practice* (pp. 3–16). Sterling, VA: Stylus.

Barkin, G. (2016). Undergraduate research on short-term, faculty-led study abroad. *Council on Undergraduate Research Quarterly*, 36 (4), 26–32.

Bathurst, L., & La Brack, B. (2012). Intervening prior to and after student experiences abroad. In M. Vande Berg, M. Paige, & H. K. Lou (Eds.), *Student learning abroad: What our students are learning, what they're not, and what we can do about it* (pp. 261–283). Sterling, VA: Stylus.

Brown, L. (2009). A failure of communication on the cross-cultural campus. *Journal of Studies in International Education*, 13(4), 439–454.

Bullock, K., Gould, V., Hejmadi, M., & Lock, G. (2009). Work placement experience: Should I stay or should I go? *Higher Education Research & Development*, 28(5), 481–494.

Coleman, J. A. (2009). Study abroad and SLA: Defining goals and variables. In A. Berndt & K. Klepping (Eds.), *Sprachlehrforschung: Theorie und empirie, festschrift für rudiger grotjahn* (pp. 181–196). Frankfurt: Peter Lang.

Crabtree, R. D. (2013). The intended and unintended consequences of international service-learning. *Journal of Higher Education Outreach and Engagement*, 17(2), 43–66.

Crealock, E., Derwing, T. M., & Gibson, M. (1999). To homestay or to stay home: The Canadian-Japanese experience. *TESL Canada Journal*, 16(2), 53–61.

Curtin, A. J., Martins, D. C., Schwartz-Barcott, D., DiMaria, L., & Ogando, B. M. S. (2013). Development and evaluation of an international service learning program for nursing students. *Public Health Nursing*, 30, 548–556.

Deakin, H. (2013). The drivers to Erasmus work placement mobility for UK students. *Journal Children's Geographies*, 12(1), 25–39.

DuFon, M. A., & Churchill, E. (2006). Evolving threads in study abroad research. In M. A. DuFon & E. Churchill (Eds.), *Language learners in study abroad contexts* (pp. 1–29). Clevedon, UK: Multilingual Matters.

Duke, C. (2000). Study abroad learning activities: A synthesis and comparison. *Journal of Marketing Education*, 22(2), 155–165.

Engle, L., & Engle, J. (2012). Beyond immersion: The American University Center of Provence experiment in holistic intervention. In M. Vande Berg, R. M. Paige, & K. Hemming (Eds.), *Student learning abroad: What our students are learning, what they're not, and what we can do about it* (pp. 284–307). Sterling, VA: Stylus.

European Commission. (2019). *Erasmus + higher education impact study*. Luxembourg: European Union. Retrieved from https://publications.europa.eu/en/publication-deta il/-/publication/94d97f.5c-7ae2-11e9-9f.05-01aa75ed71a1

Frank, V. (1997, March). *Potential negative effects of homestay*. Paper presented at the Middle Atlantic conference of the American Association for the Advancement of Slavic Studies, Albany, NY.

Gates, L. (2014). The impact of international internships and short-term immersion programs. *New Directions for Student Services*, 2014(146), 33–40.

Giovanangeli, A., Oguro, S., & Harbon, L. (2018). Mentoring students' intercultural learning during study abroad. In J. Jackson & S. Oguro (Eds.), *Intercultural interventions in study abroad* (pp. 88–102). New York: Routledge.

Godwin-Jones, R. (2016). Integrating technology into study abroad. *Language Learning & Technology*, 20(1), 1–20.

Gomez-Lanier, L. (2017). The experiential learning impact of international and domestic study tours: Class excursions that are more than field trip. *International Journal of Teaching and Learning in Higher Education*, 29(1) 129–144.

Gozik, N. (2014). The theory and practice of outcomes assessment in education abroad. In M. Hernandez, M. Wiedenhoeft, & D. Wick (Eds.), *NAFSA's guide to education abroad for advisers and administrators* (pp. 407–421). Washington, DC: NAFSA.

Hammer, M., & Bennett, M. (2003). Measuring intercultural sensitivity: The intercultural development inventory. *International Journal of Intercultural Relations*, 27, 421–443.

Hampton, C. (2015). Meeting in the virtual middle: Blending online and human resources to generate a year abroad community. In R. Mitchell, N. Tracy-Ventura, & K. McManus (Eds.), *Social interaction, identity and language learning during residence abroad* (pp. 223–240). London: Eurosla.

Hartman, E. (2016, May 12). Malia, the rise of the gap year, and ethical international engagement. *Stanford Social Innovation Review*. Retrieved from https://ssir.org/articles/entry/malia_the_rise_of_the_gap_year_and_ethical_international_engagement

He, Y., & Qin, X. (2017). Students' perceptions of an internship experience in China: A pilot study. *Foreign Language Annals*, 50, 57–70.

Iino, M. (2006). Norms of interaction in a Japanese homestay setting: Toward a two-way flow of linguistic and cultural resources. In M. A. DuFon & E. Churchill (Eds.), *Language learners in study abroad contexts* (pp. 151–173). Clevedon, UK: Multilingual Matters.

Jackson, J., & Oguro, S. (Eds.). (2018). *Intercultural interventions in study abroad*. New York: Routledge.

Jacoby, B. (2015). *Service-learning essentials: questions, answers, and lessons learned*. San Francisco: John Wiley & Sons.

Kudo, K., Volet, S., & Whitsed, C. (2018). Development of intercultural relationships at university: A three-stage ecological and person-in-context conceptual framework. *Higher Education*. Retrieved from https://link.springer.com/article/10.1007/s10734-018-0283-9

Leask, B. (2009). Using formal and informal curricula to improve interactions between home and international students. *Journal of Studies in International Education*, 13(2), 205–221.

Lee, L. (2018). Employing telecollaborative exchange to extend intercultural learning after study abroad. In J. Jackson & S. Oguro (Eds.), *Intercultural interventions in study abroad* (pp. 137–154). Abingdon: Routledge.

Lee, S., Wu, Q., Di, C., & Kinginger, C. (2017). Learning to eat politely at the Chinese homestay table: Two contrasting case studies. *Foreign Language Annals*, 50(1), 135–158.

Lough, B. J., McBride, A. M., Sherraden, M., & O'Hara, K. (2011). Capacity building contributions of short-term international volunteers. *Journal of Community Practice*, 19(2), 120–137.

Marijuan, S., & Sanz, C. (2018). Expanding boundaries: Current and new directions in study abroad research and practice. *Foreign Language Annals*, 51(1), 185–204.

McBride, A. M., & Mlyn, E. (2011). *International service and higher education: Toward a vision for the field (CSD Report No. 11–19)*. St. Louis: Washington University, Center for Social Development.

McKee, R. (2016). International service-learning: Common goals and issues among programs across disciplines. *Journal of Service-Learning in Higher Education*, 5, 28–40.

Montgomery, C. (2010). *Understanding the international student experience*. Basingstoke: Palgrave Macmillan.

Nesdale, D., & Todd, P. (2000). Effect of contact on intercultural acceptance: A field study. *International Journal of Intercultural Relations*, 24(3), 341–360.

Nilsson, P. (2020). The buddy programme: Integration and social support for international students. *Journal of Comparative and International Higher Education*.

Norris, E. M., & Dwyer, M. (2005, August). Testing assumptions: The impact of two study abroad program models. *Frontiers: The Interdisciplinary Journal of Study Abroad*, 11, 121–142.

Ogden, A. C., Streitwieser, B., & Crawford, E. C. (2014). Empty meeting grounds: Situating intercultural learning in US education abroad. In B. Streitwieser (Ed.), *Internationalisation of higher education and global mobility* (pp. 229–258). Oxford: Symposium.

Oguro, S. (2016). Facilitating students' interaction and engagement with the local society during study abroad. In L. Bleichenbacher, B. Kürsteiner, R. Frehner, & A. Kolde (Eds.), *Teacher education in the 21st century: A focus on convergence* (pp. 247–262). Cambridge: Cambridge Scholars Publishing.

Paige, M., & Vande Berg, M. (2012). Why students are not learning abroad. In M. Vande Berg, M. Paige, & H. K. Lou (Eds.), *Student learning abroad: What our students are learning, what they're not, and what we can do about it* (pp. 29–58). Sterling, VA: Stylus.

Pelligrino, V. (2005). *Study abroad and second language use: Constructing the self*. Cambridge: Cambridge University Press.

Perez-Encinas, A., & Rodriguez-Pomeda, J. (2018). International students' perceptions of their needs when going abroad: Services on demand. *Journal of Studies in International Education*, 22(1), 20–36.

Pryde, M. (2015). Teaching language learners to elaborate on their responses: A structured, genre-based approach. *Foreign Language Annals*, 48(2), 168–183.

Redden, E. (2018, November 13). Study abroad numbers grow. *Inside Higher Ed*. Retrieved from www.insidehighered.com/news/2018/11/13/study-abroad-numbers-continue-grow-driven-continued-growth-short-term-programs

Rivers, W. P. (1998). Is being there enough? The effects of homestay placements on language gain during study abroad. *Foreign Language Annals*, 31(4), 492–500.

Schmidt-Rinehart, B.C., & Knight, S.M. (2004). The homestay component of study abroad: Three perspectives. *Foreign Language Annals*, 37(2), 254–262.

Segalowitz, N. & Freed, B. (2004). Context, contact, and cognition in oral fluency acquisition: Learning Spanish in at home and study abroad contexts. *Studies in Second Language Acquisition*, 26(2), 173–199.

Sherraden, M., Lough, B. J., & Bopp, A. (2013). Students serving abroad: A framework for inquiry. *Journal of Higher Education Outreach and Engagement*, 17(2), 7–41.

Shostya, A. & Morreale, J.C. (2017). Fostering undergraduate research through a faculty-led study abroad experience. *International Journal of Teaching and Learning in Higher Education*, 29(2), 300–308.

Smith, S. (2016, January 2). World class: Boston College is at the forefront of the intercultural learning movement. *BC News*. Retrieved from www.bc.edu/bc-web/bcnews/nation-world-society/international/new-world-for-study-abroad.html

Spenader, A. J., & Retka, P. (2015). The role of pedagogical variables in intercultural development: A study of faculty-led programs. *Frontiers: The Interdisciplinary Journal of Study Abroad*, 25, 20–36.

Storti, C. (1990). *The art of crossing cultures*. Yarmouth, ME: Intercultural Press.

Strange, H., & Gibson, H. J. (2017). An investigation of experiential and transformative learning in study abroad programs. *Frontiers: The Interdisciplinary Journal of Study Abroad*, 29(1), 85–100.

Streitwieser, B. (2009). Undergraduate research during study abroad: Scope, meaning, and potential. In R. Lewin (Ed.), *The handbook of practice and research in study abroad: Higher education and the quest for global citizenship* (pp. 399–419). New York: Routledge.

Streitwieser, B., & Ogden, A. (Eds.) (2016). *International higher education's scholar-practitioners: Bridging research and practice*. Oxford: Symposium Books.

Tanaka, K. (2007). Japanese students' contact with English outside the classroom during study abroad. *New Zealand Studies in Applied Linguistics*, 13(1), 36–54.

Tarrant, M., Rubin, D., & Stoner, L. (2014). The added value of study abroad: Fostering a global citizenry. *Journal of Studies in International Education*, 18(2), 141–161.

Toncar, M. F., & Cudmore, B. V. (2003). The overseas internship experience. *Journal of Marketing Education*, 22(1), 54–63.

Van Mol, C. (2017). Do employers value international study and internships? A comparative analysis of 31 countries. *Geoforum*, 78, 52–60.

Van Mol, C., & Michielsen, J. (2015). The reconstruction of a social network abroad: An analysis of the interaction patterns of Erasmus students. *Mobilities*, 10(3), 423–444.

Vande Berg, M., Connor-Linton, J., & Paige, R. M. (2009). The Georgetown Consortium Project: Interventions for student learning abroad. *Frontiers: The Interdisciplinary Journal of Study Abroad*, 17, 1–75.

Volet, S., & Ang, G. (1998). Culturally mixed groups on international campuses: An opportunity for inter-cultural learning. *Higher Education Research and Development*, 17 (1), 5–23.

Ward, C., Okura, Y., Kennedy, A., & Kojima, T. (1998). The U-curve on trial: A longitudinal study of psychological and sociocultural adjustment during cross-cultural transition. *International Journal of Intercultural Relations*, 22(3), 277–291.

Wilkinson, S. (2002). The omnipresent classroom during summer study abroad: American students in conversation with their French hosts. *Modern Language Journal*, 86, 157–173.

Wu, S. L. (2017). The planning, implementation, and assessment of an international internship program: An exploratory case study. *Foreign Language Annals*, 50, 567–583.

Yao, C. W., & G. Mwangi, C. A. (2017). Role of student affairs in international student transition and success. *Journal of International Students*, 7(4), i–iii.

# Part 3

# Student outcomes

There are numerous factors that now make understanding the impact of international education on student outcomes so important. The pressure for universities to engage in robust internationalization has pushed education abroad as a key development strategy. Unprecedented growth of participants has been driven by myriad factors, from advanced technology and travel opportunities making it more accessible to some, to recognition that education abroad is an attractive professional profile, to seeking experience that makes one a so-called "global citizen." While we have tried to be cognizant of the fact that different countries and regions promote and value education abroad in distinct ways, the need to understand impact has never been more important. Understanding the outcomes of international educational experience on students is so relevant because they, after all, are its primary consumers.

A question that many scholars, practitioners and participants want to know is how international education impacts student learning on multiple levels, from intercultural competency and language skills to broadened horizons and changed perspectives. But empirically documenting outcomes, having confidence that empirical data has been appropriately collected and rigorously analyzed, and agreeing on its interpretation and value has been an enduring challenge for the field broadly (Hoffa & DePaul, 2010; Stearns, 2009; Terzuolo, 2018; Wildavsky, 2010; Woolf, 2007). In the U.S., the Institute of International Education (IIE) has been collecting and analyzing student mobility data since 1919; its "Open Doors" survey publishes a wide range of metrics on education abroad and international student mobility each year. More broadly, the OECD's "Education at a Glance" annual study provides further data on global mobility and broader higher education metrics. By now, each year hundreds of small-scale qualitative and quantitative studies conducted on settings around the world and looking at a wide range of factors are produced in a variety of international journals. Yet the reliability of data collection, measurement and interpretation of student outcomes, from the macro level in sources like Open Doors and the OECD, to the micro level on studies conducted on institutions, programs and individuals, continues to be a point of debate in the field (see Conclusion).

For years a common criticism of research in international education was that it lacked robust use of theory and was light on empirical analysis, particularly larger, longitudinal studies with large populations. But that began to change rapidly (Hulstrand, 2006; Comp et al., 2007), and especially over the last decade (Ogden & Streitwieser, 2016), through the development of validated and widely used assessment instruments, broad dissemination of findings of studies using them or inspired by them, and a growing prominence of journals in the field and widely attended academic conferences. That said, while some assessment instruments are largely used in the U.S. and countries with similar higher education systems, in other countries, learning outcomes for education abroad are built into the student's overall program of study (see Chapter 11 in this volume by Leask and Green). Through course, module, unit or program assessments (in the U.S. referred to as evaluation) students demonstrate whether or not those outcomes have been achieved.

Two journals in particular stand out as instrumental in establishing greater rigor and respectability for our field: *Frontiers: The Interdisciplinary Journal of Study Abroad*, established by Brian Whalen in 1995 and still an open access publication, and the *Journal of Studies in International Education*, established by Hans de Wit in 1997 and now with Sage Press. In addition, other journals have also made significant contributions to research in the field, including *The International Journal of Intercultural Relations;* the *Journal of International Students; Research in Comparative and International Education;* and the *Journal of Comparative and International Higher Education*, to name only a few. Additionally, a more solid research focus to studies of international education has been added by annual conferences of the Forum on Education Abroad (Forum), the Association for the Study of Higher Education (ASHE), the American Educational Research Association (AERA), the European Association for International Education (EAIE), the International Education Association of Australia (IEAA), the Mexican Association for International Education (AMPEI), the Brazilian Association for International Education (FAUBAI), the Canadian Bureau For International Education (CBIE), the Conference of the Americas on International Education (CAIE), and the Asia Pacific Association for International Education (APAIE), along with occasional research panels at the annual meetings of NAFSA: Association of International Educators and at the Association of International Education Administrators (AIEA)

Increasingly, those who work in international education, meaning all management and support staff in international offices, have come to accept that they are part of a field of international education research and scholarship built on a profession that is guided by an established code of ethics and recognizable competencies (Streitwieser & Ogden, 2016). Scholars of international education are increasingly pursuing lines of inquiry that have direct professional application. We argue in this book that the professionals who work in international education are also increasingly becoming recognized as content knowledge experts who need to be familiar with the existing research and able to use it to engage with competence in scholarly practice.

In the first chapter in this section on academic development, Joshua McKeown, Heather Ward, and Maria Luz Celaya lay out how academic development is conceived and applied to education abroad by asking if it is a recognized goal and what evidence there is to suggest it occurs. They find that academic development occurring from education abroad can impact, even if indirectly, students' future career success, in addition to their immediate post-secondary educational attainment

In the second chapter, on language proficiency, Jane Jackson, Martin Howard and John Schwieter explain that while more tertiary-level students are choosing to enhance their second language (L2) proficiency through some form of education abroad, a complex mix of internal and external factors must be taken into consideration that lead to significant differences in language and (inter)cultural learning and that while too many HEIs still send students abroad with limited preparation for language and culture-learning, increasing numbers of administrators and educators are familiar with research findings and the need to prepare and support their students better through innovative, learner-centered interventions.

In the third chapter on college student development, Chris Glass and Mark Holton focus on "multi-locality" or how the multi-layered and intersectional aspects of each student's identity and life history shapes their sense of place. They address the role that education abroad leaders play in helping students recognize that development of sense of place is shaped by both local and multiple experience given the pluralistic world they now inhabit with those of different cultural backgrounds, habits, perspectives, customs, religious beliefs and aspirations.

In the fourth chapter in this section, Neriko Musha Doerr, David Puente and Uichi Kamiyoshi critically examine notions of global citizenship, intercultural competence, and student identities to provide a deeper analysis of the ways these concepts have continued to drive policy discussions around curriculum policy, learning outcomes and other factors. Importantly, the authors urge us to expand the scope of who we consider in international education by focusing our attention further on diversity, inclusivity, and the identities of immigrants, stateless and other mobile border populations who are also engaging in international learning experiences.

In the last chapter in this section focused on employability, Jannecke Wiers-Jenssen, Martin Tillman and Cheryl Matherly examine the relationship between education abroad and employability in terms of the transition from higher education to the labor market, to employability skills and employer perspectives. At a time when education abroad programs are increasingly expected to demonstrate how they develop skills and competencies that prepare graduates to find work, the authors discuss the seeming disconnect between the role of education abroad programs with developing skills that employers identify as important, and evidence that these skills actually contribute to a student's employability. They find that the actual impact on a graduate's employability is mixed.

Together, these five chapters urge practitioners and scholars to revisit the ways they think about the variety of student learning outcomes that result from international educational experience. These impact factors range from beginning a sojourn and starting to rethink conceptions of life history, identity and sense of place, to ways they engage as language learners and processing complex notions of global citizenship and intercultural competence, to years later when reflecting back on international learning and experience as working professionals.

## References

Comp, D., Gladding, S., Rhodes, G., Stephenson, S., & Vande Berg, M. (2007). Literature and resources for education abroad outcomes assessment. In M. Bolen (Ed.), *A guide to outcomes assessment in education abroad* (pp. 97–136). Carlisle, PA: The Forum on Education Abroad.

Hoffa, W., & DePaul, S. (Eds.) (2010). *A history of U.S. study abroad: 1965 to the present.* Carlisle: PA: The Forum on Education Abroad.

Hulstrand, J. (2006). "Beyond anecdote: Education abroad comes of age." *International Educator,* 15(1), 52.

Ogden, A., & Streitwieser, B. (2016). A concise overview of research on U.S. education abroad. In D. Velliaris & D. Coleman-George (Eds.), *Handbook of research on study abroad programs and outbound mobility* (pp. 1–39). Adelaide: IGI Global Press.

Stearns, P. (2009). *Educating global citizens in colleges and universities: Challenges and opportunities.* New York: Routledge.

Streitwieser, B., & A. Ogden (Eds.) (2016). *International higher education's scholar-practitioners: Bridging research and practice.* Oxford: Symposium Books.

Terzuolo, E. R. (2018). "Intercultural development in study abroad: Influence of student and program characteristics." *International Journal of Intercultural Relations,* 65, 86–95.

Wildavsy, B. (2010). *The great brain race? How global universities are reshaping the world.* Princeton, NJ: Princeton University Press.

Woolf, M. (2007). "Impossible things before breakfast: Myths in education abroad." *Journal of Studies in International Education,* 11, 496–509.

# Chapter 5

# Academic development

## The impact of education abroad on students as learners

## Joshua S. McKeown, M. Luz Celaya and Heather H. Ward

### Highlights:

- This chapter examines students' academic development resulting from participation in education abroad. Academic development is defined as the *ways students progress as learners, including their academic focus, commitment to their studies, clarification of their academic and eventually career goals based on their abilities, confidence in their learning approaches, and with respect for the diversity of other learners.*
- The chapter raises two central questions, with implications for practitioners: (1) To what extent is academic development recognized as a goal or an outcome of education abroad? (2) Is there evidence that academic development occurs during education abroad?
- Evidence of academic development has been observed by international educators, and an emerging body of scholarship has attempted to define and measure these gains.
- The authors conclude that while evidence of academic development exists, it may be implied through a variety of measures of student learning and success.

### 1. Introduction and chapter overview

*Academic development*, as proposed by Morais and Ogden (2010), is defined as a broad and interdisciplinary measure of student learning. The term is not yet widely used to describe post-secondary students' development of characteristics important to their growth and sophistication as learners. However, there is increasing recognition among international educators that education abroad contributes to student learning in interesting and important ways beyond disciplinary, linguistic, and other traditional academic measures. A broader understanding of student development occurring during education abroad seems overdue. This chapter examines how academic development can be applied to, understood by, and inferred from education abroad participation.

The global literature review for this chapter sheds light on the emerging evidence for academic development during education abroad. The review does not seek to be exhaustive but rather to focus with fresh perspective on observable outcomes—using different measures and for different levels of student mobility and engagement. The evidence may be clear or inferred and draws from countries and post-secondary educational systems with different approaches to education abroad. Though academic development may not be explicitly researched in global contexts, the literature cited nonetheless provides interesting and important contributing evidence that it is occurring for students who study outside their home countries. Finally, implications for practice and new directions for research are summarized.

## 2. Key Questions to be addressed

What happens to students during education abroad is researched differently around the world, usually following the motivations and priorities important in that country. Drivers of student mobility vary considerably between countries and world regions. The very term *academic development* (defined below) has not been widely used in the context of post-secondary student development research. Even the student-centered outcomes that academic development implies may not always be stated or prioritized in different global contexts. This chapter seeks to address these questions:

- To what extent is academic development recognized as a goal or outcome of education abroad? Given that education abroad is typically considered a high-impact experience, do higher education institutions (HEIs) and societies value this goal explicitly?
- Is there evidence that academic development occurs as a result of education abroad? And if there is not, what evidence exists that education abroad supports and encourages academic development in students?

### 2.1 Definition of academic development

The term *academic development* in post-secondary education refers to ways that students enhance their ability to learn. It does not necessarily refer to academic performance, achievement, rates of graduation, or other topics important in post-secondary education research. Instead, it specifically means those ways that students themselves progress as learners, including their academic focus, commitment to their studies, clarification of their academic and eventually career goals based on their abilities, confidence in their learning approaches, and with respect for the diversity of other learners around them (Ogden, 2010).

Two important terms pertinent to this discussion are the dimensions of academic self-efficacy and academic self-concept (Morais & Ogden, 2010). *Academic self-efficacy* concerns the extent to which students are self-directed and confident about taking responsibility for their academic performance. This consists of learning with a sense of purpose, being curious and open to new experiences, and developing the self-determination to align academic and life goals. Academic self-efficacy also encompasses effort, particularly students engaging in activities linked to their learning in intrinsically pure and satisfying ways, not in pursuit of grades. Lastly, it means persistence: students show self-reliance and adapt alternative approaches to learning when faced with difficulties (Ogden, 2010).

*Academic self-concept* refers to students' perceptions of themselves and their academic ability. It incorporates both cognitive and affective responses and is influenced by social comparison. Academic self-concept consists of expanding academic interests; students become better able to locate and evaluate information and integrate knowledge from a variety of sources. It also embraces peer learning and teamwork and being able to do so in flexible ways with diverse people (Ogden, 2010).

*Academic development* might be best understood through the perspective of today's education abroad students. Consider the questions students might be asking themselves around the time they choose to have an international experience:

- What kind of student am I, and how do I learn best?
- Which subjects am I good at and not good at?
- What are my academic interests, and where are they leading me?
- How do I overcome challenges and succeed academically?
- How do I work best with others to learn what I need to learn?

The literature suggests that education abroad, like other high-impact experiences, may lead to gains in student ability suggestive of academic development as defined above. However, it should be noted that post-secondary education is a complex experience over a long period, making any cause-and-effect relationship difficult to prove. Although the term academic development itself has not been widely used in all countries and contexts to describe this type of student development, education abroad practitioners have observed changes in students reflective of it for a long time. Indeed, as the relevant global literature will show, there is some evidence that academic development is occurring worldwide during education abroad.

## 3. Review of the literature

While research in the United States has dominated the discussion of student development and other education abroad outcomes, this chapter presents findings from both U.S. and non-U.S. contexts. While the term academic development itself is not always used, and direct findings for it may be limited, many studies lend support that academic development as defined herein is occurring.

In the United States, HEIs and international education providers have developed programming following curricular and student-oriented goals. A growing body of literature assessing education abroad outside standard program evaluation tends to focus on overall quality, outcomes, and participant satisfaction. Student outcomes assessment typically measures pre/post shifts for a particular course or program. It often focuses on personal and intercultural development, student learning, and long-term effects such as further study or employment (Farrugia & Sanger, 2017).

The research shows that post-education abroad students tend to engage in academic work with greater curiosity and interest, less distraction, and more for the pleasure of learning than to achieve high grades (Hadis, 2005). This reflects students' understanding of academic ability, as presented in the definition of academic development above. Students can develop greater understanding of their academic strengths and weaknesses after studying intensively during a short period in an unfamiliar environment. Open-mindedness and independence increase (Hadis, 2005), perhaps because their ability to communicate, problem solve, and overcome difficulties without the usual support structures had been tested while abroad.

A study led by George Kuh for the American Association of Colleges and Universities (AAC&U) identified global learning, including experiences abroad, as one of 11 high-impact practices that increase student engagement (Kuh, 2008). Accordingly, many U.S. colleges and universities have introduced programs aligned with high-impact practices to improve retention and degree completion. Kuh's findings lend support to the impact of education abroad on academic development.

The National Survey of Student Engagement (NSSE) is widely used by U.S. institutions, querying students about their learning experiences and activities on campus. In 2016, NSSE introduced a global learning module, which asked students about their globally focused coursework, development of intercultural skills, participation in global experiences, and opportunities to work and learn with culturally diverse students, and understanding multiple viewpoints in an increasingly interdependent world (Kinzie, Helms, & Cole, 2017). Li, Fei, and You (2017) found evidence that Chinese students taking the Chinese College Student Survey (CCSS), which was developed from the NSSE questionnaire through collaboration between Indiana University and Tsinghua University, showed comparable outcomes. The researchers found a positive impact of education abroad on students in both countries (Li, Fei, & You, 2017). Important connections can be drawn to academic development, particularly from the questions focused on working with and learning from culturally diverse peers, and on understanding various viewpoints in the world.

One study documenting student learning and academic outcomes post-education abroad is the Georgia Learning Outcomes of Students Studying Abroad Research Initiative (GLOSSARI). From 2000 to 2010, researchers measured several areas of functional knowledge, as well as grade point average, retention, and degree completion among education abroad participants in the University System of Georgia (Sutton & Rubin, 2010). This study is an important one for education abroad generally, in that it found—across race and gender—education abroad participants more likely to complete a four-year degree and take less time to do so, and that overall they had higher grade point averages (GPAs) following education abroad than non-participants. This was particularly the case for students with lower SAT scores and lower GPA, suggesting that education abroad may have a larger benefit for low-performing students relative to their peers (Sutton & Rubin, 2010).

For academic development in particular, the GLOSSARI researchers found that education abroad students developed stronger ability to apply their knowledge (including but not limited to their knowledge of cultural practices), focus on their studies, and not just learn facts. This conceptual, big picture approach to learning (Sutton & Rubin, 2010) aligns with the broader understanding of student intellectual development (Perry, 1968) and how it can be enhanced during education abroad, particularly among students who have had less opportunity before (McKeown, 2009).

While studies of U.S. students abroad have tended to dominate this discussion, evidence from other regions supports a better understanding of how education abroad contributes to academic development in student participants. Wang (2018) studied academic experiences of a Chinese cohort in the United Kingdom, finding that initial shock stemming from misperceptions of the role of teachers and students, along with unfamiliar teaching and communication styles, over time evolved into positive outcomes. Students displayed enhanced academic confidence without emphasizing memorization and comfort with language ability despite imperfections. They formed their own understanding of academic material through discovery and independence in the learning process. In this sense, students gained new learning strategies and confident learning approaches, suggesting enhanced academic development.

Stahl (2016) found similar evidence in a sample of Chinese high school students in the United States, who developed greater academic self-concept from having their ideas heard and taken seriously, and they found freedom to grow and develop beyond the strict control typical in Chinese schools. These and other studies (Mankowska, 2018; Powell & Biederman, 2017) suggest a pattern for Chinese students traveling to the U.S. and the U.K., in that initial shock may lead to enhanced academic development as students navigate and re-negotiate their learning environments to become more confident, assured learners.

In the United States and elsewhere, there is considerable debate regarding the academic impact of shorter (eight weeks or less) and longer (semester or year) education abroad experiences (Anderson, Lorenz, & White, 2016). As institutions and providers strive to increase overall participation, and in particular the participation of traditionally under-served demographic groups, they have introduced more diverse program offerings like short-term, experiential, service-learning, embedded, and other models. Today, over 60 percent of education abroad experiences are 1–8 weeks' duration (Coker, Heiser, & Taylor, 2018). Several scholars have attempted to measure outcomes that can inform the discussion of academic development (particularly student learning, intellectual development, and intercultural skills) according to program duration. In one study, students who participated in instructor-led, short education abroad programs reported changing their academic program (e.g., switching majors, adding a foreign-language minor) because of the experience (Anderson et al., 2016). Other researchers found that those who participated in three-week programs enhanced their awareness of other cultures and languages, and improved their own identity awareness (Coker et al., 2018). Many conclude (Mellors-Bourne, Jones, Lawton, & Woodfield, 2015) that short-term offerings do produce measurable changes in terms of cognition, self-awareness, career, and intercultural development, and that the intellectual development benefit of education abroad is greatest when it is the student's first international experience, not necessarily according to program duration (McKeown, 2009). Still, many suggest that longer education abroad experiences produce deeper academic benefits (Dwyer, 2004).

In 2016, the Canadian Bureau for International Education (CBIE) undertook a comprehensive survey of 1,600 education abroad participants from 35 Canadian universities, published in the report, *A World of Learning*. Strong majorities of students surveyed said that their experience abroad influenced their career choice, and that it shaped their academic path. In addition, most students reported their self-confidence and intellectual development were greater than if they had been studying at the home campus (CBIE, 2016).

In Canada and elsewhere, there is growing emphasis on experiential learning in education abroad, typically involving internships, research, or community engagement. In a qualitative study of Mitacs, a Canadian government-funded research internship program for international students hosted at Canadian universities, and for Canadian students to conduct research at partner universities abroad, Canadian awardees said their projects resulted in important advancements, such as a new product, diagnostic model, or algorithm. Most said the experience would improve their employment prospects and that it made them better citizens of the world (Science-Metrix, 2015), reflecting a sense of confidence and autonomy as learners which are key to academic development.

In Europe, education abroad has been largely associated with the Erasmus (European Region Action Scheme for the Mobility of University Students) program, created in 1987 to promote mobility in higher education within the European Union. Since then more than 6 million students have studied abroad in Europe, and more than 4,000 institutions have been involved. In Europe, studies of the benefits of education abroad had initially focused on the relationship between the education abroad experience and language-learning (Pérez-Vidal, 2014; Regan, Howard, & Lemée, 2009).

However, since then there has been a notable shift in European interest from the focus on language acquisition toward a more analytical focus on students' personal and academic growth, and on students' understanding of their experience (Mellors-Bourne et al., 2015; Streitwieser & Light, 2018). In recent reports on mobility in Europe, many of which address the benefits for employability, students report a wide array of cognitive benefits related to their academic development following their education abroad experience. One of these is the Erasmus Impact Study (EIS, 2014), which analyzed 78,891 responses to five online surveys addressed to different sectors involved in education abroad (mobile and non-mobile students, higher education institutions, academic and non-academic staff, and employers). According to the report, the benefits of education abroad can be summarized into three broad categories: increases in leadership features and social skills as compared to those students who had not been abroad, the enhancement of employability resulting from skill-development (not just acquisition of content knowledge or foreign language ability), and the acceptance of job mobility in their prospective careers. More recently, the acquisition of competences through student mobility has been pointed out as the main aim of a high number of higher education institutions (see the Erasmus+ Higher Education Impact Study, 2019).

These results compare well to the Institute of International Education's Generation Study Abroad report (2017) on education abroad and careers in the United States (Farrugia & Sanger, 2017), and to Suleman's (2018) analysis of studies on employability skills. The latter showed that openness and self-confidence are the skills most valued by employers and graduates. Weibl (2015) goes further and claims that students' sociocultural expectations can be indicators of personal growth related to cosmopolitanism and global citizenship. Taken together, these global findings suggest enhanced academic development in students after their education abroad experience.

However, the effects of academic development resulting from education abroad may not always be experienced as positive change by students. Marijuan and Sanz (2018) state that education abroad experiences may lead to a clash between one's own national identity and sense of global citizenship. Similarly, Petzold and Moog (2018), in their analysis of education abroad intention among 307 students at a German university, found that personality development was not perceived as a possible benefit of education abroad prior to the experience. Also, Suleman (2018) points out that research is far from conclusive on the skills supposedly enhanced by education abroad, and advocates for policymakers and HEIs to focus on employability. This may be why, as stated in Van Mol's (2017) analysis of the Flash Eurobarometer, only a minority of employers consider international education for certain hiring decisions. In the Erasmus context, there is considerable support for expanding the definition and purposes of education abroad to include volunteering, global service-learning, and international internships (Marijuan & Sanz, 2018), as well as redefining the concepts of cosmopolitanism and global citizenship (Caruana, 2014) to align with the definition of academic development put forth in this chapter (de Wit, Hunter, Howard, & Egron-Polak, 2015; Jones, 2010; Jones, 2013; Jones, 2016).

Although there are developing economies and post-secondary education sectors where more immediate economic development and human capacity building agendas take precedence, there are some shifts toward valuing the intrinsic worth of international education and its impact on individual achievement. While the term academic development as defined here is not used in most of these contexts, through careful examination there is emerging evidence of its importance. In South Korea, for example, the rationale for international education has shifted from traditional, post-civil war and reconstruction period economic goals towards its social and cultural goals (Byun & Kim, 2011). Similarly, the Association of

Southeast Asian Nations (ASEAN) has called for an Erasmus-style student mobility project designed to foster students' personal development and independence, cultural discovery of their region, and a greater open-mindedness towards enrichment of their own educational pursuits (Rasplus, 2018)—a departure from the previous emphasis on education abroad for technical skills that contribute to economic development toward more student-focused outcomes. In China, following decades of increased in-bound and out-bound student mobility (Liu, 2014), a growing body of research on the impact of international education on both foreign students in China and Chinese students abroad (Wang, 2018) shows outcomes supportive of academic development in these students.

The few studies that touch on education abroad of African students (Chien & Chiteng Kot, 2011) emphasize that Africa is struggling to overcome the problem of brain drain. Many African students decide to stay in the host country after their studies abroad either to complete their education or to work, resulting in a loss of human capital. Such facts are in line with Bilecen and Van Mol's (2017: 1241) claim that "international academic mobility also produces and reproduces inequalities." Nevertheless, several programs have successfully promoted education abroad (Chien & Chiteng Kot, 2011), and some universities in South Africa, for instance, have recently focused on internationalization in their strategic plans (de Wit et al., 2015).

## 4. Implications for practice

In response to the two central questions of this chapter, the global literature review and synthesis has strong implications for practice: In terms of the first question, *To what extent is academic development recognized as a goal or outcome of education abroad? Given that education abroad is typically considered a high-impact experience, do higher education institutions (HEIs) and societies value this goal explicitly?* As stated earlier, the term academic development is not universally used and therefore not always articulated explicitly or researched directly. Although there have been efforts to observe and describe so-called *generic attributes*, particularly in Australia, to describe skills and qualities desired in graduates regardless of discipline or major (Barrie, 2006), academic development as defined here has not been widely researched. Nonetheless by surveying research and practice worldwide there is strong evidence in North America and Europe, as well as growing and emerging evidence in Asia and elsewhere, that student development akin to academic development is a goal of post-secondary education in general. Education abroad can contribute toward that goal such that, worldwide, new models and structures aim to increase education abroad participation. Academic development encompasses student success in a number of key areas, including focus, persistence, confidence, independence, and open-mindedness towards academic and career goals with growing awareness of how best to work with others in a dynamic and complex world. Education abroad can contribute to this, based on studies of students from diverse world regions. The depth of education abroad opportunity and concomitant research on outcomes in the United States and Europe, and related if indirect evidence from parts of Asia and elsewhere, support the claim that education abroad can have positive impact on students' academic development.

*Is there evidence that academic development occurs as a result of education abroad? And if there is not, what evidence exists that suggests education abroad supports and encourages academic development in students?* Based on direct and inferred evidence, there is a substantial case to be made that education abroad contributes to academic development in post-secondary students worldwide and may be an especially appropriate student outcome measure for education abroad. As others have noted (Hadis, 2005), academic achievement per se is neither reliably measurable nor useful in practice. Education abroad is often susceptible to self-selection bias, whereby higher achieving students are drawn to it and may, in fact, be the desired student demographic of program administrators. Instead, identifying outcomes related to the development of student academic success factors and traits is more accurate of the changes occurring to students having an international experience.

In fact, based on some of the research cited in this review, less high-achieving, more at-risk students may stand to gain the most from education abroad in terms of their academic development. While all students can potentially gain from an international experience in some way, those students with the greatest opportunity to develop academically may be the most productive, indeed important, focus of practitioners. Another implication for practice is that institutional and systemic support, including funding, for student-centered learning outcomes in education abroad can have a direct impact. For example, structured international exchange agreements, education abroad provider organization programming, or the Erasmus program in Europe can articulate clear goals for student development with measurable results. This is a departure from traditional policy objectives for education abroad related to economic growth and skills development, which remain prevalent in less developed regions.

## 5. Directions for future research

While some research has shown, most notably Ogden (2010), that education abroad can promote academic development, it is a relatively new concept as applied to education abroad and therefore lacks a full body of explicitly stated and intentionally designed research. Are there conclusions to be made about academic development based on inferences from existing research? As presented in this chapter, there is considerable research on related outcomes, such as confidence in contributing to class discussions, synthesizing ideas, critical thinking, comfort-level and open-mindedness working with others, and less rote memorization of course material (Coker et al., 2018), as well as increased independence, maturity, adaptability, persistence, and self-reliance (Maharaja, 2018). Can these documented results contribute to the field's understanding of academic development in education?

Researchers, particularly in North America, have consistently used proprietary instruments, such as the Intercultural Development Index (IDI), Global Awareness Profile (GAP), or the Global Perspective Inventory (GPI) in studying the impact of education abroad. A limited number of instruments focus on students' psychosocial development, such as the Beliefs, Events, and Values Inventory (BEVI). Applying the lens of academic development to existing data collected through these instruments could be a promising direction for new research.

It is important to note that widening access to higher education worldwide typically increases enrollment of underrepresented and non-traditional students. Gains related to academic development cited earlier in this chapter (particularly greater academic focus, self-confidence, self-esteem, and appreciation by students of their own capabilities) have been consistently observed in students following their education abroad experience for:

- underrepresented and community college students (Arnold, 2015; Latiner, Rhodes, & Biscarra, 2014);
- students going abroad to diverse destinations (Cai & Sankaran, 2015; Campbell, 2016);
- students from non-traditional academic majors including STEM (Jesiek, Haller, & Thompson, 2014) and business (Alexejun & D'Angelo, 2013; Black & Duhon, 2006);
- both U.S. and non-U.S. students (Han & Zweig, 2010; Komura, 2013; Luo & Jamieson-Drake, 2013; Redwine, Wagner, Rutherford, & Wingenbach, 2018).

The existing literature prompts important questions about academic development: Can education abroad help at-risk students persist in their studies? Can education abroad foster not only intercultural understanding but also enhanced learning skills and confidence? Developmental benefits from education abroad have been observed consistently for decades (Carlson, Burn, Useem, & Yachimowicz, 1990; Hansel & Grove, 1986; Kauffmann & Kuh, 1984) for traditional education abroad program models as well as experiential education programs abroad (Savage & Wehman, 2014). Evidence for its contribution to gains in intellectual development (McKeown, 2009) and academic development (Ogden, 2010) have been proven in limited but important ways. These new questions and research directions may be vital, not only for developing effective education abroad programs but also for creating learning environments that engender greater opportunities and success for all students.

Finally, it seems clear that academic development occurring from education abroad can impact, even if indirectly, students' future career success, in addition to their immediate post-secondary educational attainment. The difficulty of tracking long-term outcomes among education abroad participants is a major limitation of measuring the full impact of the experience, but several studies have asked graduates about career and life choices years after their international experience. Overall, students who participated in education abroad reported a higher level of employment and were more likely to complete an advanced degree than their peers not participating in education abroad. Mulvaney (2017) found that education abroad had an impact in raising student curiosity, stimulating intellectual growth, and encouraging academic interest beyond the requirements of a traditional four-year degree. This included higher levels of civic engagement, such as voting, advocacy, and political involvement. These results match other studies that found an over-whelming majority of education abroad alumni report enhanced interest in academic study and that it influenced subsequent educational experiences (Anderson, Hub-bard, & Lawton, 2015) and career decisions by helping to clarify values and interests in a more confident, independent manner (Kronholz & Osborn, 2016). As reported by employers in Europe and the United States, these qualities are increasingly in demand in a globally inter-connected world. This suggests, for both academic and long-term career success, that education abroad plays a substantive and multi-faceted role in career and life satisfaction, and that academic development may be one key aspect of this process. New research addressing the direct connections between aca-demic development during post-secondary education and later career and life satis-faction would benefit our understanding of the important role academic development has and how education abroad can contribute.

## Further reading

Hadis, B. F. (2005). Why are they better students when they come back? Determinants of academic focusing gains in the study abroad experience. *Frontiers: The Interdisciplinary Journal of Study Abroad*, 11, 57–70.

Latiner R. R., Rhodes, G. M., & Biscarra, A. (2014). Community college study abroad: Implications for student success. *Community College Journal of Research and Practice*, 38 (2–3), 174–183.

Li, J., Fei, G., & You, Y. (2017). Study abroad during college: Comparison between China and the United States. *Current Issues in Comparative Education*, 19 (2), 111–139.

McKeown, J. S. (2009). *The first-time effect: The impact of study abroad on college student intellectual development*. Albany: State University of New York Press.

Ogden, A. C. (2010). *Education abroad and the making of global citizens: Assessing learning outcomes of course-embedded, faculty-led international programming*. Michigan: Ann Arbor.

## References

Alexejun, K. M., & D'Angelo, A. M. (2013). International experience required: Lessons from the Carlson School of Management. *Journal of International Education in Business*, 6 (2), 80–94.

Anderson, C., Lorenz, K., & White, M. (2016). Instructor influence on student inter-cultural gains and learning during instructor-led, short-term study abroad. *Frontiers: The Interdisciplinary Journal of Study Abroad*, 28, 1–23.

Anderson, P.H., Hubbard, A., & Lawton, L. (2015). Student motivation to study abroad and their intercultural development. *Frontiers: The Interdisciplinary Journal of Study Abroad*, 26, 39–52.

Arnold, M. J. (2015). *Study abroad education and its influence on African-American college students.* Michigan: Ann Arbor.

Barrie, S.C. (2006). Understanding what we mean by the generic attributes of graduates. *Higher Education*, 51, 215–241.

Bilecen, B., & Van Mol, C. (2017). Introduction: International academic mobility and inequalities. *Journal of Ethnic and Migration Studies*, 43 (8), 1241–1255.

Black, H. T., & Duhon, D. L. (2006). Assessing the impact of business study abroad programs on cultural awareness and personal development. *Journal of Education for Business*, 81 (3), 140–144.

Byun, K., & Kim, M. (2011). Shifting patterns of the government's policies for the internationalization of Korean higher education. *Journal of Studies in International Education*, 15 (5), 467–486.

Cai, W. W., & Sankaran, G. (2015). Promoting critical thinking through an interdisciplinary abroad program. *Journal of International Students*, 5 (1), 38–49.

Campbell, R. (2016). Maintaining the Japan connection: The impact of study abroad on Japanese language learners' life trajectories and ongoing interaction with Japanese speakers. *Comparative and International Education*, 45 (2), 1–16.

Canadian Bureau for International Education. (2016). *A world of learning: Canada's performance and potential in international education.* https://cbie.ca/wp-content/uploads/2017/07/A-World-of-Learning-HI-RES-2016.pdf

Carlson, J. S., Burn, B. B., Useem, J., & Yachimowicz, D. (1990). *Study abroad: The experience of American undergraduates.* New York: Greenwood Press.

Caruana, V. (2014). Re-thinking global citizenship in higher education: From cosmopolitanism and international mobility to cosmopolitanisation, resilience and resilient thinking. *Higher Education Quarterly*, 68 (1), 85–104.

Chien, C., & Chiteng Kot, F. (2011). New patterns in student mobility in the Southern Africa development community. In C. Chien, F. Chiteng Kot, M. Mpinganjira, K. Ngamau, & E. Garwe (Eds.), *Building regional higher education capacity through academic mobility* (pp. 4–22). SARUA Leadership Dialogue Series, 3 (1). Johannesburg: Southern African Regional Universities Association.

Coker, J. S., Heiser, E., & Taylor, L. (2018). Student outcomes associated with short-term and semester study abroad programs. *Frontiers: The Interdisciplinary Journal of Study Abroad*, 30 (2), 92–105.

de Wit, H., Hunter, F., Howard, L., & Egron-Polak, E. (Eds.) (2015). *Internationalisation of higher education study.* European Parliament, Directorate-General for Internal Policies, Policy Department B: Structural and Cohesion Policies, Culture and Education.

Dwyer, M. M. (2004). More Is Better: The impact of study abroad program duration. *Frontiers: The Interdisciplinary Journal of Study Abroad*, 10, 151–163.

Erasmus Impact Study (EIS). (2014). Retrieved from https://ec.europa.eu/programmes/erasmus-plus/about_en#tab-1-5. Accessed July 2018.

Erasmus+ Higher Education Impact Study. (2019). Retrieved from https://op.europa.eu/en/publication-detail/-/publication/94d97f.5c-7ae2-11e9-9f.05-01aa75ed71a1/language-en. Accessed January 2020.

Farrugia, C., & Sanger, J. (2017). *Gaining an employment edge: The impact of study abroad on 21st century skills and career prospects in the United States, 2013–2016.* Institute of International Education, IIE Center for Academic Mobility Research and Impact. www.iie.org/Research-and-Insights/Publications/Gaining-an-employment-edge—-The-Impact-of-Study-Abroad

Hadis, B. F. (2005). Why are they better students when they come back? Determinants of academic focusing gains in the study abroad experience. *Frontiers: The Interdisciplinary Journal of Study Abroad*, 11, 57–70.

Han, D., & Zweig, D. (2010). Images of the world: Studying abroad and Chinese attitudes towards international affairs. *The China Quarterly*, 202, 290–306.

Hansel, B., & Grove, N. (1986). International student exchange programs: Are the benefits real? *NASSP Bulletin*, 70 (487), 84–90.

Jesiek, B. K., Haller, Y., & Thompson, J. (2014). Developing globally competent engineering researchers: Outcomes-based instructional and assessment strategies from the IREE 2010 China Research Abroad Program. *Advances in Engineering Education*, 4 (1). https://eric.ed.gov/?id=EJ1076148

Jones, E. (2010). 'Don't worry about the worries': Transforming lives through international volunteering. In E. Jones (Ed.), *Internationalisation and the student voice: Higher education perspectives* (pp. 83–97). London: Routledge.

Jones, E. (2013). Internationalization and employability: The role of intercultural experiences in the development of transferable skills. *Public Money and Management*, 33 (2), 95–104.

Jones, E. (2016). Mobility, graduate employability and local internationalisation. In Jones, E., Coelen, R., Beelen, J. & de Wit, H. (eds.), *Global and Local Internationalization* (pp. 107–116). Rotterdam & Boston: Sense Publishers.

Kauffmann, N. L., & Kuh, G. D. (1984, April). *The impact of study abroad on the personal development of college students*. Presented at the meeting of the American Educational Research Association, New Orleans, Louisiana.

Kinzie, J., Helms, R., & Cole, J. (2017). A glimpse of global learning: Assessing student experiences and institutional commitments. *Liberal Education*, 103 (2). Retrieved from www.aacu.org/liberaleducation/2017/spring/kinzie_helms_cole. Accessed October 2018.

Komura, K. (2013). *Borderless STEM Education: A study of both American students and foreign students*. (Ph.D. Dissertation). Published by ProQuest LLC.

Kronholz, J., & Osborn, D. (2016). The impact of study abroad experiences on vocational identity among college students. *Frontiers: The Interdisciplinary Journal of Study Abroad*, 27, 70–84.

Kuh, G. (2008). *High-impact educational practices: What they are, who has access to them, and why they matter*. Washington, D.C.: American Association of Colleges and Universities.

Latiner, R. R., Rhodes, G. M., & Biscarra, A. (2014). Community college study abroad: Implications for student success. *Community College Journal of Research and Practice*, 38 (2–3), 174–183.

Li, J., Fei, G., & You, Y. (2017). Study abroad during college: Comparison between China and the United States. *Current Issues in Comparative Education*, 19 (2), 111–139.

Liu, X. (2014). Comparison on the developmental trends between Chinese students studying abroad and foreign students studying in China. *Journal of International Students*, 4 (1), 34–47.

Luo, J., & Jamieson-Drake, D. (2013, May). *Predictors of study abroad intent, participation, and college outcomes*. Paper presented at the Annual forum of the Association for Institutional Research, Long Beach, California.

Maharaja, G. (2018). Impact of study abroad on college students' intercultural competence and personal development. *International Research and Review: Journal of Phi Beta Delta Honor Society for International Scholars*, 7 (2), 18–41.

Mankowska, A. (2018). *Studying abroad: A case study of Chinese international mobility.* BCES Conference Books, Vol. 16, Part 4: Higher Education, Lifelong Learning & Social Inclusion. https://eric.ed.gov/?id=ED586147

Marijuan, S., & Sanz, C. (2018). Expanding boundaries: Current and new directions in study abroad research and practice. *Foreign Language Annals,* 51, 185–204.

McKeown, J. S. (2009). *The first time effect: The impact of study abroad on college student intellectual development.* Albany: State University of New York Press.

Mellors-Bourne, R., Jones, E., Lawton, W., & Woodfield, S. (2015). *Student perspectives on going international.* London: UK HE International Unit.

Morais, D., & Ogden, A.C. (2010). *Measuring student learning in education abroad: Global citizenship & academic development scales.* Presented at The Forum on Education Abroad, Charlotte, North Carolina.

Mulvaney, M. (2017). The long-term impact of study abroad on honors program alumni. *Frontiers: The Interdisciplinary Journal of Study Abroad,* 29 (1), 46–67.

Ogden, A. C. (2010). *Education abroad and the making of global citizens: Assessing learning outcomes of course-embedded, faculty-led international programming.* Michigan: Ann Arbor.

Pérez-Vidal, C. (ed.). (2014). *Language acquisition in study abroad and formal instruction contexts.* Amsterdam and Philadelphia: John Benjamins.

Perry, W. G., Jr. (1968). *Forms of intellectual and ethical development in the college years: A scheme.* Cambridge, MA: President and Fellows of Harvard College.

Petzold, K., & Moog, P. (2018). What shapes the intention to study abroad? An experimental approach. *Higher Education,* 75, 35–54.

Powell, D. L., & Biederman, D. J. (2017). U.S.-based short-term public health cultural immersion experience for Chinese undergraduate students. *Journal of Student Affairs Research and Practice,* 54 (4), 454–463.

Rasplus, J. (2018). Report of the ASEAN "SHARE" (Support to Higher Education in the ASEAN Region). Retrieved from www. universityworldnews.com/ article.php?story= 20180629090604303. Accessed October 2018.

Redwine, T., Wagner, S., Rutherford, T., & Wingenbach, G. (2018). Outcomes of study abroad in three domains of human development. *NACTA Journal,* 62 (1), 77–83.

Regan, V., Howard, M., & Lemée, I. (2009). *The acquisition of sociolinguistic competence in study abroad contexts.* Bristol: Multilingual Matters.

Savage, M. P., & Wehman, T. L. (2014). Assessing the impact of international experiential education on the critical thinking skills and academic performance of college students. *International Journal of Arts & Sciences,* 7 (1), 1–18.

Science-Metrix. (2015). *Evaluation of the Mitacs Globalink Program: A qualitative study, final report.* www.mitacs.ca/sites/default/files/uploads/newsroom/evaluation_of_ the_mitacs_globalink_program_final_report.pdf

Stahl, M. L. (2016). *Chinese students in United States high schools* (Ph.D. Dissertation). Published by ProQuest LLC. Michigan: Ann Arbor.

Streitwieser, B. T., & Light, G. J. (2018). Student conceptions of international experience in the study abroad context. *Higher Education,* 75, 471–487.

Suleman, F. (2018). The employability skills of higher education graduates: Insights into conceptual frameworks and methodological options. *Higher Education,* 76, 263–278.

Sutton, R. C., & Rubin, D. L. (2010, June). *Documenting the academic impact of study abroad: Final report of the GLOSSARI Project.* Presented at NAFSA Annual Conference, Kansas City, Missouri.

Van Mol, C. (2017). Do employers value international study and internships? A comparative analysis of 31 countries. *Geoforum*, 78, 52–70.

Wang, I. K. (2018). Long-term Chinese students' transitional experiences in UK higher education: A particular focus on their academic adjustment. *International Journal of Teaching and Learning in Higher Education*, 30 (1), 12–25.

Weibl, G. (2015). Cosmopolitan identity and personal growth as an outcome of international student mobility at selected New Zealand, British and Czech universities. *Journal of International Mobility*, 1 (3), 31–44.

# Chapter 6

# Language proficiency

## Developmental perspectives and linguistic outcomes of education abroad

*Jane Jackson, Martin Howard and John W. Schwieter*

### Highlights:

- There has been a significant rise in the number of students who are participating in education abroad programmes, both short-term and long-term, and many seek to enhance their second language (L2) proficiency in the host speech community.
- From this growth come a number of key research questions discussed in this chapter, including: (a) What factors impact the language learning of higher education students who gain education abroad experience? (b) What can be done to optimize the language learning of education abroad participants? and (c) What are the implications for pedagogical interventions at all stages of education abroad (pre-departure, while abroad, and upon return)?

### 1. Introduction and chapter overview

More and more tertiary-level students are choosing to enhance their second language (L2) proficiency through some form of education abroad (e.g., study abroad, global service-learning, international internship). Even when language learning is not their primary goal, they are apt to be exposed to unfamiliar linguistic codes and practices to varying degrees. Accordingly, in the past decade, there has been a steady rise in the number of research projects and publications that centre on language and intercultural learning in diverse education abroad programmes in different parts of the world. Intercultural learning refers to the development of cultural competence that helps individuals to act and relate appropriately and effectively in a range of cultural contexts (Messner and Schäfer 2012). The growth of this body of work (both qualitative and quantitative studies) is evidenced by the publication of recent volumes (e.g., Jackson 2018; Jackson and Oguro 2018; Plews and Misfeldt 2018; Sanz and Morales-Front 2018). The findings help explain variations in the developmental trajectories of education abroad participants.

Recent research has debunked some long-held assumptions about the language and intercultural development of students who engage in some form of international education. Education abroad researchers have discovered that a complex mix of internal and external factors can lead to significant differences in language and (inter) cultural learning (Jackson 2018; Kinginger 2009, 2013). Some participants become more global-minded and significantly enhance their L2 proficiency and intercultural sensitivity during their stay abroad, whereas others limit their exposure to the host language and culture and return home with little or no desire to use their L2 or enhance their intercultural competence. Consequently, seasoned education abroad scholars increasingly advocate language and intercultural pedagogical interventions to optimize the potential of international educational experience.

After identifying the key questions that frame this chapter, definitions of core constructs are presented, followed by a brief review of developments in the field that have enriched our understanding of language learning in education abroad contexts. The discussion then centres on individual and external or environmental factors that have been found to influence the language development of student education abroad participants. This is followed by a brief review of common methodologies that are being used to track and assess the language learning of education abroad participants. After discussing pedagogical implications, this chapter concludes by identifying gaps in language learning research in education abroad and offers suggestions for future studies.

## 2. Key questions to be addressed

Drawing on contemporary education abroad research and practice, this chapter aims to address the following questions:

- What factors impact the language learning of higher education students who gain education abroad experience?
- What can be done to optimize the language learning of education abroad participants?
- What are the research implications for pedagogical interventions at all stages of education abroad?

## 3. Review of the literature

### 3.1 Overview of language learning in education abroad

Beginning with Carroll's (1967) study, applied linguists initially examined the L2 developmental gains of education abroad participants in very broad terms through the use of general proficiency tests (see Brecht, Davidson, and Ginsberg 1993); later studies also drew on learner self-reports (see Lapkin, Hart, and Swain 1995). Research findings generally pointed to greater gains in speaking and listening skills compared to reading and writing; however, the studies failed to illuminate the language learning process and general tests are subject to ceiling effects at more advanced levels. For instance, at higher levels of the ACTFL Oral Proficiency

Interview it is difficult to track language development due to a lack of specificity in the descriptors. By the 1990s, recognizing the limitations of general proficiency tests, more researchers were beginning to examine specific areas of language skills, such as oral proficiency, fluency, vocabulary, sociolinguistic and pragmatic competence, grammar, and pronunciation.

The publication of Freed's (1995a) seminal volume exemplifies the value of more focused language proficiency studies. In the case of oral proficiency, researchers have found that fluency skills are especially enhanced through education abroad. Freed (1995b) noted that education abroad learners speak more, demonstrate a faster speech rate, and are more at ease in the target language compared to their classroom counterparts who have not been abroad. Moreover, in terms of long-term retention, Huensch and Tracy-Ventura (2017) discovered that gains in speed fluency are retained a full year post-education abroad. Other work points to enhanced willingness to communicate even after a few weeks in the host environment (see Dewaele, Comanaru, and Faraco 2015). In the related area of communicative strategies, Lafford (1995) highlights how education abroad learners can develop a larger range of strategies, which helps them to deal with difficulties that arise in real-time interaction. With regard to interactional competence, Taguchi (2015) observed a range of features in education abroad participants which point to their increased ability to interact competently during their stay in the host environment. For example, they displayed a better grasp of ways to enter and end conversations in the host language, and more ability to modify their use of language and shift their communication style in different social situations.

Some education abroad research also points to vocabulary learning and the enhancement of sociolinguistic and sociopragmatic skills (see Howard 2012; Ife, Vives Boix, and Meara 2000). While sociolinguistic variation concerns sociolinguistic variables specific to a target language, sociopragmatic competence is concerned with the learner's ability to use appropriate language for the expression of universal pragmatic functions, e.g., compliments, refusals, and apologies.

Research on pronunciation and grammar in education abroad contexts has yielded more mixed results. With regard to pronunciation, Díaz-Campos (2004) found no beneficial effect for education abroad in his learners' acquisition of two difficult sounds in L2 Spanish. Mora (2008), in contrast, reported more positive development. As for grammar, a twofold approach has dominated research on grammatical skills. Some studies focus on specific grammatical concepts and items, while others are situated within the framework of Complexity, Accuracy, and Fluency (CAF) (see Housen, Kuiken, and Vedder 2012). Howard and Schwieter (2018) offered an overview of work in both areas, reporting that education abroad is especially propitious to CAF development with studies showing important gains – learner language is found to be more complex, more accurate and to evidence greater fluency both in speaking and to a lesser extent in writing (see Juan-Garau 2014, Pérez-Vidal and Juan-Garau 2011). Such work, however, does not specifically document detailed changes in the learner's production that give rise to greater complexity and accuracy. Studies exploring specific grammatical concepts offer mixed findings in relation to the benefits of education abroad compared to classroom learning. A length of stay threshold may operate such that the gains are only evident after a certain amount of time abroad.

While the above findings point to the potential of international educational experience to impact linguistic development, it is clear that development is not guaranteed. A wide range of factors, both individual and external, can lead to significant variations in the language learning and intercultural development of participants (Jackson 2018; Jackson and Schwieter forthcoming). The next section will examine some of these elements, beginning with individual or internal variables.

### 3.2 Individual factors affecting language learning in education abroad

Education abroad researchers have identified a myriad of individual elements or characteristics that can lead to profound differences in the language and inter-cultural learning of participants (Benson, Barkhuizen, Bodycott, and Brown 2013; Jackson 2018; Kinginger 2009). Agency (e.g., choices made in the host environ-ment), education abroad expectations and aspirations (e.g., belief in the ability to experience significant language learning gains in a short-term education abroad programme), learning aims (e.g., vague or focused language learning targets, rea-listic or unrealistic goals), physical appearance (e.g., race, minority status), gender, and aptitude (e.g., cognitive ability in relation to language learning) are some of the many factors that can result in different learning paths and outcomes.

A number of affective and psychological dimensions can also be influential including language and intercultural attitudes (e.g., openness to host practices, degree of positivity), personality (e.g., introversion, extroversion), motivation and investment (e.g., amount of effort expended to learn the host language), self-confidence, imagined selves/identities (e.g., the desire to be a proficient speaker of the host language), self-efficacy beliefs (e.g., confidence in one's language learning ability), willingness to communicate (e.g., initiate intercultural interactions in an L2), and anxiety or communication apprehension (e.g., fear of using an L2 to communicate with first language speakers/host nationals) (Benson et al. 2013; Jackson 2018; Jackson and Schwieter forthcoming).

### 3.3 External factors affecting language learning in education abroad

Education abroad scholars have also discovered that external or environmental elements can bring about variations in the language learning trajectories of edu-cation abroad participants and, ultimately, result in different outcomes. In parti-cular, programme and housing variations, the degree of host receptivity, and the use of technology can affect the quality of international educational experience and L2 learning (Jackson 2018; Jackson and Schwieter forthcoming).

Programmes may differ in a number of ways, including learning aims, duration, the amount of language and cultural preparation and support provided, language learning instruction, the setting, the depth of critical reflection promoted, the amount of contact with locals, and the amount and quality of debriefings, among others. Some programmes may be faculty-led with students remaining as an intact group throughout their stay abroad; other students may independently join an education abroad programme and study alongside students from other countries.

The type of accommodation during education abroad can result in divergent opportunities for social integration, language learning, and intercultural engagement. Frank (1997) and Rivers (1998) call into question the homestay as the *sine qua non* of accommodation types most conducive to development, suggesting that host families do not necessarily productively engage with students. While folk linguistic belief might hold that education abroad offers extended opportunities for L2 contact, qualitative research points to significant variability in experiences. Kinginger (2008) and Kinginger, Wu, Lee, and Tan (2016) observed that some learners find relationship-building with their host family difficult and withdraw, reducing exposure to the target language. While some hosts may make an effort to include learners in family activities, others may be less inclined to do so. Beyond the learner's type of residence, Wilkinson (1998) noted differential opportunities for students to use the target language in everyday encounters outside their place of residence, suggesting the need for classroom instruction and meaningful community-based tasks for language learners during education abroad.

Many studies have also drawn attention to the impact of host receptivity on the social integration and engagement of education abroad participants. Mitchell, Tracy-Ventura, and McManus (2017) highlight the ways in which the openness of hosts can influence the social networks and linguistic development of international exchange students. While Mitchell et al., and Magnan and Back (2007) suggest little additional benefits among learners who develop diverse social networks, Baker-Smemoe, Dewey, Bown, and Martinsen (2014) show that the dispersion, size, and density of the learner's social networks are key predictors of general proficiency gains. Dewey, Belnap, and Hillstrom (2013), for example, identified language learning benefits for education abroad students who developed intercultural friendships.

As English has become the de facto language of internationalization, more non-English speaking countries are offering courses in this language, including both language enhancement and subject matter modules. This means that some education abroad participants may primarily use English as a lingua franca in the host environment, that is, most of their intercultural interactions involve conversations with other L2 speakers who do not speak their first language.

In education abroad programmes, the accommodation arrangement can also vary (e.g., host family life; residence in a dormitory on campus; independent living in an apartment off-campus with co-nationals, host nationals, and/or a diverse group) and as mentioned earlier, this can lead to differences in the amount of exposure that the newcomers have to the host language and culture. The degree of immersion may also be affected by the use of electronic tools of communication. For example, advances in communications technology and social media (e.g., email, Facetime,

Skype, WeChat, eLearning platforms) are enabling education abroad students to keep in close contact with home; this can make an 'immersion' experience quite different from past generations (Goodwin-Jones 2016). Additionally, the quality and amount of pre-departure preparation, support in the host country, and re-entry debriefings can vary tremendously in education abroad programmes, ranging from no support to credit-bearing language and intercultural coursework at all stages.

Multiple environmental factors may also influence the language and culture-learning experiences of education abroad participants. In particular, the degree of host receptivity (openness to newcomers) and power-related issues (e.g., inequality in the host environment) can facilitate or hamper education abroad learning (Coleman 2013; Jackson 2018; Kinginger 2009). Limited L2 proficiency and a lack of familiarity with sociopragmatic norms in the host environment (use of language in socially appropriate ways) can result in newcomers feeling disadvantaged and vulnerable, especially when interacting with impatient hosts who possess limited intercultural communication skills and international experience. Lack of empathy and understanding may impede relationship-building and curtail the diversification of social networks (Mitchell et al. 2017).

Numerous other environmental elements may inhibit the language and cultural learning of education abroad participants, including an unfamiliar climate, food/diet, pollution (e.g., air, noise, water), congestion (e.g., reduction in personal space), or atmosphere for studying, among others. Moving from an urban university setting to a rural environment, and vice-versa, can also be disquieting for some, and initially some newcomers may find it difficult to concentrate on language learning and be less willing to engage in intercultural interactions.

## 4. Evaluation of research methodology

There are a number of methods, both qualitative and quantitative, which researchers can use to track and assess the language learning of education abroad participants. While some studies are designed to compare language learning in the host speech community with learning in traditional classroom settings in the home environment (e.g., Isabelli-García 2010; Segalowitz and Freed 2004), others utilize within-group analyses to explore linguistic and intercultural development in two or more timespans (e.g., Faretta-Stutenberg and Morgan-Short 2018; Grey et al. 2015; Schwieter 2013; Schwieter and Klassen 2016). The design choice depends on several factors, including the research questions, availability of research equipment and materials, the expertise of the researcher, and the structure and length of the education abroad programme. Quantitative methods may be used (e.g., questionnaire surveys) to explore learners' language learning perceptions, global development (e.g., the broad effects of education abroad on oral fluency or listening comprehension) or the acquisition of specific linguistic information (e.g., the precise effects of education abroad on grammar development or vocabulary learning). Because of space limitations, it is not feasible to discuss the many quantitative methods commonly used in education abroad research. The reader is referred to Grey (2018) to learn more.

Measures that take a qualitative approach are 'based on descriptive data that does not make (regular) use of statistical procedures' (Mackey and Gass 2005: 61). In education abroad research, qualitative methods often contain open-ended questions that call for a detailed analysis of learner experiences, interactions, and individual differences within a particular education abroad context. Given the strong tradition of socially-oriented theories such as sociocultural theory (Lantolf and Thorne 2006) and poststructuralist accounts of identity and language learning (Bourdieu 1991; Norton 2000), there has been a significant increase in qualitative education abroad research (e.g., ethnographic studies, narrative inquiry, introspective diary studies). Through these means, more is known about learner characteristics and how to systematically code and analyse learner participation in the host community abroad.

One objective of qualitative methods has been to describe learner engagement in the host community. Several concepts and foci have been introduced into this work such as communities of practice, social networks, and language socialization. Trentman (2013) used open-ended questionnaires, the Language Contact Profile (Freed, Dewey, Segalowitz, and Halter 2004), interviews, and field notes to explore overall engagement of education abroad learners in terms of how they view themselves as members of an imagined community while abroad. Churchill (2006) moderated a focus group among education abroad participants to evaluate learner engagement and determine the practices that facilitate or hinder the integration of newcomers into the host community. Longitudinal case studies are also revealing of learner engagement abroad. Umino and Benson (2016) interviewed their focal participant, who spent four years abroad at two strategic intervals: at the end of the third and fourth years. At the beginning of each interview, the researchers used photo-elicitation to encourage the participant to reflect on his scaffolded and self-managed community of practice while abroad.

Some qualitative methods focus on understanding education abroad learners' characteristics (e.g., second language identities, language learning motivation) and learning paths. Many contemporary studies have analysed education abroad journal entries and transcripts of interviews to learn how, for instance, learners perceive their language progression and the effect of certain variables (positive, negative) in the host environment (Isabelli-García 2010). Others have studied learners' perceptions of their personal goals, intercultural learning, and interaction abroad (Allen, 2010 2013). Jackson (2008) employed a rich breadth of data collection techniques to explore the evolution of education abroad participants' sociocultural identities and perceptions of language and intercultural learning. Prior to a five-week education abroad programme, the learners took two classes with the researcher, one on ethnography and one on intercultural communication. During these courses, the learners produced a home ethnography project, an intercultural reflection journal, and a cultural identity narrative. Once abroad, they conducted ethnographic fieldwork, kept diaries including a language use log, and participated in weekly surveys about their experience abroad. Upon returning to their home country, they completed a post-abroad survey and debriefing session and spent a semester developing ethnographic reports. To date, the range of methods employed in Jackson's study is among some of the most extensive found in a single project.

## 5. Implications for practice

Many institutions of higher education are still sending students abroad with limited preparation and scant awareness of language and culture-learning strategies that could enhance education abroad learning. Fortunately, this is changing as administrators and educators become more familiar with research findings that point to the need to prepare and support the language and intercultural development of education abroad participants. To enrich international educational experience, more education abroad scholars are designing innovative, learner-centred interventions (e.g., experiential learning, intercultural mentoring, individualized problem-solving, ethnographic fieldwork, host language enhancement courses) (Jackson 2019; Jackson and Oguro 2018; Plews and Misfeldt 2018). With more awareness of the many factors that can enhance or impede education abroad learning, educators increasingly recognize the benefits of developing adequate learner profiles for coping with the challenges of the education abroad experience. This is helping them to sequence materials/activities and provide appropriate mentoring. While most interventions are implemented either prior to education abroad or during the stay in the host environment, there is a pressing need to pay more attention to the post-education abroad phase. While it is encouraging that more educators are developing innovative schemes for the re-entry phase, more work is needed to extend education abroad learning.

Kolb's experiential learning cycle (Kolb and Kolb 2017; Passarelli and Kolb 2012) and Mezirow's (2009) transformative learning theory are guiding the development of many pedagogical interventions in education abroad contexts. Both stress the importance of critical reflection to deepen the language and intercultural learning and engagement of education abroad participants. In sync with learner-centred approaches to pedagogy, educators who adopt this approach serve as mentors or facilitators of language and intercultural learning rather than that of experts who seek to transmit knowledge (e.g., information about the host language and culture) (Jackson and Oguro 2018; Paige 2015). A further dimension concerns the academic structuring of education abroad programmes, as noted by Salaberry et al. (2019). These authors note that there are many opportunities in the foreign language classroom prior to education abroad that can better reflect the types of communicative interaction that students will experience in the host environment. With this preparation, the learners are more likely to benefit from those interactional opportunities. Indeed, as Salaberry et al. highlight, there is often a mismatch between the interactional focus of classroom practice and the learner's interactional needs while abroad. They call for greater awareness on the part of instructors to reflect the type of everyday interaction in classroom activities that learners will need to engage in while in the host speech community. The learner's programme of instruction while abroad should also integrate tasks which require meaningful use of the target language in intercultural situations.

Ethnographic inquiry can also help students become more thoughtful language and culture learners and better equipped for life in the host speech community (e.g., Jackson 2008; Roberts, Byram, Barro, Jordan, and Street 2001). With sufficient support and preparation, advanced language learners can investigate a cultural scene in the host environment which requires prolonged intercultural contact and a focus on sociocultural dimensions of language use, including pragmatic features (e.g., politeness norms, the use of the host language in particular contexts and situations, honorifics).

Educators are also taking advantage of developments in communication technology and social media to devise learner-centred interventions that promote language learning and intercultural engagement in education abroad settings. For example, Lee (2018) developed a telecollaborative language and intercultural exchange project to link US-American students who had recently completed an education abroad placement in Spain with first language speakers of Spanish in Spain. Drawing on her education abroad research, Jackson (2019) developed a fully online intercultural transition course for international exchange students to take while they are in their host country. Through deep reflection on language and intercultural interactions, the participants hone their sociopragmatic awareness and intercultural competence.

There is growing recognition of the need for pedagogical interventions to deepen and extend the language and intercultural learning of education abroad returnees. This has spawned the development of language and intercultural workshops and courses for the re-entry phase of the education abroad cycle (e.g., Jackson 2015; Lee 2018). As mentioned above, in some situations, this involves the use of technology such as e-Learning platforms which link returning language students with language partners in the host country (e.g., Lee 2018). Creative work of this nature is encouraging returnees to continue their learning of the host language, thereby reflecting the specificity of their learning needs during their re-integration in their home institutions post-education abroad.

In addition to advances in the design, delivery, and assessment of language and intercultural learning in education abroad programmes (e.g., learner-centred approaches) (Kinginger 2009; Savicki and Brewer 2015), more scholars are recognizing the importance of conducting systematic, comprehensive programme reviews to provide direction for the refinement of language and intercultural interventions in education abroad (e.g., investigations of summer language immersion programmes by Jackson, 2018). These developments are further enhancing education abroad. Taken together, education abroad research has much to offer by drawing programme organizers' and instructors' attention to the complexity of the individual learner experience abroad where a multitude of learner-internal and other external factors contribute to shaping the individual nature of that experience. The examples of the interventions above show how pre-education abroad training along with mentoring during the experience abroad can significantly enhance the opportunities to be availed of along with the learner's ability to deal with the various challenges that such an experience can entail.

## 6. Directions for future research

Applied linguists and scholars from related fields (e.g., cross-cultural psychology, international education, sociology, among others) have drawn on various theoretical frameworks and methodologies to make sense of differences in the linguistic and intercultural developmental trajectories of education abroad students. As well as traditional quantitative studies, mixed-method and interpretive qualitative studies (e.g., case studies, ethnographies) have been carried out to better understand what actually happens on stays abroad (Jackson 2018; Kinginger 2009). While there have been major advances in research and practice in relation to language and intercultural learning, our review has identified gaps in the literature on education abroad as well as methodological limitations in research and practice in our field. For example, more studies are needed – beyond the few that exist – that carefully document and critically examine pedagogical interventions. Also, there is the need for more ethnographic investigations and discourse analyses of language learning in homestay situations as well as in other housing situations on stays abroad. These studies should go beyond focusing on the perspectives of novice learners in new cultural settings. It is also imperative to examine post-education abroad learning in relation to linguistic and intercultural development. Much remains to be done to optimize education abroad experience.

## Further reading

Jackson, J. and Oguro, S. (eds.) (2018) *Intercultural Interventions in Study Abroad*, London and New York: Routledge.
Kinginger, C. (2009) *Language Learning and Study Abroad: A Critical Reading of Research*, London: Palgrave Macmillan.
Plews, J. and Misfeldt, K. (eds.) (2018) *Second Language Study Abroad: Programming, Pedagogy, and Participant Engagement*, New York: Springer.

## References

Allen, W. (2010) 'Language-learning motivation during short-term study abroad: An activity theory perspective', *Foreign Language Annals*, 43: 27–49.
Allen, W. (2013) 'Self-regulatory strategies of foreign language learners: From the classroom to study abroad and beyond', in C. Kinginger (ed.) *Social and Cultural Aspects of Language Learning in Study Abroad*, Philadelphia and Amsterdam: John Benjamins, pp. 47–74.
Baker-Smemoe, W., Dewey, D., Bown, J., and Martinsen, R. (2014) 'Variables affecting L2 gains during study abroad', *Foreign Language Annals*, 47 (3): 464–486.
Benson, P., Barkhuizen, G., Bodycott, P., and Brown, J. (2013) *Second Language Identity in Narratives of Study Abroad*, London: Palgrave Macmillan.

Bourdieu, P. (1991) *Language and Symbolic Power*, Cambridge: Cambridge University Press.

Brecht, R., Davidson, D., and Ginsberg, R. (1993) *Predictors of Foreign Language Gain during Study Abroad*, Washington, DC: National Foreign Language Center.

Carroll, J. (1967) 'Foreign language proficiency levels attained by language majors near graduation from college', *Foreign Language Annals*, 1: 131–151.

Churchill, E. (2006) 'Variability in the study abroad classroom and learner competence', in M. DuFon and E. Churchill (eds), *Language Learners in Study Abroad Contexts*, Clevedon, UK: Multilingual Matters, pp. 203–227.

Coleman, J. (2013) 'Researching whole people and whole lives', in C. Kinginger (ed.) *Social and Cultural Aspects of Language Learning in Study Abroad*, Philadelphia and Amsterdam: John Benjamins, pp. 17–46.

Dewaele, J.-M., Comanaru, R., and Faraco, M. (2015) 'The affective benefits of a pre-sessional course at the start of study abroad', in R. Mitchell, N. Tracy-Ventura, and K. McManus (eds.) *Social Interaction, Identity, and Language Learning during Residence Abroad*, EuroSLA Monograph Series, 4, Amsterdam: European Second Language Association, pp. 95–114.

Dewey, D. P., Belnap, R. K., and Hilstrom, R. (2013) 'Social network development, language use, and language acquisition during study abroad: Arabic language learners' perspectives', *Frontiers: The Interdisciplinary Journal of Study Abroad*, 21: 84–110.

Díaz-Campos, M. (2004) 'Context of learning in the acquisition of Spanish second language phonology', *Studies in Second Language Acquisition*, 26: 249–274.

Faretta-Stutenberg, M. and Morgan-Short, K. (2018) 'Individual differences in context: A neurolinguistic investigation of the role of memory and language use in naturalistic learning contexts', *Second Language Research*, 34 (1): 67–101.

Frank, V. (1997) '*Potential negative effects of home stay*'. Paper presented at The Middle Atlantic Conference of the American Association for the Advancement of Slavic Studies, Albany, New York.

Freed, B. (ed.) (1995a) *Second Language Acquisition in a Study Abroad Context*. Philadelphia and Amsterdam: John Benjamins.

Freed, B. (1995b) 'What makes us think that students who study abroad become fluent?' in B. Freed (ed.), *Second Language Acquisition in a Study Abroad Context*, Philadelphia and Amsterdam: John Benjamins, pp. 123–148.

Freed, B., Dewey, D., Segalowitz, N., and Halter, R. (2004) 'The lLanguage cContact pProfile', *Studies in Second Language Acquisition*, 26 (2): 349–356.

Freed, B., Segalowitz, N., and Dewey, D. (2004) 'Context of learning and second language fluency in French: Comparing regular classroom, study abroad, and intensive domestic immersion programs', *Studies in Second Language Acquisition*, 26 (2): 275–301.

Goodwin-Jones, R. (2016) 'Emerging technologies: Integrating technology into study abroad', *Language Learning and Technology*, 20 (1): 1–20.

Grey, S. (2018) 'Quantitative approaches for study abroad research', in C. Sanz and A. Morales-Front (eds.) *The Routledge Handbook of Study Abroad Research and Practice*, New York: Routledge, pp. 48–57.

Grey, S., Cox, J., Serafini, E., and Sanz, C. (2015) 'The role of individual differences in the study abroad context: Cognitive capacity and language development during short-term intensive language exposure', *Modern Language Journal*, 99 (1), 137–157.

Housen, A, Kuiken, F., and Vedder, I. (2012) 'Complexity, accuracy and fluency: Definitions, measurement and research', in A. Housen, F. Kuiken, and I. Vedder (eds),

*Dimensions of L2 Performance and Proficiency: Complexity, Accuracy and Fluency in SLA*, Language Learning and Language Teaching, vol. 32, Philadelphia and Amsterdam: John Benjamins, pp. 1–20.

Howard, M. (2012) 'The advanced language learner's sociolinguistic profile: On issues of individual differences, L2 exposure conditions and type of sociolinguistic variable', *Modern Language Review*, 96 (1): 20–33.

Howard, M. and Schwieter, J. W. (2018) 'The development of second language grammar in a study abroad context', in C. Sanz and A. Morales-Front (eds), *The Routledge Handbook of Study Abroad Research and Practice*, New York : Routledge, pp. 135–148.

Huensch, A. and Tracy-Ventura, N. (2017) 'L2 utterance fluency development before, during, and after residence abroad: A multidimensional investigation', *Modern Language Journal*, 101 (2): 275–293.

Ife, A., Vives Boix, G., and Meara, P. (2000) 'The impact of study abroad on the vocabulary development of different proficiency groups', *Spanish Applied Linguistics*, 4 (1): 55–84.

Isabelli-García, C. (2010) 'Acquisition of Spanish gender agreement in two learning contexts: Study abroad and at home', *Foreign Language Annals*, 43 (2): 289–303.

Jackson, J. (2008) *Language, Identity, and Study Abroad: Sociocultural Perspectives*, London: Equinox.

Jackson, J. (2015) 'Becoming interculturally competent: Theory to practice in international education', *International Journal of Intercultural Relations*, 48: 91–107.

Jackson, J. (2018) *Interculturality in International Education*, London and New York: Routledge.

Jackson, J. (2019) *Online Intercultural Education and Study Abroad: Theory into Practice*, London and New York: Routledge.

Jackson, J. (forthcoming) 'Intercultural education in study abroad contexts', in S. Rasinger and G. Rings (eds), *The Cambridge Handbook of Intercultural Communication*, Cambridge: Cambridge University Press.

Jackson, J. and Oguro, S. (eds) (2018) *Intercultural Interventions in Study Abroad*, London and New York: Routledge.

Jackson, J. and Schwieter, J.W. (forthcoming) 'Study abroad and immersion', in J.W. Schwieter and A. Benati (eds), *The Cambridge Handbook of Language Learning*, Cambridge: Cambridge University Press.

Juan-Garau, M. (2014) 'Oral accuracy growth after formal instruction and study abroad: Onset level, contact factors, and long-term effects', in C. Pérez-Vidal (ed.), *Language Acquisition in Study Abroad and Formal Instruction Contexts*, Philadelphia and Amsterdam: Benjamins, pp. 87–109.

Kinginger, C. (2008) 'Language learning in study abroad: Case studies of Americans in France', *TheModern Language Journal*, 92: 1–124.

Kinginger, C. (2009) *Language Learning and Study Abroad: A Critical Reading of Research*. London: Palgrave Macmillan.

Kinginger, C. (2013) 'Introduction', in C. Kinginger (ed.) *Social and Cultural Aspects of Language Learning in Study Abroad*, Philadelphia and Amsterdam: John Benjamins, pp. 3–16.

Kinginger, C., Wu, Q., Lee, S.-H., and Tan, D. (2016) 'The short-term homestay as a context for language learning', *Study Abroad Research in Second Language Acquisition and International Education*, 1 (1): 34–60.

Kolb, A. and Kolb, D. (2017) *The Experiential Educator: Principles and Practices of Experiential Learning*, Kaunakakai, Hawaii: Experience Based Learning Systems.

Lafford, B. (1995) 'Getting into, through, and out of a situation: A comparison of communicative strategies used by students studying Spanish abroad and "at home"', in B. Freed (ed.), *Second Language Acquisition in a Study Abroad Context*, Philadelphia and Amsterdam: John Benjamins, pp. 97–121.

Lantolf, J.P. and Thorne, S.L. (2006) *Sociocultural Theory and the Genesis of Second Language Development*, Oxford: Oxford University Press.

Lapkin, S., Hart, D., and Swain, M. (1995) 'A Canadian interprovincial exchange: Evaluating the linguistic impact of a three-month stay in Québec', in B. Freed (ed.), *Second Language Acquisition in a Study Abroad Context*, Amsterdam: John Benjamins, pp. 67–94.

Lee, L. (2018) 'Extending the intercultural learning after study abroad through a tele-collaborative exchange', in J. Jackson and S. Oguro (eds.), *Intercultural Interventions in Study Abroad*, London and New York: Routledge, pp. 137–154.

Mackey, A. and Gass, S. M. (2005) *Second Language Research: Methodology and Design*, New York: Routledge.

Magnan, S. S. and Back, M. (2007) 'Social interaction and linguistic gain during study abroad', *Foreign Language Annals*, 40: 43–61.

Messner, W. and Schäfer, N. (2012) *The ICCA Facilitator's Manual: Intercultural Communication and Collaboration Appraisal*. London: GloBus Research.

Mezirow, J. (2009) 'Transformative learning theory', in J. Mezirow and E. Taylor (eds), *Transformative Learning in Practice: Insights from Community, Workplace, and Higher Education*, San Francisco, CA: Jossey-Bass, pp. 18–30.

Mitchell, R., Tracy-Ventura, N., and McManus, K. (2017) *Anglophone Students Abroad: Identity, Social Relationships and Language Learning*, New York: Routledge.

Mora, J. (2008) 'Learning context effects on the acquisition of a second language phonology', in C. Pérez-Vidal, M. Juan-Garau, and A. Bel (eds.), *A Portrait of the Young in the New Multilingual Spain*, Bristol: Multilingual Matters, pp. 241–263.

Norton, B. (2000) *Identity and Language Learning: Gender, Ethnicity, and Educational Change*, Harlow, UK: Longman.

Paige, R. (2015) 'Interventionist models for study abroad', in J. Bennett (ed.), *The SAGE Encyclopedia of Intercultural Competence*, Los Angeles: Sage, pp. 563–568.

Passarelli, A. and Kolb, D. (2012) 'Using experiential learning theory to promote student learning and development in programs of education abroad', in M. Vande Berg, R. Paige, and K. Lou (eds.), *Student Learning Abroad: What our Students are Learning, what they're not, and what we can do about it*, Sterling, VA: Stylus, pp. 137–161.

Pérez-Vidal, C. and Juan-Garau, M. (2011) 'The effect of context and input conditions on oral and written development', *International Review of Applied Linguistics*, 49, 175–185.

Plews, J. and Misfeldt, K. (2018) *Second Language Study Abroad: Programming, Pedagogy, and Participant Engagement*, New York: Springer.

Rivers, W. (1998) 'Is being there enough? The effects of homestay placements on language gain during study abroad', *Foreign Language Annals*, 31 (4): 492–500.

Roberts, C., Byram, M., Barro, A., Jordan, S., and Street, B. (2001) *Language Learners as Ethnographers*, Clevedon, UK: Multilingual Matters.

Salaberry, R., White, K., and Rue Birch, A. (2019). 'Language learning and interactional experiences in a study abroad setting. An introduction to the special issue', *Study Abroad Research in Second Language Acquisition and International Education*, 4 (1): 1–18.

Sanz, C. and Morales-Front, A. (eds) (2018) *The Routledge Handbook of Study Abroad Research and Practice*, New York: Routledge.

Savicki, V. and Brewer, E. (eds) (2015) *Assessing Study Abroad: Theory, Tools, and Practice*, Sterling, VA: Stylus.

Schwieter, J. W. (2013) 'Immersion learning: Implications for non-native lexical development', in J. W. Schwieter (ed.), *Studies and Global Perspectives of Second Language Teaching and Learning*, Charlotte, NC: Information Age, pp. 165–185.

Schwieter, J. W. and Klassen, G. (2016) 'Linguistic advances and learning strategies in a short-term study abroad experience', *Study Abroad Research in Second Language Acquisition and International Education*, 1 (2): 217–247.

Segalowitz, N. and Freed, B. (2004) 'Context, contact, and cognition in oral fluency acquisition: Learning Spanish in at home and study abroad contexts', *Studies in Second Language Acquisition*, 26: 173–199.

Taguchi, N. (2015) *Developing Interactional Competence in a Japanese Study Abroad Context*, Bristol: Multilingual Matters.

Trentman, E. (2013) 'Imagined communities and language learning during study abroad: Arabic learners in Egypt', *Foreign Language Annals*, 46 (4): 545–564.

Trentman, E. (2017) 'Oral fluency, sociolinguistic competence, and language contact: Arabic learners studying abroad in Egypt', *System*, 69: 54–64.

Umino, T. and Benson, P. (2016) 'Communities of practice in study abroad: A four-year study of an Indonesian student's experience in Japan', *The Modern Language Journal*, 100 (4): 757–774.

Wilkinson, S. (1998) 'On the nature of immersion during study abroad: Some participant perspectives', *Frontiers: The Interdisciplinary Journal of Study Abroad*, 4 (2): 121–138.

# Chapter 7

# Student development

## Reflecting on sense of place and multi-locality in education abroad programmes

*Chris Glass and Mark Holton*

### Highlights:

- Student development theories are used critically to explore how education abroad programmes can develop students' understanding of the world and their sense of place within it.
- Research and practice are connected to outline how education abroad leaders might facilitate student development leading to a renewed sense of relationship to people and issues that cross local, national, and global boundaries.

Education abroad is often thought to expand a student's sense of the global. In this sense, 'being global' has strong associations with how education abroad crosses national borders and expands students' sense of being in the world (King & Ruiz-Gelices, 2003). This chapter posits that, by viewing the world from another geographic location, students develop social, cultural and emotional perspectives that would not be possible had they remained at home (Lewin, 2009). The focus of this chapter is therefore on the convergence of sociological, geographical, and psychological forces that comprise a student's *sense of place* – defined as the intimate and emotional connections with place developed through time and memory (Holloway & Hubbard, 2001) – as a way of extending traditional perspectives on student development. In doing so, this chapter emphasizes that incorporating sense of place into this way of thinking shifts notions of education abroad programmes beyond being about simply making students 'more global' citizens (Perez, Shim, King, & Baxter Magolda, 2017), to help them understand their deeper connection with the world.

To achieve this, this chapter describes how education abroad practitioners might design programmes that foster reflection on *multi-locality* – the social, cultural, political and economic relationships that result from a person's migration between countries (Thieme, 2008) – so that students might develop a more complex sense of place. Education abroad leaders play a significant role in helping students recognize that development of sense of place is shaped by experience – and crucially, that their experience is both local and multiple.

This chapter argues that drawing the complexities of sense of place into student development theory is vitally important in prompting education abroad participants (and practitioners) to question their sense of national, geographic-bound sense of belonging and to develop multiple national, regional, city, or university-based identities that shift and recombine as a result of short-term mobility. The stress that is associated with negotiation of a more complex sense of place produces a renewed sense of relationship to people and issues that cross local, national, and global boundaries. A critical approach to student development in this chapter is essential for education abroad leaders to consider as student mobilities are often structured along lines of social and economic class that encompass specific routes from school to university and into the workplace (Findlay, 2012; Salisbury et al. 2009). This approach follows broader shifts in contemporary student development theory that situates student development in webs of relationships and roles, and nested within broader social systems, including geopolitical contexts of power and privilege (Perez, 2019; Perez et al., 2017).

- To what extent does short-term mobility foster the development of students' sense of place?
- In what ways can education abroad programming be leveraged to foster the development student's sense of place?

This chapter begins with a review of traditional theories of student development. It then considers how education abroad programmes might foster student development with a focus on the development of a more critical consciousness of how students perceive their sense of place. The chapter concludes by outlining new and alternative directions for how programmes might be leveraged to propel student development based on emerging evidence.

### 3.1 Student development

Traditional theories of student development have been guided by three primary assumptions (Evans et al., 2009). First, that students operate as separate individuals, with unique and contrasting motivations, expectations, needs, and goals. Second, that learning does not just exist in the classroom but comprises all dimensions of a students' life (e.g. peer and familial influences) and the totality of a student's environment needs to be considered as educational. Third, that students must be considered active agents in their educational biographies. While this places responsibility upon students to 'get educated' it also means that educators must not treat students as passive learners. Indeed, many argue that engaging with these dimensions in a local setting are not enough, as alluded to in this quote by Braskamp et al., (2009): 'In a pluralistic world, students now need to develop a global perspective while enrolled in tertiary education. They need to think and act in terms of living in a world in which they meet, work, and live with others with very different cultural backgrounds, habits, perspectives, customs, religious beliefs, and aspirations' (p. 101).

Hence, providing students with the tools, knowledge and experiences associated with 'thinking globally' may prepare them to more confidently (and self-reflexively) advance into their post-student lives as graduates.

As a field of study, student development contains a broad array of theories that have been predominately developed in the US and thus reflect primarily Western understandings of the self (Evans et al., 2009). The fundamental thread that drives traditional theories is that students operate on an individualized pathway through various stages of development. Development includes multiple dimensions, such as the acquisition of basic and complex life skills, subject-specific knowledge, and broader life experience. Abraham Maslow's (1954) *Hierarchy of Needs*, for example, presents a framework for ordering the relative phases of development of an individual that consists of five categories: physiological; safety/security; love/belongingness; self-esteem; and self-actualization. The first three of these categories are considered essential for students in developing well-being and in understanding their 'fit' within the university structures and among their peer group, while the latter two relate to more self-directed approaches that require deeper engagement. This approach becomes problematic when relating it to education abroad, principally as the former needs may become destabilized if the environment that a student has travelled is unfamiliar to them. This is particularly related to notions of friendship, which links to Maslow's third dimension – love and belongingness.

Another traditional student development framework applied to education abroad programmes is Chickering's (1993) *Seven Vectors of Student Development* theory. Chickering proposes that students' identities undergo seven tasks based upon intellectual, technical (manual) and interpersonal competences – developing competency, managing emotions, moving through autonomy towards interdependence, developing mature interpersonal relationships, developing identity, developing purpose, and developing integrity (Chickering & Reisser, 1993). Like Maslow, Chickering's psychosocial approach to understanding student development is fundamentally individual and sequential, focusing upon issues that correspond to chronological age and that relate to the accomplishment of tasks at specific 'life stages' (Maekawa Kodama et al., 2002). Chickering's theory aligns closely with education abroad strategies, and Drexler and Campbell (2011) agree that education abroad programmes play a vital role in student development – specifically in relation to the cultivation of Chickering's competences and the deepening of interpersonal relationships – meaning students can become increasingly self-aware and self-reflexive. More specifically, Fine and McNamara (2011) focus on the 'autonomy towards interdependence' competency as a crucial dimension of the effects of education abroad upon student development. They argue that '[i]nterdependence is marked by a commitment to the welfare of the larger community, with the larger community now being a global and pluralistic one' (p. 260). This relates closely to the ways in which studying abroad involves effective interactions with diverse communities – specifically in understanding how and where students might envisage themselves in a globalized society (cf. Dolby, 2007; Teichler, 2004).

Finally, Mezirow's (1991) *Transformative Learning* theory begins to provide an alternative approach to understanding student development, focusing on three dimensions that encompass the psychological, convictional, and behavioural changes involved in education. Mezirow's constructive-developmental approach hinges on an appreciation of learning in more meaningful ways – specifically through an explicit kind of experiential learning (Kolb, Boyatzis, & Mainemelis, 2001) – while also recognizing the importance of self-reflection in operationalizing knowledge in practical ways. Perry et al. (2012) argue that this form of self-reflection, linked with the disorientation associated with being among the 'unfamiliar', provides students who have engaged with education abroad programmes a unique ability to consider their understanding of global issues, cultures, societies etc. in the context of their home environment. Yet, as Rowan-Kenyon and Niehaus (2011) argue, education abroad experiences are acutely temporal, and as such, for transformations to have lasting benefit they need to be repeated through subsequent trips. However, these opportunities may not be available to all students, highlighting the socioeconomic imbalances involved in access to education abroad programmes. Opportunities arise then to question then whether those participating on a programme are legitimately 'becoming' global citizens or if their experiences are merely symbolic (Leracitano, 2014).

Beyond these more theoretical permutations of student development, others have adapted these concepts for more practical gains. For example, in developing these ideas into a practical framework, Malmgren (2007) presents a useful set of categorizations that can support and signpost students outlining three sets of goals: *academic learning outcomes* (those that relate directly to the programme of study and develop subject-specific and methodological skills); *ability learning outcomes* (those skills related to critical thinking and flexibility); and *attitudes/awareness learning outcomes* (those more affective skills that promote self-reflexivity, worldliness, and self-awareness). A crucial benefit from adopting this type of approach is to critique the assumption that students (should) acquire all or any of these skills naturally through education abroad programmes. This type of approach is vital in problematizing the essentialized student identity (White, male, young, heterosexual and able-bodied) and instead acknowledging how education abroad might be witnessed differently by different groups (Shin, 2014). For example, Willis (2015) argues that the levels of oppression experienced by Black women on home campuses are reflected in education abroad programmes, ranging from (un)intentional isolation and discrimination to sexual harassment or assault.

### 3.2 Sense of place and multi-locality in education abroad programmes

This next section considers how education abroad programmes might foster student development. Beyond the attributes drawn from being mobile learners, little is understood about how students' experiences of education abroad programmes might relate to their sense of place in and around the confines of their home or host university. This chapter approaches understanding sense of place using the constructive-developmental theories of human development, pioneered by Jean Piaget (Wadsworth, 1996), that also serve as the underpinning of transformative learning theory (Mezirow, 1991). Constructive developmentalism is the underpinning of popular assessment instruments of education abroad programmes, such as the Global Perspective Inventory (GPI), which assesses the cognitive, intrapersonal, and interpersonal dimensions of student development (Braskamp, 2009; Merrill, Braskamp, & Braskamp, 2012). Constructive developmentalists posit that students actively make constructions of the world and those constructions become more complex and multifaceted through experience (Barber, King, & Baxter Magolda, 2013). Constructive-developmental theory is therefore *constructive* in that it explores the way students make meaning from everyday experience. It is *developmental* in that it focuses on experiences that prompt qualitative shifts in making meaning so that humans develop a multi-layered view of the world characterized by nuance and complexity. This nuance and complexity is extremely important when considering the intersectionalities of race, gender, ethnicity, sexuality, age, and disability that comprise many students' relational identities and how, at a period of most students' lives where identities are forming, reforming, and being challenged, education abroad programmes can at best nurture, or at worst undermine these intersectional identities.

That said, constructive developmentalists are less concerned with the content and geographic location of the student on an education abroad programme and more concerned with the *features* of the experience that prompt shifts in perspective-taking. This subtle, but important, difference in emphasis suggests that education abroad programmes might add greater complexity to a person's sense of place, rather than simply expanding it (Perez, Shim, King, & Baxter Magolda, 2017). This thinking therefore challenges the notion that education abroad is necessarily about expanding one's perspective from a localized view of the world to a more globalized one. Rather, it suggests that education abroad involves moving from uncritical locality to multi-locality as students develop a critical consciousness of the ways they perceive their social surroundings and their sense of place within it. Rather than ask, 'Where are you from?' A multi-local perspective encourages educators to ask, 'Where are you local?' (Selasi, 2014).

A focus on multi-locality therefore permits a more complex image of student development to emerge for education abroad practitioners (Glass, 2018). This perspective allows for a multiplicity of trajectories of development, as we are all multi-local in different ways, as opposed to the standard linear progression of moving from a 'local' to a 'global' perspective, which implies a more universal trajectory of development. Multi-locality encourages education abroad practitioners to consider how the multi-layered and intersectional aspects of each student's identity and life history shapes their sense of place. Moreover, this focus on multi-locality recognizes that crossing cultural boundaries does not always entail crossing national borders. While this is often referred to as developing a global perspective that generates a greater capacity to move back and forth between culturally distinct places with greater ease, such nuanced thinking may inspire students to understand their place in the world more critically in relation to others. Finally, with the rise of globalization, interconnectivity makes global cities separated by great distance more culturally similar than adjacent urban and rural regions located nearby one other. A temporary migrant's country of origin is important to their sense of place, but so is their identity, their sense of locality, and the multiple locations where they feel like members of the local community.

According to Baxter Magolda et al. (2010), the majority of students enter tertiary education with a *socialized* form of mind. They make meaning of the world through other perspectives that they have acquired through socialization, whether it be from their family of original, political, and social affiliations, or social and intersectional identities and community organizations. They have internalized these expectations and social norms as a way of experiencing the world. Cognitively, socialized individuals take on the beliefs of the social network in which they are embedded. Intrapersonally, their sense of identity is shaped both by the expectations of other people and their own self-reflexive positionalities. Interpersonally, the socialized mind includes expectations of how they may be treated abroad and the way they position themselves with those they expect to interact with on their international sojourn. The socialized mind reflects an uncritical locality. Uncritical locality is a sense of place that sees the local world, whether it be their hometown or a city they visit during education abroad, through a lens of the social norms and expectations of others without a consciousness of the lens through which they interpret these unfamiliar experiences. This can be witnessed through discourses of othering that comprise what Nairn (2005, p. 295) defines as a 'politics of position'. Here, challenging students' viewpoints from 'how are others different to me?' to 'how am I different to others?' provides an important lesson in self-reflexivity, specifically in situations where unfamiliar places may be juxtaposed with the familiar and normal where students experience a sense of comfort and a sense of home (cf. Holton, 2015 for a UK perspective).

As students' understanding becomes more complex, they develop a *self-authored* mind (Baxter Magolda et al., 2010). Self-authored persons are capable of developing an internalized set of principles that are consciously chosen. Cognitively, they recognize that their social group has a preferred way of knowing and it is important to critically assemble new knowledge. Intrapersonally, they recognize their identity as complex and evolving and negotiate multiple identities in different settings and contexts. Interpersonally, they relate their own positionality to develop a natural desire and curiosity to form relationships with those who have different social, political, or cultural perspectives than their own. The self-authored mind reflects a critical locality. Critical locality involves a sense of place that recognizes exploring multiple, local worlds develops a more critical and complex sense of place. The experience of new cultures, political structures, and social customs allows students to critically examine their own culture, political structure, and social customs. This critical sense of place allows students to pick up the pen and understand their subjectivity, question their socialization, and make conscious decisions designed to shape their own development.

In advanced stages of development, humans develop *self-transforming* minds, often in the post-university middle stages of life, where they are capable of recognizing that no single system or perspective, even when it is a perspective they have developed and believe, is sufficient to understand the complexity and diversity they experience in the world (Baxter Magolda et al., 2010). While this may appear to deviate from student development, it is mentioned here because the outcomes of education abroad too often focus on how education abroad prepares university graduates for engaged citizenship and meaningful careers, but rarely on the lifelong – and often ineffable – impacts of the experience throughout the course of students' post-university lives (cf. Rowan-Kenyon and Niehaus, 2011). Self-transforming individuals continue to take intellectual risks and seek-out experiences that challenge their self-authored perspective. They recognize that multiple systems of meaning are required to understand the vast diversity of people and social groups they encounter. They identify their responsibility to explore systems that are unfamiliar and continuously adapt their understanding of the world. The self-transforming mind reflects a complex sense of multi-locality. Multi-locality acknowledges that experience is both multiple and local; it recognizes that humans live simultaneous existences that transcend time and space. Students who develop this sense of multi-locality over a time therefore embrace a multiplicity of identities and ways of knowing and feel at home in multiple locations with different local cultures, social structures, and customs.

As stated at the beginning of this chapter, research and practice are bridged by describing how education abroad practitioners might create programmes that foster students' reflection on multi-locality so that students might develop a more complex picture of their lives (Selasi, 2014). Educational abroad leaders will, of course, recognize that no two programmes are alike, e.g. some programmes are short-term, others are long-term; some involve first-year students who recently graduated from secondary school, others involve adults attending graduate school; some comprise travel to destinations with culture quite different from the student's home country, others involve countries with a similar heritage etc. With all of these forms of difference, it is important to strive for what might be universal about human experience and view student development as a long-term endeavour, where the education abroad experience is not separate from the longer-term trajectory of a person's development. This section outlines some practical ideas for the pre-departure and on-site stages of education abroad programme design.

### 4.1 Pre-departure programme design

Pre-departure orientations often focus on the culture of the country students will travel to, which positions the participants as visitors who see themselves as 'from' one country on a sojourn to another. Education abroad leaders may foster student development by challenging this nation-based way of seeing the world by inviting students to discuss 'where they are from', not in terms of citizenship or country of origin, but by responding to the more probing question, 'Where are you local?' A focus on students' locality pre-departure invites a shift in perspective so they might move beyond a single response of a nation or city, i.e. 'I'm from the United States' or 'I'm from Cleveland', to a multitude of responses comprising the many places and people to which they are connected simultaneously. This focus allows students to recognize the people they will encounter while abroad may reside in the host country, but they too are local in the same sense.

To probe multi-locality more deeply pre-departure, education abroad leaders might invite students to discuss the three aspects of locality as recommended by Selasi (2014): the rituals, relationships, and restrictions that shape their daily lives. For rituals leaders might ask: What does a typical day look like from when it begins to when you come home at night? What do meals look like and who are they shared with? What holidays, festivals, and traditions mark importance milestones over a year? For relationships, leader might ask: To whom do you speak on a regular basis whether it be in-person or online? Who do you miss and look forward to seeing? For restrictions, leaders might ask: What places do you feel like an unwelcomed guest? Are there places where you are unable to travel – or it is unsafe to travel – even if you wished? Are communities that you hope to belong to but are unable to fully participate? After exploring students' sense of locality, leaders might invite students to share about the people they expect to encounter abroad whose daily lives are, too, shaped by such rituals, relationships, and restrictions. This focus on localities, and not nations and cities, prompts a richer set of pre-departure discussions marked by contrasts and commonalities that unearths a richer set of experiences students might explore during their time abroad.

This review of student development theory highlights how transitions from simple to more complex ways of making meaning are often marked by struggle, loss, uncertainty, and confusion. The human mind and body have been hardwired over millions of years to prefer simple, local ideas and perspectives to more complex, global ones. Education abroad leaders can also prepare students' pre-departure by encouraging them to discuss how the experience of the unfamiliar feels in their bodies. Bodies naturally tense up when they experience the unfamiliar and people experience stress when they feel uncertainty. Greater awareness of the bodily sensations that arise when students experience the unfamiliar pre-departure allows them to be more mindful, rather than reactionary, when they no longer feel local as they encounter the unfamiliar during their on-site programme. They learn to notice how uncertainty feels, and it empowers them to use that awareness and respond to the unfamiliar in more open-minded ways and, perhaps, begin to develop a more complex sense of their sense of place.

## 4.2 On-site programme design

Education abroad leaders can design courses to foster the development of a sense of multi-locality. Student development theory emphases learning that stimulates a shift in mind, not just the content of knowledge itself, educational interventions that are the most powerful are those that prompt reflect on how one thinks, not just knowledge and information. There are well-established approaches to high-quality education abroad programme design that align with this chapter's focus on the features of experience that prompt such shifts in perspective-taking. For example, interacting with individuals from the host country outside the classroom and speaking the host country's language fosters an understanding of the relationships that shape those individual's lives. Exploring new habits and behaviours while studying abroad and immersing oneself in the culture of the host country fosters an exploration of the rituals of the local communities that students encounter. Interacting with students from other racial or ethnic communities may raise awareness of the restrictions different groups encounter.

Education abroad leaders can include assignments that require students to gather information from their surrounding community while abroad to counter the 'Google-it' approach to learning about culture that has become the default of professors and students alike. Travel creates space for relaxed conversations that lead in unexpected directions. To learn about culture in a more premodern, conversational way requires asking questions to locals with patience and lack of hurry, as well as an attitude of respect and learning. It necessitates a sense of genuine curiosity in the other person and humility that allow them to be the first to speak. Purposeful engagement provides a dynamic, multi-layered, and personal understanding of the 'nearby' history in contrast to the one-dimensional 'Google-it' approach.

To engage with their communities successfully, students learn to appreciate nearby history. Rather than identify this past as 'local' or 'community' history as some have done and limit it to a concept of place, or call it 'family history' and restrict it to a concept of relationship, or talk about material culture and confine the discussion to objects, the term 'nearby history' is chosen here to include the entire range of possibilities in a person's immediate environment (Doberneck, 2007, p. 68).

By definition, students who travel abroad do not face restrictions on their mobility to the host country, but the inverse may not be the same. The people they encounter may not experience such freedom of movement to travel to another country or even within their own communities. Education abroad leaders can incorporate reflections on four types of restrictions students experience through journaling or group discussion: First, students put restrictions on themselves due to discomfort or fear. Second, students may have experience due to their race, gender, or other salient identity that is more or less salient in a new cultural and geographic context. Third, students may observe restrictions experienced by others in their group or in the host community. Finally, students may experience discomfort from the lack of restrictions they experience, as compared with others in the group or host community, due to economic and social privilege inherent in their gender, ethnicity, citizenship, or socioeconomic status. Not all people are equally free to move as they please or experience such ease in movement from place to place. As students develop a sense of multi-locality, they recognize the restrictions that shape their existence and the existence of others. They may be free to move about a rural community in Europe, but face restrictions in urban cities in North America; they may enjoy the daily rituals of everyday life in an African city, while feeling unwelcomed or overlooked when they travel abroad to Asia.

Learning to see the world from multiple perspectives is one of the most powerful tools in developing more complex forms of making meaning of the world. Education abroad leaders can also encourage students to see local rituals and traditions from an insider's point of view, not from the perspective of itinerant traveller. To counteract the tendency of students to see themselves as educational tourists, leaders can encourage students to capture photographs from different vantage points, then reflect on how those photographs exemplify different perspectives towards the local community. Leaders can help students develop multi-layered understandings by asking them to view a situation through multiple perspectives, or "gazes", each constructed through 'non-tourist forms of social experience' (Urry, 2002, p. 1). Reflections can include, but are not limited to, five potential ways of seeing a situation: the tourist gaze – how 'we' see 'them'; the local gaze – how 'they' see the 'nearby'; the mutual gaze – how 'they' see 'us'; the global gaze – how 'I' see 'the global'; and the positional gaze – how 'I' see 'myself'. Leaders can encourage students to reflect on the specific conditions or economic, political, and social forces that have shaped the subjects or situations captured in the photos (Perez, 2019), as well as the student's own intercultural development, including the ways in which power and privilege affect their interactions with others (McCabe, 2005; Perez et al., 2017). These five ways of positioning themselves in a local community helps students become more self-aware of the hierarchical power relations that exist for them and then explore ways their actions may challenge or perpetuate these relations (Urry, 2002). The next chapter in this volume explores identity and intercultural competence in greater detail.

This chapter has advanced an understanding of student development in education abroad by exploring the influence of multi-localities – the iterative movements between home, university, and an international placement – upon which mobile students' experiences of place and identity intersect. It positions this focus on multi-locality as a crucial future agenda for education abroad research and practice to develop a more complex sense of place in the world – one that recognizes that experience is local and multiple (Gargano, 2009). The chapter argues that this emphasis prompts students to question their sense of national, geographic-bound sense of belonging and develop multiple national, regional, city, or university-based identities that continue to shift and recombine as a result of short-term mobility. The stress associated with this negotiation process produces a renewed sense of relationship to people and issues that cross local, national, and global boundaries. Moreover, this negotiation of multi-locality is a necessary and important aspect of the exploration, expansion, and integration of a more complex, global identity and sense of inhabiting the world. While linkages between multi-locality and sense of place add weight to student development through education abroad, it is also important to recognize that more needs to be achieved here – particularly in relation to empirical studies. Notwithstanding this, the perspectives shared in this chapter illustrate how forms of movement affect students' identities and senses of belonging, and in doing so, critique to what extent education abroad contexts might foster development and change, and if so, whether there is parity in how this is achieved. Future research must consider how the geopolitics of short-term mobility is linked to student development and how short-term mobility has become a crucial and highly politicized driver for student development.

## Further reading

Evans, N. J., Forney, D. S., Guido, F. M., Patton, L. D., & Renn, K. A. (2009). *Student development in college: Theory, research, and practice*. Hoboken, NJ: John Wiley & Sons.

Perry, L., Stoner, L., & Tarrant, M. (2012). More than a vacation: Short-term study abroad as a critically reflective, transformative learning experience. *Creative Education*, 3 (5), 679–683.

Rowan-Kenyon, H. T., & Niehaus, E. K. (2011). One year later: The influence of short-term study abroad experiences on students. *Journal of Student Affairs Research and Practice*, 48(2), 213–228.

## References

Barber, J. P., King, P. M., & Baxter Magolda, M. B. (2013). Long strides on the journey toward self-authorship: Substantial developmental shifts in college students' meaning making. *The Journal of Higher Education*, 84(6), 866–896.

Baxter Magolda, M. B., Creamer, E. G., & Meszaros, P. S. (2010). *Development and assessment of self-authorship: Exploring the concept across cultures*. Sterling, VA: Stylus Publishing.

Braskamp, L. A., Braskamp, D. C., & Merrill, K. (2009). Assessing progress in global learning and development of students with education abroad experiences. *Frontiers: The Interdisciplinary Journal of Study Abroad*, 18, 101–118.

Campbell, K. (2016). Short-term study abroad programmes: Objectives and accomplishments. *Journal of international Mobility*, 1, 189–204.

Chickering, A. W., & Reisser, L. (1993). *Education and identity* (2nd ed.). San Francisco: Jossey-Bass.

Doberneck, D. M. (2007). Community engagement in rural Ireland: A lecturer's perspective, in L. McIlrath, A. Farrell, J. Hughes, S. Lillis & A. Lyons (Eds.), *Mapping civic engagement within higher education in Ireland*. Dublin: AISHE and Campus Engage.

Dolby, N. (2007). Reflections on nation: American undergraduates and education abroad. *Journal of Studies in International Education*, 11(2), 141–156.

Drexler, D. S., & Campbell, D. F. (2011). Student development among community college participants in study abroad programs. *Community College Journal of Research and Practice*, 35(8), 608–619.

Evans, N. J., Forney, D. S., Guido, F. M., Patton, L. D., & Renn, K. A. (2009). *Student development in college: Theory, research, and practice.* Hoboken, NJ: John Wiley & Sons.

Findlay, A. M., King, R., Smith, F. M., Geddes, A., & Skeldon, R. (2012). World class? An investigation of globalisation, difference and international student mobility. *Transactions of the Institute of British Geographers*, 37(1), 118–131.

Fine, J. B., & McNamara, K. W. (2011). Community redefined: School leaders moving from autonomy to global interdependence through short-term study abroad. *Frontiers: The Interdisciplinary Journal of Study Abroad*, 21, 254–274.

Gargano, T. (2009). (Re) conceptualizing international student mobility: The potential of transnational social fields. *Journal of Studies in International Education*, 13(3), 331–346.

Glass, C. R. (2018). International students' sense of belonging: Locality, relationships, and power. *Peer Review*, 20(1), 27–30.

Grabowski, S., Wearing, S., Lyons, K., Tarrant, M., & Landon, A. (2017). A rite of passage? Exploring youth transformation and global citizenry in the study abroad experience. *Tourism Recreation Research*, 42(2), 139–149.

Green, W., Gannaway, D., Sheppard, K., & Jamarani, M. (2015). What's in their baggage? The cultural and social capital of Australian students preparing to study abroad. *Higher Education Research & Development*, 34(3), 513–526.

Holloway, L., & Hubbard, P. (2001). *People and place: The extraordinary geographies of everyday life.* Harlow: Pearson.

Holton, M. (2015). Learning the rules of the 'student game': Transforming the 'student habitus' through immobility. *Environment and Planning*, 47(11), 2373–2388.

Ieracitano, F. (2014). New European citizens? The Erasmus generation between awareness and scepticism. *European Journal of Research on Social Studies*, 1(1), 16–21.

King, P. M., & Baxter Magolda, M. B. (2005). A developmental model of intercultural maturity. *Journal of College Student Development*, 46(6), 571–592.

King, R., & Raghuram, P. (2013). International student migration: Mapping the field and new research agendas. *Population, Space and Place*, 19(2), 127–137.

King, R., & Ruiz-Gelices, E. (2003). International student migration and the European 'year abroad': Effects on European identity and subsequent migration behaviour. *International Journal of Population Geography*, 9(3), 229–252.

Kolb, D. A., Boyatzis, R. E., & Mainemelis, C. (2001). Experiential learning theory: Previous research and new directions. *Perspectives on Thinking, Learning, and Cognitive Styles*, 1(8), 227–247.

Leracitano, F. (2014). New European citizens? The Erasmus generation between awareness and scepticism. *European Journal of Research on Social Studies*, 2(1), 16–21.

Lewin, R. (2009). *The handbook of practice and research in study abroad: Higher education and the quest for global citizenship.* New York: Routledge.

Lörz, M., Netz, N., & Quast, H. (2016). Why do students from underprivileged families less often intend to study abroad? *Higher Education*, 72(2), 153–174.

McCabe, S. (2005). 'Who is a tourist?': A critical review. *Tourist Studies*, 5(1), 85–106.

Maekawa Kodama, C., McEwen, M. K., Liang, C. T., & Lee, S. (2002). An Asian American perspective on psychosocial student development theory. *New Directions for Student Services*, 2002(97), 45–60.

Malmgren, J. (2007, December). Goal-setting for study abroad learning outcomes. *Academic Advising Today*, 30(4). Retrieved from www.nacada.ksu.edu/Resources/Academic-Advising-Today/View-Articles/Goal-Setting-for-Study-Abroad-Learning-Outcomes.aspx

McKeown, J. S. (2009). *The first-time effect: The impact of study abroad on college student intellectual development.* New York: SUNY Press.

Maslow, A. H. (1954). *Motivation and personality.* New York: Harper & Row.

Merrill, K. C., Braskamp, D. C., & Braskamp, L. A. (2012). Assessing individuals' global perspective. *Journal of College Student Development,* 53(2), 356–360.

Mezirow, J. (1991). *Transformative dimensions of adult learning.* San Francisco: Jossey-Bass.

Nairn, K. (2005). The problems of utilizing 'direct experience' in geography education. *Journal of Geography in Higher Education,* 29(2), 293–309.

Perez, R. (2019). Paradigmatic perspectives and self-authorship: Implications for theory, research, and praxis. *Journal of College Student Development,* 60(1), 70–84.

Perez, R. J., Shim, W., King, P. M., & Baxter-Magolda, M. (2017). Refining King and Baxter-Magolda's model of intercultural maturity. *Journal of College Student Development,* 56(8), 759–776.

Perry, L., Stoner, L., & Tarrant, M. (2012). More than a vacation: Short-term study abroad as a critically reflective, transformative learning experience. *Creative Education,* 3 (5), 679–683.

Potts, D. (2015). Understanding the early career benefits of learning abroad programs. *Journal of Studies in International Education,* 19(5), 441–459.

Rowan-Kenyon, H. T., & Niehaus, E. K. (2011). One year later: The influence of short-term study abroad experiences on students. *Journal of Student Affairs Research and Practice,* 48(2), 213–228.

Salisbury, M. H., Umbach, P. D., Paulsen, M. B., & Pascarella, E. T. (2009). Going global: Understanding the choice process of the intent to study abroad. *Research in Higher Education,* 50(2), 119–143.

Salisbury, M. H., An, B. P., & Pascarella, E. T. (2013). The effect of study abroad on intercultural competence among undergraduate college students. *Journal of Student Affairs Research and Practice,* 50(1), 1–20.

Selasi, T. (2014). Taiye Selasi: Don't ask where I'm from, ask where I'm a local. TED video. www.ted.com/talks/taiye_selasi_don_t_ask_where_i_m_from_ask_where _i_m_a_local

Shin, H. (2014). Social class, habitus, and language learning: The case of Korean early study-abroad students. *Journal of Language, Identity & Education,* 13(2), 99–103.

Teichler, U. (2004). Temporary study abroad: the life of ERASMUS students. *European Journal of Education,* 39(4), 395–408.

Thieme, S. (2008). Sustaining livelihoods in multi-local settings: Possible theoretical linkages between transnational migration and livelihood studies. *Mobilities,* 3(1), 51–71.

Urry, J. J. (1990/2002). *The tourist gaze.* London: Sage.

Wadsworth, B. J. (1996). *Piaget's theory of cognitive and affective development: Foundations of constructivism.* London: Longman Publishing.

Willis, T. Y. (2015). 'And still we rise …': Microaggressions and intersectionality in the study abroad experiences of Black women. *Frontiers: The Interdisciplinary Journal of Study Abroad,* 26, 209–230.

Chapter 8

# Global citizenship, identity and intercultural competence

## Student identities in education abroad

*Neriko Musha Doerr, David Puente and Uichi Kamiyoshi*

### Highlights

- This chapter reviews and critically examines notions of global citizenship, intercultural competence, and student identities.
- The chapter also suggests new perspectives in these areas—meta-level analyses of these concepts and incorporation of insights from immigrant studies—and shows how these perspectives can be applied in education abroad practices.

### 1. Introduction and chapter overview

This chapter introduces existing literature on global citizenship, intercultural competence, and the identities of education abroad students and suggests expanding the discussion through meta-level analyses and incorporating insights from immigrant studies, whose benefit will be illustrated with a case study from Japan. This broadened conception of the field creates opportunities for wider collaboration, for instance, with equity and diversity offices.

### 2. Key questions to be addressed

There are four key questions in this chapter:

1 How is global citizenship currently approached and measured and how can it be improved?
2 How is intercultural competence currently approached and measured and how can it be improved?
3 How does the notion of student identity function within the education abroad literature?
4 How can the scope of existing literature on these concepts be expanded by including insights from immigrant studies?

## 3. Review of the literature

### 3.1 Global citizenship

Global citizenship is increasingly at the center of educational policy discussions, driving curriculum policy and informing learning outcomes at the national (American Association of Colleges and Universities, American Council on Education) and international (OECD, UNESCO, Young & Commins, 2002) levels. Though it remains a "highly contested topic" (Ogden, 2015, p. 34) with contextual variations—developing countries (Jooste & Heleta, 2017) or Europe or Australia (Beelen & Jones, 2015; Lilley et al., 2017)—there are some underlying common threads that most experts accept. This section introduces four such threads identified by Darla Deardorff (2009, 348), critically examining each of them.

The first is "global knowledge," which can encompass foreign language, facts about foreign countries, cultures and contexts (Lambert, 1994) and various forms of self-knowledge (Lewin & Van Kirk, 2009). Here, what is important is asking fundamental yet rarely asked questions: which "knowledge" is considered important, hence to be taught, and who gets to decide (Bourdieu & Passeron, 1977)? Some possible answers will be discussed later in this chapter.

The second common thread is, "understanding the interconnectedness of the world" (Deardorff, 2009, p. 348). Some researchers theorized "global connectivity"—how individuals come to feel distant places are routinely accessible (Tomlinson, 1999)—and "global assemblage," where events are shaped by the global distribution of capital and technological expertise, though regulated by national institutions (Collier & Ong, 2005). Global citizenship involves awareness of how such interconnectedness shapes our daily lives. The power relations, hierarchies, and asymmetries involved in such interconnections are rarely discussed in education abroad.

The third common thread is "engagement on the local and global level around issues that impact humanity" (Deardorff, 2009, p. 348), moving beyond knowledge, attitudes, and awareness toward the ability to behave across cultural differences (Deardorff, 2011; Harvey, 2018a; Skelly, 2009). The focus here is on bringing about positive outcomes—what Ogden (2015, p. 1) has called "operationalizing" global citizenship—cast as an urgent call to action, involving political commitments to "social justice" (Womack-Wynne, 2017, p. 22), or "civic responsibility" (Ogden 2015, p. 1). Students become "proactive contributors" of change (UNESCO, 2014, p. 15) or action-oriented "global stewards" (Womack-Wynne, 2017, p. 22), with teaching as a "moral practice" (Lilley, 2014, p. 15). This action can include both voting as citizens who enact political power to endorse or offset effects of regulations and trade agreements, and behaving as ethical consumers who "vote with their money."

Insights about actual citizenship, for instance from Critical Citizenship Studies, need to be included here. Rygiel defines citizenship as "a social process through which individuals and social groups engage in claiming, expanding and losing rights" (2010, p. 21). Stateless or border populations experience citizenship as a dystopian "regime of control" (2010, p. 22), a "biopolitical" tool used to manage their identities (2010, p. 106). Various dispossessed and stateless populations (at least 3.9 million in 2018 per the United Nations) interrupt facile developmental narratives of citizenship. For example, Abrahamian (2015) contrasts ultra-wealthy tax evaders who buy citizenships of convenience at Swiss auctions with the bureaucratic plight of Kuwait's Bidoons (literally the *withouts*, in Arabic) who, as stateless people, find themselves *in*, but not *of*, Kuwait, obtaining identity papers only through recourse to a cash-strapped foreign third party that sells them passports. Such examples raise questions about the arbitrariness not just of rights, but of national identity.

Global citizenship, as a call to push individuals to manage their own emotions and sensibilities, can be a form of neoliberal project. Neoliberalist regimes do not explicitly oppress individuals but make "free" individuals targets of influence. Such regimes produce individuals as independent, enterprising, self-interested, and "free" consumers who invest in themselves as a project, such as through one's own affect management in pursuit of "happiness." As such, global citizenship can, ironically, end up endorsing a shift from collectivist, social values toward the more individualistic pursuit (Sugarman, 2015) of professional skills and prosperity (Lilley et al., 2017).

The fourth common thread is "intercultural competence," discussed separately below as the fourth common thread of global citizenship and our second key question of the chapter.

### 3.2 Intercultural competence

Intercultural competence can be defined, though there is no clear consensus, as the capacity for "effective and appropriate behavior and communication in intercultural situations" (Deardorff, 2017, p. 66) or "the ability to communicate and act appropriately and effectively across cultural differences" (Harvey, 2018a, p. 4). Traits commonly seen as correlating with intercultural competence include empathy, adaptability, and propensity for perspective-taking/frame-shifting.

In practice, this understanding of intercultural competence involves deep self-analysis of our own behavior, best facilitated by guided interventions. For example, Vande Berg et al. (2012) designed (co-)curricula to develop four "core intercultural competences": awareness of our own meaning-making and behavior; awareness of others' meaning-making and behavior; management of our emotions in the face of ambiguity, change, and challenge; and bridging of cultural gaps by shifting perspective and adapting behavior.

Increasingly, intercultural competence is also more broadly defined as interactions occurring across differences of personal and group identity (gender, generational, socio-economic, etc.) (Deardorff, 2017; OECD, 2017). As such, intercultural learning can be built upon what students have already experienced (Doerr, 2018b). Not only can this help reduce the anxiety of those who may be intimidated by new overseas environments, giving them confidence in their own ability to leverage their subject positions; it might also broaden the pedagogical scope, making the home campus community part of a learning zone for pre- and post-program education abroad participants as well as non-participants with diverse backgrounds to interact with, and potentially learn from, each other (Bathurst & La Brack, 2012). It is important to expand the notion of intercultural competence not only to learn from insights in research about skills students may develop outside formal education settings, as is recognized in the literature on internationalization at home (for example see Beelen & Jones, 2015) but also to better account for the intercultural competence of immigrant and other trans-border students and to learn from insights suggested in immigrant studies about these populations' cross-border experiences.

### 3.3 Measuring global citizenship and intercultural competence

Many methods exist for measuring global citizenship and intercultural competence, which are often overlapping and intertwined depending on how they are defined. Among those focused more on global citizenship, some measure a "global" dimension of the subject's attitudes but not behavior. One commonly used instrument, the Global-Mindedness Scale (GMS; Hett, 1993), is a Likert-style response to thirty statements about global-mindedness. Some, such as the Global Awareness Profile (GAP; Corbitt, 1998), leave aside attitudes and focus on positive "global" knowledge, assessing the subject's worldview according to size, complexity, and diversity of intercultural experiences. Others emphasize a behavioral aspect: the OECD Program for International Student Assessment refers to conflict resolution as a competency, and references "actions" and "behavior" as learning objectives. Similarly, the Global Citizenship Scale (Morais & Ogden 2011) focuses on three subdimensions—social responsibility, global competence, and civic engagement—that also include behavioral aspects.

Instruments that foreground "global" skills may helpfully connect strategic initiatives around global citizenship *qua* competencies with the more extensive literature around intercultural competence assessment. The Global Perspectives Inventory (GPI; Braskamp & Braskamp, 2018) measures student viewpoint and attitude with questions grouped as cognitive, intrapersonal, and interpersonal. The Global Competence Inventory (GCI) assesses seventeen competencies—with subdimensions of perception management, relationship management, and self-management, which are related to working effectively across cultural differences.

There are now over 140 self-report instruments for assessing intercultural competence (Ogden, 2015, p. 16) in the US context which this chapter mainly focuses on.[1] Some measure external outcomes, emphasizing social agency. Others prioritize internal or attitudinal traits such as openness, empathy and ethno-relativistic worldview. There are also indirect assessment tools such as surveys, interviews, e-portfolios, and direct assessment such as observation by faculty, host families, supervisors (Deardorff, 2015; Harvey, 2018b) and measured through rubrics. The focus here is on the former, which predominate in professional assessment while representing an area of overlap with global citizenship. Given the complexities involved in defining intercultural competence, researchers suggest a multi-measure, multi-perspective assessment approach, often aligning multiple methods with programmatic goals (Deardorff, 2015). Many, such as those listed below, have theoretical underpinnings in educational or psychological theories of personal development or self-authorship that conceive of learning as a process (Deardorff, 2011), hence the tendency for pre- and post-program testing that casts gains in competence as "growth" (or "regression") along a defined spectrum.

An example of a pre- and post-education abroad instrument used in more than thirty countries is the Intercultural Development Inventory (IDI), a 50-item instrument based on the Developmental Model of Intercultural Sensitivity (DMIS). It identifies "intercultural sensitivity" by locating individuals on a continuum from highly ethnocentric to highly ethnorelative (Vande Berg et al., 2009), assessing the traits of openness, tendency to stereotype and receptivity to otherness based on level of agreement with numerous belief-value statements (Anderson et al., 2008).

Other tools measuring subjects' attitude include the Cross-Cultural Adaptability Inventory (CCAI), assessing emotional resilience, flexibility and openness, perceptual acuity, and personal autonomy; and the Intercultural Effectiveness Scale (IES), assessing hardiness, continuous learning, and interpersonal engagement. These tools can be used to predict overall success in college or in job placements abroad and enjoy wider popularity outside education abroad.

The tools above, when used with a multiple measure assessment approach, may provide a more holistic picture of student development in education abroad. However, practitioners do well to subject positivistic ideals of these measurement to critical scrutiny. Do attitudes lead necessarily to correspondingly appropriate behaviors? Some interculturalists (Bennett, 2014; Molinsky, 2013) have discussed the paradox of subject behaviors that, outwardly, could be construed as effective and appropriate, yet might not feel "authentic." Similarly, a subject pursuing a desirable social cause and effecting societal change can be doing so as an automatic response to social pressures. Also, there is a danger that some measurement approaches may in unwelcome ways impose Western, or indeed American, values and beliefs even where claiming to measure others' values and beliefs.

Such methodological impasses are in fact a common obstacle to assessment practices that rely on subject self-reporting. Ken Plummer (1995) argues that our self-description is shaped by "coaxers" who ask particular types of questions (e.g., assessment instruments for intercultural competence), audiences for whom we dialogically describe ourselves (e.g., educators), and available vocabularies and narratives (e.g., response choices in the assessment instruments). Therefore, results of such measurement often reflect culturally arbitrary (Bourdieu & Passeron, 1977) assumptions and even orthodoxies about what students feel they should have learned (Doerr, 2018b). Many instruments reflect what assessors view as important and hence desire to impart, thus shaping the students' responses via a self-fulfilling structural imperative about what the ideal competent actor is presumed to know. Things learned that are outside of educators' purview—e.g., becoming proficient at Instagram storytelling—may often go unacknowledged or be dismissed as detrimental.

This issue, fundamental to any educational project, may be described, following Bourdieu and Passeron (1977), as "symbolic violence": imposing the educator's view of what is worth knowing. In the education abroad context, for example, Trentman and Diao (2017) argue that some of the goals implicit in nurturing global citizenship and intercultural competence, such as aspiring to succeed in the global marketplace and/or wanting to be an ambassador for world peace, are compatible with a status quo of US hegemony in the world.

Letting students set and take ownership of overseas learning goals is one way to mitigate symbolic violence (Deardorff, 2015; Doerr, 2018b). Guided intervention along the lines of S-M-A-R-T (Specific, Measurable, Action-oriented, Relevant, Timely) goals setting (Deardorrf & Arasaratnam-Smith 2017, p. 123) represents a promising trend, as long as care is taken to foster intrinsic motivation rather than mere compliance (Morisano et al., 2010; Reeve, 2014). Also, the process of self-narrative described above (Plummer, 1995) can still prevail in such practices, making even well-intentioned efforts to produce global citizens become an imposition of a certain worldview upon students.

One way to avoid this process is to reframe the act of measuring: instead of seeing the measured results prima facie as objective data, we might treat the data as an occasion for reflection and Socratic inquiry about the merits and pitfalls of our own "regimes" of pedagogy in education abroad and beyond.

### 3.4 Identities

This chapter identifies three approaches to discussions of "identities" in education abroad. In the first, student identity appears as an aspiration, that which can be gained through education abroad experience. Students are encouraged to *become* "global citizens" by pursuing the various paths indicated by different researchers. Some argue for putting students in an unfamiliar environment and making them "strangers" and objects of others' gaze, prompting questioning of their own assumptions (Palmer, 2015), an important aspect of global citizenship. Many education abroad programs make this kind of identity a stated goal, although some have questioned building grandiose aspirations into education abroad program design (Woolf, 2010; Zemach-Bersin, 2009). Others view development of national/ethnic identification as part of global/world citizenship (Lewin & Kirk, 2009), suggesting the importance of knowing one's subject position and its effects on our viewpoints.

A second approach involves examining student identities as reflecting relations of power that both pre-exist and are further enhanced by education abroad. Ogden (2007) critiques "colonial students" who do not learn local customs and expect amenities with a sense of entitlement. Other participant identities critiqued using this approach include "saviors," in the context of service work (Sin, 2009), and "explorers" and "adventurers" who treat the world as their playground (Zemach-Bersin, 2009). This approach encourages education abroad researchers and practitioners to critically examine the language and imagery used to recruit students.

A third category of identity discourse has been critiqued for making monocultural, monolingual, white and middle-class identity normative for education abroad participants. This approach can be seen in the discourse of crossing cultural borders that do not consider potential prejudice students may encounter. Talbert and Stewart (1999) emphasize how one's race, class, and gender lead to diverse participant experiences, stressing the importance of student discussions about their implications for deepened understanding of the host society's social dynamics as well as effects of subject positions in their education abroad experiences.

Yet challenging this normative monocultural/monolingual image of education abroad students—such as calling for increased minority participation (e.g., Butler, Madden, & Smith, 2018; Simon & Ainsworth, 2012)—needs to avoid a "deficit approach" that views such students as being at risk of missing out on intercultural competence. Since "minority" students may already possess intercultural competence from their experiences as cultural "other" even at home, as will be discussed below (also, see Doerr 2018a), recognizing and reflecting these in program design and goal setting is important. And acknowledging this diversity of individuals in our midst besides education abroad students, such as immigrants, stateless and other mobile border populations, can enrich the discussion of education abroad in general.

In the section below, some possible ways to respond to the critiques summarized above through incorporating works in immigrant studies are suggested.

### 3.5 Immigrant studies

In their work on "regimes of mobility," Glick Schiller and Salazar (2013, p. 189) note the disparities in the treatment of global human mobility. The mobility of the rich is deemed cosmopolitan; that of middle-class college students enacts global learning. Meanwhile, poor and non-white populations' mobility is seen negatively, as suspect. Scholarly research may unwittingly participate in such regimes of mobility when immigrant studies and education abroad research fails to acknowledge a shared interest in issues of individual and group adjustment to new sociocultural environments (Doerr, 2018a; Doerr & Suarez, 2017). Focusing only on education abroad students when discussing global citizenship and intercultural competence risks perpetuating the separation accomplished by these regimes, leaving intact the relations of power underlying them.

Some emerging literature does seek to move away from this exclusive student focus: by recognizing diverse contours of minority immigrants' global citizenship and intercultural competence (Doerr, 2012a); giving attention to their little-discussed education abroad experiences utilizing such competence (Doerr, 2018a); and suggesting pedagogies that acknowledge alternative paths toward intercultural competence (Deardorff & Arasaratnam-Smith, 2017). This greater inclusivity is also seen in education abroad research on community-based service-learning work with refugees

(Reisinger, 2017), in UNESCO initiatives bringing together members of local communities for formal/informal learning (Deardorff, 2019), in the discussion of education abroad that includes education of refugees and other displaced individuals in their new homeland (Streitwieser, 2019), and "Internationalization at Home" in Europe and beyond, which focuses on nurturing employable "intercultural skills" in those without access to border-crossing opportunities (Beelen & Jones, 2015) not only through curriculum content that focuses on global issues but also through utilizing local diversity (Beelen & Jones, 2015), similar to the notion of "study away" in the US.

We build on these approaches and further suggest engaging more with immigrant studies, giving centrality to discussion of the competencies already possessed by students who have *not* studied abroad. To invest ourselves in making global citizenship a meaningful construct, we need to account for diverse contours of the immigrant and minority experience of adapting to various mainstream cultures. It is important to celebrate these oft-ignored forms of border-crossing experience (Doerr, 2018a) as well as drawing on existing literatures developed separately, such as immigrant studies scholarship.

There are three ways this incorporation of immigrant studies can enhance education abroad practices. First, research on immigrants' adjustment process is useful in revisiting common practices in education abroad that discourage students from spending time with their compatriot students. Portes and Rambaut (2001) have made a powerful case for staying within one's own group, in spite of some risks of insulation, noting that such practice helps smooth adjustment to new environments by providing coping strategies, especially where there are prejudices to overcome. Portes and Zhou (1993) have highlighted a wide range of effective, research-backed immigrant adjustment processes, correlating them by group size (e.g., Cubans in Miami with their own microcosm, allowing for more social mobility); length of stay (e.g., newly arrived Mexicans tend to have more faith in the system—hence higher motivation—than the third generation Mexican Americans); and social assimilation context (e.g., sense of resignation among those adjusting to low-income inner-city communities with the sense of helplessness vs. relative hopefulness of those assimilating to wealthy suburban areas). Adaptation processes also vary according to the legal status of the immigrants, such as Deferred Actions for Childhood Arrival (DACA) individuals and undocumented individuals (Chen & Rhoads, 2016; Pérez, 2014). Awareness of such research allows the discussions in education abroad to consider how the ethnic background and group size of a given education abroad cohort can impact interactions with "locals" in pursuit of intercultural competence.

Second, comparison of immigrant acculturation and education abroad adaptation may throw into relief new dimensions of intercultural learning abroad. For example, immigrant adjustment to the host society is often about survival, whereas education abroad students seek to gain soft skills for cultural capital back home. Immigrants' original culture and language are often considered a hindrance to their adjustment to their new home based on a zero-sum model of "cultural replacement," whereas education abroad students' learning about the host culture and language is considered an additive enrichment. Too complete an adjustment to the destination for education abroad students is sometimes viewed as problematic because it can lead to "home" country re-entry problems, whereas such adjustment by immigrants is usually celebrated (Doerr & Suarez, 2017). Such students who adjusted to the destination so much that they decide to stay—what Doerr, Poole, and Hedrick (2020) call "post-study-abroad students"—are rarely discussed in education abroad literature in the US context.[2]

Third, immigrants and education abroad students, despite any differences in legal status or positioning within aforementioned regimes of mobility, are in practice located on a continuum. Arbitrary differentiation based on hastily applied labels can have a detrimental impact on the students' identities (Doerr, 2018a). Class discussions acknowledging diverse paths to intercultural skills can mitigate this issue, heightening awareness of regimes of mobility but also forging connections between immigrant students and education abroad participants. Leveraging immigrant students' self-awareness of their own intercultural competence could broaden program participation among non-traditional students (Doerr, 2018b).

In order to clearly illustrate the importance of expanding the scope of analyses to the continuum of education abroad students and immigrants—the continuum sometimes so dense and complex that separating these constituents risks ignoring an important aspect of education abroad politics—introduced below is a case from Japan, where xenophobia against immigrants is shaping the contours of education abroad policies and practices, a possible future direction in some other countries.

### 3.5.1 Education abroad and immigration: A case from Japan

Japan, with its conservative immigration policy despite declining birth rates and an aging population, presents an intriguing mobility paradox that lends itself to an analysis combining education abroad and immigrant studies viewpoints. Its dire need for an infusion of young skilled workers and inflexibility about accepting immigrants makes the incoming education abroad participant (*ryugakusei*)[3] take on a heightened significance.

Historically, Japan has welcomed education abroad students: first, for educating human resources for developing countries (Takeda, 2006), later to enhance "international understanding" (Yamamoto, 2014), and currently, as a way to compensate for a declining labor force (Yokota & Shiratsuchi, 2004).

Education abroad students contribute to Japan's workforce in two ways. The first is by staying after their education abroad, to work in Japan. The Career Development Program for Foreign Students in Japan, begun in 2007, helps foreign students do so. In 2008, the "300,000 Study Abroad Students Plan" created streamlined policies for supporting them to find employment. In 2017, the "International Student Employment Promotion Program" was launched in twelve universities to support education abroad students' employment through industry-university cooperation.

The second way international students contribute is by working part-time during their studies. Japan's Immigration Control and Refugee Recognition Act of 1989 allows education abroad students to work up to 28 hours per week during the semester and eight hours per day during school vacation. As of 2015, 74.8% of education abroad students in Japan worked in this category (JASSO, 2015). Reasons for this include limited availability of Japanese government scholarships; the struggle to afford Japan's high living cost and school fees; and the attractiveness of Japan as an employment destination (Nishi-Nippon Shinbun, 2017).[4]

A symbiotic relationship has developed between Japan's labor shortage and foreign student demand for work opportunities. Smaller universities with declining domestic enrollments may enroll foreign students to fill the classes and promote the college as "global" (Kamiyoshi, work in progress). Urban convenience stores often rely on *ryugakusei* as part-time workers, and factory jobs may be filled by those with limited Japanese proficiency (Nishi-Nippon Shinbun, 2017). In rural communities with decreasing youth populations, education abroad students are sought after as health care workers for the elderly. Local vocational schools offer programs to become health care workers along with Japanese language programs. Some communities entice foreign students with scholarships, on the condition that they work in the community upon graduation for certain number of years.

Though research on this linkage is only starting to emerge (e.g., Iwakiri, 2017; Kamiyoshi, 2020; Debnar, 2020; Sato, 2018), this example of the merging destinies of mobile students and immigrants shows the need for the expansion of both fields of research in order to clearly understand the dynamics described above.

## 4. Implications for practice

In reviewing the existing literature, this chapter has sought to add meta-level examination of common notions and practices in education abroad regarding global citizenship, intercultural competence, and identity formation. This approach has some practical implications, which are discussed in this section. In terms of global citizenship, education abroad programming can go beyond the provision of "global knowledge" by raising certain critical questions. Why *this* knowledge *here*? Whose viewpoint is being privileged by learning it? What other viewpoints should be considered, and how? To foster students' awareness of the interconnectedness of the world, directing their attention to otherwise mundane consumer transactions, such as buying a shirt from a local Zara retailer, may be useful. Are they aware the shirt may contain materials imported from Turkey and sewn by Bangladeshis and distributed by Italians working for a Spaniard (i.e., Inditex founder and billionaire Amancio Ortega), or that this purchase implicates them in a web of behaviors involving remote others' working conditions and the environmental impact their material productions create? In encouraging student engagement in "global issues," education abroad programs can ask them what makes the issues "global," what kind of solution a global citizen, as variously defined by the experts cited in 3.1 above, might seek, and how their preferred forms of activism stand to gain, if at all, from being considered global.

Regarding intercultural competence, in order to avoid the imposition of the dominant group's views in deciding what constitutes "intercultural competence," students can set their own goals, as mentioned. The occasion of intercultural competence assessment can also be used as an opportunity for reflection and conversation regarding the practice itself—its agenda, assumptions, and unintended consequences—rather than treating the result as an objective outcome, as discussed in 3.3.

As for identities, we can ask what kinds of participants current education abroad program materials assume, summon, or claim to produce; whether students are encouraged to see themselves on a developmental model of growth or something more static; whether the pedagogy used to foster and demonstrate learning (e.g., blog prompts) encourages critical self-reflection of participants' sometimes already intercultural identity dynamics. Program design, mission, and vision should embrace the diversity and existing cultural competence of its student body.

To expand the scope of discussions of global citizenship, intercultural competence, and student identities, this chapter suggested incorporating the experiences and vocabularies of immigrants, ethnic minorities, and others who have experiences in border-crossing. For example, have home campuses organize discussion panels where education abroad alumni and immigrant students are given conceptual tools to compare their cross-cultural experiences. These tools can include exercises about labelling some things "global" and others "multicultural," an item in educators' intercultural toolkits that are rarely used to engage other campus "cultures." Comparing differences between immigrants and education abroad students in terms of cultural adjustment may allow both groups see new connections to each other, potentially nurturing intercultural competence in novel ways. Programs can also be modified to address ways to make use of and enrich immigrant students' existing intercultural competence and multicultural and multilingual skills during their education abroad. For example, some Spanish/English bilingual students in conventional education abroad programs report taking on leadership roles in Spain, acting as translators for fellow students and gaining confidence in their bilingual identities for the first time (Doerr, 2018a). Preparing bilingual students for such leadership roles—for instance, fine-tuning their social skills prior to education abroad and creating concrete role options within the program such as "bilingual leaders"—could enhance their experience.

Another possible way to expand the scope of discussions of global citizenship, intercultural competence, and student identities is to apply holistic, big picture frameworks for contextualizing global mobility, as introduced with the case from Japan in 3.5.1. Practical application of this more inclusive approach to global citizenship, intercultural competence, and identities might take forms of talks and roundtables by immigration experts as well as education abroad researchers, whose results can inform education abroad program designs.

## 5. Directions for future research

This chapter reviewed existing literature on the notions of global citizenship, intercultural competence, and student identities and added meta-level analyses of these concepts. One path for future research is to help nurture students' "structural competence"—the ability to understand how wider historical and current structural forces situated in relations of power shape "differences" (Doerr, 2018b). This approach allows us to move away from static notions of "culture" common in discourses of "intercultural competence." For example, ramen noodles are often seen as "Japanese food culture." However, they were popularized in the post-WWII Cold War context where the US provided flour to ease the hunger of poor Japanese in order to prevent them from radicalizing into communists. This flour was made into ramen noodles to render it more familiar to the Japanese palate (Solt, 2014). Practitioners can examine similarly static cultural assumptions that may be embedded into programming, designing programs that encourage students to gain greater sensitivity to ways "cultural" practices are shaped by broader structural forces.

A second kind of student learning to which researchers can turn their attention is "social competence" (Doerr, 2018b)—that is, broader abilities to deal with human differences at all scales, rather than only when national "culture" is foregrounded. Reframing "intercultural competence" as "social competence" allows us to acknowledge divergent identities—race, gender, class, etc.—and skills honed in crossing such borders, which goes along with including insights from immigrant studies. It also helps redress inequalities in the respective burdens assumed by different groups seeking to adjust among others (i.e., minority groups tend to be the ones having to adjust to the dominant group norms). Making social competence an object of critical scrutiny could also serve to make mundane domestic power relations, not just those encountered during education abroad, relevant for reflection and analyses by students, helping prepare them for education abroad as well as make the experience abroad more relevant to daily life upon their return.

It may be that, ironically, the kind of reflective practice that is most needed will require us to rethink our commitments to the technical-rationalist assumptions behind intercultural measurement, and instead to focus our attention on more mundane practices that currently fall outside the scope of our expertise. Critical reflection about possible ideological underpinnings of our current practice can go hand in hand with our field's renewed attention to diversity, inclusivity, and the identities of those who are marginalized.

## Notes

1 International educators in the US, however, may want to take steps to emulate assessment practices from Europe and elsewhere, where learning outcomes meant to reflect the competencies discussed here tend to be built into the curriculum rather than added on.
2 This differs slightly in the European context where ERASMUS programs were developed focused on partnerships among countries and "mobility" of students (Brandenburg, Berghoff & Taboadela, 2014).

3  Here, education abroad students are degree-seeking students rather than short-term credit-seeking students.
4  The Immigration Control and Refugee Recognition Act went into effect in April 2019, allowing non-Japanese nationals with certain in-demand skills to live and work in Japan without having to study. Some predict the number of *ryugakusei* to Japan will decrease as they may prefer to work rather than study in Japan. Some fraud cases have been reported as well: in 2016–2018, 1,400 out of 5,700 *ryugakusei* (mainly from Vietnam, Nepal, and Sri Lanka) at Tokyo University of Social Welfare left the university to work full time illegally. Some predict that the crackdown on such cases will result in more *ryugakusei* entering Japan under the legal category of "specified skilled worker" instead. Also, according to data released in August 2019 by the Immigration Services Agency of Japan, the number of cases of revocation of the status of residence drastically increased from 385 in the previous year (2017) to 832 in 2018. Especially, foreign students account for half (412 cases) in this data (Status 2018).

## Further reading

Deardorff, D.K., & Arasaratnam-Smith, L.A. (Eds.) (2017). *Intercultural competence in higher education*. Routledge.
Doerr, N. (2018b). *Transforming study abroad*. Berghahn Books.
Glick Schiller, N.M., & Salazar, N.B. (2013). Regimes of mobility across the globe. *Journal of Ethnic and Migration Studies* 39(2), 183–200.
Kortegast, C.A., & Boisfontaine, M.T. (2015). Beyond "it was good." *Journal of College Student Development* 56(8), 812–828.
Root, E. & Ngampornchai, A. (2012). "I came back as a new human being": Student descriptions of intercultural competence acquired through education abroad experiences. *Journal of Studies in International Education* 17(5), 513–532.

## References

Abrahamian, A.A. (2015). *The cosmopolites: The coming of the global citizen*. Columbia Global Reports.
Anderson, P., Hubbard, A., Lawton, L., & Rexeisen, R. (2008). Study abroad and intercultural development. *Frontiers*, 17, 1–20.
Beelen, J., & Jones, E. (2015). Redefining internatinalization at home. In A. Curaj, L. Matei, R. Pricopie, J. Salmi & P. Scott (Eds.), *The European higher education area: Between critical reflections and future policies*. Springer.
Bennett, M. (2014, June 12). What is dangerous of DOS and DON'TS in the intercultural context [Video file]. Retrieved from https://www.youtube.com/watch?v=NvuU34kZDrg
Bourdieu, P., & Passeron, J.-C. (1977). *Reproduction in education, society and culture*. Sage.
Brandenburg, U., Berghoff, S., & Taboadela, O. (2014). *The ERASUMS impact study*. Publications Office of the European Union.
Braskamp, L.C., Braskamp, D., & Carter Merrill, K. (2018). Global perspectives inventory (GPI). Retrieved from www.researchgate.net/publication/239931705_Global_Persp ectives_Inventory_GPI_Its_Purpose_Construction_Potential_Uses_and_Psychometric_ Characteristics
Butler, P.E., Madden, M., & Smith, N. (2018). Undocumented student participation in education abroad. *Frontiers: The Interdisciplinary Journal of Study Abroad*, 2, 1–31.

Chen, A.C., & Rhoads, R.A. (2016). Undocumented student allies and transformative resistance. *The Review of Higher Education*, 39(4), 515–542.

Collier, S.J., & Ong, A. (2005). Global assemblages, anthropological problems. In A. Ong & S.J. Collier (Eds.), *Global assemblages* (pp. 3–21). Blackwell Publishing.

Corbitt, N.J. (1998). *Global awareness profile: Gaptest: facilitator's manual*. Boston: Nicholas Brealey Publishing.

Deardorff, D.K. (Ed.) (2009). *The SAGE handbook of intercultural competence*. Sage.

Deardorff, D.K. (2011). Assessing intercultural competence. *New directions for Institutional Research*, 149, 65–79.

Deardorff, D.K. (2015). *Demystifying outcomes assessment for international educators*. Stylus.

Deardorff, D.K. (2017). The big picture of intercultural competence assessment. In D.K. Deardorff & L. Arasaratnam-Smith (Eds.), *Intercultural competence in higher education*. Routledge.

Deardorff, D.K. (2019). *UNESCO manual on intercultural competences based on human rights*. UNESCO/Routledge.

Deardorff, D.K., & Arasaratnam-Smith, L.A. (Eds.) (2017). *Intercultural competence in higher education*. Routledge.

Debnar, M. (2020). "Ryūgakusei" as students, workers or migrants? Multiple meanings and borders of the international students in Japan. In N.M. Doerr (Ed.), *The global education effect and Japan: Constructing new borders and identification practices*. Routledge.

Doerr, N.M. (2012a). Producing American citizens with "global competence." In A.W. Wiseman, A. Chase-Mayoral, T. Janis, & A. Sachdev (Eds.), *Community colleges worldwide* (pp. 71–98). Emerald Group Publishing Inc.

Doerr, N.M. (2012b). Study abroad as "adventure." *Critical Discourse Studies*, 9(3), 257–268.

Doerr, N.M. (2018a). "Global competence" of minority immigrant students. *Discourse*. doi:10.1080/01596306.2018.1462147

Doerr, N.M. (2018b). *Transforming study abroad*. Berghahn Books.

Doerr, N.M., & Suarez, R.J. (2017). Immersion, immigration, immutability. *Educational Studies*. doi:10.1080/00131946.2017.1356309

Doerr, N.M., Poole, G., & Hedrick, R. (2020). "Post study abroad students," "never study abroad students," and the politics of belonging: The global education effect of Japan's English-medium campus. In N.M. Doerr (Ed.), *The global education effect and Japan: Constructing new borders and identification practices*. Routledge.

Durden, W.G. (2015). *Embracing the new globalism*. The Forum on Education Abroad Annual Conference, San Diego, CA, April 2, 2015.

Glick Schiller, N., & Salazar, N.B. (2013). Regimes of mobility across the globe. *Journal of Ethnic and Migration Studies*, 39(2), 183–200.

Harvey, T.A. (2018a). An educator's guide to intercultural learning. Retrieved from https://www.truenorthintercultural.com/p/educators-guide-to-intercultural-learning

Harvey, T.A. (2018b). Challenges and practical realities of assessing intercultural learning. Retrieved from https://www.truenorthintercultural.com/blog/challenges-practical-realities-of-assessing-intercultural-learning

Hett, E.J. (1993). Development of an instrument to measure global-mindedness. *Dissertation Abstracts International* 54(10), 3724.

Iwakiri, T. (2017). Foreign students adapting to Japanese cultural context in their working place in Japan. *Kagoshima Women's College Bulletin*, 53, 15–24.

JASSO. (2015). Lifestyle survey of privately-financed international students 2015. Retrieved from www.jasso.go.jp/about/statistics/ryuj_chosa/h27.html

Jooste, N., & Heleta, S. (2017). Global citizenship versus globally competent graduates: A critical view from the South. *Journal of Studies in International Education*, 21 (1), 39–51.

Kamiyoshi, U. (2020). Japan's new "immigration" policy and the society's responses. In N. M. Doerr (Ed.), *The global education effect and Japan: Constructing new borders and identification practices*. Routledge.

Lewin, R., & Kirk, G.V. (2009). It's not about you. In R. Lewin (Ed.). *The handbook of practice and research in study abroad* (pp. 543–564). Routledge.

Lilley, K., Barker, M., & Harris, N. (2014). Unravelling the rhetoric of the global citizen. *Internationalisation of Higher Education*, 1, 7–19.

Lilley, K., Barker, M., & Harris, N. (2017). The global citizen conceptualized: Accommodating ambiguity. *Journal of Studies in International Education*, 21 (1), 6–21.

Molinsky, A. (2013). *Global dexterity*. Harvard Business School Press.

Morais, D.B., & Ogden, A. (2011). Initial development and validation of the global citizenship scale. *Journal of Studies in International Education*, 15(5), 445–466.

Morisano, D.Hirsh, J.B., Peterson, J.B., Pihl, R.O., & Shore, B.M. (2010). Setting, elaborating and reflecting on personal goals improves academic performance. *Journal of Applied Psychology*, 95(2), 255–264.

Nishi-Nippon Shimbun. (2017). *The new era of immigration*. Retrieved from www.fukuoka-now.com/en/new-era-immigration-kyushu/

OECD. (2017). *Preparing our youth for an inclusive and sustainable world*. OECD. Retrieved from www.oecd.org/education/Global-competency-for-an-inclusive-world.pdf

Ogden, A. (2007). The view from the veranda. *Frontiers*, 15, 35–55.

Ogden, A. (2015). *Toward a research agenda for U.S. education abroad*. AIEA.

Palmer, N.W. (2015). Inverting the object of study. *Teaching Theology and Religion*, 18(1), 63–72.

Pérez, Z.J. (2014). Removing barriers to higher education for undocumented students. Center for American Progress. Retrieved from: www.americanprogress.org/issues/immigration/reports/2014/12/05/101366/removing-barriers-to-higher-education-for-undocumented-students/

Plummer, K. (1995). *Telling sexual stories*. Routledge.

Portes, A., & Rambaut, R.G. (2001). *Legacies: The story of the immigrant second generation*. University of California Press.

Portes, A., & Zhou, M. (1993). The new second generation. *The Annals of the American Academy of Political and Social Science*, 530, 74–96.

Reeve, J.M. (2014). *Understanding motivation and emotion*. Wiley & Sons.

Reisinger, D.S. (2017). Issues in global displacement. In D. Deardorff & L.A. Arasaratnam-Smith (Eds.), *Intercultural competence in higher education* (pp. 249–253). Routledge.

Rygiel, K. (2010). *Globalizing citizenship*. University of British Columbia Press.

Sato, Y. (2018). International student policy as de facto entry point of immigration and refugee policy in Japan. *Migration Policy Review*, 10, 29–43.

Shimmi, Y., & Otu, H. (2018). Super short-term study abroad in Japan. *International Higher Education*, 94. doi:10.6017/ihe.2018.0.10559

Simon, J., & Ainsworth, J.W. (2012). Race and socioeconomic status differences in study abroad participation. *ISRN Education*, 1–21. doi:10.5402/2012/413896

Sin, H.L. (2009). Who are we responsible to? Locals' tales of volunteer tourism. *Geoforum*, 41, 983–992.

Skelly, J.M. (2009). Fostering engagement: The role of international education in the development of global civil society. In R. Lewin (Ed.), *The handbook of practice and research in study abroad* (pp. 21–32). Routledge.

Solt, G. (2014). *The untold history of ramen*. University of California Press.

Status of reporting on the employment of foreign workers by employers. (2018). www.mhlw.go.jp/content/11655000/000472892.pdf. Accessed on November 3, 2019.

Streitwieser, B. (2019). International education for enlightenment, for opportunity and for survival: Where students, migrants and refugees diverge. *Journal of Comparative and Higher Education*, 11, 4–9.

Sugarman, J. (2015). Neoliberalism and psychological ethics. *Journal of Theoretical and Philosophical Psychology*, 35(2), 103–116.

Takeda, S. (2006). Transition of the roles of Japan's international policy, *Nihon University GSSC Journal*, 7, 77–88.

Talbert, S., & Stewart, M. (1999). What's the subject of study abroad? Race, gender and living culture. *Modern Language Journal*, 82, 163–175.

Tomlinson, J. (1999). *Globalization and culture*. University of Chicago Press.

Trentman, E., & Diao, W. (2017). The American gaze east. *Study Abroad Research in Second Language Acquisition and International Education*, 2(2), 175–205.

UNESCO Global Citizenship Education Working Group. (2014). *Global citizenship education: Preparing learners for the challenges of the 21st century*. UNESCO.

Vande Berg, M., Connor-Linton, J., & Paige, R.M. (2009). The Georgetown Consortium Project: Interventions for student learning abroad. *Frontiers: The Interdisciplinary Journal of Study Abroad*, 18, 1–75.

Vande Berg, M., Paige, R.M., & Lou, K.H. (2012). *Student learning abroad*. Stylus.

Womack-Wynne, C. (2017). Creating global citizens. *The Forum Focus*, 4(2), 6–8.

Womack-Wynne, C. (2018). Global citizenship 2.0. *International Education*, May–June, 20–26. Retrieved from www.gpi.hs.iastate.edu/documents/nafsa_ie_20180506.pdf

Woolf, M. (2010). Another mishegas. *Frontiers*, 19, 47–60.

Yamamoto, S. (2014). *Post-war nation-state and Japanese language education*. Tokyo: Kuroshio Shuppan.

Yokota, M., & Shiratsuchi, S. (2004). *International student advising*. Nakanishiya.

Young, M., & Commins, E. (2002). *Global citizenship*. Oxfam.

Zemach-Bersin, T. (2008). American students abroad can't be global citizens. *Chronicle of Higher Education*, 54(26), A34.

Zemach-Bersin, T. (2009). Selling the world. In R. Lewin (Ed.), *The handbook of practice and research in study abroad* (pp. 303–320). Routledge.

# Chapter 9

# Employability

## How education abroad impacts the transition to graduate employment

*Jannecke Wiers-Jenssen, Martin Tillman and Cheryl Matherly*

## Highlights:

- The relationship with employability and education abroad is mixed and sometimes overstated. Although employers seek traits associated with outcomes from education abroad, the research is inconclusive about the impact on employability or salary.
- Purposefully designed education abroad programs can be viewed as high-impact co-curricular learning experiences that contribute to developing skills and competencies that are desired by employers.
- This chapter underscores the need for more comparative research on labor market outcomes of student mobility, comparing countries, and comparing mobile and non-mobile students and program models. There is also need for research that controls for student background characteristics (selectivity) when analyzing the effects of education abroad.

## 1. Introduction and chapter overview

Education abroad, which includes study, internship, volunteering, non-credit internships, and directed travel (Forum on Education Abroad, 2011), is well understood to contribute to student learning along several dimensions. While it has been shown that internationally mobile students develop language proficiency, cultural skills, greater self-efficacy, and enhanced interpersonal skills (see e.g. Murphy-Lejeune, 2002; Wiers-Jenssen, 2003; Spitzberg & Changnon, 2009; Brooks & Waters, 2011, Malicki & Potts, 2013; European Comission, 2016; as well as previous chapters in this volume), this chapter will address the following question: In what ways does an education abroad experience impact student employability?

The term 'employability' has become part of mainstream discourse about expected outcomes for higher education, and increasingly, education abroad programs are expected to demonstrate how they develop skills and competencies that contribute to preparing graduates to find work (Matherly & Tillman, 2015; British Council, 2013; Farugia & Sanger, 2017). Indeed, international student mobility has become a part of institutional and national knowledge policies in many countries over the past three decades, first in Europe, but more recently, in the United States, Australia and Asia (Gribble & Tran, 2016; Farugia & Sanger, 2017; Potts, 2018). The rationales for this are complex and overlapping, but are generally associated with economic, academic, cultural and political goals (see e.g. Knight & de Wit, 1997).

The most widely cited definition describes employability in terms of the transition from higher education to the labor market. It is the "capability to gain initial employment, maintain employment and obtain new employment if required. It is also, ideally, about the quality of such work or employment" (Hillage & Pollard, 1998). Others, however, define employability in terms of the ability to get a job. It is "a set of achievements – skills, understandings and personal attributes – that makes graduates more likely to gain employment and be successful in their chosen occupations, which benefits themselves, the workforce, the community, and the economy" (Yorke, 2004). This distinction is important. While little research suggests a *causal* relationship between education abroad and ease of finding a job or impact on salary, there is an ample body of survey research that does demonstrate a *correlation* with sets of employable skills preferred by employers, some of which are associated with outcomes from education abroad (British Council, 2013; Tillman, 2012).

This chapter will examine the particular relationship between education abroad and employability from three perspectives: the transition from higher education to the labor market; employability skills; and employer perspectives. The authors will discuss the seeming disconnect between the role of education abroad programs with developing skills that employers identify as important, and evidence that these skills actually contribute to a student's employability. Addressing this issue has particular relevance for the way practitioners should advise students about marketing their education abroad experiences to prospective employers. The chapter concludes with recommendations for future research, especially as they relate to international internships and work-integrated learning, which may be better recognized as experiences that contribute to a graduate's employability.

## 2. Key questions to be addressed

- What research evidence is there that education abroad strengthens skills and competencies that employers value?
- What is the research evidence that education abroad provides students an advantage in terms of their career development?
- What is the research evidence that the employability outcomes of education abroad are related to selectivity?

## 3. Review of the literature

Is an education abroad an advantage in terms of pursuing a career? This chapter examines this question using two frameworks. Using a human capital framework

(Becker, 1993), one might assume that education abroad prepares students with additional competencies that make them more valuable to an employer, such as foreign language proficiency and intercultural skills. An alternative framework, the signaling theory, suggests that education abroad may benefit a student for its signaling effects (Spence, 1973). Education abroad may indicate to an employer that a student possesses specific, desired hard and soft skills, due to an assumption that mobile students constitute a select group in the first place (e.g. regarding motivation and potential productivity). This chapter will explore research related to both frames that conclude the actual impact on a graduate's employability is mixed.

### 3.1 Transition from higher education to employment

A significant body of literature examines the relationship between education abroad and its impact on post-graduate employment. Waibel, Rüger, Ette, and Sauer (2017) conducted a systematic literature review of career consequences of international education, summing up results from sixty-five research contributions. They find that in studies based on self-assessment (subjective measures), mobile students report that they have a smoother transition from higher education to work, and that education abroad contributed to their ability to get their first jobs. Similar findings are observed in other studies based on self-assessment (see Farugia & Sanger, 2017; Liwiński, 2018; Yokota, 2016). However, Waibel et al. (2017) also observe that most studies that compare graduates with education abroad experience to graduates without such experience, applying objective measures, such as employment rates or time between graduation and first jobs, find limited effects on students' transition into employment. Only two studies in their systematic review documented shorter transitions from higher education to work for graduates with international mobility experience, involving students from Southern Europe, Italy (Cammelli, Ghishelli & Mignoli, 2008) and Greece (Lianos, Asteriou & Agiomirgianakis, 2004) respectively. In a study of Italian graduates, Di Pietro (2013) finds positive effects of education abroad on employment rates three years after graduation, finding that students with lower socio-economic background benefit more.

The paragraph above suggests education abroad might be valued differently in different countries. In comparative studies of ERASMUS students, students from Southern Europe, and to some extent Eastern Europe, with education abroad experience, have a lower risk of unemployment compared to students without such experience, while this difference is far less pronounced among students from Northern Europe (Janson, Schomburg & Teichler, 2009; European Commission, 2016). The factors that may contribute to this difference, such as how common it is in a particular country to undertake education abroad or the quality of domestic vs. foreign education, are not obvious. Teichler (2015) distinguishes between vertical mobility, which refers to undertaking education in an institution or a country with more favorable academic and economic standards, and horizontal mobility, which refers to education sojourns in countries with similar academic qualities and economic conditions. Teichler assumes that vertical mobility is more likely to enhance employment prospects. An alternative perspective could be that students who choose institutions and countries very different from home are exposed to more cultural challenges, and thereby benefit from a higher added value. Further, conditions in the student's home country may play an important role. A study of ERASMUS students show that students from more peripheral countries in Europe more often are motivated to study abroad due to poor labor market prospects in their home country (Van Mol & Timmerman, 2014). Hence, potential benefits of education abroad may be influenced by an interplay between prestige hierarchies and the national labor markets. Effects of education abroad may also be related to type of study program, though few studies have focused on this. Based on data from Germany, Waibel, Petzold & Rüger (2018) find that status returns to international student mobility is higher in what they label "occupationally unspecific fields of study," compared to "specific fields of study."

Studies that examine the relationship between education abroad and wages suggest some correlation (e.g. Kratz & Netz, 2018; Liwiński, 2016; Teichler, 2015; Jacob, Kühhirt & Rodrigues, 2019; Waibel et al., 2017). The systematic review of Waibel et al. (2017), for example, indicated a moderate positive effect of education abroad on wages. The authors see this in relation to the fact that graduates who have studied abroad more often work in larger, private companies. Furthermore, Kratz and Netz (2018) indicated that German graduates with education abroad experience have a steeper wage development in early career. Interestingly, their analysis also shows this is partly due to the fact that those who have studied abroad are a select group and partly due to more frequent employer changes. In a similar vein, Liwiński (2016) showed a high correlation between education abroad and wages in the first jobs of Polish graduates, but this wage premium is reduced when abilities are controlled for. Furthermore, his results indicated that wage premiums only exist in the private sector, and that short (less than one semester) stays abroad are not correlated with wage premiums. In addition, Liwiński finds that males earn a higher wage than females, and that students with poor qualifications and low social origin benefit more. Schmidt and Pardo (2017) made a similar conclusion that the incomes of United States' graduates who have studied abroad are similar to those who have studied in the USA only.

A recent study of German students finds positive correlations between education abroad and occupational status (using the International Socio-Economic Index ISEI) three years after graduation (Waibel, Petzold & Rüger, 2018). However, this is partly related to the fact that graduates with better occupational prospects self-select to participate in education abroad programs. Further, Waibel et al. (2018) find that occupational status returns to mobility are only found for graduates from generic fields of education, not for more specific/professional study programs. Altogether, these studies indicate that wage effects, and potentially also other outcomes of education abroad, may be heterogeneous: some groups are more likely to benefit than others.

Finally, several studies indicate that graduates who participated in education abroad have jobs that are different from those who have not. For example, it has been shown that graduates who have studied abroad are more likely to have jobs where they use foreign language skills and that involve more business travel abroad (Bracht, Engel, Janson, Over, Schomburg & Teichler, 2006; Wiers-Jenssen, 2008). Furthermore, graduates who have been mobile are more likely to search for, and find, work abroad after graduation (Wiers-Jenssen, 2008; Parey & Waldinger; 2010, Oosterbeek & Webbink; 2011, Jacob, Kühhirt & Rodrigues, 2019; Teichler 2015; Kaplan, 2016). Hence, education abroad may serve particularly as a steppingstone for an international career.

In sum, the research in the field demonstrates mixed conclusions about the impact of education abroad on the ability to get a job, wages and career advancement. Further, it is methodologically challenging to distinguish effects of education abroad from characteristics of the students that were already present before going abroad. Mobile students might have different characteristics from non-mobile students, such as socio-economic background, age, gender, race or ethnicity, school performance or personality (see e.g. Teichler, 2015; Kratz & Netz, 2018; Waibel et al., 2017; Schmidt & Pardo, 2017), which may impact employment outcomes.

### 3.2 Employability skills

Although overall empirical research does not identify a strong causal relationship between education abroad and a student's time to get a job upon graduation, it is more encouraging with regard to the correlation between the employability skills that students are able to develop during (well designed) education abroad programs.

Malicki & Potts' (2013) meta-analysis of research conducted over a span of fifty years determined that overseas education programs promoted the development of critical international skills and competencies, including: understanding of the complexity of global issues; applying disciplinary knowledge in a global context; ability and comfort, to work with people from other cultures; intercultural awareness; adaptability and tolerance; cognitive skills (in those who have not travelled previously); self-confidence and self-reliance; open-mindedness and independence in students; and general and culturally-specific creativity.

The Institute of International Education completed the largest survey of US education abroad alumni investigating the connection between students' perceptions of their participation in education abroad programs and the development of skills that contribute to employment and career development, surveying over 4,500 program alumni between the academic years of 1999–2000 and 2016–17 (Farugia & Sanger, 2017). The authors reported an increase in soft skills and competencies that students identified in three categories: intrapersonal competencies, cognitive competencies and interpersonal competencies.

Importantly, most research suggests that students are more likely to develop these employability skills as part of programs that are designed to foster a connection with student career development (Farugia & Sanger, 2017; Vande Berg et al. 2012). Potts (2018) finds in her summary of ten research studies (from the United States, Japan, the EU, United Kingdom, Australia and Italy) that education abroad experiences provide environments in which students can apply new and existing skills that she identifies as transferable to the workplace, especially when students are encouraged to engage in reflection and articulate the relationship of their skills developed while abroad to other situations.

The research included in this section identifies a consistent set of skills and competencies that students indicate they develop as part of an education abroad experience. However, most of these studies are based on surveys that ask respondents to self-report on a range of employability outcomes from their international experiences instead of using objective measures; and they do not control for selectivity into education abroad programs. Furthermore, as education abroad has grown in popularity and more institutions have identified such programs as central to their internationalization strategies, the linkage of education abroad with employability outcomes has, on occasion, been exaggerated. This has led to a notable disconnect between campus goals to widen education abroad opportunities for students and the value attached to these programs by employers seeking specific transferable skills (as explained in the next section) when hiring new graduates (Tillman, 2012, p. 194).

### 3.3 Employer perceptions and the disconnect with labor market mobility

Employers' perceptions of education abroad is at the crux of how these programs contribute – or not – to employability. Research consistently suggests that employers value cross-cultural skills (Bikson & Law, 1994; Crossman & Clarke, 2010; Spitzberg & Changnon, 2009). In the QS Global Employer Survey (Moloney, Sowter & Potts, 2011), 10,000 respondents from 116 countries reported that they value education abroad for the knowledge, skills and attitudes that such experience help mobile students to develop. A transnational survey of employers by the British Council (2013) identified skills that employers actively screen for, including: demonstrating strong communication skills, linguistic competence and cultural sensitivity.

In an evaluation of the ERASMUS program, employers were asked to assess the competencies and abilities of young graduates in their companies. Results show that graduates who had undertaken education abroad were perceived to have higher abilities not only in foreign languages and intercultural understanding but also regarding adaptability and initiative (Janson et al., 2009). However, regardless of the value placed on such competencies and cross-cultural skills, studies also consistently show that experience abroad, per se, is not considered a particularly important or valuable learning experience by employers when compared with other criteria (Humburg & van der Velden, 2015; Van Mol, 2017; Hart Research,

2018). For example, in a study among German employers, Petzold (2017) found that employers value education abroad experience only if they want to recruit for international jobs.

A survey completed by Hart Research among 500 hiring managers in the US is particularly useful to illustrate this contradiction (Hart Research, 2018). The hiring managers rated the following global learning skills as very important: ability to effectively communicate orally; ethical judgment and decision making; ability to work effectively in teams; ability to apply knowledge and skills to real world settings; ability to analyze and solve complex problems; and the ability to analyze and solve problems with people of different backgrounds and cultures. It is noteworthy that these skills align closely with those identified as outcomes from education abroad in the previous section. However, hiring managers ranked education abroad *last* in a list of experiences they considered important when evaluating candidates, after internships, projects with people from diverse backgrounds, research projects completed collaboratively, a senior thesis, and service learning projects (Hart Research, 2018).

This list provides some insight as to why employers may not place the same value on education abroad as other types of international experience for preparing employable graduates. The literature is clear that employers look for recent graduates who have the ability to apply a broad range of skills and in-depth knowledge to "real-world settings," and internships are used widely by employers to assess whether new graduates have such specific skills and knowledge to be effective in the workplace (Callanan & Benzing, 2004; Malerich, 2009; Lowden et al., 2011; Gudofsky, Zukin & Van Horn, 2011; Hart Research Associates, 2018; O'Higgins & Pinedo, 2018). A meta-analysis of research studies on the effect of educational internships on US and European students' abilities to get a job, conducted by the International Labour Organization, concludes that these experiences positively affect student employment outcomes, correlate with higher wages, and reduce a students' time from graduation to employment (O'Higgins & Pinedo, 2018). It is not surprising, then, that some research suggests that employers similarly value how well constructed and carefully supervised international internships prepare employable graduates (Tillman, 2012; Trooboff & Berg, 2008). In a study with education, industry and academic experts designed to define 'globally competent engineering graduates,' for example, participants rated international internships as a most important educational experience (Streiner et al., 2014). In a study of recruitment preferences of European employers, Van Mol (2017) finds that internships abroad are more highly valued than study sojourns.

Hence, this is the conundrum. The preponderance of research shows that employers, seeking new talent with a range of skills and competencies, find such skills are developed and strengthened through international experience, yet they do not place the same value on all types of such experience. They place a higher value on the skills and competencies gained through internships as opposed to education abroad, per se.

## 4. Evaluation of research methodology

Investigating the career impacts of education abroad involves several challenges. Three challenges stand out particularly, namely the issue of selectivity, the reliance on subjective measurements, and limited generalizability of reported results.

First, as indicated earlier, many studies do not take selectivity issues into account (Waibel et al., 2017; Schmidt & Pardo, 2017), which may lead to inconclusive findings. Favorable labor market impacts of an education abroad experience may be attributed to the fact that mobile students represent a highly self-selective group, more pre-disposed to maximizing the advantages of an international experience. Mobile students tend to come from more privileged socio-economic backgrounds than do non-mobile students (Blanck & Börjesson, 2008; Brooks & Waters, 2011, Wiers-Jenssen, 2013; Jacob, Kühhirt, & Rodrigues, 2019; European Commission, 2016). UK research has also shown that they are less likely to have an immigrant background (King, Findlay & Ahrens, 2010). It has also been shown that mobile students have better intake scores (King et al., 2010) and different personality traits (Zimmermann & Neyer, 2013) compared to non-mobile students. These characteristics are likely to enhance employability, independent of the education abroad experience. Research that takes selectivity into account (such as Liwiński, 2016; Waibel et al., 2017; Kratz & Netz, 2018), finds less difference in labor market outcomes between mobile and non-mobile students than those that do not, which illustrates the need to apply more sophisticated analyses such as multivariate regression, fixed effects models and propensity score matching.

Second, education abroad research is often based on self-reported information by students. As the Waibel et al. (2017) study shows, studies based on such assessments give a different picture than studies that use more objective measures and comparative data. Traditionally, there have been relatively few studies comparing students with and without mobility experience, hence it is difficult to know if and how career outcomes of graduates with education from abroad diverge from career outcomes of studies without such experiences.

Finally, many surveys have a low response rate. This seems to be particularly true for employer surveys that sometimes have response rates as low as 5–10 percent. This implies that results are not generalizable, and that caution is needed when interpreting the validity and reliability of results.

## 5. Implications for practice

The fact that research in the field shows mixed results regarding career outcomes suggests a need for increased caution regarding how education abroad is promoted on campuses or by outside provider organizations. The research examined in this chapter suggests that while there is a relationship between employability and education abroad experience, its magnitude is simply not clear. Moreover, no research suggests that education abroad should be considered an exclusive strategy for developing employability skills, or that it is better than other campus or community-based experiences. Rather, education abroad can be considered of value alongside other educational experiences such as internships, service learning or research with a faculty member, as a learning experience with potential for high impact that contributes to developing traits desired by employers (Kuh, O'Donnell & Reed, 2013).

The fact that employers do not place a high value on education abroad, per se, when hiring, despite the importance they place on traits associated with education abroad, suggests the importance for specialized career advising for students who are planning to study abroad. Specifically, students should be advised on how to present the skills they think they developed while abroad in ways that are meaningful to employers, on their resumes, in social-media profiles and during interviews. This advising should begin before students go abroad, and education abroad programs should articulate such specific skills as expected program outcomes (Vande Berg et al., 2012; Farugia & Sanger, 2017). Potts (2018) stresses the importance of preparing students to identify the transferrable skills they developed when abroad and to reflect on how to apply them to other situations after they return.

Although the research related to international internships is limited, it does suggest that these experiences may favorably impact students' time to employment because employers use such practical experience to assess a graduates' readiness to confront 'real world problems' (ILO, 2018; Malerich, 2009). The number of students completing international internships is growing (IIE, 2018), and this may represent an education abroad model that may be most directly correlated with improving graduates' employability.

Finally, knowing that internationally mobile students tend to constitute a highly self-selected group, it is important to reach out to groups that traditionally are less likely to participate in education abroad, including students from lower-income backgrounds, students whose parents did not participate in higher education, students with average or poor academic performance, or students of diverse ethnic, and immigrant backgrounds. A promising thread of research identifies education abroad as a high-impact learning experience, characterized by frequent and substantive interaction with faculty members, frequent feedback, collaboration among students and engagement with difference, and opportunities to apply and test learning in new contexts (AAC&U, 2007; Kuh, 2008; Kuh, O'Donnell & Reed, 2013). The research that connects high-impact learning with employability is scarce, but it is very compelling with its impact on improving academic success, including graduation rates of under-represented minority students and low-income students (Sutton & Rubin, 2004). The Institute for International Education is leading the Consortium for Analysis of Student Success Through International Education survey (CASSIE) in partnership with the University of Georgia System to assess the impact of education abroad on college completion and GPA, especially for minority and at-risk students. Studies such as this may eventually lead to a better understanding of the connection of education abroad experience with employability.

## 6. Directions for future research

This chapter suggests several areas for additional research. The impacts of various education abroad program models should be reviewed to assess their impact on employability skills. Variables such as duration of sojourn, overall structure and organization and how purposefully students are prepared prior to departure to maximize the impact of their experience abroad, should be taken into account. It is important to investigate to what extent the student's institution, as well as home and host country, influence employability outcomes. The sparse research about the specific impact of international internships on employability, as compared with research on the impact of internships in general, presents a particularly important area for future inquiry. Differences by type of study program need to be addressed, as education abroad may be of varying demand and benefit across subject fields and segments of the labor market.

The authors also think that it may be interesting to look at career trajectories over a longer time span. That would probably require the use of data from national registers. Some countries, such as those in Scandinavia, have applicable data, while in most countries such data are not available. Hence, this is a challenging task.

As a third area, the authors note that a higher awareness of correlation versus causality in research findings is needed. This is especially important as we seek to understand factors unique in education abroad that can – and do – affect employability; for example, the need to acknowledge that findings are influenced by traits that students possess because of their background and previous experiences. This chapter underscores the need for more comparative research on labor market outcomes of student mobility, comparing countries, and comparing mobile and non-mobile students. National graduate surveys are often good data sources, but international graduate surveys have larger potential for more comparative research, though declining survey response rates represents a challenge.

There is also a need for developing more well-designed studies which apply more advanced techniques for analysis to fully understand the effects of education abroad on employability. In recent years, the authors have observed more studies using multivariate analyses including fixed effects models and propensity score matching. This trend is promising and will hopefully provide more research that can help students, faculty, higher education leaders and policy makers, make more informed decisions regarding education abroad strategies.

Finally, this chapter suggests that the notion of employability challenges both the traditional role of tertiary education and the focus of classroom learning outcomes – traditionally, subject knowledge and understanding, or learning how to learn. A growing critique of the emerging "employability agenda" is that it is too driven by government policy and employers' marketplace needs. However, economic globalization and the expansion of institutional policies and practices that impact internationalization give rise to important questions and further areas for inquiry by higher education policy makers. How should campuses prepare students to succeed in the global economy? How should universities align campus internationalization priorities and strategies with expectations of the global marketplace? Should preparing global-ready graduates be solely the domain and responsibility of colleges and universities? What is the role of business and industry in contributing to the applied knowledge and skill development of students?

## Further reading

Farugia, C. & Sanger, J. (2017). *Gaining an Employment Edge: The Impact of Education Abroad on 21st Century Skills & Career Prospects in the United States, 2013–2016*. New York: Institute of International Education.

Jacob, M., Kühhirt, M. & Rodriguez, M. (2019). Labour market returns to graduates' international experience: Exploring cross-country variations in Europe. *European Sociological Review*, 1–15. doi:10.1093/esr/jcz022

Van Mol, C. (2017). Do employers value international education and internships? A comparative analysis of 31 countries. *Geoforum*, 78, 52–60.

Waibel, S., Rüger, H., Etter, A. & Sauer, L. (2017). Career consequences of transnational educational mobility: A systematic literature review. *Educational Research Review*, 20, 81–98.

Yokota, M. (2016). Survey of global personnel development and long-term impact of study abroad. Research Project No. 25245078, School of Global Japanese Studies, Meiji University.

## References

Association of American Colleges & Universities (AAC&U). (2007). *College Learning for the New Global Century: A Report from the National Leadership Council for Liberal Education & America's Promise (LEAP)*. Washington, D.C.: AAC&U. Retrieved from www.aacu.org/sites/default/files/files/LEAP/GlobalCentury_final.pdf

Becker, G. (1993). *Human Capital: A Theoretical and Empirical Analysis, with Special Reference to Education*, 3rd edition. Chicago: University of Chicago Press.

Bikson, T.K. & Law, S.A. (1994). *Global Preparedness and Human Resources*. Santa Monica, CA: RAND Institute on Education and Training.

Blanck, D. & Börjesson, M. (2008). Transnational strategies in higher education and cultural fields: The case of the United States and Sweden in the 20th century. *American Studies in Scandinavia*, 40 (1–2), 80–89.

Bourner, T. & Millican, J. (2011). Student community engagement and graduate employability. *Widening Participation and Lifelong Learning*, 13 (2), 68–85.

Bracht, O., Engel, C., Janson, K., Over, A., Schomburg, H. & Teichler, U. (2006). *The Professional Value of ERASMUS Mobility: Final Report*. Brussels: DG Education and Culture.

British Council. (2013). Culture at work: The value of intercultural skills in the workplace. Retrieved from www.britishcouncil.org/sites/default/files/culture-at-work-report-v2.pdf

Brooks, R. & Waters, J. (2011). *Student Mobilities, Migration and Internationalization of Higher Education*. Basingstoke: Palgrave Macmillan.

Callanan, G. & Benzing, C. (2004). Assessing the role of internships in career orientated employment of graduating college students. *Education + Training*, 46, (2), 82–89.

Cammelli, A., Ghishelli, S. & Mignloi, G.P. (2008). Education experience abroad: Italian graduate characteristics and employment outcomes. In M. Bryam & F. Dervin (Eds.),

*Students, Staff and Academic Mobility in Higher Education* (pp. 217–236). Newcastle: Cambridge Scholars Publishing.

Crossman, J.E. & Clarke, M. (2010, May). International experience and graduate employability: Stakeholder perceptions on the connection. *Higher Education*, 59 (5), 599–613.

Di Pietro, G. (2013). *Do Education Abroad Programs Enhance the Employability of Graduates?* IZA discussion paper series 7675. Bonn: Forschungsinstitut zur Zukunft der Arbeit.

European Commission. (2016). *The Erasmus Impact Study: Regional Analysis*. Luxemburg: European Union.

Farugia, C. & Sanger, J. (2017). *Gaining an Employment Edge: The Impact of Education Abroad on 21st Century Skills & Career Prospects in the United States, 2013–2016*. New York: Institute of International Education.

Forum on Education Abroad. (2011). *Education Abroad Glosssary*. Carlisle, PA: The Forum on Education Abroad. Retrieved from https://forumea.org/wp-content/uploads/2014/10/Forum-2011-Glossary-v2.pdf

Gribble, C. & Tran, L. (2016). *International Trends in Learning Abroad: Information and Promotions Campaigns for Student Mobility*. Melbourne: International Education Association of Australia.

Gudofsky, J., Zukin, C. & Van Horn, C. (2011). Unfulfilled expectations: Recent college graduates struggle in a troubled economy. John J. Heidrich Center for Workforce Development, Rutgers, The State University of New Jersey. Retrieved from www.heldrich.rutgers.edu/sites/default/files/content/Work_Trends_May_2011.pdf

Hart Research Associates. (2018). Fulfilling the American dream: Liberal education and the future of Work. Washington DC: American Association of Colleges and Universities. Retrieved from www.aacu.org/sites/default/files/files/LEAP/2018EmployerResearchReport.pdf

Hillage, J. & Pollard, E. (1998). Employability: Developing a framework for policy analysis. Institute for Employment Studies, Research Brief No. 85, London. Retrieved from www.researchgate.net/publication/225083565_Employability_Developing_a_framework_for_policy_analysis_London_DfEE

Humburg, M. & van der Velden, R. (2015). Skills and the graduate recruitment process: Evidence from two discrete choice experiments. *Economics of Education Review*, 49, 24–41.

Institute for International Education. (2018). Open Doors. www.iie.org/Research-and-Insights/Open-Doors/Data

International Labor Organization. (2018) The regulation of internships: A comparative study. Working paper No. 240. Retrieved from www.ilo.org/employment/Whatwedo/Publications/working-papers/WCMS_629777/lang–en/index.htm

Jacob, M., Kühhirt, M. & Rodriguez, M. (2019). Labour market returns to graduates' international experience: Exploring cross-country variations in Europe. *European Sociological Review*, 1–15. doi:10.1093/esr/jcz022

Janson, K., Schomburg, H. & Teichler, U. (2009). The professional value of ERASMUS mobility. ACA Papers on International Cooperation in Education. Bonn: Lemmens. Retrieved from www.aca-secretariat.be/fileadmin/aca_docs/images/members/2009_The_Professional_Value_of_ERASMUS_Mobility_01.pdf

Kaplan. (2016). Going global: Are graduates prepared for a global workforce? Economist Intelligence Unit. Retrieved from https://kaplan.com/wp-content/uploads/2016/09/Going-Global-Are-graduates-prepared-for-a-global-workforce-EIU-Kaplan-WhitePaper-2016.pdf

King, R., Findlay, A. & Ahrens, J. (2010). *International Student Mobility Literature Review*. London and Bristol: Higher Education Funding Council for England (HEFCE).

Knight, J., & de Wit, H. (Eds.). (1997). *Internationalisation of Higher Education in Asia Pacific Countries*. Amsterdam: European Association for International Education.

Kratz, F. & Netz, N. (2018). Which mechanisms explain monetary returns to international student mobility? *Studies in Higher Education*, 43 (2), 375–400.

Kuh, G.D. (2008). *High-Impact Educational Practices: What They Are, Who Has Access to Them, and Why They Matter*. Washington, DC: American Association of Colleges & Universities.

Kuh, G., O'Donnell, K. & Reed, S. (2013). *Ensuring Quality and Taking High-Impact Practices to Scale*. Washington, DC: American Association of Colleges & Universities.

Lianos, T.P., Asteriou, D. & Agiomirgianakis, G. (2004). Foreign university graduates in the Greek labour market: Employment, salaries and over-education. *International Journal of Finance and Economics*, 9 (6), 151–164.

Liwiński, J. (2016.) Does it pay to study abroad? Evidence from Poland. Working Paper no. 25. Warsaw: Faculty of Economic Sciences.

Liwiński, J. (2018). Does studying abroad enhance employability? *Economics of Transition*. Retrieved from https://onlinelibrary.wiley.com/doi/epdf/10.1111/ecot.12203

Lowden, K.*et al.* (2011). Employer perceptions of the employability skills of new graduates. Edge Foundation, London. Retrieved from www.educationandemployers.org/wp-content/uploads/2014/06/employability_skills_as_pdf_-_final_online_version.pdf

Malerich, J. (2009). The value of international internships in global workforce development. Arizona State University. Retrieved from www.aieaworld.org/assets/docs/Issue_Briefs/thevalueofinternationalinternshipsinglobalworkforcedevelopment_malerich.pdf

Malicki, S. & Potts, D. (2013). The outcomes of outbound student mobility: A summary of academic literature. Retrieved from file:///C:/Users/owner/Desktop/UAAsia BoundOutcomesResearch%20Final.pdf

Matherly, C.A. & Tillman, M.J. (2015). Higher education and the employability agenda. In J. Huisman, H. de Boer, D.D. Dill & M. Souto-Otero (Eds.), *The Palgrave International Handbook of Higher Education Policy and Governance*. London: Palgrave Macmillan.

Moloney, J., Sowter, B. & Potts, D. (2011) QS global employer survey report: How employers value an international education experience. Retrieved from http://content.qs.com/qs/qs-global-employer-survey-2011.pdf

Murphy-Lejeune, E. (2002). *Student Mobility and Narrative in Europe*. London: Routledge.

O'Higgins, N. & Pinedo, L. (2018). Interns and outcomes: Just how effective are internships as a bridge to stable employment? International Labour Organization, Employment Policy Department Employment Working Paper, No. 241.

Oosterbeek, H. & Webbink, D. (2011). Does studying abroad induce a brain drain? *Economica* 78, 347–366.

Parey, M. & Waldinger, F. (2010). Studying abroad and the effect on international labour market mobility: Evidence from the introduction of ERASMUS. *The Economic Journal*, 121, 194–222.

Petzold, K. (2017). The role of international student mobility in hiring decisions: A vignette experiment among German employers. *Journal of Studies in International Education*, 30 (8), 893–911.

Potts, D. (2018). Learning abroad and employability: Researching the connections. Research Digest 13, International Education Association of Australia. www.ieaa.org.au/documents/item/1267

Schmidt, S. & Pardo, M. (2017). The contribution of education abroad to human capital formation. *The Journal of Higher Education*, 88 (1), 135–157.

Spence, M. (1973). Job market signaling. *The Quarterly Journal of Economics*, 87 (3), 355–374.

Spitzberg, B. & Changnon, G. (2009) Conceptualizing intercultural competence. In D. Deardorff (Ed.), *The SAGE Handbook of Intercultural Competence* (pp. 2–52). Thousand Oaks, CA: SAGE.

Streiner, S., Cunningham, S., Levonisova, S., Huang, S., Matherly, C., Besterfield-Sacre, M., Ragusa, G., Shuman, L. & Kotys-Schwartz, D. (2014). *Moving toward a research informed conceptual model of engineering global preparedness.* American Society for Engineering Education Annual Conference and Exposition, Indianapolis, IN, June 2014.

Sutton, R. & Rubin, D.L. (2004). The GLOSSARI project: Initial findings for a system-wide research initiative on study abroad learning outcomes. *The Interdisciplinary Journal of Study Abroad*, 10, 65–81.

Teichler, U. (2015). The impact of temporary education abroad. In R. Mitchell, N. Tracy-Ventura & K. McMansus (Eds.), *Social Interaction, Identity and Language Learning during Residence Abroad*. Eurosla Monographs Series, 4 (pp. 15–32). Amsterdam: The European Second Language Association.

Tillman, M. (2012). Employer perspectives on international education. In D.K. Deardorff, H. de Wit, J.D. Heyl & A. Adams (Eds.), *The SAGE Handbook of International Higher Education* (pp. 191–206). Thousand Oaks, CA: SAGE.

Trooboff, S. & Berg, V. (2008). Employer attitudes toward study abroad. *Frontiers: The Interdisciplinary Journal of Study Abroad*, 15, 17–33.

Van Mol, C. (2017). Do employers value international education and internships? A comparative analysis of 31 countries. *Geoforum*, 78, 52–60.

Van Mol, C. & Timmerman, C. (2014). Should I stay or should I go? An analysis of the determinants of intra-European student mobility. *Population, Space and Place*, 20, 465–479.

Vande Berg, M., Paige, R. M. & Lou, K. (2012). *Student Learning Abroad: What Our Students Are Learning, What They're Not and What We Can Do About It*. Sterling, VA: Stylus Publishing.

Waibel, S., Petzold, K. & Rüger, H. (2018). Occupational status benefits of studying abroad and the role of occupational specificity: A propensity score matching approach. *Social Science Research*. doi:10.1016/j.ssresearch.2018.05.006

Waibel, S., Rüger, H., Etter, A. & Sauer, L. (2017). Career consequences of transnational educational mobility: A systematic literature review. *Educational Research Review*, 20, 81–98.

Wiers-Jenssen, J. (2003). Norwegian students abroad.: Experiences of students from a linguistically and geographically peripheral European country. *Studies in Higher Education*, 28, 391–411.

Wiers-Jenssen, J. (2008). Does higher education attained abroad lead to international jobs? *Journal of Studies in International Education*, 12, 101–130.

Wiers-Jenssen, J. (2013). Degree mobility from the Nordic countries: Background and employability. *Journal of Studies in International Education* 17, 471–491.

Yokota, M. (2016). Survey of global personnel development and long-term impact of study abroad. Research Project No. 25245078, School of Global Japanese Studies, Meiji University.

Yorke, M. (2004). Employability in the undergraduate curriculum: Some student perspectives. *European Journal of Education*, 39 (4), 409–427.

Zimmermann, J. & Neyer, F.J. (2013). Do we become a different person when hitting the road? Personality development of sojourners. *Journal of Personality and Social Psychology*, 105 (3), 515–530

# Part 4

# Institutional outcomes

For decades, international educators around the world have urged government officials and university leaders alike to prioritize education abroad programming as a means through which students can acquire 21st-century knowledge and skills. Although increasing student participation has often been confused as a goal rather than as a methodology through which to foster student learning outcomes, advocacy efforts have nevertheless been largely successful with capturing the attention of government and university leaders who have increasingly supported and invested in expanded education abroad programming. Today, these leaders may however be more responsive to advocacy efforts that position education abroad programming as a high-impact educational practice that contributes to advancing institutional outcomes, such as boosting student recruitment, retention and graduation rates, enhancing the undergraduate curriculum and the quality of education, and encouraging increased faculty engagement in international research and collaboration.

Deardorff and van Gaalen (2012) offer a useful framework in this regard by drawing a compelling connection between how an institution allocates resources for education abroad programming with desirable institutional outcomes, such as enhanced student success, expanded faculty international engagement, financial growth, enhanced reputation and global rankings, etc. Specifically, they framed the impact of internationalization around a logic model to demonstrate the importance of looking beyond student level outputs, such as the number of students studying abroad, to understanding broader institutional outcomes. In other words, institutions must determine what resources are needed to develop and implement specific activities that will generate measurable outputs (e.g., enrollment growth, diverse participations, etc.) and desirable institutional outcomes (e.g., retention and graduation rates, alumni loyalty, etc.). By allocating resources for education abroad specifically, institutions can achieve clear and measurable outcomes for the institution generally.

This fourth section, inclusive of three distinct chapters, focuses on the existing research examining institutional outcomes associated with education abroad and the implications that can be drawn for practice. Chapter 10, authored by John

Haupt and Santiago Castiello-Gutiérrez of the University of Arizona, begins by demonstrating a clear and positive relationship between education abroad participation and student success, as defined by first to second year retention rates and persistence to graduation. The chapter discusses emerging research demonstrating that education abroad participation is not only positively correlated with student success indicators but may actually be a causal variable in enhancing student success, an institutional outcome of high importance. The chapter also discusses the many financial benefits to an institution that come with investing in education abroad, specifically around alumni and donor giving. The authors also demonstrate that robust education abroad programming is an increasingly important factor influencing an institution's reputation, particularly with respect to national and global university rankings. As ranking schemes begin to factor education abroad metrics into calculations, it is to be expected that student decision making patterns when selecting an institution will be impacted.

In Chapter 11, Betty Leask and Wendy Green look specifically at internationalization of the undergraduate curriculum and challenges the mostly U.S. concept of *curriculum integration* by presenting the broader notion of a *continuum of integration*. Whereas curriculum integration has largely been focused on the integration of major-specific education abroad programming into undergraduate degree plans, these authors build a compelling case from existing research in this area which argues that broadly integrating international learning into the curriculum enhances student learning for all as opposed to only those students who engage in such programming. By integrating international learning into the curriculum at home, all students are able to engage in international and intercultural learning experiences. One end of the continuum focuses on leveraging education abroad for an exclusive minority of students and at the other universal international and intercultural learning is prioritized. Integrating international learning, whatever its form, enhances educational quality overall and contributes to graduating competent students who have a deeper understanding of the international nuances of their chosen disciplines.

The final chapter in this section, Chapter 12, looks at ways to encourage greater faculty engagement in education abroad programming. According to chapter authors, Betty Leask, Craig Whitsed, Hans de Wit and Jos Beelen, most international educators have long focused their efforts on students; after all, student learning and development is the *raison d'être* of higher education. However, faculty own and control the curriculum and any real success in further integrating education abroad into the curriculum is arguably found by working with, and through, the faculty. A key to working successfully with the faculty is to bridge international engagement with other driving factors that are of concern to the faculty, such as how to leverage education abroad programming as a means to support the faculty with shaping and realizing the international education goals they have for their students. Some faculty members on nine-month contracts may be attracted to summer salary supplements which may be available through faculty-directed programming, but many more will have an interest in how engagement in education abroad relates to promotion and tenure aspirations, research and funding opportunities, international and interdisciplinary research networks, and so on. Institutional support for faculty international engagement can be significant in attracting and retaining high-quality faculty and as this chapter demonstrates, also has the potential to enhance important student success metrics, internationalize the curriculum and boost international research output.

## References

Deardorff, D., & van Gaalen, A. (2012). Outcomes assessment in the internationalization of higher education. In D. Deardorff, H. de Wit, J. Heyl, & T. Adams (Eds.), *The Sage handbook of international higher education* (pp. 167–190). Thousand Oaks, CA: Sage.

# Chapter 10

# Institutional impact

## Degree completion, alumni giving, quality, and reputation

*John P. Haupt and Santiago Castiello-Gutiérrez*

### Highlights:

- Research has shown a positive relationship between Education Abroad (EA) participation and retention and degree completion.
- University alumni who participated in EA are more likely to donate to educational institutions than their peers who did not study abroad.
- Involvement in EA programs has pushed institutions to seek institutional accreditations from abroad as a form of legitimacy and quality assurance.
- EA programming has also been linked to institutional outcomes such as improved reputation and prestige as measured in international rankings and employers' surveys.

## 1. Introduction and chapter overview

Higher education institutions are increasingly considering how education abroad (EA) can support achieving broader institutional goals. Through an analysis of existing literature, this chapter demonstrates a mainly positive relationship between EA and four institutional outcome measures: student retention and degree completion, institutional finances, institutional policies, and prestige and reputation. The chapter also calls on practitioners to expand their conceptualization of EA's impact and to establish relationships across campus to better leverage EA programming to support and extend institutional goals. Lastly, it ends by identifying areas for future research needed to strengthen claims and produce generalizable findings on the broader institutional impact of EA.

The purpose of education abroad (EA) at higher education institutions (HEIs) is multi-faceted and has evolved over time. As previous chapters show, researchers have investigated the connection between EA and student development on key learning outcomes, such as academic development (Chapter 5), second language acquisition (Chapter 6), identity and affective skills (Chapter 7), intercultural and global competencies (Chapter 8), and career advancement (Chapter 9). While student growth and development is indeed an important outcome of EA, HEIs are increasingly considering how EA can be leveraged to support broader institutional goals. This expanded purpose for EA has emerged in part because of the increased pressure for institutional accountability by governing boards, regional and national governments, and students and their parents. However, capitalizing on EA's impact as an institutional outcome has been surprisingly absent from the literature and remains a confusing and contradictory conversation among practitioners. This chapter contributes to this conversation by framing the impact of EA in terms of HEIs' broader goals and discussing the impact and potential of EA to help institutions succeed in accomplishing their goals. The range of possible impacts and outcomes that EA can have at the institutional level is diverse. The scope of this chapter is limited to a review of common practices and academic literature around the relationship between EA and the following topics: retention and degree completion, institutional finances, institutional policies, and reputation and global standings. These topics are of central importance to HEIs throughout the world, and institutions use measures related to these topics to demonstrate institutional development, quality, and success. Thus, research findings on the relationship between EA and these topics can allow for advocates of EA to discuss the role it can play promoting broader goals of HEIs.

## 2. Key questions to be addressed

- To what extent is EA a high-impact experience that enhances and supports student retention and degree completion?
- What direct and indirect financial benefits do institutions receive as a result of student participation in EA?
- Are (and in what ways) institutional policies affected as a result of changing tendencies in EA?
- To what extent (if any) does EA participation affect institutional reputation and global standings?

## 3. Review of the literature

### 3.1 Education abroad, retention, and degree completion

Governments, particularly those in Western countries, have placed growing importance on increasing the number of students who persist through their studies and complete university degrees (Cherastidtham & Norton, 2018; European Commission, 2015b; Kolster & Kaiser, 2016). Governments investing in education want to ensure that HEIs are generating results that produce a highly educated and skilled workforce (Alexander, 2000) that can provide a competitive advantage in knowledge-based industries and contribute to sustainable economic growth (Kolster & Kaiser, 2016). As a result, higher education leaders and managers have started to prioritize and explore ways to increase degree completion rates (Cherastidtham & Norton, 2018; European Commission, 2015b; Kelly & Schneider, 2012; Kolster & Kaiser, 2016; Sneyers & De Witte, 2018). This has led to pressure for programs and activities to demonstrate how they directly relate to student learning and success (Seifert, Gillig, Hanson, Pascarella, & Blaich, 2014).

Within higher education, there continues to exist a widely held perception that EA participation will delay students' time to complete their degree. In the U.S. context, one study found that 46% of all students feared that participation in EA might delay their graduation (Xu, de Silva, Neufeldt, & Dane, 2013). Likewise, in the European context, Van Mol and Timmerman (2014) found that for some students, the fear of delaying their graduation was a factor that influenced them not to participate in EA. Although this view is still present on many campuses worldwide, research, primarily out of the U.S., has sought to demonstrate the impact that EA participation has on retention and degree completion. Utilizing samples from single institutions and U.S. state-wide higher education systems, studies have investigated differences in graduation rates between students who participated in EA and those who have not as well as whether participation in EA increases the probability of students graduating.

Scholars have investigated the link between EA participation, retention, and graduation by comparing the graduation rates of EA participants and non-participants. Researchers have demonstrated that, in general, a significantly higher proportion of students who participate in EA graduate in the expected number of years for degree completion (i.e. four, five or six years in the case of the U.S.) compared to their peers who do not participate in EA (Hamir, 2011; Malmgren & Galvin, 2008; O'Rear, Sutton, & Rubin, 2012). Additionally, participation in EA has been shown to increase the odds of graduating. At bachelor's degree institutions, research has shown that EA participation significantly increases the odds of graduating within five and six years (Hamir, 2011; O'Rear, Sutton, & Rubin, 2012; Xu, de Silva, Neufeldt, & Dane, 2013), and at technical or vocational institutions, research has demonstrated that EA participation increases the odds of being retained through the first and second year, earning a degree or certificate within three years, and transferring to a four-year institution within three years (Raby et al., 2014). Moreover, preliminary results from the Consortium for Analysis of Student Success through International Education (CASSIE), a U.S. federally funded inter-institutional collaborative research project, have shown that students who studied abroad are 10% more likely to graduate in four years compared to students who did not (Shiflet & Bhatt, 2019). These results taken together show that participation in EA does not slow a student's time to degree, but in fact, might actually increase the probability that a student will be retained and graduate within four, five, and six years at bachelor's degree granting intuitions and three years at technical or vocational institutions.

### 3.2 Financial impact of education abroad

Student participation in EA can financially impact an HEI directly and indirectly in both positive and negative ways. To date, there are few studies that have investigated the direct financial effects of EA to an HEI. For example, there are no

known empirical studies in the USA which have investigated the financial implications of direct enroll programs, or programs in which students pay tuition
directly to the foreign host institution, and how HEIs have the potential to
increase their net tuition revenue from hosting direct enroll students from abroad,
or possibly lose net tuition revenue if their students participate on direct enroll
programs at foreign institutions. Additionally, there are no known studies in the
USA investigating how EA is being leveraged as a recruitment tool to attract and
maintain high achieving students. For example, some institutions are offering EA
scholarships to recruit students instead of offering high cost tuition scholarships
and discounts. Part of the reason for a lack of research related to the direct financial benefits of EA is due to the variations in financial structures of universities
around the world, which would make it difficult to conduct analyses and generate
generalizable findings.

One increasingly common strategy for HEIs to generate revenue is to seek out
private sources of funding, including donations from university alumni (Perez-
Esparrells & Torre, 2012; Rohayati, Najdi, & Williamson, 2016). Although
research into this area is increasing throughout the world, most studies on the
topic are focused on the U.S. context. These studies have sought to establish
relationships between alumni giving and student characteristics, such as age, year
of graduation, income, occupation, gender, involvement in co-curricular and
extra-curricular activities, emotional attachment, and satisfaction with education
experience (Clotfelter, 2003; Monks, 2003; Moore, 2008). Additionally, through
attempts to understand the long-term impact of EA on students, researchers have
attempted to measure the impact of EA on alumni giving. Researchers have
examined the relationship between EA and alumni giving as part of studies that
investigate the association between co and extra-curricular activities and alumni
giving. Monks (2003), in an analysis of alumni giving at 28 U.S. institutions,
focused on the importance of student experiences on and off campus and found
that participation in EA was not significantly correlated with alumni giving.
Moreover, in an unpublished doctoral dissertation, Golz (2013) using the
National Survey of Student Engagement (NSSE), investigated the impact of
enriching education experiences (EEE), which includes activities such as EA,
international internships, and global service-learning, on alumni giving at a small
liberal arts college in the U.S. The findings of the study indicate a positive significant relationship between participation in EEE and alumni giving. Following a
similar methodology, Moore (2008) used NSSE data to analyze experiences on
campus and alumni giving rates at 45 U.S. institutions. Unlike Golz (2013),
Moore (2008) found a small significant negative correlation between participation
in EEE and alumni giving.

Additional research has focused exclusively on the relationship between EA and
alumni giving (Mulvaney, 2017; Murphy, Sahakyan, Yong-Yi, & Magnan, 2014;
Paige, Fry, Stallman, Josic, & Jon, 2009). These studies have investigated both
levels of alumni donations to society at large and levels of donations to the institution from which alumni graduated. Paige, Fry, Stallman, Josic, and Jon (2009)

investigated the impact of EA on student's global engagement and identified phi-lanthropic giving as one dimension of global engagement. They found that 37.6% of EA participants reported that their level of involvement in donating money was influenced by their participation in EA. Amongst the respondents who said they donated money, 50% indicated that they frequently or sometimes gave donations to educational organizations. Building on Paige et al. (2009) study, Murphy, Sahakyan, Yong-Yi, and Magnan (2014) investigated whether EA participants and non-participants donated to different types of organizations. They found that EA participants were significantly more likely to donate to organizations in the arts, education, environmental, human rights, international development, and social justice; whereas, non-EA participants were significantly more likely to donate to youth organizations and religious organizations.

Expanding upon the research conducted by Paige et al. (2009) and Murphy et al. (2014), Mulvaney (2017) investigated the long-term impact of EA on a select group of students, Honors program alumni. Mulvaney surveyed 78 Honors alumni who participated in EA and 87 who did not from a small liberal arts college in the U.S. seeking to gather information on how participation in EA impacted the student's future civic engagement behaviors, including self-reported donating behaviors to the university. Mulvaney found that 28% of alumni who participated in EA indicated they frequently provide financial assistance to the college; whereas only 17% of alumni who did not participate in EA reported the same behavior.

### 3.3 Institutional policies

Since EA is primarily an academic endeavor, academic policies related to the quality of the programs abroad and the recognition and transferring of credits earned abroad have a large indirect impact on HEIs. These policies promote or hinder a successful implementation of EA programs as well as the number of par-ticipating students in as much as EA programs push for flexibility on institutional policies. These policies tend to be established at the institutional level; however, there are some instances where policies have been implemented at national and supranational levels. A clear example of the latter was the creation and imple-mentation of the European Credit Transfer System (ECTS) which is used nowa-days as an international equivalent unit for measuring the volume of students' learning and workload across different countries (European Commission, 2015a). Students returning from academic studies abroad where the host institution is responsible for providing evidence of the student's performance, can transfer the credits earned while studying abroad. Other evolving institutional policies that have impacted EA programs are those related to requiring students to learn a language different from the institution's main language of instruction. HEIs with stronger foreign language teaching, tend to do better in the number of students participating in EA programs (Bartha & Gubik, 2018; Lau & Lin, 2017); how-ever, more research in this area is also needed. Specific policies at a national or supranational level are discussed more thoroughly in Chapter 13.

EA has also impacted other policies such as the ones measured by institutional accrediting agencies (in countries where there is no national institutional accreditation system). With an increasing number of students participating in short-term programs abroad in which students enroll in courses at foreign institutions, HEIs have started to question the quality of learning their students are receiving as they have no control over the teaching and grading. This concern has pushed institutions to become more selective when choosing an international partner to establish an EA program. Partly for this reason, the past decades have seen an exponential increase in universities seeking recognition from accrediting agencies outside their national borders (Blanco Ramírez & Berger, 2014; Blanco Ramírez, 2015a, 2015b). Accreditation from a known accrediting agency signals the quality of a program or institution, and HEIs often use this information to select partners for EA. In some cases, HEIs may choose to permit their students to study abroad and earn transferable credits only at institutions which share the same accreditation. Thus, obtaining accreditation provides HEIs with additional opportunities to develop EA programming for both inbound and outbound EA students.

### 3.4 Institutional reputation and prestige

The quest for international recognition has become almost an obsession for many HEIs (Brewer, Gates, & Goldman, 2002; Collins & Park, 2016; Hazelkorn, 2017). Internationalization in general, is seen as a tool to enhance the prestige or profile of an institution (Delgado-Márquez, Escudero-Torres, & Hurtado-Torres, 2013; Egron-Polak & Hudson, 2014). EA programs, as a prime tool for internationalization, may also be used by institutions to advance their prestige measured by their position in both world and national rankings. Most of the more renowned international rankings include two key indicators: reputation and international outlook. The former is measured by asking leaders at HEIs to name other institutions outside their country which they think are reputable, and the latter is measured by the presence of international faculty and students on campus as well as international research collaborations. For example, Times Higher Education's *World University Ranking* uses an international reputation survey to ask HEIs around the world to name other institutions known for their excellence in teaching (with a weight of 15% on an institution's overall grade) as well as institutions known for their research (18%). Moreover, at 7.5% of an institution's grade, it measures the proportion of international faculty and students on campus and the proportion of a university's journal publications with at least one international co-author. Thus, a total of 40% of an institution's ranking is dependent on its international reputation and outlook (Times Higher Education, 2019). Similarly, the QS world ranking allots 45% of its grade to a university's reputation in teaching and research and the proportion of international faculty and students on campus (QS, 2019). Recently, at a national level, the U.S. News & World Report launched a ranking of the "Top Colleges for Study Abroad" (US News, 2019). This ranking relies solely on the opinion of "college presidents, provosts and admissions deans … [who] are asked to nominate up to 15 schools … with stellar examples [of education abroad programs]" (US News, 2019). These examples demonstrate how both reputation and international outlook are key indicators that could potentially be improved by an institution's EA activities.

There are few empirical studies that demonstrate a direct impact on rankings and reputation of EA programs. Using a sample of 77 research universities in the U.S., Jang (2009) found a statistically significant and positive relation between the number of students who participated in EA programs (as reported by the Open-Doors survey) and their institution's reputation (measured by the peer assessment results of the US News and World Report 2005 ranking). In contrast, another study conducted using the Academic Ranking of World Universities (ARWU) and the Times Higher Education (THE) rankings found mixed results on the effect of the internationalization measures of an institution and its position on the ranking (Delgado-Márquez, Hurtado-Torres, & Bondar, 2011). The authors found that given the formulas used by these rankings, the most prestigious universities are less affected by their internationalization ratios than lower ranked institutions.

## 4. Evaluation of research methodology

Although limited in scope, the research presented above sheds light on the mostly positive relationship between EA and several institutional outcomes. However, there are several methodological limitations that need to be taken into consideration. The studies presented demonstrate the need for sophisticated statistical analyses through which researchers will be better able to isolate the impact of EA and control for factors that might also influence the outcomes under investigation (Haupt, Ogden, & Rubin, 2018). Additionally, there are still relatively few large-scale, multi-institutional, multi-country studies that are able to provide clear evidence on the relationship between EA and the outcomes discussed above. Moreover, in the retention and degree completion research as well as the alumni giving research, EA has been conceptualized as homogeneous. In the studies, there is no differentiation between program types, such as faculty-directed, exchange, or direct enroll programs and how these might lead to different outcomes. Also, there are no attempts to differentiate programs by the length of time a student is abroad or other programmatic features, such as living with a host family. Incorporating the differential effects of program type and program features is necessary to fully understand the impact that EA has on outcome measures. Finally, specifically regarding the studies from the broader field of higher education and alumni giving, none attempted to isolate the impact of EA by isolating it as a unique variable in their analyses. Each study in this category of research grouped EA participation with other types of on and off campus, co-curricular and extra-activities to form a single variable. This limits the generalizations that can be made regarding EA's impact on alumni giving as some alumni in the sample may not have participated in EA and only participated in other activities.

## 5. Implications for practice

The mostly positive relationship between EA and the institutional outcomes of student retention and degree completion, alumni giving, quality assurance, and institutional prestige and rankings can also provide practitioners with the ability to engage with members of their campus communities and outside stakeholders to demonstrate the broader impact that EA can have. However, due to the limitations associated with the research results presented, particularly their generalizability, practitioners should not attempt to overgeneralize the findings but instead should use the research as a guide to gather data at their own institutions which will allow them to present results to various stakeholders that best reflect the realities of their institution. In order to assist practitioners in the process, this chapter has provided suggestions related to the importance of reconceptualizing EA's impact, utilizing partnerships to collect and analyze data, and for developing options for alumni to donate to EA directly.

Some suggestions for practitioners include:

- *Expanding the conceptualization of EA's impact*: Traditionally, EA offices serve HEIs by managing and providing international education opportunities for students. The success of this work is usually tied to the number of students participating in programs and student learning outcomes. This chapter discusses the idea of EA serving HEIs in a much broader way, which ultimately requires practitioners to expand their understanding of their role on campus. The research points to external influences that are driving institutional policies, which means that for EA to support HEIs in achieving their goals, practitioners must become aware or remain up-to-date on the trends that are influencing institutional goal setting and decision making. By doing this, practitioners will be able to identify key priorities of the institution and use data to demonstrate how EA is helping an HEI achieve its goals. However, this is only possible if EA practitioners move beyond the traditional conceptualizations of the impact EA has and begin to prioritize how EA as an integrated part of the large campus community can be leveraged to help achieve broader institutional goals.
- *Partnering across campus for data collection and analysis*: The research discussed in this chapter requires data analysis techniques in which most practitioners have not received training as well as access to information that EA offices do not traditionally collect. For example, one can assume that most EA offices worldwide do not have access to information on alumni giving as it is out of the purview of an EA office's responsibilities. Additionally, practitioners do not have the time to engage in such research because of their already full workloads. Because of this, for EA practitioners to be able to gather and analyze data at their own institutions, they will need to partner with various individuals and offices across campus. Who or which offices practitioners should partner with will vary depending on the HEI; however, in order for practitioners to be able to demonstrate the broader impact of EA, these

partnerships are crucial and should be established and utilized by EA practitioners moving forward.

- *Developing a mechanism through which EA alumni can donate*: Since research demonstrates that students who participate in EA have a tendency to donate to educational organizations in the future, EA offices may benefit from engaging in fundraising activities with alumni to support operations or provide scholarships for students. This engagement can take the form of EA offices independently soliciting alumni donations, such as via their website, or collaborating with the office at their institution that manages fundraising to set up a specific fund for EA. Thus, instead of alumni donating to the university in general, past EA participants can specifically choose to donate to EA. EA offices can reach out to past participants to raise awareness of the opportunity to give, and EA offices can plant the seed of giving in the minds of students when they return from their experience abroad as a way to promote EA and help others have similar, enriching experiences abroad.

- *Just as EA programs must comply with institutional policies, such policies likewise need to adapt to serve the needs of evolving programs*: EA programs have evolved greatly since the traditional semester abroad. Institutions need to be flexible enough to accommodate innovative internationalization practices. Assessing students' learning and development should be prioritized over compliance with rigid academic policies, such as those on credit transfer, grading, and graduation requirements, among others, that were not designed with an experiential learning approach in mind.

- *EA programs are a tool to increase an institution's reputation and prestige*: Practitioners need to bear in mind that factors associated with EA programs such as who the international partners are, how they engage with their partners, the number of students participating, and the learning outcomes of participating students can enhance key indicators to advance their position in world rankings (Delgado-Márquez, Escudero-Torres, & Hurtado-Torres, 2013). Thus, practitioners should prioritize the cultivation of positive, mutually beneficial partnerships with universities abroad not only to benefit student learning but also to help enhance the reputation of one's university.

## 6. Directions for future research

There are numerous areas in which research can further and more strongly demonstrate a relationship between EA and broader institutional outcomes. Related to retention and degree completion, one area ripe for investigation is the impact that first year EA programs have on student retention from first to second year. First year experiences can be defined as an EA program that a student participates on during their first year at the university. Determining the impact of EA on retaining students from first to second year is important due to the large number of students who drop out of college during this time period. In the U.S., it is estimated that almost 30% of students drop out before they reach their second year (NSC Research Center, 2018), and recent reports from Australia indicate that roughly 15% of students drop out before they reach their second year (Burke, 2016). Thus, being able to establish a positive relationship between EA participation and first to second year retention can further demonstrate the value of EA for helping HEIs achieve their retention and degree completion goals.

There is also a need for studies that compare the effects of different EA program types and program features on institutional outcomes. Both researchers and practitioners recognize that variations in EA program types and program features can have differential effects on outcomes under investigation (Haupt & Ogden, 2019; Vande Berg, Connor-Linton, & Paige, 2009). For example, students who participate on short-term faculty-directed programs may have a vastly different experience abroad than students who participate on semester long exchange programs, which may lead to differences in learning outcomes, such as language proficiency. This same logic can be applied to research on retention and degree completion, alumni giving, and prestige and rankings. Such questions worth investigating may include: does the experience of studying abroad with a cohort of your peers and a faculty member from your institution lead to stronger feelings of attachment to your university, compared to a direct enroll program or exchange program at a foreign institution? Or does studying abroad, conducting research abroad, engaging in service-learning abroad, or interning abroad result in significantly different likelihoods of a student completing their degree in four, five, or six years? Understanding these differences can help practitioners identify the best program options for students to maximize the benefits of EA for broader institutional goals.

Moreover, there is a lack of empirical research that investigates the impact of EA on institutional finances either directly or indirectly. However, there is a long line of research that has investigated the financial implications of degree-seeking international students on HEIs from which EA scholars could borrow research methodologies (Kelly, 2012; Winkler, 1984; Zhang, Worthington, & Hu, 2017). Ideally, research in this area would engage in multi-country, multi-institutional studies that would allow for international generalizations to be made about research findings. Studies could investigate topics such as the implications of different types of programming on HEIs' financial structures and how changes in program types offered or the number of students participating in EA impacts those structures over time, financial incentives and disincentives for universities to offer certain types of EA programs, factors that make EA profitable or at least cash-neutral for a university, and opportunity costs for HEIs associated with EA.

Finally, more empirical research is needed to better understand how EA programming can be leveraged to enhance an institution's reputation or ranking position. Research in this area should be comprehensive and control for other institutional factors that affect the international outlook of a HEI. EA programs are often part of comprehensive institutional partnership agreements that include other types of programming, such as faculty exchanges or research collaborations. These additional types of programming may also impact the reputation and prestige of a university, and therefore, must also be accounted for in the analysis.

This chapter began with an assumption that HEIs, more than ever before, are leveraging EA to achieve broader institutional goals. Evidence is provided on how this expanded purpose for EA has emerged as a result of external pressures placed on HEIs from various stakeholders, such as federal governments and accrediting agencies. The chapter also discussed the impact of EA on four institutional outcome measures: retention and degree completion, institutional finances, institutional policies, and institutional reputation and prestige. The results of the literature review demonstrated a mostly positive relationship between EA and the four outcome measures. The results allow practitioners to engage in dialogue with various stakeholders across campus about the role EA can play in supporting broader institutional goals. However, the literature review also revealed that additional research is needed to ensure the generalizability of the findings and to better account for the variability in EA programming which may impact the outcomes under investigation.

In the end, the outcomes discussed in this chapter extend beyond the traditional ways that EA scholars and practitioners have conceptualized the impact of EA. They demonstrate that the role of EA offices on campuses is bigger than providing international learning opportunities for students. Helping to achieve broader institutional outcomes should not be seen as competing with traditional EA outcome measures, but instead, they should be seen as complimentary to them. In combination, they allow EA scholars and practitioners to demonstrate the scope of EA's impact and the important role that EA plays on university campuses worldwide. Moving forward, EA scholars and practitioners must engage with the wider campus community to identify ever changing institutional priorities to investigate and establish a relationship between EA and broader institutional goals.

## Further reading

Blanco Ramírez, G., & B. Berger, J. (2014). Rankings, accreditation, and the international quest for quality. *Quality Assurance in Education*. http://doi.org/10.1108/QAE-07-2013-0031

Mulvaney, K. (2017). The long-term impact of study abroad on honors program alumni. *Frontiers: The Interdisciplinary Journal of Study Abroad*, 29(1), 46–67.

O'Rear, I., Sutton, R. L., & Rubin, D. L. (2012). The effect of study abroad on college completion in a state university system. Retrieved from http://glossari.uga.edu/wpcontent/uploads/%0Adownloads/2012/01/GLOSSARI-Grad-Rate-Logistic-Regressions-040111.pdf

University System of Georgia. (2019). CASSIE: The Consortium for Analysis of Student Success through International Education. Retrieved from https://www.usg.edu/cassie

## References

Alexander, F. K. (2000). The changing face of accountability. *The Journal of Higher Education*, 71(4), 411–431.

Bartha, Z. & Gubik, A. S. (2018). Institutional determinants of higher education students' international mobility within the Erasmus Programme countries. *Club of Economics in Miskolc: Theory, Methodology, Practice*, 14(2), 3–13.

Blanco Ramírez, G. (2015a). International accreditation as global position taking: An empirical exploration of U.S. accreditation in Mexico. *Higher Education*. doi: doi:10.1007/s10734-014-9780-7

Blanco Ramírez, G. (2015b). Translating quality in higher education: US approaches to accreditation of institutions from around the world. *Assessment and Evaluation in Higher Education*, 40(7), 943–957.

Blanco Ramírez, G., & B. Berger, J. (2014). Rankings, accreditation, and the international quest for quality. *Quality Assurance in Education*. http://doi.org/10.1108/QAE-07-2013-0031

Brewer, D., Gates, S., & Goldman, C. (2002). *In pursuit of prestige: Strategy and competition in U.S. higher education*. New Brunswick, NJ and London: Transaction.

Burke, L. (2016, September 6). University attrition rates: Why are so many students dropping out? News.com.au. Retrieved from https://www.news.com.au/finance/work/careers/university-attrition-rates-why-are-so-many-students-dropping-out/news-story/3e491dd119e1249a5a3763ef8010f.8b5

Cherastidtham, I., & Norton, A. (2018). University attrition: What helps and what hinders university completion. Retrieved from https://grattan.edu.au/wp-content/uploads/2018/04/University-attrition-background.pdf

Clotfelter, C. T. (2003). Alumni giving to elite private colleges and universities. *Economics of Education Review*, 22(2), 109–120.

Collins, F. L., & Park, G. S. (2016). Ranking and the multiplication of reputation: Reflections from the frontier of globalizing higher education. *Higher Education: The International Journal of Higher Education Research*, 72(1), 115–129.

Delgado-Márquez, B. L., Escudero-Torres, M. A., & Hurtado-Torres, N. E. (2013). Being highly internationalised strengthens your reputation: An empirical investigation of top higher education institutions. *Higher Education: The International Journal of Higher Education and Educational Planning*, 66(5), 619–633.

Delgado-Márquez, B., Hurtado-Torres, L., & Bondar, N. (2011). Internationalization of higher education: Theoretical and empirical investigation of its influence on university institution rankings. *Revista de Universidad y Sociedad del Conocimiento*, 8(2), 265–284.

Egron-Polak, E., & Hudson, R. (2014). *IAU 4th global survey. Internationalization of higher education: Growing expectations, fundamental values*. Paris, FR: International Association of Universities.

European Commission. (2015a). ECTS key features. Retrieved from: http://ec.europa.eu/education/ects/users-guide/key-features_en.htm

European Commission. (2015b). Dropout and completion in higher education in Europe. Retrieved from https://cdn.studyinternational.com/news/wp-content/uploads/2016/01/ec.europa.eu_education_library_study_2015_dropout-completion-he_en.pdf

Golz, C. (2013). The impact of student engagement on alumni giving (Doctoral dissertation). The Chicago School of Professional Psychology. Available from ProQuest Dissertations and Theses database (UMI No. 3602956).

Hamir, H. B. (2011). Go abroad and graduate on-time: Study abroad participation, degree completion, and time-to-degree (Doctoral dissertation). University of Nebraska—Lincoln. Retrieved from https://digitalcommons.unl.edu/cgi/viewcontent.cgi?article=1065&context=cehsedaddiss

Haupt, J., & Ogden, A. C. (2019). Education abroad as a high impact practice: Linking research and practice to the cumulative collegiate experience. In E. Brewer & A. C. Ogden (Eds.), *Critical perspectives on education abroad: Leveraging the educational continuum*. Sterling, VA: Stylus Publishing, LLC.

Haupt, J., Ogden, A. C., & Rubin, D. (2018). Toward a common research model: Leveraging education abroad participation to enhance college graduation rates. *Journal of Studies in International Education*, 22(2), 91–107.

Hazelkorn, E. (Ed.). (2017). *Global rankings and the geopolitics of higher education: Understanding the influence and impact of rankings on higher education, policy and society*. Abingdon: Routledge, Taylor & Francis Group.

Ingram, M. (2005). Recasting the foreign language requirement through study abroad: A cultural immersion program in Avignon. *Foreign Language Annals*, 38(2), 211–222.

Jang, J. (2009). Analysis of the relationship between internationalization and the quality of higher education (Doctoral dissertation). Retrieved from ProQuest Dissertations and Theses.

Kelly, S. (2012). Economic impact of international students attending an institution of higher education in the United States (Doctoral dissertation). Louisiana State University, LA. Retrieved from http://etd.lsu.edu/docs/available/etd-01202012-124540/unrestricted/Economic_Impact_of_International_Students_S_Kelly.pdf

Kelly, A. P., & Schneider, M. (2012). *Getting to graduation: The completion agenda in higher education*. Baltimore, MD: Johns Hopkins University Press.

Kolster R., & Kaiser F. (2016). Study success in higher education. In C. Sarrico, P. Teixeira, A. Magalhães, A. Veiga, M. J. Rosa, & T. Carvalho (Eds.), *Global challenges, national initiatives, and institutional responses*. Rotterdam: Sense Publishers.

Lau, K., & Lin, C. (2017). Internationalization of higher education and language policy: The case of a bilingual university in Taiwan. *Higher Education*, 74(3), 437–454.

Malmgren, J., & Galvin, J. (2008). Effects of study abroad participation on student graduation rates: A study of three incoming freshman cohorts at the University of Minnesota, Twin Cities. *NACADA Journal*, 28(1), 29–42.

Monks, J. (2003). Patterns of giving to one's alma mater among young graduates from selective institutions. *Economics of Education Review*, 22(2), 121–130.

Moore, J. V. (2008). Predicting collegiate philanthropy student engagement as a correlate of young alumni giving. *Journal of the Student Personnel Association at Indiana University*, 39–55. Retrieved from https://scholarworks.iu.edu/journals/index.php/jiuspa/article/view/4655

Mulvaney, K. (2017). The long-term impact of study abroad on honors program alumni. *Frontiers: The Interdisciplinary Journal of Study Abroad*, 29(1), 46–67.

Murphy, D., Sahakyan, N., Yong-Yi, D., & Magnan, S. S. (2014). The impact of study abroad on the global engagement of university graduates. *Frontiers: The Interdisciplinary Journal of Study Abroad*, 22, 1–19.

NSC Research Center. (2018). Persistence & retention – 2018. Retrieved from https://nscresearchcenter.org/snapshotreport33-first-year-persistence-and-retention/

O'Rear, I., Sutton, R. L., & Rubin, D. L. (2012). The effect of study abroad on college completion in a State university system. Retrieved from http://glossari.uga.edu/wpcontent/uploads/%0Adownloads/2012/01/GLOSSARI-Grad-Rate-Logistic-Regressions-040111.pdf

Paige, R. M., Fry, G., Stallman, E. M., Josic, J., & Jon, J. (2009). Study abroad for global engagement: The long-term impact of mobility experiences. *Intercultural Education*, 20, S29–S44.

Perez-Esparrells, C., & Torre, E. M. (2012). The challenge of fundraising in universities in Europe. *International Journal of Higher Education*, 1(2), 55–66.

Quacquarelli Symonds (QS). (2019). World university ranking 2019. Methodology. Retrieved from https://www.topuniversities.com/qs-world-university-rankings/methodology

Raby, R. L., Rhodes, G. M., & Biscarra, A. (2014). Community college study abroad: Implications for student success. *Community College Journal of Research and Practice*, 38(2–3), 174–183. http://doi.org/10.1080/10668926.2014.851961

Rohayati, M. I., Najdi, Y., & Williamson, J. C. (2016). Philanthropic fundraising of higher education institutions: A review of the Malaysian and Australian perspectives. *Sustainability*, 8(6), 541. https://doi.org/10.3390/su8060541

Seifert, T. A., Gillig, B., Hanson, J. M., Pascarella, E. T., & Blaich, C. F. (2014). The conditional nature of high impact/good practices on student learning outcomes. *The Journal of Higher Education*, 85(4), 531–564. http://doi.org/10.1353/jhe.2014.0019

Shiflet, C., & Bhatt, R. (2019, March). *The proof is in the data: Harnessing the power of 'Big Data' to examine the effects of education abroad*. Paper presentation at the 15th annual meeting of the Forum on Education Abroad Conference, Denver, CO.

Sneyers, E., & De Witte, K. (2018). Interventions in higher education and their effect on student success: A meta-analysis. *Educational Review*, 70(2), 208–228.

Times Higher Education. (2019). World university ranking 2019. Retrieved from https://www.timeshighereducation.com/world-university-rankings/methodology-world-university-rankings-2019

US News and World Report. (2019). Programs to Look for. Retrieved from https://www.usnews.com/education/best-colleges/articles/programs-to-look-for

Van Mol, C., & Timmerman, C. (2014). Should I stay or should I go? An analysis of the determinants of intra-European student mobility. *Population, Space, and Place*, 20, 465–479.

Vande Berg, M., Connor-Linton, J., & Paige R. M. (2009). The Georgetown Consortium Project: Interventions for student learning abroad. *Frontiers: The Interdisciplinary Journal of Study Abroad*, 18, 1–75.

Winkler, D. R. (1984). The cost and benefits of foreign students in United States higher education. *Journal of Public Policy*, 4(2), 115–138.

Xu, M., de Silva, C. R., Neufeldt, E., & Dane, J. H. (2013). The impact of study abroad on academic success: An Analysis of first-time students entering Old Dominion. *Frontiers: The Interdisciplinary Journal of Study Abroad*, 23, 90–103.

Zhang, L. C., Worthington, A. C., & Hu, M. (2017). Cost economies in the provision of higher education for international students: Australian evidence. *Higher Education*, 74(4), 717–734.

# Chapter 11

# Curriculum integration

## Maximizing the impact of education abroad for all students

*Betty Leask and Wendy Green*

## Highlights:

- Education abroad is increasingly regarded as an insufficient approach to internationalizing student learning when it is conceptualized and practised as a discrete elective activity engaging a minority of students.
- Curriculum integration of education abroad may be conceptualized along a continuum, where the focus at one end of the continuum is on optional international studies for an exclusive minority of students, and at the other on inclusive, universal international and intercultural learning outcomes.
- A pedagogy for curriculum integration will be transformative (Mezirow, 1995) and experiential (Kolb 1984), intentionally designed to support all students to make sense of complex phenomena inside and outside the classroom.
- Curriculum integration in the context of education abroad requires a collaborative exercise of co-creation involving students, faculty, administrative staff and communities.

## 1. Introduction and chapter overview

The term 'curriculum integration' as it relates to education abroad is understood in different ways. Parcells and Woodruff (2016, np) describe the integration of education abroad into the curriculum as 'a variety of institutional approaches designed to fully integrate education abroad *options* (emphasis added) into the college experience and academic curricula for students in all majors'. Brewer and Cunningham (2009, p. 230) describe it as 'a vehicle for transforming faculty members, students, and educational institutions, *and* for teaching and learning abroad and at home', while Green and Mertova (2014, p. 670) describe it as 'the integration of students' *international learning experiences* into the curriculum at home for the benefit of *all students* (emphasis added)'. In this chapter different interpretations of the term *curriculum integration* are conceptualized as being on a *continuum of curriculum integration*. At one end of this continuum, there is a focus on 'exclusive integration'. Here the goal is to *maximize the international/ intercultural learning of students undertaking optional education abroad experiences*, a select minority. At the other end of the continuum, the focus is on 'inclusive integration'. Here the goal is *to maximize the international/inter-cultural learning of all students* by integrating mobile students' international experiences and intercultural learning into the curriculum at home. Approaches along the continuum are differentiated in terms of the focus of activities that are undertaken, the actors that are engaged in them and the scope of the impact of those activities.

At the 'exclusive integration' end of the continuum, strategy and activities are focused on maximizing opportunities for a small number of students to study abroad and on assisting those students to integrate their learning abroad into their life and learning experiences at home. This often occurs as an add-on to the main course of study and preparation, with support and returning home activities frequently organized and run by international office staff. The emphasis for faculty may be on matching course descriptions to determine if they will recognize credit earned abroad toward the home institution degree. Alternatively, they may be focused on the scheduling of course modules or units to create a 'mobility window', elective space for students to pursue a semester abroad without prolonging the duration of study required to complete the degree. International officers and faculty will often work together to negotiate options for education abroad with partner institutions. The primary goal of these activities is to optimize the learning for those who go abroad. The focus of international staff and faculty may be on interacting with the cohorts of mobile students who have returned in order to help them to make sense of the experiences they had whilst they were abroad. Students at this 'exclusive integration' end of the continuum will be focused on practical concerns (such as organizing their lives prior to departure, completing the work required of them while abroad and readjusting to life at home once they return) as well as on maximizing opportunities for learning through their international experience.

At the 'inclusive integration' end of the continuum the goal is not only to assist those who have been abroad to maximize their learning but to use their learning to enrich the learning of those who stayed at home. This goal requires different types of activity specifically designed to ensure that students and staff who have been abroad not only maximize their own learning but also share their experiences and their learning in meaningful ways with the students and staff who stay at home. For example, faculty may be involved in working collaboratively with colleagues in partner institutions to co-design rigorous education abroad curricula with the potential to enrich learning at home, as opposed to simply matching existing course descriptions. This 'inclusive integration' end of the continuum, invites efforts to include all students in some way in the education abroad experience. Perhaps those who stay at home are engaged in planning or in connecting with their mobile peers while they are abroad, interviewing them at different stages of the experience as part of a class project. When the mobile students return they may deliver seminars to their own or junior classes using the knowledge they gained while abroad as an activity. This in itself will enhance their own learning, as well as that of their peers, and may even encourage their peers to undertake an education abroad experience themselves. It is at this end of the continuum where there is the strongest alignment between curriculum integration and recent developments in integrative learning, international higher education and internationalization of the curriculum.

This chapter briefly discusses the limitations of existing approaches to education abroad and explores different interpretations of and approaches to curriculum integration in the context of recent trends in international higher education, and reimagines education abroad as a rich learning resource for all faculty, staff and students for the entire institution and the communities it serves. Finally, implications for practice and areas requiring further research are discussed.

## 2. Key questions to be addressed

- What are the limitations of existing approaches to education abroad?
- How might curriculum integration be re-conceptualized to harness the potential of education abroad to enrich all students' learning?
- What are the implications of this reconceptualization for practice?
- What are the implications for future research?

## 3. Review of the literature

There is abundant literature on education abroad written by researchers and scholar-practitioners from different countries, regions and types of institution. Much of this literature is focused on exploring ways to increase the number of students studying abroad and improve the learning of those who do.

### 3.1 Some limitations of existing approaches to education abroad

Education abroad is seen as an important component of an international education by governments and universities in countries across the world. Assumptions that studying abroad automatically deepens students' understanding of the world and themselves drive large numbers of faculty, staff and institutions worldwide to dedicate their time and energy to increasing the percentage of students who undertake part of their education abroad. Despite this effort however, education abroad today only engages a small percentage of students, often white, female and economically advantaged. Some argue that education abroad is inherently elitist, involving 'a selected group regarding social origin and mobility capital (exposure to international experiences)' (Wiers-Jenssen, 2011). Studies in Europe (Murphy-Lejeune, 2017) and Australia (Green et al. 2015) show the same tendency for mobility opportunities to attract those with higher levels of social and cultural capital. In this regard education abroad is seen by many as primarily an exclusive activity.

A number of studies also question the assumed impact of education abroad on students' learning, personal development and transformation (Pence & Macgillivray, 2008; Van Hoof & Verbeeten, 2005), cultural understanding (Dolby, 2007), linguistic development (Goldoni, 2013), academic benefits (Van Hoof & Verbeeten, 2005), and 'global citizenship' (Clarke et al. 2009; Mernard-Warwick & Palmer, 2012, see also Chapter 8, this volume). There is a range of practical guides to the many policy, operational and administrative tasks associated with these programmes, typically covering topics such as seeking approval through to evaluating the programme and all that is required in between, such as finances and budgets, managing risk and emergencies, handling logistics and preparing students and faculty for the abroad experience. However, there are 'few resources on designing rigorous education abroad curricula' (Pasquarelli, Cole & Tyson, 2017, p. 2).

Perhaps one of the strongest criticisms of approaches to international education has been the failure to better integrate education abroad and international experiences into the curriculum (Mestenhauser & Ellingboe, 1998). Historically, the gap between students' studies abroad and their curriculum at home has been wide. Clyne and Rizvi (1998) observed that once students returned from abroad, 'lecturers showed little or no ... interest in hearing about their exchange or any inclination to make use of the exchange experience' (p. 43). More recently, a US study found that students 'perceived no connection between their education abroad experiences and the curriculum at the home institution' (Hill & Green, 2008, p. 4) and a New Zealand study found only a few examples of academics linking education abroad to the curriculum at home in any way (Doyle et al., 2010). The cultural and linguistic knowledge students acquire through international travel (Gothard, Downey & Gray, 2012) is rarely recognized as valuable cultural capital that could inform the design and experience of learning at home.

Education abroad touches a small minority of students, and its impact on individuals is variable. Hence education abroad is increasingly regarded as an insufficient approach to internationalizing student learning *unless* it is integrated into the curriculum in such a way that it ensures students maximize their learning from their own education abroad experience and also bring that learning home to enrich the learning of their peers, the majority of whom will not have had the benefit of that experience abroad.

### 3.2 Reconceptualizing education abroad to enrich all students' learning

Broadly speaking, curriculum integration can be seen as an institutional response to the untapped educational potential of learning abroad. However, it is understood in various ways. At the most basic level, curriculum integration involves recognizing credit earned abroad toward home institution degrees, a practice which has been implemented for some time in many countries. In some cases, the concept of integration is taken further, to include the incorporation of coursework taken abroad into the academic context of the home campus [by] weaving study abroad into the fabric of the on-campus curriculum through activities such as course matching, academic advising, departmental and collegiate informational and promotional materials, and the structuring of degree requirements. (Forum on Education Abroad, 2015, p. 11)

Significantly, this definition aligns with the principles on which the European exchange scheme Erasmus+ is based (European Commission, 2014).

Some have long argued for more radical integration of education abroad into the formal curriculum; for example, thirty years ago Carlson, Burn, Useem and Yachamowicz (1990) envisaged faculty being more involved in linking education abroad to students' academic interests, by integrating it into students' majors, and a number of institutions now aim to fully integrate education abroad options into the curricula for students in all majors (Parcells & Woodruff 2016).

While these are positive developments, many such comprehensive and ambitious definitions of curriculum integration continue to target the minority of students who can travel abroad. In contrast, Brewer and Cunningham (2009, p. 230) argue that education abroad has the potential to impact more broadly on faculty members, students, and educational institutions, including those at home, while Green and Mertova (2014, p. 670) call for an approach to curriculum integration that will benefit all students. Thus, the literature suggests a *continuum of integration*. At one end of the continuum, the focus is on *exclusive integration* of optional international experiences for a minority of students), at the other on *inclusive integration* which maximizes the benefits of education abroad for all students and enables them to achieve *international and intercultural learning outcomes.* This suggests a shift towards conceptualizing approaches to curriculum integration as being on an *Integrated International Learning Continuum.*

It is useful to consider recent developments in integrative learning before discussing the concept of the continuum further. Rhodes (2010, p. 51) defines integrative learning as 'an understanding and a disposition that a student builds across the curriculum and co-curriculum, from making simple connections among ideas and experiences to synthesizing and transferring learning to new, complex situations within and beyond the campus'. Education abroad – as well as for example, multicultural education and service learning at home – place students in complex situations, where they can, with the appropriate support, integrate disciplinary knowledge with experiential insights (Newell, 2010). Additionally, curriculum integration can mean supporting students to integrate learning from courses not available at home and apply disciplinary knowledge and skills in new, unfamiliar contexts.

Integrative learning, thus understood, is consistent with the subtle but important developments in the broader field of internationalization of higher education. While education abroad has long been assumed to be the cornerstone of international higher education, the latter is now more clearly focused on the end goal of making a 'meaningful contribution to society' (de Wit et al. 2015) by focusing on the development of *all* students as 'global citizens' (Leask, 2015; Landorf, Doscher & Hardrick 2018). Internationalization at Home (IaH) was specifically devised as a strategy to address this aim. Wächter (2003) argued that education abroad and IaH should not be conceived as mutually exclusive activities, but rather, that the whole of education abroad and at home, 'is larger and more meaningful than the sum of its parts' (2003, p. 10). Leask (2015) also highlights the importance of being purposeful in the way student learning is supported in both the formal and informal curriculum at home and focusing specifically on how to enhance *all* students' international and intercultural learning as preparation for life in a globalized world. She argues that on campus and off campus informal learning activities organized for or by students are an important component of internationalization of the curriculum.

These recent developments in integrative learning, internationalization of higher education and internationalization of the curriculum suggest that 'curriculum integration' in relation to education abroad needs recalibration. First and foremost, it should be seen as a process specifically designed to enrich the international and intercultural learning of students who go abroad *as well as those who do not*.

## 4. Implications for practice

Improving the practice of curriculum integration – so that learning from education abroad is extended into the curriculum at home for all students – has implications for institutions as well as individual faculty, administrators and international officers, and the relationship between all of these actors.

The literature clearly suggests that if students are to develop global and intercultural knowledge, skills and attributes through education abroad, and then share that learning with students at home, their attainment of specific global learning outcomes needs to *designed for*, rather than assumed. While articulating intended learning outcomes (ILOs) is increasingly recognized as an important, if not critical, aspect of the curriculum design process, there is little agreement about what the ILOs of international education are, or should be. This issue will be discussed in more detail in the section on future directions for research. Here the discussion focuses on implications for the practice of curriculum integration at both ends of the continuum described in this chapter, and consideration of who needs to be involved in its realization.

### 4.1 Designing education abroad support programmes that foster deep global learning and prepare students to share that learning back home

Designing a successful education abroad programme to support the learning of even a small percentage of students is a complex project (Pasquarelli, Cole & Tyson, 2017). In order to foster deep global learning through education abroad, students need to be supported to reflect on their experiences while overseas and find ways to 'anchor' their new knowledge in the curriculum at home (Gothard, Downey & Gray, 2012). Jackson and Oguro (2018) note increasing calls for empirical research into what students actually learn while abroad and how to deepen that learning, along with calls from scholars for research-driven and theory based intercultural interventions in education aboard at all stages of the process. These should focus on guiding students, assisting them to make deeper connections between intercultural experiences, course work and course theory. When based on principles drawn from transformative (Mezirow, 1995) and experiential learning (Kolb, 1984) such guidance will enable students to recognize and make use of their experiences in foreign environments to develop greater awareness of self and others. They will be helped to 'build on structured experiences rather than classroom content' (Gothard et al., 2012, p. 5) and supported through the 'disorienting dilemmas' they confront while overseas in ways that enable them to critically question their assumptions and ultimately change the way they understand and interact with the world (Mezirow, 1995).

Two recent approaches to curriculum design for education abroad exemplify how these principles can be put into practice. The first, Gothard et al.'s (2012) 'Bringing the learning home' programme conceptualizes education abroad as a rite of passage. Inspired by van Gennep's work (2004, originally 1909), Gothard et al. (2012) argue that the experience of education abroad is analogous to that of initiates in traditional societies who move through a process of separation (from their old life), transition (through new, disorienting experiences), and finally incorporation (of new knowledge to be shared for the benefit of their community). Learning modules in this programme are designed to prepare students prior to their departure, orient them towards potential learning opportunities while abroad, and deepen and consolidate their learning once back home. Observing that 'failure to mark [students'] return often characterises the study abroad experience', Gothard et al. (2012, p. 16) give particular attention to the post-abroad period as an 'important opportunity to reinforce and validate global competence'.

Secondly, Townsin and Walsh's (2016) 'border-crossing pedagogy' presents a comprehensive model for international education curriculum design. This model weaves in post-intercultural theory, such as Giroux' (1992) concept of border crossing to challenge the current focus on intercultural competence and establish fresh conceptual territory in education abroad research. Moreover, Townsin and Walsh's 'border crossing pedagogy' encompasses encounters with the other/others at home as well as abroad. Thus, they avoid the reification of travel and open up the possibility of a pedagogy for border crossing for all students, both those who are able to travel (the minority) and those who are not (the majority). This possibility will be taken up below in the second implication for practice.

These two examples are indicative of recent developments in designing for deep learning through international education. Such programmes not only help the minority of students who go abroad consolidate and continue to develop their learning, they also prepare those students to share their learning with their peers at home. The design, teaching and support for such programmes have implications for faculty, international office staff, students, whole institutions (both host and home), and local communities (Brewer & Ogden, 2019).

## 4.2 Developing teaching and learning practices that support the integration of students' international and intercultural experiences into the curriculum at home

Studies in several countries have found that students are frustrated about the lack of opportunity to incorporate their cultural and linguistic knowledge into learning activities. For example, Heffernan et al.'s (2018) UK-based study concluded that faculty and curriculum committees charged with internationalizing the curriculum need to 'engage with student views effectively' in the process (2018, p. 14). Recent work on engaging 'students as partners' (SaP) in internationalization (Green, 2019a) provides one theoretically informed and empirically evaluated approach to engaging students as genuine contributors to the formal and co-curriculum. As a metaphor, SaP 'challenges traditional assumptions about the identities of, and relationships between, learners and teachers'; in practice, it repositions teachers and learners in relation to each other and to the work they undertake at university (Matthews, 2017, pp. 6–7). As an approach to curriculum design, SaP has been shown to value and use students' diverse cultural and linguistic perspectives, knowledge, skills and experiences for curriculum internationalization and enhanced global learning outcomes for all students (e.g., Green, 2019a). Green's analysis of 13 student–staff partnerships in internationalization – at home and abroad, in the formal and co-curriculum – shows that the students and staff involved in such partnerships became increasingly aware of, and interested in the impact of globalization in their lives, personally and professionally; more committed to pursuing global learning in the future; and more empathetic towards and interested in those considered culturally different from themselves. Inclusive curriculum integration of education abroad offers rich opportunities to engage SaP in curriculum co-design.

While the integration of students' rich cultural and linguistic knowledge into the formal and co-curriculum at home is an emergent practice, the current literature indicates that it must embrace the following principles;

- Curriculum integration must be based on a pedagogy for all students – the minority who are able to travel and the majority who are not (Townsin & Walsh, 2016).
- The curriculum at home must be experiential (Kolb, 1984) and transformative (Mezirow, 1995) in intent.
- Students must be positioned as genuine contributors to the internationalization of learning and teaching.

A number of studies have suggested the importance of collaboration between key stakeholders in teaching, learning and internationalization during the design of curricula. Hence, the application of these design principles should involve at least consultation, and ideally collaboration, between for example, faculty, students, learning designers and international office staff, as well as community organizations where appropriate.

### 4.3 Supporting broader engagement in curriculum design and production

Faculty 'are in the unique position of being able to support students' disciplinary and cultural learning by integrating the education abroad experiences of the small number of students into the learning and teaching programme at home' (Green & Mertova, 2014, p. 672). However, *requiring* faculty to integrate education abroad into the curriculum they teach – effectively asking them to teach differently, in areas they consider outside their expertise – is often met with resistance (Leask, 2015; Brewer & Cunningham, 2009). Engaging faculty in the integration of education abroad into the curriculum will require support for the active involvement of a broad range of actors in curriculum design and production.

An integrated, internationalized curriculum – whether specifically for those going abroad or for all students – is dynamic and multi-faceted and is necessarily co-constructed. Faculty, international staff and students all offer diverse perspectives of immense value for the task. The process of internationalization of the curriculum requires that everyone recognizes the value, and the limits, of their own, and others' cultural capital (Green, 2019b; Singh, 2010). In this space, no one can be regarded as the expert; rather new understandings need to be continually co-produced through discussion, debate and reflection, from the multiple perspectives of all those involved. International staff, international officers and students from diverse backgrounds are rich curriculum resources. Yet, all are largely excluded from curriculum internationalization processes in relation to the formal curriculum. Similarly, faculty and students are often excluded from the development of co-curricular programmes which therefore remain disconnected from the formal curriculum.

Fostering genuine collaborations between faculty, international office staff, students and even those external to the university will disrupt established assumptions about the processes of curriculum production and who is responsible for it. It will question traditional notions of academics' disciplinary identity and authority, based as it is on disciplinary expertise (Leask, 2013; Green, 2019a). Just as the emerging work on student–staff partnerships shows, the success of collaborations which include multiple stakeholders in curriculum design depend in large part on the development of shared understandings of how each can 'contribute equally, although not necessarily in the same ways' to the formal and informal curriculum (Cook-Sather et al., 2014, p. 6). There is little evidence of such collaborations in the education abroad literature (a fact which is considered in more depth in the final section of this chapter). However, future faculty-international office staff-student collaborations would do well to adopt good practice principles developed in the context of student–staff and community-student–staff partnerships, namely;

- fostering inclusion and power-sharing between those who are positioned differently within an institutionally and culturally entrenched hierarchy (Matthews, 2017);
- focusing on the process while accepting that outcomes may be uncertain (Matthews, 2017);

- negotiating a shared understanding of what any particular curriculum partnership means; 'partnership' is itself a cultural construct, so while there may be some shared meaning across cultures, disciplines, and occupations, 'partnership' can mean different things to different people (Green, 2019b);
- embracing cultural ignorance productively and creating spaces where each person is valued and empowered to actively participate in decision-making (Green, 2019b); and
- engaging in 'affable' conversations (Appiah, 2007) where participants can find common ground between apparent cultural, disciplinary or other differences.

### 4.4 Developing comprehensive policy and strategies that support the collaborative development and enactment of internationalized curriculum

Developing an integrated internationaliszd curriculum cannot be left to individual enthusiasts. As Klein (2005, p. 8) argues, integrative learning requires a systemic, whole-of-institution response involving the 'structures, strategies, and activities that bridge numerous divides ... experiences inside and outside the classroom, theory and practice, and disciplines and fields'.

Faculty, international office staff and students must be empowered, supported and recognized for their contribution to this work through institutional policies and strategies. One of the major barriers to curriculum integration is that curriculum, teaching and learning are often located in academic/disciplinary institutional silos (and the broader academic portfolio), and internationalization in another (the international office/international portfolio). To change this typical siloed scenario, institutions need to build an 'ethos that manifestly connects' the local, national and global dimensions of its mission, while at the same time, providing 'guidance and ensuring accountability' (Hudzik, 2011, p. 34). Building such an ethos can only occur through affable conversations involving faculty, other university staff and students. Curriculum integration will have little chance of success if it lacks 'support from those who are supposed to implement it and those who are supposed to benefit from it' (Landorf et al. 2018, p. 26).

## 5. Directions for future research

### 5.1 Comprehensive literature reviews of key terms as they are operationalized in the learning outcomes for an integrated internationalized curriculum

It is now commonly accepted that good curriculum design begins with defining what students are expected to achieve (their outcomes) before teaching takes place. Teaching activities, learning resources and assessment can then be designed in order to best support and measure those outcomes (Biggs, 2014) and to create relevant learning experiences. However, the intended learning outcomes of internationalization, whether through education abroad programmes or internationalization of the curriculum at home are typically ambiguous and/or difficult to measure. Practitioners debate the purpose of education abroad: is it 'intercultural learning? maturation? serious academic study?' (Brewer & Cunningham, p. xi). Likewise, faculty charged with responsibility for internationalizing degree programmes often feel under-confident when it comes to determining the outcomes for internationalization of the curriculum and designing for learning accordingly. As Rizvi and Lingard (2010, p. 173) observe,

> While the appeal of the idea of internationalisation of the curriculum appears ubiquitous it is not always clear what it means and how it might represent a new way of prioritizing and organizing learning.

To complicate the issue further, it is not possible to construct a universally relevant set of learning outcomes for international education. Various factors – disciplinary, institutional, local, national, regional as well as global – interact in different ways to drive and shape the way in which learning outcomes are defined, taught and assessed (Leask & Bridge, 2013), whether in the formal or co-curriculum. How it is to be operationalized needs to be decided in situ through a dialogic process involving all stakeholders.

Such conversations need to develop shared understandings of key concepts found in the discourse of international education (Landorf et al. 2018). Hence, one productive direction for future research would be systematic literature reviews that identify current descriptions of key constructs as they are operationalized in the learning outcomes of curricula in different disciplinary, institutional and geopolitical contexts. Such a resource could form a useful starting point for any curriculum team or indeed, a whole institution wanting to develop authentic and collaborative approaches to internationalizing learning and teaching.

## 5.2 Exploring more productive ways for faculty, international office staff and students to collaborate on curriculum integration

Articulating locally and globally relevant learning outcomes for internationalization and subsequently designing a curriculum that will enable students to reach these intended outcomes requires a team effort. Whilst having disciplinary relevance, such a curriculum must also target a different kind of learning, one that involves an interdisciplinary 'triple engagement' of knowing, acting and being – reflexively – in the world (Barnett & Coate, 2005). As argued above, internationalization, whether focused on deepening the learning of those students who travel abroad and/or extending that learning into the curriculum for all students calls for a paradigm shift in universities, a revaluing of experiential as well as different disciplinary knowledges, and therefore a revaluing of the contribution which the international office, other staff such as learning designers and academic developers, and students can make to curriculum design (Brewer & Cunningham, 2009; Green, 2019a). Such a paradigm shift points to the second direction for future research.

Multi-disciplinary team-based approaches to teaching and learning design are rare in the academy, and those examples available highlight a range of challenges as well as potential gains (e.g., Voogt et al., 2011). Leask's (2015) action research on engaging faculty revealed a range of individual, cultural and institutional barriers to collaborative approaches to internationalizing the curriculum. Emerging research on team-based curriculum design in e-learning – another area which demands expertise beyond that normally held by faculty – reveals similar barriers, but little concrete advice on effective collaboration (Burrell et al., 2015; Voogt et al., 2011). Recent work on 'students as partners', which puts forward a number of propositions for building ethical partnerships across the traditionally entrenched hierarchies between faculty and students (e.g., Cook-Sather et al. 2014; Matthews, 2017) will be relevant to those exploring broader collaborative possibilities in curriculum integration of education abroad. However, further research is needed to clarify the roles and expertise different stakeholders bring to integrating education abroad experiences into the curriculum and to seek out and learn from examples of good collaborative practice.

Amidst a growing sense of urgency to ensure that the transformative potential of international education is open to *all* students, inclusive integration of education abroad into the curriculum at home offers a promising way forward. This requires reimagining curriculum integration as a transformative learning resource for all faculty, staff and students – for the entire institution and the communities it serves. This must not be left to individual enthusiasts. Curriculum integration must be approached as a collectivist rather than individualistic enterprise, one that brings international office staff, students and faculty together in hitherto unheard of internal partnerships and alliances.

This chapter has identified both implications for practice and areas requiring further research. Perhaps the greatest implication for practice is the need for international officers, staff and faculty to recognize and respect the unrealized potential of education abroad for those at home and the important roles that they each play in the process of reimagining and re-enacting education abroad as a transformative experience for all students and staff.

## Further reading

Brewer, B. & Cunningham, K. (2009). *Integrating study abroad into the curriculum*. Sterling, VA: Stylus.

Green, W. (2019). Engaging students as partners in global learning: Some possibilities and provocations. *Journal of Studies in International Education*, 23 (1), 10–29.

Landorf, H., Doscher, S. & Hardrick, J. (2018). *Making global learning universal*. Sterling, VA: Stylus.

Leask, B. (2015). *Internationalizing the curriculum*. Abingdon: Routledge.

## References

Appiah, K.A. (2007). *Cosmopolitanism: Ethics in a world of strangers.* New York: Norton.

Barnett, R. & Coate, K. (2005). *Engaging the curriculum in higher education.* London and New York: Routledge.

Biggs, J. (2014). Constructive alignment in university teaching. In P. Kandlbinder (Ed.), *Review of higher education,* Vol. 1 (pp. 5–22). Hammondville, NSW: HERDSA.

Brewer, B. & Cunningham, K. (2009). *Integrating study abroad into the curriculum.* Sterling, VA: Stylus.

Brewer, B. & Ogden, A. (2019). *Education abroad and the undergraduate experience: Critical perspectives and approaches to integration with student learning and development.* Sterling, VA: Stylus.

Burrell, A.R., Cavanagh, M., Young, S. & Carter, S. (2015). Team-based curriculum design as an agent of change. *Teaching in Higher Education,* 20(8), 753–766. doi:10.1080/13562517.2015.1085856

Carlson, J., Burn, B.B., Useem, J. and Yachimowicz, D. (1990). *Study abroad: The experience of American undergraduates.* Westport, CN: Greenwood Press.

Clarke, I., Flaherty, T., Wright, N. & McMillen, R. (2009). Student intercultural proficiency: From study abroad programs. *Journal of Marketing Education,* 31(2), 173–181.

Clyne, F. & Rizvi, F. (1998). Outcomes of student exchange. In D. Davis & A. Olsen (Eds.), *Outcomes of international education: Research findings (a set of commissioned research papers presented at the 12 Australian International Education Conference, Canberra, 1998* (pp. 35–49). Canberra: IDP Education Australia.

Cook-Sather, A., Bovill, C. and Felten, P. (2014). *Engaging students as partners in learning and teaching: A guide for faculty.* San Francisco, CA: Jossey-Bass.

de Wit, H., Hunter, F., Egron-Polak, E. & Howard, L. (Eds.) (2015). *Internationalization of higher education: A study for the European Parliament.* Brussels: EU Parliament.

Dolby, N. (2007). Reflections on nation: American undergraduates and education abroad. *Journal of Studies in International Education,* 11(2), 141–156.

Doyle, S., Gendall, P., Meyer, L.H., Hoek, J., Tait, C., McKenzie, L., *et al.* (2010). An investigation into factors associated with student participation in study abroad. *Journal of Studies in International Education,* 14 (5), 471–490.

European Commission. (2014). Erasmus + Programme guide. http://sepie.es/doc/con vocatoria/2014/erasmus-plus-programme-guideen.pdf.

Forum on Education Abroad. (2015). Education abroad glossary. https://forumea.org/wp-content/uploads/2014/10/Forum-2011-Glossary-v2.pdf.

Giroux, H. (1992). *Border crossing: Cultural workers and the politics of education.* London & New York: Routledge.

Goldoni, F. (2013). Students' immersion experiences in study abroad. *Foreign Language Annals,* 46 (3), 359–376.

Gothard, J., Downey, G. & Gray, T. (2012). Bringing the learning home: Re-entry programs to enhance study abroad programs in Australian universities. www.olt.gov.au/project-bringing-learning-home-murdoch-2010

Green, W. (2019a). Engaging students as partners in global learning: Some possibilities and provocations. *Journal of Studies in International Education,* 23(1), 10–29.

Green, W. (2019b). Stretching the cultural-linguistic boundaries of 'students as partners'. *International Journal for Students as Partners,* 3(1), 84–88.

Green, W. & Mertova, P. (2014). Enthusiasts, fence-sitters and sceptics: Faculty perspectives on study abroad in Australia and the Czech Republic. *Higher Education Research & Development*, 34(4), 670–683.

Green, W., Gannaway, D., Sheppard, K. & Jamarani, M. (2015). What's in their baggage?: The cultural and social capital of Australian students preparing to study abroad. *Higher Education Research & Development*, 34(4), 513–526.

Heffernan, T., Morrison, D., Magne, P., Payne, S. & Cotton, D. (2018). Internalising internationalisation: Views of internationalisation of the curriculum among non-mobile home students. *Studies in Higher Education*, doi:10.1080/03075079.2018.1499716

Hill, B.A., & Green, M.A.( 2008). *A guide to internationalization for chief academic officers*. Washington, DC:American Council on Education.

Hudzik, J. (2011). *Comprehensive Internationalization: From concept to action*. Washington, D.C: NAFSA Association of International Educators.

Jackson, J. & Oguro, S. (2018). Enhancing and extending study abroad learning through intercultural interventions. In J. Jackson & S. Oguro (Eds.), *Intercultural interventions in study abroad* (pp. 1–17). Abingdon: Routledge.

Klein, J.T. (2005). Integrative learning and interdisciplinary studies. *Peer Review*, 7(4), 8–10.

Kolb, D. (1984). *Experiential learning: Experience as the source of learning and development*. Englewood Cliffs, NJ: Prentice-Hall.

Landorf, H., Doscher, S. & Hardrick, J. (2018). *Making global learning universal*. Sterling, VA: Stylus.

Leask, B. (2009). Using formal and informal curricula to improve interactions between home and international students. *Journal of Studies in International Education*, 13(2), 205–221. http://jsi.sagepub.com/cgi/content/abstract/13/2/205

Leask, B. (2015). *Internationalizing the curriculum*. Abingdon: Routledge.

Leask, B. & Bridge, C. (2013). Comparing internationalisation of the curriculum in action across disciplines: Theoretical and practical perspectives. *Compare: A Journal of Comparative and International Education*, 43(1), 79–101.

Lewin, R. (2009). *The handbook of practice and research in study abroad: Higher education and the quest for global citizenship*. New York and London: Routledge.

Matthews, K. (2017). Five propositions for genuine students as partners practice. *International Journal for Students as Partners*, 1(2), 1–9.

Mernard-Warwick, J. & Palmer, D. (2012). Eight versions of the visit to La Barranca: Critical discourse analysis of a study-abroad narrative from Mexico. *Teacher Education Quarterly*, Winter, 121–138.

Mestenhauser, J. (2011). *Reflections on the past, present and future of internationalizing higher education: Discovering opportunities to the meet the challenges*. Minneapolis: Global Programs and Strategy Alliance, University of Minnesota.

Mestenhauser, J. & Ellingboe, B. (1998). *Reforming the higher education curriculum: Internationalizing the campus*. Phoenix, AZ: American Council on Education/Oryx Press.

Mezirow, J. (1995). Transformation theory of adult learning. In M. Welton (Ed.). *In defense of the lifeworld: Critical perspectives on adult learning* (pp. 37–90). New York: State University of New York Press.

Murphy-Lejeune, E. (2017). *Student mobility and narrative in Europe: The new strangers*. Boca Raton, FL: CRC Press.

Newell, W. (2010). *Educating for a complex world: Integrative learning and interdisciplinary studies*. Washington, DC: Association of American Colleges and Universities.

Parcells, C. & Woodruff, G. (2016). Curriculum integration: Best practices. NAFSA. www. nafsa.org/Professional_Resources/Browse_by_Interest/Education_Abroad/Network_ Resources/Education_Abroad/Curriculum_Integration__Best_Practices/

Pasquarelli, S., Cole, R. & Tyson, M. (2017). *Passport to change: Designing academically sound, culturally relevant, short-term, faculty-led study abroad programs.* Sterling, VA: Stylus Publishing.

Pence, H.M. & Macgillivray, I.K. (2008). The impact of an international field experience on preservice teachers. *Teaching and Teacher Education*, 24, 14–25.

Rhodes, T. (2010). *Assessing outcomes and improving achievement: Tips and tools for using rubrics.* Washington, DC: Association of American Colleges and Universities.

Rizvi, F. & Lingard, B. (2010). *Globalizing education policy.* London & New York: Routledge.

Singh, M. (2010). Connecting intellectual projects in China and Australia: Bradley's international student-migrants: Bourdieu and productive ignorance. *Australian Journal of Education*, 54(1), 31–45.

Townsin, L. & Walsh, C. (2016). A new border pedagogy: Rethinking outbound mobility programs in the Asian century. In D. Valliarus & D. Coleman-George (Eds.), *Handbook of research on study abroad programs and outbound mobility* (pp. 215–247). Hershey, PA: IGI Global.

Van Gennup, A. (1960). *The rites of passage,* trans. M. Vizedom & G.L. Caffee. London: Routledge & Kegan Paul.

Van Hoof, H.B. & Verbeeten, M.J. (2005). Wine is for drinking, water is for washing: Student opinions about international exchange programs. *Journal of Studies in International Education* 9(1), 42–61.

Voogt, J., Westbroek, H., Handelzalts, A., Walraven, A., McKenney, S., Pieters, J. and de Vries, B. (2011). Teacher learning in collaborative curriculum design. *Teaching and Teacher Education*, 27, 1235–1244.

Wächter, B. (2003). An introduction: Internationalization at home. *Journal of Studies in International Education*, 7(1), 5–11.

Wiers-Jenssen, J. (2011). Background and employability of mobile vs. non-mobile students. *Tertiary Education and Management*, 17(2), 79–100.

# Chapter 12

# Faculty engagement

## Moving beyond a discourse of disengagement

*Betty Leask, Craig Whitsed, Hans de Wit and Jos Beelen*

### Highlights:

- Engagement of faculty in internationalization, including education abroad, has repeatedly been identified as a critical obstacle to institutions achieving their internationalization goals. This discourse of disengagement is problematic.
- Faculty engagement is complex and multifaceted with cognitive, emotional and behavioral dimensions. It is important for practitioners and researchers to explore this complexity in greater depth.
- Faculty engagement in education abroad is best approached as an integral part of broader institutional strategies that connect internationalization with teaching, research and service missions.
- In doing this it will be essential to challenge assumptions and strongly held beliefs about faculty motivation and the nature of engagement in order to move beyond the current problematic discourse of disengagement.

## 1. Introduction and chapter overview

There is general agreement in the literature that faculty play a vital role in higher education internationalization. However, faculty engagement has repeatedly been identified as an obstacle to institutions achieving their internationalization goals (Knight, 2004). Respondents in successive International Association of Universities (IAU) global surveys have suggested that faculty are insufficiently engaged in internationalization, and the reasons for this include lack of preparation, capacity and expertise.

This chapter looks at a specific aspect of faculty engagement: the engagement of faculty with education abroad. Faculty engagement in education abroad is constructed as a subset of their engagement in teaching, research and service activities associated with internationalization. Therefore, to gain insights into faculty engagement, two strands in the literature are considered: that related to faculty engagement in internationalization generally, and also the literature related specifically to faculty engagement in education abroad.

The chapter explores three dimensions of faculty engagement with education abroad: cognitive, emotional and behavioral. Strategies to address concerns with the level of faculty engagement in education abroad and their implications for policy makers and practitioners are discussed. The chapter concludes that engaging faculty in education abroad requires thinking differently about the very nature of engagement and the integration of education abroad into broader institutional strategies associated with teaching, research and service.

## 2. Key questions to be addressed

Drawing on contemporary literature on the internationalization of higher education, education abroad and faculty development, this chapter addresses the following questions:

- Why is faculty engagement in education abroad important?
- How engaged are faculty in education abroad?
- How might faculty engagement in education abroad be described?
- How can we better understand faculty engagement in education abroad?

## 3. Review of the literature

The literature review below informs answers to the key questions described above.

### 3.1 Why faculty engagement in education abroad is important

The literature on education abroad identifies numerous reasons why faculty engagement is important for education abroad.

First, faculty are seen to play a significant role in students' participation in education abroad. Stohl (2007) argues that the low level of student participation in education abroad is a key indicator of academics' lack of engagement. Education abroad in its various forms including study abroad, undergraduate research abroad, international internships and global service-learning, are often used as proxy measures of internationalization in higher education institutions, especially throughout Europe and the US. Hence levels of participation in education abroad assume high importance and much attention in strategy and planning documents.

Second, education abroad is associated with opportunities for significant learning opportunities for students. Outcomes may impact the intellectual, social and emotional growth of a student (Ritz, 2011), through the development of skills, knowledge and attitudes of relevance to future employment and life as 'global citizens' (Diamond, Walkley, & Scott-Davies, 2011). Mezirow (1991) argues that the perspectives and frames of reference through which individuals understand the world and themselves, are enabled by involvement in uncomfortable situations or what he terms, "disorienting dilemmas." Education abroad is essentially experiential in nature (Perry, 2011; Perry, Stoner, & Tarrant, 2012) and offers many disorienting dilemmas and enormous potential for transformative learning. However, effective programming, for which faculty are responsible, is important for student learning (Strange & Gibson, 2017). Furthermore, because faculty have also been identified as critical to student participation in education abroad, who can both explicitly and implicitly inspire and discourage their participation (Fielden et al. 2007; Malicki and Vaughn, 2004; Gore, 2009), it is crucial that faculty are supportive and actively involved in education abroad.

The third reason that faculty engagement is important is that faculty are in the "unique position of being able to support students' disciplinary and cultural learning by integrating it into curricula at home" (Green and Mertova, 2011, p. 672), thereby enriching all students' learning. Curriculum integration is discussed in more detail in Chapter 11 of this volume. In short, faculty engagement is critical not only to ensuring students go abroad, and make sense of that learning when they return but also in ensuring that their experiences enrich the curriculum 'at home' and hence the learning of the vast majority of students who do not go abroad.

In summary, faculty play a critical role before, during and after students' education abroad experiences (Gothard, Downey & Gray, 2012; Jackson & Oguro, 2018; Lou & Bosley, 2009). They have an impact on how students use their education abroad experience, on how they make sense of their experiences in the context of their past and their possible futures, and how they integrate them into their identity, their life, and their worldview (Rizvi, 2005).

The learning potential of education abroad, the central role that faculty play in programming and managing student learning, and the evidence suggesting that faculty exert significant influence on student decision-making in relation to participation in education abroad, means that faculty engagement is critically important to the success of education abroad.

### 3.2 A discourse of disengagement

The *Global Surveys* of the International Association of Universities (IAU) have consistently identified faculty engagement as one of the main obstacles faced by institutions in the achievement of their internationalization goals. To date, five Global Surveys have been undertaken and published, the first in 2003, the most recent in 2018, published in 2019. In her report on the 2nd Global Survey, Knight (2006) concluded that issues related to staff interest, involvement, expertise and recognition were the biggest obstacles to the implementation of internationalization. In the 3rd Global Survey (Egron-Polak & Hudson, 2014) lack of engagement, skills and expertise of faculty were again identified as significant obstacles to internationalization and in the 5th Global Survey (Marinoni, 2019), faculty engagement, together with language skills and faculty capacity, was once again identified as a significant impediment to internationalization. In summary, these surveys indicate that respondents in universities have a persistent perception of low levels of faculty engagement in internationalization over a 15-year period. The surveys do not, however, shed light on how the respondents, usually a senior international officer, or faculty themselves, understand *engagement* in internationalization, including education abroad, or how to improve faculty engagement.

A range of obstacles to and enablers of faculty engagement in internationalization, of which education abroad is one component, have been identified in the scholarly literature (Clifford, 2009; Childress, 2010; Friesen 2013; Leask 2015). Childress (2010, pp. 28–29), identifies six levels of engagement, ranging from champions, advocates, latent champions and advocates, to skeptics and opponents. Leask (2015) identifies *cultural blockers, institutional blockers and personal blockers* to faculty engagement. *Cultural blockers* derive from the values, beliefs and dominant ways of thinking in the discipline, and their influence on faculty priorities. For example, whether intercultural sensitivity and skills are regarded as peripheral or essential to success in the field and the extent to which "other ways of seeing the world" are considered relevant or interesting. *Institutional blockers* are those over which the institution has some control, such as the profile of the staff it employs, the type of support and development opportunities provided, and promotion criteria. *Personal blockers*, related to the "mindset, skillset and heartset" (Bennett, 2008) of individual faculty members may also influence the willingness of faculty to engage in internationalization activities, including the integration of education abroad into the curriculum (see Chapter 11).

In summary, the literature positions faculty as key players (Leask 2015), the "stewards" of internationalization across teaching, research and service agendas (Childress 2010, p. 27) but also as resistant to change, intransigent, unmotivated and lacking the required cognitive competence (Ellingboe, 1998; Bond, 2003; Green & Olson, 2003; Knight, 2006). This literature constitutes a discourse of faculty engagement in internationalization and it is at least as much about their *disengagement* as it is about their engagement.

This discourse of disengagement diminishes faculty, constructing them in large part as a problem, a major obstacle to internationalization due, in part at least, to their own deficiencies. The assumptions and traditional beliefs embedded in this discourse of educational researchers and scholar-practitioners require critical evaluation (Webster-Wright, 2009; Fairclough, 2013; Streitwieser and Ogden, 2016). They have affected how faculty are defined, the power they have and the decisions they make (Brockbank et al., 2002 in Webster-Wright, 2009). They may, therefore, have a negative impact on faculty engagement.

Discourse practices could also be used to reposition and empower faculty, bringing about social change through "conscious intervention" (Fairclough, 1992, p. 200). A positive discourse of faculty engagement requires an understanding of engagement from multiple perspectives including what it means to faculty, and the ways in which they are engaged that are not currently observed or measured. It also requires acceptance that current implicit assumptions about what constitutes engagement are insufficient or inappropriate in the light of precursors and drivers of engagement (Kahn, 1990). The discussion in the next section suggests ways in which the term "faculty engagement" might more usefully be understood, both in general terms and more specifically in relation to education abroad.

### 3.3 Describing faculty engagement in education abroad

One of the issues with describing "faculty engagement" is that there is no clear description or definition of "engagement" in psychological terms (Kahn, 2010), even though the term has been much used in teaching and learning literature. Barnett and Coate (2005) suggest engagement of staff is a measure of a successful curriculum, without describing what that engagement might look like. Is it participation? Enthusiasm? Commitment? Action? There have been a number of studies of faculty engagement in internationalization activities related to teaching, research and service (see for example, Childress, 2010; Leask, 2015; Nyangau, 2018). However, what faculty engagement looks like is not described in any detail in this literature either, although the assumption seems to be that "engagement" is a commitment to and active involvement in a range of activities, and that a number of factors support or inhibit faculty engagement.

In contrast, much has been written on the meaning of the term "student engagement." Cook-Sather, Bovill and Felton (2014, p. 101), citing literature from 2001 through to 2007, define "student engagement" as "serious interest in, active taking up of, and commitment to learning." Martin and Torres (2016, section I) discuss the multi-dimensional nature of engagement, the three dimensions being behavioral, emotional and cognitive engagement, all of which they argue may vary in intensity and duration, depending on a range of factors. This literature, in combination with the literature on faculty engagement, offers a useful framework for thinking differently about and describing faculty engagement in education abroad in the future.

Faculty engagement in education abroad might be considered across three dimensions:

- *Cognitive engagement* – the level of intellectual and academic interest faculty have in education abroad as a learning opportunity for their students and also for themselves;
- *Emotional engagement* – the balance of positive and negative emotional reactions faculty have to education abroad as a learning experience for their students and for them;
- B*ehavioral engagement* – the extent to which faculty participate in activities related to education abroad.

Forms of engagement may then be described in different ways such as: 'understanding of the learning potential' (cognitive engagement), 'belief in the power of' (emotional engagement); and 'leadership of' education abroad activities, at home or abroad (behavioral engagement). Cognitive engagement might take various forms such as connecting with faculty abroad, integrating education abroad learning into the curriculum at home (see Chapter 11), or reading literature on education abroad; emotional engagement might take the form of urging or supporting students or other faculty to participate in education abroad; and behavioral engagement might be demonstrated by organizing or leading activities.

In summary, faculty engagement in education abroad may be described as complex and multifaceted with cognitive, emotional and behavioral dimensions. Some forms of engagement will be less apparent than others, but all will be based on a commitment to the learning possibilities education abroad offers to students and faculty.

Recognizing that faculty may be engaged in education abroad in a variety of hitherto overlooked or undervalued ways suggests ways to better understand faculty engagement in the internationalization of education abroad as well as internationalization more generally.

### 3.4 Understanding faculty engagement in education abroad

A number of participatory action research projects conducted over the last decade have found that faculty engagement at institutional and programme level is influenced to a large degree by disciplinary, institutional, national, regional and global contexts (Clifford 2009; Childress 2010; Leask & Bridge 2013). Education abroad is a central component of institutional strategies, and is also connected to internationalization of the curriculum, hence the following discussion focuses on practical strategies to engage faculty in education abroad across a wide range of activities cognitively, emotionally and behaviorally.

*Cognitive engagement.* Levels of intellectual and academic interest in education abroad are influenced by a number of factors. Academic leadership, emanating from the words and actions of leaders including the president, heads of discipline and respected colleagues are important influencers. Anderson and Johnson (2006) found that key leaders in faculties and schools "influence, motivate and enable" the practices of their colleagues (pp. 2–3). Green and Mertova (2011) found that faculty involved in education abroad in Australia and the Czech Republic valued support provided by leaders for them to teach and research for short periods overseas.

In a study undertaken at the University of Minnesota, Beatty (2013) found that lecturers considered experiences abroad meaningful for their professional development when they provided them with new knowledge, greater opportunities for collaboration and research, and enhanced intercultural skills. Green and Mertova (2011) also found that faculty valued cross-cultural training before departure and guided reflection upon return from their experiences abroad for the purpose of teaching and research.

On the negative side, faculty may be discouraged from engaging in education abroad if they consider it lacks intellectual rigor and academic quality. In the Netherlands some faculty saw education abroad as having a negative impact on students' progress through a course of study (Statistics Netherlands, 2018). In a US study, faculty who were concerned that the academic quality of education abroad was inferior to that at home were less likely to be engaged (Childress, 2010).

These studies suggest that to increase cognitive engagement faculty need to understand and respect the academic content of the programmes that students undertake whilst they are abroad, as well as the theories and concepts on which the programme is based. They need to value the learning that students will bring home from the experience. This is more likely when they have a direct connection with those who design and teach the programmes, or they are connected in some way to faculty in the host organization. It suggests that engaging faculty in education abroad must go well beyond mechanistic curriculum/content matching activities. It also makes sense to provide opportunities for faculty to strengthen and build international academic connections as part of education abroad program development because it is also possible that it will benefit research and scholarship beyond the immediate programme.

*Emotional engagement*, the balance of positive and negative emotional reactions faculty have to education abroad as a learning experience is also influenced by several factors. While the prior international experience of faculty may logically be seen as a positive influence on a faculty members' emotional engagement with education abroad, Woodruff (2009) found that a "faculty member's own prior international experience" alone did not result in their encouraging students to study abroad (pp. 5–6). Mestenhauser (2011) highlighted the moderating effect of faculty dispositions (qualities of mind and character) over which formal education may have a significant influence, but over which travel, employment and relationships with cultural others at home and abroad are also influential. Dispositions are relevant to the questions of if, and to what extent, faculty will engage emotionally with internationalization, including education abroad.

Another factor of importance identified in the literature is the perceived alignment between the institutions' motivations for education abroad and student learning. Friesen (2013) found that where lecturers viewed the institution's motives to be chiefly focused on the university's reputation and economic returns, rather than on promoting intercultural understanding and enhancing educational quality, they were less likely to support education abroad. Green and Mertova (2011) found Australian academics were more likely to be engaged in education abroad if it were not seen as an end in itself but as a means to an end, and Childress (2010) concluded that institutions needed to connect institutional goals for internationalization with the scholarly agendas of faculty.

These studies suggest that increasing faculty members' emotional engagement requires awareness of and attention to their disposition towards 'others' which will have an impact on the extent to which they see personal and academic value in interacting with and learning about and from culturally different ideas and people. Supporting faculty to travel to international conferences and to teach and research with colleagues from different cultural backgrounds, and rewarding them for it through the tenure and promotion processes, are possible ways to influence faculty dispositions worthy of further investigation.

Institutions also need to ensure that they demonstrate integrity in their approach to education abroad. The setting of seemingly random targets, unrelated to academic goals, is not likely to result in high levels of emotional engagement and may in fact result in disengagement.

*Behavioral engagement* in education abroad may both stimulate cognitive and emotional engagement, and be stimulated by cognitive and emotional engagement. Faculty may engage in behaviors such as encouraging students to undertake education abroad opportunities; organizing short trips and managing relationships with partners; teaching abroad; inviting returning students to share reflections on their experiences formally in class; and designing or redesigning programmes specifically to enable students to spend a semester abroad without interruption to their study plan. These activities provide valuable opportunities to deliberately and strategically stimulate cognitive and emotional engagement.

It may also be useful to understand behavioral engagement as an outcome of cognitive and emotional engagement; and cognitive and emotional engagement as precursors to or pre-requisites for behavioral engagement. This may lead to different types of strategies being employed to support faculty engagement.

A multi-dimensional understanding of faculty engagement in education abroad suggests a number of implications for practice, described in the next section.

## 4. Implications for practice

The implications for practice described below provide starting points for institutions to move away from the current deficit discourse of faculty engagement in education abroad. They are grounded in the existing literature but also suggest the need for significant changes in ways of thinking about, talking about and supporting faculty engagement in education abroad. A more positive discourse will privilege faculty agency and control over the ways in which they and their students engage cognitively, emotionally and behaviorally in education abroad. It will simultaneously support faculty and students across these three domains of engagement.

### 4.1 Engage faculty as partners

Childress argues that engagement in internationalization requires knowledge, skills and attitudes as well as institutional support (Childress, 2010). It is beyond the scope of this chapter to discuss the specific knowledge, skills and attitudes identified as desirable and/or required for faculty to be involved in education abroad. Suffice it to say they are wide-ranging and the knowledge, skills and attitudes each faculty member brings with them will be different, influenced by their unique personal and professional experience and disciplinary culture, which will interact with the institutional culture and context in unique ways. Ultimately however, as Kahn (2010, p. 22) observes, "people engage when, on balance, it matters to do so." For faculty it is more likely to "matter" if education abroad is seen to have a positive impact on their students' learning, that is, on the quality of education they provide to their students. It is important, therefore, that faculty have many opportunities to communicate with program leaders in partner institutions to ensure they have a sound knowledge of and respect for the academic work students will undertake while they are abroad. These interactions are rich opportunities for professional learning and personal growth. It is important to involve faculty in conversations and negotiations around research partnerships and teaching programmes at an early stage, and to sustain those conversations.

A key determinant of engagement is meaningful collaboration across and within organizational groups (Khan, 2010). Thus it is important to propagate and sustain an environment marked by a sense of "we" in both internal and external conversations around education abroad. This is essentially engaging staff as agentic partners in education abroad, rather than occasional participants or respondents. Faculty will "look for signals" to see if leaders are actually interested in internationalization, value their perspectives, welcome them as experts and respected partners, and are curious about and interested in their views and in what they are doing (Cook-Sather, Bovill & Felten, 2014; Kahn, 1990).

### 4.2 Make education abroad matter

Faculty engagement begins with a strong institutional narrative that provides a clear, shared vision for the institution and the place and value of education abroad as a core dimension of its purpose and mission. Green and Mertova (2011) identified potential for increased faculty *buy-in* if the institutional narrative provides a clear line of sight between faculty, education abroad, the espoused values of the institution and educational outcomes for students. A clearly expressed narrative, which explains the purpose of education abroad in the context of the institution, why it is important, and the role of faculty (MacLeod & Clarke, 2012) is essential.

Policy and strategy development provide the institutional framework within which conversations around education abroad, student learning outcomes and curriculum design take place. Voice is at the heart of engagement (Kahn, 2010). The development of institutional policy around education abroad, including the setting of goals and targets, should be an enabling conversation, one in which the voices of faculty are heard and the agency and resources they need to implement policy are recognized. Institutional policies and strategies should communicate a clear educational rationale for education abroad developed in collaboration with, rather than in isolation from, faculty.

If education abroad is indeed a core part of the internationalization strategy, faculty will expect not only to be consulted but also to see institutional leaders:

- aligning efforts and resources with strategy;
- helping people grow to support achievement of the strategy;
- providing support and recognition for faculty participation where appropriate;
- promoting and encouraging teamwork and collaboration;
- empowering individuals to lead and participate in existing initiatives and innovation. (Based on the Development Dimensions International, 2005.)

### 4.3 Approach education abroad as a continuing professional learning opportunity for faculty as well as students

Professional development is widely recognized as a driver of engagement (Kahn, 1990). Webster-Wright (2009) argues that continuing professional learning (CPL) occurs through "practice, experience and critical reflective action within contexts that may pose dilemmas; that CPL is situated, social and constructed … and support for CPL should reflect these assumptions" (p. 724). While ways to capture and evaluate the transformative power of education abroad for students are often discussed, in comparison little consideration has been given to the transformative potential of education abroad programmes for faculty, and therefore of the need to engage them as whole people in their "knowing, acting and being." In essence, professional learning for faculty in education abroad should be as much about ontology (who the professional is) as it is about epistemology (what the professional knows), seeking first to listen to, then engage them emotionally and cognitively as well as behaviorally.

Approaching education abroad as an opportunity for faculty to participate in transformative continuing professional learning, rather than as a means to an end (an increase in the number of students participating in education abroad programmes) is consistent with the findings of a number of studies involving faculty in internationalization of the curriculum which found that, "internationalizing the academic self" is a precursor to faculty engagement in internationalizing the curriculum, and parochialism amongst faculty impedes their ability to internationalize the curriculum at home (Sanderson, 2008).

What might this look like in practice? Institutional partnerships would be built from and around faculty teaching, research and service interests, rather than being primarily built around institutional agendas or organized by external providers, in isolation from the academic programme. At the very least, faculty with responsibilities for teaching and research would be included in negotiations and discussions in the early stages so that the education abroad experience for students is constructed as an integral part of a broader and deeper academic relationship, rather than an end in itself.

### 4.4 Support faculty to use education abroad as an opportunity to improve the quality of the programme provided to all students

An important aspect of curriculum integration, a concept discussed in detail in Chapter 11, is the integration of the learning of students who are abroad, or who have recently returned, into the curriculum at home. There is a pressing need to "engage academics in ongoing conversations about the place of study abroad in the contemporary university, including its integration with the curriculum at home" (Green & Mertova, 2011, p. 681). This requires the active involvement of a broad range of actors in curriculum design and production. Staff and faculty from teaching and learning units, professional developers and learning designers all have important contributions to make in ensuring education abroad experiences are integrated into the curriculum at home in ways that enrich the learning of all students.

The options are many and include, for example, "returning home" seminars in which students share reflections on their experiences and learning of specific relevance to the programme of study with their peers. Faculty may connect home and abroad students and facilitate structured online conversations around key course themes while one group are abroad and others are at home. Students who are abroad can create online blogs on core topics in a course which can later be used as valuable learning resources. Such options offer rich possibilities for deep learning for all students as well as faculty. Nyangau (2018) highlighted the importance of intrinsic rewards for faculty engagement. Rewards that are focused on improving the quality of all students' learning are effective intrinsic rewards for faculty that are likely to increase cognitive and emotional engagement.

## 5. Directions for future research

There are numerous possible research directions and questions raised by the discussion above. A few are proposed here.

First and foremost, rigorous studies that investigate the nature of cognitive, emotional and behavioral engagement specifically in relation to education abroad would provide greater clarity on the concept itself. Such studies should be led by faculty in cross-disciplinary teams (e.g. psychology, human resources, education) to ensure they have academic credibility with faculty.

The extant literature on faculty engagement in education abroad draws heavily upon educational research and observations made by practitioners and researchers exploring faculty participation in and commitment to aspects of higher education internationalization, including education abroad. Future research should continue not only to explore links between international education research in different areas such as internationalization of the curriculum at home and faculty engagement in education abroad but also connect with research in areas outside international education. For example, the literature on employee engagement from the management and human resources disciplines may offer more nuanced understandings of the dynamic interactions between higher education institutions as organizational structures and faculty as employees performing roles and duties within complex workplace settings. Further exploration of this literature may illuminate drivers of engagement that have hitherto been overlooked across the discourses of faculty engagement in education abroad specifically, and higher education internationalization more generally. In summary no single theoretical or disciplinary lens is likely to be sufficient to gain a full understanding of complex issues in internationalization, such as faculty engagement in education abroad.

There is also need for scholarly investigation of interventions to engage faculty in collegial conversations leading to successful education abroad programmes, including local action research projects. The work of Childress (2010) and Landorf, H., Doscher, S. and Hardrick, J. (2018) are two examples of detailed case studies of single institutions in the US which have provided valuable insights into faculty engagement. More such studies are needed in different national and institutional contexts. It is also important to engage directly with faculty to explore their views on education abroad in comparative international studies such as that of Green and Mertova (2011).

Collation of existing and new case studies could usefully be employed to explore answers to the following questions:

- What international and intercultural learning outcomes related to education abroad do faculty value for their students?
- What frameworks and models have been successfully used by leaders and SIOs to give faculty a voice in education abroad programme negotiations? What principles can be deduced from successful models?
- What intrinsic and extrinsic rewards do faculty gain from the different ways they engage in education abroad programmes, in comparison with other forms of international engagement?

Faculty engagement in education abroad is a complex issue in its own right, best approached as an integral part of broader institutional strategies that connect internationalization with teaching, research and service missions. This requires challenging assumptions and strongly held beliefs about faculty motivation and the nature of engagement, drawing on international and interdisciplinary research, which is inclusive of multiple perspectives, and approaching education abroad as a rich learning opportunity for students, faculty and staff rather than an end in itself.

## Further reading

Beatty, M. (2013). Factors influencing faculty participation in internationalization at the University of Minnesota's Schools of Nursing and Public Health: A case study (Doctoral dissertation). Minneapolis, University of Minnesota.

Friesen, R. (2013). Faculty member engagement in Canadian university internationalization: A consideration of understanding, motivations and rationales. *Journal of Studies in International Education* 17(3), 209–227.

Green, W., & Mertova, P. (2011). Engaging the gatekeepers: Faculty perspectives on developing curriculum for globally responsible citizens. In V. Clifford, & C. Montgomery (Eds.), *Moving towards internationalisation of the curriculum for global citizenship in higher education* (pp. 69–92). Oxford: The Oxford Centre for Staff and Learning Development.

Kahn, W. A. (1990). Psychological conditions of personal engagement and disengagement at work. *Academy of Management Journal*, 33(4), 692–724.

## References

Agnew, M. (2013). Strategic planning: An examination of the role of disciplines in sustaining internationalization of the university. *Journal of Studies in International Education*, 17(2), 183–202. doi:10.1177/1028315312464655

Anderson, D., & Johnson, R. (2006). Ideas of leadership underpinning proposals for the Carrick Institute: A review of proposals for the leadership for excellence in teaching and learning program. Australian Learning & Teaching Council (ALTC). Retrieved from www.altc.edu.au/resource-ideas-of-leadership-underpinning-proposals-altc-2006

Barnett, R., & Coate, K. (2005). Engaging the curriculum in higher education. *British Journal of Educational Studies*. doi:10.1111/j.1467-8527.2008.00402_3.x

Beatty, M. (2013). Factors influencing faculty participation in internationalization at the University of Minnesota's Schools of Nursing and Public Health: A case study (Doctoral dissertation). Minneapolis, University of Minnesota.

Bennett, J. M. (2008). On becoming a global soul. In V. Savicki (Ed.), *Developing intercultural competence and transformation: Theory, research, and application in international education* (pp. 13–31). Sterling, VA: Stylus.

Bond, S. L. (2003). *Engaging educators: Bringing the world into the classroom, guidelines for practice*. Ottawa: Canadian Bureau for International Education.

Bond, S. L., Qian, J., & Huang, J. (2003). *The role of faculty in internationalizing the undergraduate curriculum and classroom experience* (CBIE research millennium series, Research Paper No. 8 ed.). Ottawa: Canadian Bureau for International Education.

Brewer, E., & Leask, B. (2012). Internationalization of the curriculum. In D. Deardorff, H. de Wit, D. Heyl & T. Adam (Eds.), *The Sage handbook of international higher education* (pp. 245–266). Thousand Oaks, CA: Sage.

Childress, L. K. (2010). *The twenty-first century university: Developing faculty engagement in internationalization*. New York: Peter Lang Publishing Group.

Clifford, V. (2009). Engaging the disciplines in internationalising the curriculum. *International Journal for Academic Development*, 14(2), 133–143.

Cook-Sather, B., Bovill, C., & Felten, P. (2014). *Engaging students as partners in learning and teaching: A guide for faculty*. San Francisco, CA: Jossey-Bass.

Development Dimensions International. (2005). Predicting employee engagement MRKSRR12–100. Development Dimensions International, Inc., MMV. Retrieved from www.ddiworld.com

Diamond, A., Walkley, L., & Scott-Davies, S. (2011). *Global graduates into global leaders*. London: Council for Industry and Higher Education (CIHE). Retrieved from www.ncub.co.uk/index.php?option=com_docman&view=download&category_slug=publications&alias=43-global-graduates-into-global-leaders-executive-summary&Itemid=2728

Egron-Polak, E., & Hudson, R. (2014). *Internationalization of higher education: Growing expectations, essential values. IAU 4th global survey report*. Paris: IAU.

Ellingboe, B. (1998). Divisional strategies to internationalise a campus portrait. In J. Mestenhauser & B. Ellingboe (Eds.), *Reforming higher education curriculum: Internationalising the campus*. Phoenix, AZ: Oryx Press.

European Union. (2014). *The Erasmus impact study: Effects of mobility on the skills and employability of students and the internationalisation of higher education institutions*. Brussels: EU.

Fairclough, N. (1992). *Discourse and social change*. Cambridge: Polity Press.

Fairclough, N. (2013). *Critical discourse analysis: The critical study of language*. Abingdon: Routledge.

Fielden, J., Middlehurst, R., & Woodfield, S. (2007). *Global horizons for UK students*. London: CIHE.

Friesen, R. (2013). Faculty member engagement in Canadian university internationalization: A consideration of understanding, motivations and rationales. *Journal of Studies in International Education*, 17(3), 209–227.

Gacel-Ávila, J., Bustos-Aguirre, M., & Celso Freire, J. (2017). Student mobility in Latin America and the Caribbean: Latest trends and innovative programs. In H. de Wit, J. Gacel-Ávila, E. Jones, and N. Jooste (Eds.), *The globalization of internationalization: Emerging voices and perspectives* (pp. 61–72). Abingdon: Taylor & Francis.

Giovanangeli, A., Oguro, S., & Harbon, L. (2018). Mentoring students' intercultural learning during study abroad. In J. Jackson & S. Oguro (Eds.), *Intercultural interventions in study abroad* (pp. 88–102). New York: Routledge.

Gore, J. E. (2009). Faculty beliefs and institutional values: Identifying and overcoming these obstacles to education abroad growth. In R. Lewin (Ed.), *The handbook of practice and research in study abroad: Higher education and the quest for global citizenship* (pp. 282–303). New York: Routledge.

Gothard, J., Downey, G., & Gray, T. (2012). *Bringing the learning home: Programs to enhance study abroad outcomes in Australian Universities*. Sydney: Office for Learning and Teaching, Australian Government.

Green, M. F., & Olson, C. (2003). *Internationalizing the campus: A user's guide*. Washington, DC: ACE.

Green, W., & Mertova, P. (2011). Engaging the gatekeepers: Faculty perspectives on developing curriculum for globally responsible citizens. In V. Clifford & C. Montgomery (Eds.), *Moving towards internationalisation of the curriculum for global citizenship in higher education* (pp. 69–92). Oxford: The Oxford Centre for Staff and Learning Development.

Green, W., & Whitsed, C. (Eds.) (2015). *Critical perspectives on internationalising the curriculum in disciplines: Reflective narrative accounts from business, education and health*. Rotterdam: Sense Publishers.

Jackson, J., & Oguro, S. (2018). *Intercultural interventions in study abroad*. New York: Routledge.

Kahn, W. A. (1990). *Psychological conditions of personal engagement and disengagement at work. Academy of Management Journal*, 33(4), 692–724.

Kahn, W. A. (2010). The essence of engagement: lessons from the field. In S. Albrecht (Ed.), *Handbook of employee engagement: Perspectives, issues, research and practice* (pp. 20–30). Cheltenham: Edward Elgar Publishing.

King, R., Findlay, A., & Arens, J. (2010). *International student mobility literature review: Report to HEFCE, and co-funded by the British Council, UK National Agency for Erasmus*. London: Higher Education Funding Council for England.

Knight, J. (2004). Internationalization remodeled: Definition, approaches, and rationales. *Journal of Studies in International Education*, 8(1), 5–31. doi:10.1177/1028315303260832

Knight, J. (2006). *Internationalization of higher education: New directions, new challenges. 2005 IAU global survey report*. Paris: International Association of Universities.

Landorf, H., Doscher, S. and Hardrick, J. (2018). *Making global learning universal: Promoting inclusion and success for all students*. Sterling, VA: Stylus.

Leask, B. (2008). Teaching for learning in transnational courses and programs. In L. Dunn and M. Wallace (Eds.), *Teaching in transnational higher education* (pp. 120–132). Melbourne: Routledge.

Leask, B. (2013). Internationalizing the curriculum in the disciplines: Imagining new possibilities. *Journal of Studies in International Education*, 17(2), 103–118.

Leask, B. (2015). *Internationalizing the curriculum*. London: Routledge.

Leask, B., & Beelen, J. (2010). Enhancing the engagement of academic staff in international education. In *Proceedings of a joint IEAA-EAIE symposium* (pp. 28–40). Melbourne: International Education Association of Australia.

Lou, K., & Bosley, G. (2009). Dynamics of cultural contexts. In V. Savicki (Ed.), *Developing intercultural competence and transformation* (pp. 276–296). Sterling, VA: Stylus.

MacLeod, D., & Clarke, N. (2012). Engaging for success: Enhancing performance through employee engagement. Retrieved from http://dera.ioe.ac.uk/1810/1/file52215.pdf

Malicki, R., & Vaughn, L. (2004). Promoting outbound exchange. ISANA International Education Association. Retrieved from www.isana.org.au/index. php?option=com_con tent&view=category&layout=blog&id=38&Itemid=60&limitstart=5

Marinoni, G. (2019). *5th IAU global survey, internationalization of higher education: An evolving landscape locally and globally*. Berlin: DUZ Academic Publisher.

Martin, J., & Torres, A. (2016). *User's guide and toolkit for the surveys of student engagement: The High School Survey of Student Engagement (HSSSE) and the Middle Grades Survey of Student Engagement (MGSSE)*. Washington, DC: National Association of Independent Schools. Retrieved from www.nais.org

Mestenhauser, J. (2011). *Reflections on the past, present and future of internationalizing higher education: Discovering opportunities to meet the challenges*. Minneapolis: University of Minnesota.

Mezirow, J. (1991). *Transformative dimensions of adult learning*. San Francisco: Jossey-Bass.

Nyangau, J. (2018). A qualitative study of faculty motivations of engagement in internationalization (Doctoral dissertation). Kent State University.

Perry, L. (2011). A naturalistic inquiry of service-learning in New Zealand classrooms: Determining and illuminating the influence on engagement. (Doctoral dissertation). University of Canterbury, Christchurch, New Zealand.

Perry, L., Stoner, L., & Tarrant, M. (2012). More than a vacation: Short-term study abroad as a critically reflective, transformative learning experience. *Creative Education*, 3(5), 679–683.

Ritz, A. (2011). The educational value of short-term study abroad programs as course components. *Journal of Teaching in Travel & Tourism*, 11(2), 164–178.

Rizvi, F. (2005). Identity, culture and cosmopolitan futures. *Higher Education Policy*, 18 (4), 331–339.

Saarikallio-Torp, M., & Wiers-Jenssen, J. (Eds.) (2010). *Nordic students abroad: Student mobility patterns, student support systems and labour market outcomes*. Helsinki: The Social Insurance Institution of Finland.

Sanderson, G. (2008). A foundation for the internationalization of the academic self in higher education. *Journal of Studies in International Education*, 12(3), 276–307.

Sandström, A.-M., & Hudson, R. (2018). *The EAIE barometer: Internationalisation in Europe* (2nd ed.). Amsterdam: EAIE.

Statistics Netherlands. (2018, January 23). Studiepuntmobiliteit hoger onderwijs 2015/16 [Credit mobility higher education 2015/16]. Retrieved from www.cbs.nl/nl-nl/maa twerk/2018/04/studiepuntmobiliteit-hoger-onderwijs-2015-16

Stohl, M. (2007). We have met the enemy and he is us: The role of the faculty in the internationalization in the coming decade. *Journal of Studies in International Education*, 11(3), 359–372.

Strange, H., & Gibson, H. J. (2017). An investigation of experiential and transformative learning in study abroad programs. *Frontiers: The Interdisciplinary Journal of Study Abroad*, 29(1), 85–100.

Streitwieser, B., & Ogden, A. C. (2016). Heralding the scholar-practitioner in international higher education. In B. Streitwieser & A. C. Ogden (Eds.), *International higher education's scholar-practitioners: Bridging research and practice* (pp. 19–38). Oxford: Symposium Books.

Sursock, A. (2015). *Trends 2015: Learning and teaching in European universities*. Brussels: European University Association.

Webster-Wright, A. (2009). Reframing professional development through understanding authentic professional learning. *Review of Educational Research*, 79, 702–739. doi:10.3102/0034654308330970

Woodruff, G. (2009). *Curriculum integration: Where we have been and where we are going* (Internationalizing the curriculum and campus paper series). Minneapolis: University of Minnesota, Office of International Programs.

# Part 5

# Societal outcomes

For the concluding section of this book, we stop and ask ourselves one critical, remaining question. After all the considerations around the purposes, goals, values and aspirations for why students, administrators and institutions should engage in and support education abroad, is it worth it if it does not leave a positive imprint on society? Anecdotally, few people question that engaging in education abroad could be anything but positive. But, as some of the chapters in the previous sections have shown, empirically documenting that value added in valid and measurable ways is much more challenging (Velliaris & Coleman-George, 2016; Deardorff, DeWit, Heyl & Adams, 2012). When thinking about the broader impact of education abroad programming on society, multiple factors intersect: the global impact of student mobility, its impact on countries, communities, institutions and individuals, and its interpersonal impact on participants' academic development, intercultural competency, and changed personal perspectives (Braskamp, Braskamp & Merrill, 2009; Sutton & Rubin, 2004). These factors add up not just to leave an impression on the person who is engaging in international learning but also on those involved in facilitating that learning, administrators and host communities.

The first chapter in this section by Adinda van Gaalen, Jeroen Huisman and Ravinder Sidhu looks at national policies on education abroad outcomes. Reflecting on the values of people, planet and prosperity articulated in the UNESCO's 2030 Sustainability Development Goals, they consider the unintended consequences and negative aspects of education abroad. That is an unusual and much needed approach for a field that is too often patting itself on the back (a theme we return to in our Conclusion). The authors find that despite national policies for education abroad and increasing participation, social and economic inequality is still being reproduced in some of the current programming and practices. While they find growing efforts to make education abroad more inclusive, it is less clear whether policy initiatives are truly advancing education abroad while also fostering diversity and inclusion, environmental sustainability and economic equality. The authors argue that further research is needed to understand why there remains a noticeable disconnect between national policies on education abroad and progress that needs to be made on sustainability, inclusion and diversity.

The second chapter in the section, on host community impact by Christopher Ziguras and John Lucas, looks at the still relatively understudied issue of how education abroad impacts local hosting communities. The authors find that the learning objectives of education abroad activities today have become increasingly diverse and reflective of the wider range of participating institutions, disciplines, destinations and also that the nature of host community engagement varies significantly. How universities engage with their host communities is mediated by whom they partner with in-country, which in turn has a significant impact on shaping the success of the international engagement experience. While community impacts have largely been overlooked in the past, international education professionals have more recently become eager to take steps to ensure positive impact on both sides. Shaping this impact will require greater reflection on the differences and similarities between the social worlds that students inhabit, and an openness to learning about the experience of others in the process. Explicit consideration of the positioning of the host community, partner institutions and visiting students can go a long way to improving the overall quality of engagement. While the field still has much to understand about the needs of the many diverse communities with which students engage, choosing local partners carefully and establishing close working relationship with them can foster more mutually beneficial interactions.

Together, both of the chapters in this section articulate that while many aspects of international education today are being done right and the field has come a long way, some trouble spots also remain that still need to be addressed. Programming and practice need to continue paying careful attention to how they can sensitively address issues related to environmental sustainability and inclusion and diversity, and providers must continue to foster interactions with their host communities that will make the experience of engagement mutually beneficial.

## References

Braskamp, L. A., Braskamp, D. C., & Merrill, K. (2009). "Assessing progress in global learning and development of students with education abroad experiences." *Frontiers: The Interdisciplinary Journal of Study Abroad*, 18, 101–118.

Deardorff, D. K., de Wit, H., Heyl, J. D., & Adams, T. (Eds.) (2012). *The SAGE handbook of international higher education*. Thousand Oaks, CA: Sage.

Sutton, R. C., & Rubin, D. L. (2004). "The GLOSSARI project: Initial findings from a system-wide research initiative on study abroad learning outcomes." *Frontiers: The Interdisciplinary Journal of Study Abroad*, 10, 65–82.

Velliaris, D. M., & Coleman-George, D. (Eds.) (2016). *Handbook of research on study abroad programs and outbound mobility*. Adelaide: IGI Global.

# Chapter 13

# National policies on education abroad outcomes

## Addressing undesired consequences

*Adinda van Gaalen, Jeroen Huisman and Ravinder Sidhu*

### Highlights:

- National policies on education abroad are widely present, and there is a focus on quantitative goals but very little attention on measuring impact.
- Education abroad policies are mostly stand-alone policies that do not generally refer to related policy fields such as environmental protection and equal opportunities.
- Inclusion is an exception, because it is increasingly addressed in education abroad policies at national and supranational levels, particularly in Europe and North America.

## 1. Introduction and chapter overview

Since the 1970s, national governments, and at a later stage individual higher education institutions (HEIs) and supranational organizations, started to develop policies, programs and strategies for education abroad (de Wit, Hunter, Howard, & Egron-Polak, 2015). Existing programs are inspired by various rationales, ranging from diplomacy and capacity building to motivations related to improving academic quality and economic benefits (Helms et al., 2015, pp. 7–9), and supported by various policy instruments, including regulation (e.g. credit recognition), information (e.g. study portals for education abroad) and funding (e.g. grants for students).

With increasing numbers of students participating in education abroad programs, it is tempting to declare these policies successful. Indeed, research often indicates that this form of internationalization leads to positive effects for students, HEIs, and nation states (see e.g. Clarke, 2014; Deloitte Access Economics, 2015; Richard et al., 2017). But at the same time, these studies are also criticized, both from a methodological (limited amount of longitudinal research and quasi-experimental designs, impact primarily being based on subjective perceptions, see e.g. Tarrant et al., 2013, p. 154) and conceptual perspective (focus on the positives, not the potential downsides and inconveniences of education abroad, see e.g. Trahar et al., 2016). This chapter particularly focuses on such undesired consequences or downsides of education abroad. As it is impossible to list all undesired impacts, the chapter uses three United Nations (UN) values presented in the 2030 agenda for sustainable development as a lens. The first value, *people*, states that 'all human beings can fulfil their potential in dignity and equality.' In higher education this is, among other things, related to striving for inclusion and diversity. The second value, *planet*, aims to 'protect the planet from degradation,' which refers to environmentally sustainable actions. The third value, *prosperity*, advocates that 'all human beings can enjoy prosperous and fulfilling lives,' which in terms of higher education could be translated into (economic) equality (United Nations, 2015).

Using this lens, the following issues frequently emerge in the literature. First, education abroad may homogenize rather than diversify education and experience. Partner institutions are often selected from among a limited number of preferred countries and their most valued HEIs (EAIE, 2013). In addition, curricula and languages of some countries are often preferred over others, reflecting historical, geopolitical, cultural and institutional relations rather than an attempt to get acquainted with less familiar countries (Sidhu & Dall'Alba, 2017). This results in ample opportunities for some, and fewer opportunities for other countries, including their HEIs and students, thereby reinforcing global inequalities. Second, education abroad is generally known to have a negative effect on environmental sustainability due to the high level of fossil fuel consumption and carbon emissions caused by travelling (Dvorak et al. 2011). Third, education abroad appears to benefit particularly those who are already privileged in their system (Lörz, Netz, & Quast, 2016). Some HEIs actively promote education abroad as a strategy of distinction (Sidhu & Dall'Alba, 2017) rather than as an opportunity for all. This promotion may enhance even further the reproduction of social and economic inequality (see also Chapters 1 and 2, this volume).

This chapter focuses on a selection of countries on three different continents: Europe, North America and Asia. The point of departure is to paint a broad picture with examples from across the globe. Europe is included because national policies on education abroad are common, partly as a result of European supranational education abroad programs. In North America, education abroad has been advocated at institutional level and by professional organizations for decades. Finally, the sheer population size and demography of Asia is an important reason to include this region as well. Without aiming at representativeness for their region, this chapter analyzes the policy rationales and initiatives of three distinctly different countries – in terms of the scope and nature of their engagement with education abroad – in each region. In recognition of the fact that internationalization of higher education (IoHE) is increasingly taking place in a global context, the section includes supranational policies, where they exist.

Although the term 'education abroad' is used throughout this chapter, it should be noted that national policies use a mix of terms for education abroad activities. These include, for instance, study abroad, student mobility, outbound mobility, learning abroad, student exchange and internship (abroad), global education and international education. This chapter is built on a search of the most relevant policy documents that have addressed education abroad through websites of ministries or departments of (higher) education, internationalization agencies and in the academic literature. It looked at two major elements of existing education abroad policies (Helms et al., 2015): its ideology (general goals, a set of guiding ideas) and its practical elements (a plan for action). Searching for relevant academic literature in both Web of Science and Scopus, search criteria were based on the previously mentioned terms in combination with terms such as 'higher education, policy, national, Europe, North America and Asia.' Although the research relied mainly on literature in English, since evaluations of national policies can be written in the national language, some documents in German and Spanish were also consulted.

## 2. Key questions to be addressed

This chapter explores three key questions:

- What do education abroad policies on national and supranational levels aim to achieve?
- What roles do respect for diversity and inclusion, environmental sustainability and economic equality play in these policies?
- Which (supra)national policy initiatives are promising in terms of advancing education abroad while serving diversity and inclusion, environmental sustainability and economic equality?

## 3. Review of the literature

Despite arguments and claims about the homogenization of internationalization policies – of which education abroad is often a part of – there is considerable variety in how national governments and supranational bodies view and operationalize education abroad (see e.g. Brooks, 2018). These are illustrated below in the following sections.

### 3.1 Europe

The specific domestic contexts of countries and their higher education systems, e.g. official language(s), level of economic development, size of the systems, investments in higher education, (perceived) levels of quality of education, all affect how and when governmental internationalization policies were shaped (see e.g. Huisman & Van der Wende, 2004). This is also visible in the more specific education abroad policies (Brooks, 2018).

#### Rationales

For the United Kingdom (UK), policies cannot be separated from the long-standing attention to higher education as an "export industry," with considerable emphasis on attracting fee-paying overseas students (see e.g. Lomer, 2018). Other rationales, related to foreign policy and diplomacy and to development coopera- tion are important, but are far less visible (e.g. Williams & Coate, 2004). For Germany, both older and recent analyses (Hahn, 2004; Wahlers, 2018) emphasize the mixture of different rationales, ranging from political and cultural to economic motivations, both also stress that the latter gain importance (including the accompanying activities of marketing and representative offices abroad). The prime rationale for education abroad in Luxembourg has been capacity building for the national economy (Kmiotek-Meier et al., 2018). At the European level, the rationales for international cooperation are strongly economic, although social and academic rationales feature as well.

### Concrete policies

In Germany, the mix of rationales is visible in the country's education abroad policies, with financial support for both intra-European mobile students and those seeking education outside of Europe. Regarding intra-European mobility, there is explicit attention to contributing to tolerance, European cohesion, and a Eur- opean political identity and combatting nationalism (Brooks, 2018).

In the UK's policy documents there is much less emphasis on education abroad. For instance, the 2013 policy paper "International Education: Global growth and prosperity" dedicates only half a page to education abroad. That said, the UK Higher Education International Unit (2013) stresses the impor- tance of global competencies, international cultural awareness and more gen- erally acquiring skills for life and work. Also, the benefits of mobility for (further) academic collaboration with international partners are mentioned. The overall policy target is to double the percentage of (full-time, first degree, under- graduate) students having an international experience by 2020. The strategy relies heavily on promoting the benefits of education abroad, monitoring trends in mobility, and building capacity to facilitate outward mobility and share best practices. The Universities UK, through its "Go International" program, sup- ports and operationalizes the government's strategy.

Another example comes from Luxembourg, where Kmiotek-Meier et al. (2018) show how competitiveness, innovation, and a desire to secure the education of their elite drove its internationalization agenda and the establishment of the Uni- versity of Luxembourg in 2003. Their analysis shows that this university is a highly Europeanized institution that emphasizes both education abroad *and* attracting foreign students. At the supranational level, since 1987 the Erasmus+ program has been financially supporting students in the European Union (EU) to travel to a foreign institution, ensuring the transferability of credits earned abroad. It also emphasizes European cultures and values, language learning, employability skills, inter-institutional cooperation and quality improvement. Also, more recently, the enhancement of social inclusion has been more explicitly mentioned in the Eur- opean Commission's policy documents (e.g. European Commission, 2017).

*Level of mobility and impact*

In the UK, fewer than 1% of the student population – among the lowest in the European Union – embark on an education abroad journey, half of the students through Erasmus+. Several studies indicate the socially embedded nature of mobility. Students from disadvantaged and underrepresented groups participate at lower rates, although they also benefit more from an international experience (UUK, 2017), a reason for more attention to these groups and sharing best practices to stimulate their participation (UUK, n.d.).

In Germany, outgoing mobility numbers (15–18% of total students enrolled in recent years) were already exceeding the European targets in the early 2000s. From 2001 onwards, the financial study support system is portable and also international mobility for students from lower socio-economic backgrounds is supported through the grant system. German students appear to share the same concerns about education abroad – e.g. financial burden, delayed study progress and separation from family – as do their counterparts in Austria, the Netherlands and Switzerland (Netz, 2015). More importantly, despite the supportive mechanisms of the government, social selectivity in education abroad has not decreased between 1992 and 2012 (Netz & Finger, 2016).

With the establishment of the University of Luxembourg in 2003, the immediate necessity of going abroad diminished in that country, but it can still pride itself for a very high level of mobility (e.g. through an obligatory mobility semester for all undergraduates), driven by national policies, even after domestic university education became available. Rohstock and Schreiber (2013), however, also highlight the exclusive nature of mobility, pointing at the important positions that returning students take up in industry and government.

At the supranational level, around 300,000 European students are annually supported through Erasmus+. The literature on Erasmus mobility does stress the benefits (e.g. Teichler, 2002), but also stresses the administrative burden, the low levels of grants and highlights inequality in participation (e.g. Netz, 2015), leading to conclusions that funds are not effectively used (with those benefiting most – also in terms of post-graduation earnings – being supported at the cost of those not participating). But so far, the policies are not adjusted. The policy documents do, however, acknowledge the existence of the participation inequalities (European Commission, 2017) and the European Commission (EC) actively monitors progress made by European countries in promoting, and removing obstacles to, learning mobility.

### 3.2 North America

The three countries of North America each have their own large and complex higher education system and therefore are not easily captured in generalizations. States/provinces within these countries each have their own ministry of education, or equivalent. Consequently, the national ministries of education share their responsibilities for education abroad policies. In Canada there is in fact no federal ministry of education. In Mexico education abroad is also the responsibility of the Ministry of External Relations. Private foundations and professional associations operating at the national level such as the Association of International Educators (NAFSA), the Institute of International Education (IIE) and the Association of Canadian Deans of Education (ACDE) have developed their own policies on education abroad. In North America there is no supranational policy making body equivalent to the EU. The Consortium for North American Higher Education Collaboration (CONAHEC), however, is a network of HEIs which stimulates education abroad.

### Rationales

In the United States, the Departments of State, of Education and of Defense each have developed initiatives on education abroad with various, partially overlapping rationales, including graduates' labor market position, the multicultural society, international relations, global challenges, national security and peace (Helms, 2015; U.S. Department of Education, 2012; U.S. Department of State, 2018).It is therefore complicated to speak of a 'US rationale' for education abroad.

In Canada, the most recent national level policy on IoHE was compiled by the Department for Foreign Affairs, Trade and Development (2014). It is based on an economic rationale and strongly focuses on recruiting full degree students while casually referring to education abroad. Over the last thirty years, with the increase of IoHE and the connection made to diplomatic relations of Canada, national actors have become increasingly involved (Viczko & Tascón, 2016). These include Universities Canada and the Canadian Board on International Education (CBIE), who also employ an economic rationale, but in addition view global citizenship and mutual benefit in intercultural cooperation as crucial.

Whereas internationalization policies in the US and Canada focus mainly on incoming fee-paying students, in Mexico the emphasis of internationalization is on education abroad. The government combines economic and cultural rationales: developing language skills and cultural competences in students in order to enhance their chances on the labor market (Nuño Mayer, 2016). The Mexican government considers education abroad a tool for capacity building (Secretaría de Relaciones Exteriores, 2014) and for strengthening the quality of Mexican HEIs (Secretaría de Educación Pública, 2014). The Mexican National Development Plan for 2013–2018 (Nieto, 2013) stressed the need to increase the cohesion between the curriculum and the education abroad program.

### Concrete policies

There are efforts to systematically increase participation of underrepresented groups in North America. In the US and in Mexico, these efforts aim at strengthening their position in the national labor market and society (Navarrete,

2017). In Mexico, for example, some scholarship programs aim to particularly increase participation in education abroad by students from indigenous populations (Navarrete, 2017) or female students (Proyecta 100.000). In the US, the Generation Study Abroad initiative aims to both increase education abroad participation (from 283,000 to 600,000 students) and to reduce barriers for underrepresented and disadvantaged groups of students. The Canadian CBIE launched the Learning Beyond Borders initiative with the aim of making education abroad an integral part of education rather than a luxury, hinting at inclusion without framing it as such. The Mexican government supports the development of joint programs through the *Programa de apoyo al desarollo de la educación superior* (PADES) program (Subsecretaría de Educación Superior, 2015). In Canada efforts are also visible at the meso-level, the "Accord on the internationalization of education" of ACDE publishes guidelines for HEIs on inclusion and access in internationalization such as regularly examining ethics and social accountability in education abroad initiatives and considering environmental costs in terms of pollution through travel (ACDE, 2014). Language diversity is being promoted by the US through participation in language programs abroad (Department of Defense, 2011).

### Level of mobility and impact

According to IIE, only a small percentage of students in North America participate in education abroad. The number of US students participating in education abroad shows a steady increase (IIE, 2018). The proportion of US students from underrepresented ethnic minorities in education abroad increased significantly between 2006 and 2016 (IIE, 2018). Data on education abroad participation in Mexico show a significant increase of 23% on average in the 2013–2016 period (Maldonado-Maldonado et al., 2017). The number of Canadian students participating in education abroad was rather steady between 2008 and 2014 (IIE, n.d.). Contrary to US and Mexican students, Canadian students tend to study abroad in a country where one of the two official Canadian languages, English and French, are spoken.

Scholarship programs are key policy instruments in North America for education abroad, and the corporate sector contributes to financing a number of them. Compared to e.g. the size and scope of the Erasmus+ program in the EU, these programs are modest.

Data is scarce on the number of students from underrepresented groups obtaining a scholarship except for programs specifically supporting students of limited financial means, such as the Gilman International Scholarship program in the US.

Executive agencies or foundations implementing scholarship programs (e.g. CBIE, NAFSA and IIE) often also offer information on education abroad, training or research. In Mexico such independent organizations at the national level barely exist.

Education abroad policies in North America include a focus on priority countries (e.g. 100,000 Strong programs in the US and Mexico). A focus on priority countries, preferred partners and selected students is, however, not without critique. It may mask the fact that other countries, institutions and individuals are systematically being excluded, and that education abroad is offering limited diversity (Trilokekar, 2016).

Both the US and Mexican governments are aware that education abroad may lead to outgoing degree mobility. The Mexican government requires scholarship recipients to return home and aims to repatriate Mexican researchers abroad to minimize brain drain (Secretaría de Educación Pública, 2013). Concurrently, Education USA runs education abroad centers in Mexico as part of their recruitment strategy (Helms et al., 2015).

### 3.3 Asia

Sustained student mobility in Asia must be read as part of a policy response towards "modernization" for political and economic sovereignty in the wake of Euro-American political, economic and cultural dominance over the 19th and 20th centuries. Subsequently, in higher education and in other spheres, the spatial imaginary of Asia as a marketized space has foregrounded "national prosperity" over social equity and planetary sustainability. Amidst concerns about rising inequality, ethnonationalism and ecological challenges, there are calls to urgently reconsider the appropriateness of this discursive materialization of "Asia as a market" (Breaden, 2018; Kubota, 2016).

### Rationales

Because education abroad schemes are resource-intensive, they are found in relatively wealthy countries and institutions. China, Japan, Singapore, South Korea and Taiwan have been able to make stronger investments in research performance and internationalization including education abroad schemes compared to other Asian countries (Marginson, 2018). Their national education abroad policies are shaped by a mix of political, economic and cultural rationales, which in different combinations, aim to develop a citizenry capable of dealing with the vicissitudes of economic globalization. Education abroad in Japan is folded into a long-standing platform of *kokusaika* (internationalization) to produce and recruit "global talent" (*gurobaru jinzai*) including "Asian talent" (*Asia jinzai*). Education abroad in China's internationalization project is part of a 'national rejuvenation' project to become a credible economic power within the liberal internationalist order. Accordingly, education abroad programs seek to cultivate scientific acumen and a people with "a global vision" (State Council of the People's Republic of China, 2010). Singapore's internationalization policies are driven by its economic, cultural and foreign policy aspirations to position itself as a regional hub specializing in innovation and high-end manufacturing, services and logistics (see Sidhu, Ho & Yeoh, 2011).

## Concrete policies

Japan's most recent education abroad policy, introduced in 2013, is Tobitate! (Leap for Tomorrow). It is part of a platform to "internationalize" Japanese youth through 'international experience' and English competencies to meet the workforce requirements of the country's multinational firms. Japan's Ministry of International Trade and Industry (MITI) plays an important role formulating these broader policy schemes (see Breaden, 2018).

Identifying the key actors in education abroad policies in China is difficult; funding regimes by China Scholarship Council gesture to the importance of elite Chinese universities and high performing academic achievers (mainly postgraduates) in education abroad programs (Gribble & Tran 2016, 17).

Singapore's universities have education abroad programs for undergraduates and postgraduates in partnership with "like-minded institutions." These are allied to targeted national policies introduced under the Global Schoolhouse platform and six subsequent Science and Technology Masterplans (Sidhu, Ho & Yeoh, 2014). Financial support for students depends on need and academic merit (Gribble & Tran, 2016). Because regionalization is an important economic policy, intra-Asia mobility receives special support, funneled through government departments like International Enterprise (within the Ministry of Trade and Industry), and government linked companies like the Temasek Group.

Aside from bilateral projects in education abroad, all three countries are also involved in supranational initiatives. Singapore participates in regional projects sponsored by the Association of Southeast Asian Nations (ASEAN). Japan, China and Korea began the trilateral Campus Asia initiative in 2010 to overcome stubborn war-related animosities ('mutual understanding'), and re-orient their international connectivities beyond Anglo-centric spheres (Breaden, 2018; Yonezawa & Meerman, 2012).

## Levels of mobility and impact

Japan's education abroad programs, mainly short-term, are increasingly Asia-focused and draw participants from the Humanities and Social Sciences, in contrast to earlier periods dominated by US-centric, long-term, science and technology-based mobility programs (Breaden, 2018, p. 35). To further the country's innovation capacity, elite Chinese universities, prioritize postgraduate research-driven placements in education abroad programs, setting student participation targets ranging from 10% to 90%. Singapore's education abroad programs are well resourced, include short and long-term under- and postgraduate programs, with an estimated 70–90% of students reported to participate in some kind of mobility initiative (Gribble & Tran, 2016). Tensions between Singapore's regionalization and world-class aspirations have manifested in students choosing the countries of the Global North ahead of Asia for education abroad. Universities have recently prioritized short-term Asia-bound mobility programs to enhance graduate employability.

Overall, education abroad schemes, bilateral and supranational, through their emphasis on generic 'quality' considerations, have marginalized questions of equity and environmental agendas, despite their significance to Asia's populations. Little longitudinal evidence exists on the effects of education abroad on social mobility, intercultural awareness and graduate employability. Massification trends, where present, are driven by surplus capacity in higher education rather than policy commitments towards widening participation (Marginson, 2018). Anglophonism, the preserve of the upper stratum of societies, also raises barriers to broadening participation, reinforcing the low regard in which regional languages are held.

## 4. Implications for practice

### 4.1 Rationales of national and supranational policies

In each setting considered in this chapter, a wide variety of rationales is visible. In the European Union, a policy imaginary concerned with regional identity-making over the past decades has provided the impulse and momentum for Erasmus. It has been the main driving force behind domestic education abroad policies. In Asia, the number and outreach of supranational initiatives have been limited in comparison, whereas they are virtually nonexistent in North America. In these regions, there is a more prominent role for state/provincial governments. In addition, in the US, professional associations have high relevance. The pre-eminence of economic rationales in framing education abroad policies in countries in Asia and North America can be partially attributed to the oversight and budgetary control exercised by ministries of trade or their equivalents over their Education counterparts, if they are in existence. This is not to suggest that the curriculum encountered by education abroad students is necessarily limited to instrumental economic concerns. For instance, one of the priorities of the Mexican government is clearly capacity building.

### 4.2 Diversity and inclusion, environmental sustainability and economic equality

Efforts to make education abroad more inclusive seem to be the only promising aspect of the three themes of our 3P framework in terms of currently active education abroad policies. Diversity and inclusion figures high on the agenda of most European and North American countries but receives less attention in the Asian countries. Contributing forces that have been identified include the primacy of an economic development paradigm focusing on export-driven industrialization and a legacy of state policing of civil society (see Kim, 2006). The US, Mexico, the UK and Germany for instance intend to increase the number of students from marginalized groups in scholarship programs. In the UK inclusion is being monitored and supported by sharing best practices of institutional initiatives. At supranational level the European Commission also asks for attention on this issue and monitors policy measures. There is, however, little known about the implementation and outcomes of these policies.

Environmental sustainability is absent in the (supra)national policies. Economic equality in terms of preventing brain drain was only mentioned in Mexican policies. Education abroad is in some national policies portrayed as a tool for talented students to distinguish themselves from other students (e.g. China) likely leading to more inequality and in others as a way to support mobility of disadvantaged students (e.g. US, Germany) aimed at achieving more equality.

One national association, the ACDE in Canada, does link its education abroad policies directly to the UN's 3Ps by striving to increase awareness. In a number of countries concerns are raised that education abroad programs lead to an increase in English taught (parts of) programs which may result in reduced accessibility of those programs for domestic students.

### 4.3 Promising education abroad policies

The current literature on education abroad policies offers rather limited solid research on effectiveness, particularly in considering the undesired effects of education abroad. Long-standing scholarship programs, such as Erasmus+ and Fulbright, as well as capacity building programs engage in evaluation processes to trace effects (Mawer, 2017). However, these reports predominantly focus on effects at the microlevel only and/or are based on perceptions rather than more objective measurements. Hence, still little is known about the macro level effects of national education abroad policies. Goal attainment is further complicated by a lack of specified aims. Another complicating factor to the selection of promising policies is the fact that contexts between regions and between countries within the same region may differ considerably. It is difficult to say which of the policy initiatives presented in this chapter are promising in terms of advancing education abroad while serving diversity and inclusion, environmental sustainability and economic equality.

This research, however, also finds glimpses of what could work. First, the analysis clearly shows a lack of connection to related policy such as diversity, environmental or equality policies. Second, it is recommended that efforts be made to discover undesired consequences and the reasons behind them in order to develop ethically sound and sustainable policies, such as targeted scholarship programs. Third, policies on education abroad need to pay proper attention to structurally embedding education abroad in the curriculum rather than remaining an extracurricular project. National policies could also specify which sustainability and ethical indicators they use to define the aims of education abroad policies. A fourth and final glimpse of what could work is the sharing of good practices in education abroad, such as done by Universities UK (UUK, n.d.), although such actions should include an explanation of the effects of these practices and explain how one arrives at discerning good from not so good practices.

## 5. Directions for future research

International comparisons are necessary for developing policies that are informed by research. This, however, requires that policies are clear on their objectives and measurable results. Furthermore, national governments are not necessarily the most influential level in terms of education abroad policies. Different levels (state/provincial and supranational) as well as different types of organizations (foundations and corporations) are interesting intermediate levels on which to focus future research.

Policy evaluation research should also consider longitudinal designs, generally allowing for better insight into cause and effect relations. In addition, more variance is needed in conceptual perspectives of research, as the focus is generally on positive effects, whereas there is a need to also look at the potential downsides and inconveniences of education abroad. Further research is also needed to get a better understanding of the reasons why national policies on education abroad are largely disconnected from policies in related fields such as sustainability, inclusion or diversity.

Contemporary and historical initiatives of education-related activism to further social justice, labor rights, science-driven environmental action, peace education and gender equity point to a long-standing ethic of care and responsibility (see e. g. Ide, 2017; Jackson, 2017). How such projects might inform education abroad programs deserves closer empirical and policy attention (see Kolb et al., 2017). Of crucial importance is the value of comparative and intercultural approaches to enable diverse philosophies of justice and sustainability to be brought to bear on national education abroad policies.

## Further reading

Courtois, A. (2018). 'It doesn't really matter which university you attend or which subject you study while abroad.' The massification of student mobility programmes and its implications for equality in higher education. *European Journal of Higher Education*, 8 (1), 99–114.

Kenway, J., & Fahey, J. (2009). Academic mobility and hospitality: The good host and the good guest. *European Educational Research Journal*, 8(4), 555–559.

Ferencz, I., & Wächter, B. (eds.) (2012). *European and national policies for academic mobility: Linking rhetoric, practice and mobility trends.* Bonn: Lemmens.

## References

ACDE (2014). Accord on the internationalization of education. Association of Canadian Deans of Education. https://csse-scee.ca/acde/wp-content/uploads/sites/7/2017/08/Accord-on-the-Internationalization-of-Education.pdf

Breaden, J. (2018). *Articulating Asia in Japanese higher education: Policy, partnership and mobility*. Abingdon and New York: Routledge.

Brooks, R. (2018). Higher education mobilities: A cross-national European comparison. *Geoforum*, 93(May), 87–96.

Clarke, M. (2014). The impact of international student mobility on the development of entrepreneurial attitudes (Ph.D. thesis). Loughborough University. https://repository. lboro.ac.uk/account/articles/9495338

de Wit, H., Hunter, F., Howard, L., & Egron-Polak, E. (2015). Internationalisation of higher education. In H. de Wit, F. Hunter, L. Howard & E. Egron-Polak (Eds.), *European Parliament's Committee on Culture and Education*. Brussels: European Union.

Deloitte Access Economics (2015). *The value of international education to Australia*. Canberra: Australian Government. https://internationaleducation.gov.au/research/ research-papers/Documents/ValueInternationalEd.pdf

Department of Defense (2014). *Implementation Plan for Language Skills, Regional Expertise, and Cultural Capabilities*. Washington: Department of Defense.

Dvorak, A., Christiansen, L., Fischer, N., & Underhill, J. (2011). A necessary partnership: Study abroad and sustainability in higher education. *Frontiers: The Interdisciplinary Journal of Study Abroad*, 21(Fall), 143–166.

EAIE (2013). Diplomacy and education: Internationalisation or neo-colonialism? In *Executive summary dialogue*, 1. Istanbul: EAIE.

European Commission (2017). *Communication on a renewed EU agenda for higher education*. Brussels: European Commission.

Foreign Affairs Trade and Development Canada (2014). *Canada's international education strategy: Harnessing our knowledge advantage to drive innovation and prosperity*. Foreign Affairs, Trade and Development Canada.

Gribble, C., & Tran, L. (2016). *International trends in learning abroad: Information and promotions campaign for student mobility*. Melbourne: IEAA & Universities Australia.

Hahn, K. (2004). Germany. In J. Huisman & M. van der Wende (Eds.), *On cooperation and competition: National and European policies for the internationalisation of higher education*. Bonn: Lemmens.

Helms, R., Rumbley, L., Brajkovic, L., & Mihut, G. (2015). *Internationalizing higher education worldwide: National policies and programs*. Washington: American Council on Education.

Huisman, J., & Van der Wende, M. (Eds.) (2004). *On cooperation and competition: National and European policies for the internationalisation of higher education*. Bonn: Lemmens.

Ide, K. (2017). Rethinking the concept of sustainability: Hiroshima as a subject of peace education. *Educational Philosophy and Theory*, 49(5), 521–530.

IIE (2018). Open Doors 2018 fast facts. Retrieved from www.iie.org/Research-and-In sights/Open-Doors/Fact-Sheets-and-Infographics/Fast-Facts

IIE (n.d.). Infographics and data Canada. Retrieved from www.iie.org/Research-and-In sights/Project-Atlas/Explore-Data/Canada/Outbound-Mobility—-Past-Years

Jackson, L. (2017). Asian perspectives on education for sustainable development. *Educational Philosophy and Theory*, 49(5), 473–479.

Kim, J. (2006). The environmental impact of industrialization in East Asia and strategies toward sustainable development. *Sustainability Science*, 1(1), 107–114.

Kmiotek-Meier, E., Karl, U., & Powell, J. (2018). Designing the (most) mobile university: The centrality of international student mobility in Luxembourg's higher education policy discourse. *Higher Education Policy*, 33, 21–44. doi:10.1057/s41307-018-0118-4

Kolb, M., Fröhlich, L., & Schmidpeter, R. (2017). Implementing sustainability as the new normal: Responsible management education – From a private business school's perspective. *International Journal of Management Education*, 15(2), 280–292. https://doi. org/10.1016/j.ijme.2017.03.009

Kubota, R. (2016). The social imaginary of study abroad: Complexities and contradictions. *The Language Learning Journal*, 44(3), 347–357.

Lomer, S. (2018). UK policy discourses and international student mobility: The deterrence and subjectification of international students. *Globalisation, Societies and Education*, 16 (3), 308–324.

Lörz, M., Netz, N., & Quast, H. (2016). Why do students from underprivileged families less often intend to study abroad? *Higher Education*, 72(2), 153–174.

Maldonado-Maldonado, A., Bustos-Aguirre, M., Camacho Lizárraga, M., Castiello-Gutiérrez, S., Rodríguez Betanzos, A., Cortes Velasco, C. I., & Ibarra Cázares, B. (2017). *Patlani Encuesta Mexicana de movilidad internacional estudiantil 2014/2015 y 2015/2016*. Mexico City.

Marginson, S. (2018). Higher education, economic inequality and social mobility: Implications for emerging East Asia. *International Journal of Educational Development*, 63, 4–11.

Mawer, M. (2017). Approaches to analyzing the outcomes of international scholarship programs for higher education. *Journal of Studies in International Education*, 21(3), 230–245.

Navarrete, D. (2017). *Movilidad internacional estudiantil para todos. Avances y perspectivas desde experiencias de inclusión de posgraduados indígenas*. Mexico City: RIMAC 2o Seminario sobre Movilidad Científica Transnacional.

Netz, N. (2015). What deters students from studying abroad? Evidence from four European countries and its implications for higher education policy. *Higher Education Policy*, 28, 151–174.

Netz, N., & Finger, C. (2016). New horizontal inequalities in German higher education? Social selectivity of studying abroad between 1991 and 2012. *Sociology of Education*, 89 (2) 79–98.

Nieto, E. (2013). Plan nacional de desarollo 2013–2018. Diaro Official de La Federación, Segunda Sección (20–25–2013), 4–129.

Nuño Mayer, A. (2016). *Mensaje del secretario de Educación Pública*. Mexico City: Secretariá de Educación Pública.

Richard, N., Lowe, R., & Hanks, C. (2017). Gone international: Mobility works. www.go.international.ac.uk/gone-international-mobility-works

Rohstock, A., & Schreiber, C. (2013). The Grand Duchy on the Grand Tour: A historical study of student migration in Luxembourg. *Paedagogica Historica*, 49(2), 174–193.

Secretaría de Educación Pública (2013). *Programa Sectoral De Educación*. Mexico City: Secretaría de Educación Pública.

Secretaría de Educación Pública (2014). *Diagnóstico S245 Programa de fortalecimiento de la calidad en institutiones educativas*. Mexico City: Secretaría de Educación Pública.

Secretaría de Relaciones Exteriores (2014). *Programa de Cooperación Internacional para el Desarrollo 2014–2018. Diaro Official de La Federación*. Mexico City: Secretaría de Relaciones Exteriores.

Sidhu, R. Ho, K.-C., & Yeoh, B. (2011). Emerging education hubs: Singapore. *Higher Education*, 61, 23–40.

Sidhu, R., Ho, K.-C., & Yeoh, B. (2014). Singapore: Building a knowledge and education hub. In J. Knight (Ed.), *International education hubs: Student, talent, knowledge-innovation models* (pp. 121–143). Dordrecht: Springer.

Sidhu, R., & Dall'Alba, G. (2017). "A strategy of distinction" unfolds: unsettling the undergraduate outbound mobility experience. *British Journal of Sociology of Education*, 38(4), 468–484.

State Council of the People's Republic of China (2010). Outline of China's national plan for medium and long-term education reform and development (2010–2020). https://internationaleducation.gov.au/News/newsarchive/2010/Documents/China_Education_Reform_pdf.pdf

Subsecretaría de Educación Superior (2015). *Lineamentos para la operación del programa de apoyo al desarrollo de la educación superior (PADES) 2015*. Mexico D.F.: Secretaría de Educación Pública.

Tarrant, M., Rubin, D., and Stoner, L. (2013). The added value of study abroad: Fostering a global citizenry. *Journal of Studies in International Education*, 18(2), 141–161.

Teichler, U. (Ed.) (2002). *ERASMUS in the SOCRATES programme: Findings of an evaluation study*. Bonn: Lemmens.

Trahar, S., Green, W., de Wit, H., & Whitsed, C. (2016). The internationalisation of higher education. In J. M. Case & J. Huisman (Eds.), *Researching higher education: International perspectives on theory, policy and practice* (pp. 23–41). London and New York: Routledge.

Trilokekar, R. (2016). Strategic internationalization: At what cost? *Trends & Insights: NAFSA*, (Feburary), 1–6.

UK HE International Unit (2013). *UK strategy for outward mobility*. London: UK.

United Nations (2015). *Transforming our world: The 2030 Agenda for Sustainable Development*. Pub. L. No. A/RES/70/1, Resolution adopted by the General Assembly on 25 September 2015. New York: United Nations.

U.S. Department of Education (2012). *U.S. Department of Education international strategy 2012–2016. Succeeding globally through international education and engagement*. U.S. Department of Education.

U.S. Department of State (2018). *ECA functional bureau strategy 2018–2022*. U.S. Department of State.

UUK (2017). *UK Strategy for outward student mobility 2017–2020*. London: UUK.

UUK (n.d.). *Widening participation in outward student mobility: A toolkit to support inclusive approaches*. London: UUK.

Viczko, M., & Tascón, C. (2016). Performing internationalization of higher education in Canadian national policy. *Canadian Journal of Higher Education*, 46(2), 1–18.

Wahlers, M. (2018). Internationalisation of universities: The Germany way. *International Higher Education*, 92, 9–11.

Williams, G., & Coate, K. (2004). United Kingdom. In J. Huisman & M. van der Wende (Eds.), *On cooperation and competition: National and European policies for the internationalisation of higher education* (pp. 113–137). Bonn: Lemmens.

Yonezawa, A. & Meerman, A. (2012). Multilateral initiatives in the East Asian arena and the challenges for Japanese higher education. *Asian Education and Development Studies*, 1(1), 57–66.

# Chapter 14

# Host community impact

## From harm-minimization to positive impact

*Christopher Ziguras and John S. Lucas*

## Highlights:

- Mobile students impact host communities in many ways (e.g. economic, political, educational, cultural), especially when there is a wide disparity of income between the visitors and those visited.
- Not all impacts are easily identified as positive or negative, and many may be ambiguous or contested.
- The concepts of reciprocity and mutuality derived from the international development field are helpful in improving outcomes and ensuring benefit for all partners in an international engagement.
- Outsiders can never truly understand the needs of host communities; therefore, choosing local partners wisely and working with them closely is key to success.

## 1. Introduction and chapter overview

For decades, large numbers of students have undertaken exchange semesters abroad, usually travelling from one high-income country to another, without provoking much concern about their impact on host communities (apart from the occasional complaint by residents about drunk students making too much noise in the streets at night). However, more serious concerns have been expressed about students from high-income countries who travel to low-income countries, such as those engaged in international service learning. As long ago as 1968, Ivan Illich famously used his keynote address at the Conference on InterAmerican Student Projects in Cuernavaca, Mexico to implore those gathered there to stop sending students to Latin America because of the harm they invariably do to local communities. Instead, he suggested, "use your money, your status and your education to travel in Latin America. Come to look, come to climb our mountains, to enjoy our flowers. Come to study. But do not come to help" (Illich 1968, 6). Students did, of course, continue to travel to low-income countries to work on development projects and there is a significant body of literature we can draw on today to understand how to avoid potential negative impacts and ensure instead that such study experiences will be mutually beneficial (Dear and Howard 2016; Hartman 2016; Schroeder et al. 2009).

Recent decades have seen a major shift in patterns of student mobility. While the numbers of students undertaking a semester or year abroad are slowly increasing, there has also been rapid growth of short-term student mobility from high-income countries to low- or middle-income countries, and more recently between middle-income countries. This often takes the form of study tours, work placements, summer schools and short courses. These fleeting engagements are often promoted to students, institutions and governments on the basis of the benefits that will accrue to mobile students – particularly heightened employability through the development of intercultural communication skills and knowledge of international professional practice in one's field. But amongst those designing and leading such programs, the research suggests that little thought is given to the impact they have on host communities (Schroeder et al. 2009; Wood et al. 2011).

## 2. Key questions to be addressed

- What impacts do our education abroad programs have on the host communities with which we engage?
- To what extent should we care about the impact of our programs on host communities?
- How can we improve the impact of our programs on host communities and enhance the value of international education to its various stakeholders, and how can local hosts contribute?

Each of these questions is explicated below. This chapter explores the range of ways in which internationally mobile students affect the communities in which they study. For the purposes of this investigation, this chapter looks at students from high or middle-income industrialized nations participating in study abroad programs of one year or less. The first question asks international education practitioners: What impacts do our education abroad programs have on the host communities with which we engage? On one level it is a simple empirical question, but it is usually quite difficult to answer in practice. While these impacts may sometimes be clearly perceived as positive or negative by the host community, in many cases they may not be obvious to those involved, or they may be ambiguous, or contested. The impacts may be economic, educational, cultural, or political, or lead to changes in organizational capacity made by various institutions.

The second question is ethical, namely to what extent should we care about the impact of our programs on host communities? One might argue that our primary responsibilities are to our students and to our home communities, and that the communities and partners with whom we engage are free to cease the relationship if it is not in their interests. Indeed, national strategies for internationalization usually focus on recruiting international students or providing an experience for the mobile students abroad and this is also true of the mission statements and strategic plans of many of the associations that support international education.

The third question in this chapter is: How can practitioners improve the impact of programs on host communities and enhance the value of international education to its various stakeholders? And here the chapter asks how local hosts can contribute, particularly through exercising greater agency in making decisions about the objectives and design of short-term mobility experiences.

The final section presents practical strategies for education abroad practitioners, conscious of two fundamental characteristics of contemporary education abroad that frame work with communities. First, the learning objectives of education abroad activities are increasingly diverse, reflecting the broader range of institutions, disciplines, destinations and students involved; and the nature of host community engagement will vary enormously depending on what is desirable and achievable in each case. The authors seek to avoid making well-meaning but self-important pronouncements about the "proper" objectives and approaches for learning abroad, of the kind that are all too common in the literature. Second, the authors recognize that universities' engagement with communities of all kinds is mediated by partner organizations, and that these partnerships are especially significant in international engagements. It is important to recognize how little we can ever understand of the needs of the many host communities we engage with and instead choose our local partners wisely and work with them closely.

## 3. Review of the literature

The impact of global student mobility programs on host communities was until recently an understudied topic in the learning abroad literature. While there is a significant body of literature on the benefits that accrue to mobile students and their home societies, little attention was paid to the impact of these programs on the host community. As Illich (1968) wryly noted, "How odd that nobody ever thought about spending money to educate poor Mexicans in order to prevent them from the culture shock of meeting you?" The first wave of interest in host community impact was motivated by a recognition that even with the best of intentions, the consequences of mobility experiences could be damaging, particularly from short-term programs in developing countries.

### 3.1 First do no harm

Since around the mid-2000s a body of literature has emerged, authored mainly by scholars and education abroad practitioners working in US universities, which argues that the growth of short-term education abroad poses new risks to host communities, articulating three distinct concerns.

First, the design of short-term programs involved new risks, arising from more intensive engagement by larger groups of students undertaking immersive experiences, such as study tours and field placements, that sometimes involve close contact with a wide range of people in a host community, and yet involve little in the way of preparation or gradual acculturation. Schroeder et al. (2009), for example, warn that these are "much more likely to have negative impacts on host communities than individual or small groups of students who go on semester or yearlong study abroad at a foreign university" (p. 147).

The second reason for concern was that the growth of short-term mobility has facilitated a 'massification' of learning abroad, since the early 2000s in the United States, and more recently in Japan and Australia, as detailed in other chapters in this volume. Ogden (2007) observed that with the rise of short-term mobility "the typical student is noticeably changing" and warned of the rise of "the colonial student" who seeks to "take full advantage of all the benefits studying abroad offers, but is not necessarily open to experiencing the less desirable side of being there" (p. 37) and has little interest in the social or cultural complexities of host communities. Woolf (2006) similarly lamented that among students travelling to non-traditional destinations, "rarely is there an attempt to get beyond the first-person. The host location exists as a space through which students travel with the objective of expanding their perceptions. While this is not a bad or demeaning objective, there is rarely a sense of serious exploration beyond the self." (p. 136) Universities that catered to this group to expand participation, Ogden warned, were at risk of implementing a colonial system of learning abroad, "which supports the privileged position of the student over the local" (p. 40). By focusing on benefits to mobile students, the argument goes, international educators risk replicating exploitative relationships.

The third reason for concern about the impact of short-term mobility was the rise of "non-traditional" destinations, and particularly developing countries, where inequalities between the visitor and the visited are often extreme (Schroeder et al. 2009; Wood et al. 2011; Woolf 2006). Governments began to support an expansion of mobility to low-income countries as a way to boost engagement with "emerging economies," many of which had adopted liberal economic policies after the end of the Cold War (Keith 2005). For example, in the United States, the Lincoln Commission in the early 2000s proposed to dramatically expand mobility to a wider range of destinations, while in Australia a succession of government schemes since the late 1990s has supported mobility to Asia and the Pacific. Wood et al.'s (2011) research with learning abroad coordinators found that "the potential for negative community impacts of [international service learning] and other study abroad programs are highest where there are substantial "disparity of income, disparity of lifestyle, disparities in values" between students and hosts" (p. 10). Woolf (2006) worried that students were attracted to these destinations for the wrong reasons, cautioning that, "the equation of non-traditional with developing too often signifies that the demand is based on the travel agent's attraction to the exotic allied with a quasi-missionary zeal to engage with poverty" (p. 136). The question of how we deal with structural inequalities between travelling students and host communities remains a central issue.

So, what exactly were the unintended negative impacts of education abroad on host communities that these writers were concerned about? The work of Wood et al. (2011) and Dear and Howard (2016) helps to distinguish between economic and material impacts on the one hand, and cultural and social impacts on the other. The list of concerns below is adapted from Schroeder et al. (2009) and captures most of the issues raised in the literature by a wide range of authors. In relation to material and economic impacts we may inadvertently:

- impose hardships by exploiting economic and environmental resources that would otherwise be available to local communities;
- exacerbate inequalities by working with already privileged members of the local community;
- disrupt sustainable economic activity and create a dependency on foreign visitors.

And in relation to cultural and social impacts, we may:

- disrupt local cultural traditions through our behavior, dress, or drug and alcohol use;
- disrespect local traditions, values and systems resulting in conflict or negative self-images within host communities;
- set expectations for levels of comfort, and service for mobile students that are beyond the reach of local students, thereby reinforcing a colonial relationship.

The Forum on Education Abroad's (2011) Code of Ethics for Education Abroad similarly focuses on minimizing harmful cultural and environmental impacts. According to the Forum, we should "be aware of and sensitive to host community cultural norms and expectations in program planning and execution" and minimize any negative impact on the host society and community, including through adequate orientation for participants, and the enforcement of a code of conduct (p. 7)." The Code requires that we be aware of and minimize any "harmful individual and program-related environmental and social impact," including through "preparing for the environmental, economic, and social consequences of the presence (or departure) of the program, in both program design and management" (p. 8). While the Code hints at positive contributions to the host society (as will be discussed below), its primary intended beneficiaries are mobile students.

In recent years there have been two notable campaigns to address harm to local communities from education abroad – one focused on orphanage tourism and one focused on the "white saviour" complex. Regarding the first of these, the London School of Economics, among others, has been campaigning to stop educational institutions from sending individual students or groups to visit or work in orphanages in developing countries (Coles 2016). This has been part of a global movement in response to the commercialization of orphanages which has seen vulnerable children used to generate income from well-meaning international visitors. The orphanage boycott has been taken up by many individual institutions and some entire systems. In early 2018, for example, the Australian government announced a campaign to end orphanage tourism that will, "work with states and territories and universities to ensure school groups and students are not unwittingly visiting or volunteering in programs that exploit children" (Bishop and Birmingham 2018).

A different and more diffuse problem is posed by the prominence of the "white saviour" complex in international higher education, a concept popularized in media studies to refer to the portrayal of heroic white protagonists coming to the rescue of anonymized non-white victims (Cole 2012; Hughey 2010). In higher education this is manifested in superficial forms of international service that allow privileged participants to feel they are "making a difference" while undertaking menial activities that provide little benefit to the communities they are supposed to be serving. Illich's (1968) critique of the Conference on InterAmerican Student Projects is perhaps as apt today as it was 50 years ago, "Your reports on past summers prove that you are not even capable of understanding that your do-gooding in a Mexican village is even less relevant than it would be in a U.S. ghetto" (p. 5).

Today, such critiques are directed towards educational voluntourism, which McGloin & Georgeou (2016) define as "a tour operator whose business is based in the Global North and who profits from sending others to developing countries and communities." Similar critiques have been levelled against many forms of recreational visits to impoverished communities, sometimes referred to as "poorism" or "slum tourism." The language of humanitarian development is appropriated by voluntourism companies, including those that service the higher education sector, who "trade on the idea that they send people to 'help' others in dire need of assistance" (p. 3). Kushner (2016), for example, describes the spectacle of affluent college students travelling to Haiti to undertake post-disaster construction work while locals watch on bemused. He wonders how much more effective those students' funds would have been if spent on materials and local labor rather than on airfares and hotel rooms.

Kushner suggests that we have an obligation to temper the aspirations of well-meaning young volunteers and, "abandon the assumption that we, simply by being privileged enough to travel the world, are somehow qualified to help ease the world's ills." Nevertheless, we still hear of groups of students getting on planes at great expense to lay bricks or paint school classrooms in far-flung locations. Clearly there is a difference between "voluntourism" and what McGloin and Georgeou (2016) refer to as "volunteering for development," which does indeed make a valued contribution to communities.

A different concern has emerged in some popular Western destinations in recent years, where local residents have felt displaced by a flood of visitors, many of them students. While there does not appear to be any scholarly literature addressing this issue, local governments and media struggle to address the ways accommodation for short-term visitors displaces residents; businesses serving tourists replace businesses serving locals; and the character of neighborhoods is transformed to cater to the culinary, entertainment and aesthetic tastes of visitors. One salient example is Barcelona, where some quarters of the city have seven hotel rooms for every ten residents, not to mention informal accommodation providers (Bosch 2017). Some classify the presence of large numbers of Erasmus students in the city as a particular form of "studentification," a term coined by urban planners to describe the effects that large numbers of tertiary students have on particular localities, analogous to the process of gentrification that results from the entry of high-income residents into a locality (Calvo 2017). Studentification has been more commonly attributed to national students relocating to college towns (Hubbard 2009) or full degree international students who represent a significant segment of the youth populations of cities such as Auckland, Sydney and Melbourne (Collins 2010; Ziguras 2018). Large numbers of short-term students mostly likely impacts residents in other popular destinations, such as Florence and Perugia. Considered next are the types of positive contributions education abroad might be able to make.

### 3.2 Focusing instead on reciprocity

The term reciprocity is used in the education abroad literature extensively to describe the principle that activities should benefit both visitor and host. For example, The Forum on Education Abroad's (2011) Code of Ethics requires that, "reciprocal opportunities that benefit the sending and receiving country's educational institutions, students and broader communities should be explored." For several decades the international service learning community has been developing the concepts of mutuality and reciprocity as a way of understanding and improving the impact of their programs on host societies (Alonso Garcia and Longo 2017; Dear and Howard 2016; Keith 2005). Today, definitions of international service learning, and development volunteering more broadly, almost always insist that the host community is integrally involved in identifying priorities, designing and overseeing the activity. Hartman (2016) uses the term "fair trade learning" to describe approaches that simultaneously serve community and students without privileging either group.

While notions of reciprocity and mutuality may have become core principles in international service learning and development-oriented education abroad, the idea of benefiting local communities remains largely absent in the minds of many education abroad practitioners (Wood et al. 2011) and in the rhetoric of many governments' outbound mobility funding programs (Manathunga 2017). There is therefore much that the broader education abroad community can learn from development studies.

Economic and material outcomes of hosting mobile students are often the most significant benefits identified by host communities, including expenditure on accommodation, meals, local transport, guides and donations of materials. The Forum on Education Abroad's (2011) Code of Ethics advises organizers to focus their spending on goods and services consciously, advocating, "soliciting community input and utilizing local experts, resources, goods and services, when appropriate [and] supporting local community assets such as schools, libraries, health programs, and conservation projects, when feasible" (p. 8).

Education abroad organizers often assume that contact with our students is what local communities value most, but our partners may have more pressing concerns. For example, Toms Smedley (2016) found that host communities in Costa Rica saw little or no benefit from the services performed by visiting student volunteers, but rather identified income from hosting students to be most valuable to them. And while it seems reasonable to assume that longer duration stays allow the visiting volunteer to learn more of the language and become more conversant in cultural norms thus leading to greater impact, many host families prefer shorter-term volunteers since these students pay a higher daily rate for accommodation. Kanani (2000) similarly describes how education abroad host coordinators in Kenya gain financially and are able to employ and train support staff while home-stay host families receive a financial allowance and may develop mutually beneficial friendships.

And it is not just in low- and middle-income countries that visiting students on semester and short-stay programs contribute to local economies, as is obvious in popular destinations such as Barcelona, Perugia and Florence. More destinations are now actively courting mobile students for this reason. For example, Townsville Enterprise, a business and investment promotion agency in Northern Australia, developed an edutourism consortium to coordinate the activities of small businesses and government agencies and to promote a wide range of short-term study options to universities abroad (Townsville Enterprise 2018). A moderate public investment in supporting the consortium has resulted in a large boost in educational visitor numbers and edutourism revenue that has benefited local businesses and education providers. With regard to longer-term internationally mobile students, many receiving countries now regularly publish data on the positive economic and employment impact of incoming students which run to the billions of dollars and hundreds of thousands of jobs created (Deloitte Access Economics 2015; NAFSA 2019; Universities UK 2017). Where collected, such data usually include short-term students, but these are dwarfed by the large numbers of students undertaking full degrees.

### 3.3 Working with partners

As education abroad professionals, we must recognize how little we know about the social and cultural priorities of many of the communities we engage with, and instead rely on trusted intermediaries who have much closer and longstanding connections. Educational abroad partners can take many forms – local universities, non-government organizations, private providers, community-based tourism operators and so on – but the critical factors are whether they share the values of the education abroad provider, are able to engage effectively with local community groups, and can sustain a mutually beneficial relationship over time.

For universities around the globe, community engagement has become an expected aspect of institutional mission, alongside teaching and research. As Alonso Garcia and Longo (2017) note, maintaining reciprocity and mutuality in university community relationships is challenging, even with communities that are closely connected with the home campus of the institution. When dealing with geographically and culturally distant communities through a succession of short-term engagements, this is rarely possible. "With the best of intentions," they conclude, "short-term trips face the risk of becoming transactional, 'a series of one-way transfers of goods' that meet immediate needs and then dissolve" (p. 44).

A helpful illustration of the significance of local partners is the model developed by Michigan State University, which has long had a high-level commitment to community engagement that it carries across to its international activities through its "engaged" study abroad model (Berquist and Milano 2019). There are four characteristics of community-engaged programs across the university – domestic and international – which operate as underlying principles shaping the nature of relationships with partners:

1   Reciprocal relationships with community-based partners will characterize MSU's work.
2   Community voice and expertise will be recognized and respected.
3   Students will be educated about the reasons that led to establishing the partnership and why the effort is important from a community point of view.
4   Benefits will be bi-directional and balanced – for the community and for the university (Fear and McKnight Casey 2019).

For our educational partner institutions worldwide, it is becoming easier to predict the kinds of engagement that will be valued, since campus internationalization is now a global trend (Egron-Polak and Marmolejo 2017). Considering how few of the world's university students have the opportunity to learn abroad, receiving visiting students provides a more inclusive opportunity for intercultural engagement. In our experience, more than learning from visiting students, it is the act of teaching visitors that is valued by local students and other community members, especially if they are able to share their experience with outsiders in ways that generate pride and respect.

Working with community-based partners can help to support social enterprises that channel resources back into communities. Such initiatives may be popular with local governments because they support inclusive growth, whereas mainstream tourism operators and accommodation providers tend to do the opposite. The Association of South East Asian Nations, for example, has developed standards for community-based tourism that serve as a resource for organizations as well as a starting point for educational and training providers (ASEAN Secretariat. 2016; Novelli, Klatte and Dolezal 2017).

Deep long-term partnerships may be possible in some cases, but for universities operating large-scale education abroad programs, most partnerships will be much less intensive with most responsibility delegated to the local partner. While this practice entails risks, it is also the hallmark of a mature relationship in which the partner is trusted and local approaches are valued.

## 4. Implications for practice

How should one translate these insights into practical measures for designing and leading mobility programs? The good news is that while community impacts may have been overlooked in the past, once the issue is raised, international education professionals are generally keen to take steps to ensure a positive impact (Wood et al. 2011). Ogden, Streitwieser, and Crawford (2014) identify three principles for good practice in education abroad – positionality, reciprocity and intentionality – that provide a clear conceptual framework for thinking about the types of practices that are likely to benefit host communities.

### 4.1 Positionality

Education abroad practitioners should help students, educators and community members to appreciate their own position in relation to broader social, cultural and economic structures that shape their experience. Positive engagement with host communities requires all involved to reflect on the differences (and similarities) between the social worlds they inhabit, and to be open to learning about the experience of others.

Students may feel the power relations involved in education abroad relationships more than we might realize but are often not able to analyze and reflect on these clearly without guidance by program leaders. Zemach-Bersin (2008), for example, recalled being surprised and confused about the engagement between her American education abroad group and local partners. Through reflection, she became critical of the sanitized version of intercultural engagement focused on superficial aspects of language and culture that left her struggling to understand these relationships: Why had we not analyzed race, identity, and privilege when those factors were informing every one of our interactions? ... Was there nothing to be said about the power dynamics of claiming global citizenship? (p. A34)

Explicitly considering the positioning of the host community and partner institutions and the positioning of the mobile students may improve the quality of engagement. Ogden and Harman (2019) provide an excellent learning plan for a pre-departure activity for students to enhance community-engaged learning in this way, and partner organizations are often keen to be involved.

### 4.2 Reciprocity

A consistent research finding is that a commitment to reciprocal and mutually beneficial outcomes is a prerequisite for rewarding and ongoing engagement with host communities and partner organizations. This includes a commitment to learning with and from each other, as well as ensuring that there is an open consideration of the material and practical benefits for those involved. The interests of host communities and local partners need to be explicitly considered in the design, planning, operation and evaluation of learning abroad programs, preferably through their direct participation, but where not logistically possible then through meaningful consultation.

Hartman (2016, 226–229) provides a detailed Fair Trade Learning Rubric, which provides a set of indicators to assess the strength of an education abroad partnership, including such measures as common purpose, host community program leadership and participation, and theories of change. Hartman's ideal is to maintain long-term, deeply engaged partnerships, a common aspiration in much of the international service learning literature. While many partnerships may be less intensive than the deep engagement Hartman advocates, this rubric nevertheless provides a useful framework for thinking through various possibilities.

### 4.3 Intentionality

In recent decades there has been increasing pressure for all educators to make their intentions explicit, through learning objectives. This is increasingly common also in learning abroad, and it is important to include intentions in working with host communities and local partners in such statements. By making a commitment to reciprocity an explicit feature of programs' rationale and promotions, we signal to our students, our partners and host communities that our international collaborations are driven by the desire to achieve beneficial outcomes for all involved.

One final point to make is that mobile students also benefit from our efforts to ensure that host community needs are central in education abroad, so there need not be a tension between our concern with social justice and our concern with educational outcomes. Students learn from observing how we engage with others and enact the values of mutual respect, openness to collaboration, and reciprocity in international engagements. As Tan et al. (2015) point out, developing intercultural capability and a sense of global citizenship in graduates is now a key aspiration of most universities. This chapter argues that there is no better way to enact these in our practice than through considered, explicit and reflective engagement with host communities.

## 5. Directions for future research

Many studies of education abroad programs that describe benefits to local communities must be treated cautiously since they are often self-reports by organizers of the activity, while the voices and experiences of local communities are significantly under-represented (see Dixon 2015). There is a need for research which treats the host community as the unit of analysis rather than the individual mobility program. For example, little is known about local community impacts in locations where high-volume exchange and education abroad programs have contributed to the "studentification" of neighborhoods, or about the impacts of growing student visitor numbers on capacity building in developing countries. In relation to partners, there is a need for further research into the ways in which community organizations, NGOs, social enterprises and education providers engage strategically with foreign universities over time and what benefits they may generate for their own organizations and the communities in which they operate.

Most of the host community impact research undertaken to date has examined global service learning (e.g. Larsen 2016; MacDonald and Vorstermans 2016), which constitutes a small proportion of contemporary activity. There is a need for more detailed case studies of host community engagement with study tours, professional internships and summer schools, all of which are rapidly increasing in scale.

## Acknowledgements

The authors would like to thank José Celso Freire Junior and the external reviewers for their valuable input during the drafting of this chapter, and the team at ActionAid Myanmar – Shihab Uddin Ahamad, Saw Lin Htet, Ko Aung Min Naing and David Awng – whose wise guidance in partnership with RMIT has profoundly shaped the ideas presented here.

## Further reading

Illich, Ivan. 1968. *"To Hell with Good Intentions."* In Conference on InterAmerican Student Projects, Cuernavaca, Mexico. www.uvm.edu/~jashman/CDAE195_ESCI375/To Hell with Good Intentions.pdf

Larsen, Marianne A., Ed. 2016. *International Service Learning: Engaging Host Communities.* London: Routledge.

Ogden, Anthony C., and Eric Hartman. 2019. "To Hell and Back with Good Intentions: Global Service-Learning in the Shadow of Ivan Illich." In *Conflict Zone, Comfort Zone: Ethics, Pedagogy, and Effecting Change in Field-Based Courses*, eds. Agnieszka Paczyńska and Susan F. Hirsch. Athens: Ohio University Press.

Ogden, Anthony C., Bernhard Streitwieser, and Emily R. Crawford. 2014. "Empty Meeting Grounds: Situating Intercultural Learning in US Education Abroad." In *Internationalisation of Higher Education and Global Mobility*, ed. Bernhard Streitwieser. Oxford: Symposium Books, 229–258.

## References

Alonso Garcia, Nuria, and Nicholas V. Longo. 2017. "Doing More with Less: Civic Practices for Longer-Term Impact in Global Service-Learning." *Frontiers: The Interdisciplinary Journal of Study Abroad* 29 (2): 35–50.

ASEAN Secretariat. 2016. "ASEAN Community Based Tourism Standard." Jakarta. www.asean.org/storage/2012/05/ASEAN-Community-Based-Tourism-Standard.pdf (December 5, 2018).

Berquist, Brett, and Joy Milano. 2019. "Intersections between Service Learning and Study Abroad: A Framework for Community Engagement Abroad." In *Community Engagement Abroad: Perspectives and Practices on Service, Engagement, and Learning Overseas at Michigan State University*, eds. P. Crawford and Brett Berquist. Michigan State University Press.

Bishop, Julie, and Simon Birmingham. 2018. "New Campaign to Tackle Orphanage Tourism." Australian Government Department of Education and Training Media Release. https://ministers.education.gov.au/new-campaign-tackle-orphanage-tourism (December 6, 2018).

Bosch, Rosa M. 2017. "El Barri Gòtic Acull Fins a Set Turistes per Cada Deu Residents." La Vanguardia. www.lavanguardia.com/encatala/20170806/43375177879/barri-gotic-turistes.html

Calvo, Daniel Malet. 2017. "Los Estudiantes Erasmus y La Transformación de La Ciudad." El País. https://elpais.com/elpais/2017/05/24/seres_urbanos/1495657618_127416.html

Cole, Teju. 2012. "The White-Savior Industrial Complex." The Atlantic. www.theatlantic.com/international/archive/2012/03/the-white-savior-industrial-complex/254843/

Coles, David. 2016. "Universities Have a Duty to Stop Promoting Orphanage Volunteering LSE Careers Blog." London School of Economics Careers. http://blogs.lse.ac.uk/careers/2016/05/19/universities-have-a-duty-to-stop-promoting-orphan-volunteering/ (December 3, 2018).

Collins, Francis Leo. 2010. "International Students as Urban Agents: International Education and Urban Transformation in Auckland, New Zealand." Geoforum 46 (1): 940–950.

Dear, Samantha, and Ryan Howard. 2016. "Many Meanings: Moving Reciprocity towards Interdependence." In International Service Learning: Engaging Host Communities, ed. Marianne A.Larsen. New York and London: Routledge, 162–174.

Deloitte Access Economics. 2015. "The Value of International Education to Australia." Canberra. https://internationaleducation.gov.au/research/research-papers/Documents/ValueInternationalEd.pdf (February 15, 2019).

Dixon, Brett. 2015. "International Service Learning: Analytical Review of Published Research Literature." Frontier: The Interdisciplinary Journal of Study Abroad 23 (c): 107–131. https://frontiersjournal.org/wp-content/uploads/2015/09/DIXON-FrontiersXXV-InternationalServiceLearningAnalyticalReviewofPublishedResearchLiterature.pdf

Egron-Polak, Eva, and Francisco Marmolejo. 2017. "Higher Education Internationalisation: Adjusting to New Landscapes." In The Globalization of Internationalization: Emerging Voices and Perspectives, eds. Hans de Wit, Jocelyne Gacel-Avila, Elspeth Jones, and Nico Jooste. London and New York: Routledge, 7–17.

Fear, Frank A., and Karen McKnight Casey. 2019. "The Story of Place: What We Learned about Engaged Study Abroad Work at Michigan State University." In Community Engagement Abroad: Perspectives and Practices on Service, Engagement, and Learning Overseas at Michigan State University, eds. P. Crawford and Brett Berquist. East Lansing, MI: Michigan State University Press.

Forum on Education Abroad. 2011. Code of Ethics for Education Abroad. 2nd Edition. Carlisle, PA. www.aomonline.org/aom.asp?ID=&page_ID=240

Hartman, Eric. 2016. "Fair Trade Learning: A Framework for Ethical Global Partnerships." In International Service Learning: Engaging Host Communities, ed. Marianne ALarsen. London and New York: Routledge, 215–234.

Hubbard, Phil. 2009. "Geographies of Studentification and Purpose-Built Student Accommodation: Leading Separate Lives?"Environment and Planning A 41 (8): 1903–1923.

Hughey, Matthew W. 2010. "The White Savior Film and Reviewers' Reception." Symbolic Interaction 33 (3): 475–496. http://doi.wiley.com/10.1525/si.2010.33.3.475

Illich, Ivan. 1968. "To Hell with Good Intentions." In Conference on InterAmerican Student Projects, Cuernavaca, Mexico. www.uvm.edu/~jashman/CDAE195_ESCI375/To Hell with Good Intentions.pdf

Kanani, Simeon S. 2000. "Study Abroad in Kenya: Now and in the Future." *African Issues* 28 (1/2): 84–88. http://links.jstor.org/sici?sici=1548-4505(2000)28:1/2%3C84: SAIKNA%3E2.0.CO;2-4

Keith, Novella Zett. 2005. "Community Service Learning in the Face of Globalization: Rethinking Theory and Practice." *Michigan Journal of Community Service Learning* 11 (2): 5–24. www.eric.ed.gov/ERICWebPortal/detail?accno=EJ848468%5Cnwww.eric. ed.gov/PDFS/EJ848468.pdf

Kushner, Jacob. 2016. "The Voluntourist's Dilemma." *The New York Times.* www.nytimes. com/2016/03/22/magazine/the-voluntourists-dilemma.html

Larsen, Marianne A. 2016. "International Service Learning in a Tanzanian Host Community." In *International Service Learning: Engaging Host Communities*, ed. Marianne A. Larsen. London: Routledge, 94–107.

MacDonald, Katie, and Jessica Vorstermans. 2016. "Struggles for Mutuality: Conceptualizing Hosts as Participants in International Service Learning in Ghana." In *International Service Learning: Engaging Host Communities*, ed. Marianne A.Larsen. London: Routledge, 131–144.

Manathunga, Catherine. 2017. "Excavating Cultural Imperialism in Student Mobility Programmes." *Discourse* 39 (4): 564–574.

McGloin, Colleen, and Nichole Georgeou. 2016. "'Looks Good on Your CV': The Sociology of Voluntourism Recruitment in Higher Education." *Journal of Sociology* 52 (2): 403–417.

NAFSA. 2019. "NAFSA International Student Economic Value Tool." NAFSA: Association of International Educators. www.nafsa.org/Policy_and_Advocacy/Policy_Resour ces/Policy_Trends_and_Data/NAFSA_International_Student_Economic_Value_Tool/ (June 11)

Novelli, Marina, Nia Klatte, and Claudia Dolezal. 2017. "The ASEAN Community-Based Tourism Standards: Looking beyond Certification." *Tourism Planning and Development* 14 (2): 260–281. www.tandfonline.com/action/journalInformation?journalCode=rthp 21 (December 5, 2018)

Ogden, Anthony C. 2007. "The View from the Veranda: Understanding Today's Colonial Student." *Frontiers: The Interdisciplinary Journal of Study Abroad* 15 (Fall/Fall/ Winter): 35–55.

Ogden, Anthony C, and Eric Hartman. 2019. "To Hell and Back with Good Intentions: Global Service-Learning in the Shadow of Ivan Illich." In *Conflict Zone, Comfort Zone: Ethics, Pedagogy, and Effecting Change in Field-Based Courses*, eds. Agnieszka Paczyńska and Susan F. Hirsch. Athens: Ohio University Press. www.ohioswallow.com/book/ Conflict+Zone%2C+Comfort+Zone

Ogden, Anthony C, Bernhard Streitwieser, and Emily R.Crawford. 2014. "Empty Meeting Grounds: Situating Intercultural Learning in US Education Abroad." In *Internationalisation of Higher Education and Global Mobility*, ed. Bernhard Streitwieser. Oxford: Symposium Books, 229–258.

Schroeder, Kathleen, Cynthia Wood, Shari Galiardi, and Jenny Koehn. 2009. "First, Do No Harm: Ideas for Mitigating Negative Community Impacts of Short-Term Study Abroad." *Journal of Geography* 108 (3): 141–147.

Tan, B-K, Helen Flavell, Sonia Ferns, and Joanne Jordan. 2015. *Australian Outbound Student Mobility: Quality Dimensions for International Fieldwork in Health Sciences.* Perth, Australia.

Toms Smedley, Cynthia. 2016. "The Economic Circle: Impacts of Volunteerism and Service Learning on Three Rural Communities in Costa Rica." In *International Service Learning: Engaging Host Communities*, ed. Marianne A.Larsen. London and New York: Routledge, 65–79.

Townsville Enterprise. 2018. "Edutourism: Townsville North Queensland." www.town svilleenterprise.com.au/tourism/edutourism/ (December 7, 2018).

Universities UK. 2017. "Universities UK The Economic Impact of International Students." www.universitiesuk.ac.uk/policy-and-analysis/reports/Documents/2017/brief ing-economic-impact-international-students.pdf

Wood, Cynthia*et al.*2011. "Community Impacts of International Service-Learning and Study Abroad: An Analysis of Focus Groups with Program Leaders." *Partnerships: A Journal of Service-Learning & Civic Engagement* 2 (1): 1–23. http://geo.appstate.edu/ sites/default/files/communityimpacts.pdf

Woolf, Michael. 2006. "Come and See the Poor People: The Pursuit of Exotica." *Frontiers: The Interdisciplinary Journal of Study Abroad* 13 (Fall): 135–146. http://frontiersjourna l.org/wp-content/uploads/2015/09/WOOLF-FrontiersXIII-ComeandSeethe PoorPeople.pdf

Zemach-Bersin, Talya. 2008. "American Students Abroad Can't Be 'Global Citizens'." *The Chronicle of Higher Education* 54 (26): A34. https://search-proquest-com.ezproxy.lib. rmit.edu.au/docview/214652955?accountid=13552&rfr_id=info%3Axri%2Fsid%3Aprim o (December 3, 2018).

Ziguras, Christopher. 2018. "International Academic Mobility in Australia and New Zealand." In *Encyclopedia of International Higher Education Systems and Institutions*, eds. Pedro Teixeira and Jung Cheol Shin. Dordrecht: Springer Netherlands, 1–3. https:// doi.org/10.1007/978-94-017-9553-1_239-1

# Conclusion

## Future directions and scholarship

*Christof Van Mol, Anthony C. Ogden and Bernhard Streitwieser*

Over the past decade, the study of education abroad has significantly expanded, attracting scholars from a wide range of disciplines (see e.g. Pisarevskaya et al. 2019). Consequently, a wide array of aspects related to education abroad are covered by scientists, including the decision-making process to participate in education abroad, students' experiences while being abroad, and the outcomes of their participation (Van Mol 2019). The chapters in this book have provided a synthesis of this burgeoning field of research, as well as some of the main implications that existing scholarship has for practice. However, they also provide directions for how the field of education abroad might develop in scholarly terms. In this concluding chapter, seven directions for future research are discerned from the individual chapters, with a particular emphasis on the methodological side, as the different chapter authors have already indicated relevant research questions for future research related to their respective topics. We acknowledge that these methodological issues are particularly relevant for researchers in the field of education abroad. Yet we believe it is also important practitioners know about these methodological issues, in order to be able to assess the quality of empirical studies that are published on education abroad.

First, it is clear that social stratification in education abroad is one of the most significant challenges for policymakers and practitioners, but also for scholars (see e.g. Chapters 1, 2, 5 and 13). However, existing research on education abroad does not always pay sufficient attention to how selectivity processes might have an impact on education abroad decisions, experiences, and outcomes. Nevertheless, it is clear that education abroad is a selective process, not only in terms of socio-economic background of students (see e.g. Chapters 1 and 2, this volume; Lörz et al. 2016; Netz 2015; Netz and Finger 2016; Salisbury et al. 2009) but also in terms of students' predispositions towards certain outcomes (see e.g. Chapters 7, 8 and 9, this volume; Kratz and Netz 2018; Kuhn 2012; Van Mol 2018). Taking this selectivity into account when conducting studies on the dynamics of education abroad is therefore of paramount importance in future studies on education abroad.

Second, globally there is an overly positive policy rhetoric about education abroad (Van Mol 2015), which is often uncritically adopted in scientific studies as well. Nevertheless, several chapters (e.g. Chapters 11 and 13) indicate that instead of focusing on quantity and always championing only the positive aspects of international education, it is also necessary to pay more attention to the quality of education abroad experiences and possible negative experiences and/or consequences. This means that scholars and practitioners of education abroad should try to adopt a more objective stance towards their subjects (see Chapter 4), which admittedly can often be very difficult as many researchers and practitioners have strong personal opinions about education abroad.

Third, going beyond the general inquiry of interest of international students' experiences, more research is needed on in-depth analyses around why certain patterns, experiences or outcomes exist. This means that, for example, instead of focusing on *whether* disadvantaged groups are less likely to participate in mobility, the focus should be shifted towards *why* this is the case. As such, future research should focus more on the mechanisms that explain education abroad decisions, experiences and outcomes, rather than staying on a descriptive level of analysis. Such analyses, however, require education abroad scholars to engage more in-depth with existing theories when building their scientific inquiry. These theories can originate from a very diverse set of scientific fields but can help to specify the mechanism at play. Furthermore, comparative approaches might also be beneficial in this regard (see e.g. Chapters 3, 4 and 12).

Fourth, much of the education abroad research is based on cross-sectional research designs, whereby students are interviewed or surveyed at one particular point in time. Nevertheless, if we aim to advance our understanding of the mechanisms explaining education abroad decisions, experiences, and outcomes, then there is also a real need to develop and rely more on longitudinal analyses, whereby actors are followed over a longer period of time (see e.g. Chapters 5, 9 and 13). Such analyses permit controlling for time and cohort effects, which might introduce significant bias in reported research results. For quantitative scholars, repeated cross-sectional data in the form of national student or alumni surveys could be used to this end. That kind of data is available in several European countries, such as Denmark, Finland, the Netherlands, Norway, Sweden and Switzerland. Additionally, in some countries, national register data would also permit investigating education abroad dynamics longitudinally, as they sometimes allow matching student or alumni surveys with registration data (for an example see Lombard 2019).

Fifth, education abroad research and scholarship often relies on subjective measurements, in which students are asked to indicate what they believe the impact of an education abroad experience is on certain outcomes. Nevertheless, subjective experiences can stand in sharp contrast with the results of objective measurements (see e.g. Chapter 9, this volume; Waibel et al. 2017). From a scientific viewpoint, it is clear that studies on education abroad should rely more on such objective measurements to advance the field, as they provide us with the most reliable information on what works, and why it works. Furthermore, as several chapters in this book illustrate, besides relying on self-reports, many quantitative and qualitative studies do not include control/comparison groups in their research designs, which are essential if we aim to uncover the specific dynamics, mechanisms and processes of education abroad. Relying solely on the reports of those who participate in education abroad only provides a limited picture. This is particularly important if scholars aim to detect or analyze causal relationships between education abroad and certain experiences and/or outcomes.

Sixth, several chapters (e.g. Chapters 3, 4, 9, 10, 12, 13 and 14) illustrate the need for more comparative research designs, whereby scholars more systematically focus on or compare, for example, different policy-levels (international, national, regional, institutional), types of organizations (e.g. public/private, research intensive/applied sciences), home and host country/institution context, education abroad programs, program components, and characteristics of students. Furthermore, future research should also consider a broader array of actors and environments that are involved in education abroad processes, such as employers, NGOs, education providers, the built environment, etc. Future research could therefore extend the scope of research towards other actors as well as in environments that enable or restrain education abroad dynamics. Extending the scope of education abroad research towards other disciplines such as Business Studies, the Cognitive Sciences, Economics, Geography, Migration Studies and Sociology, where there is a genuine interest in research on education abroad but where the scientific literature is developing separately from the international education literature, can be beneficial and inspiring in this regard. Taking the relationship between the built environment and students' experiences abroad as an example, scholars could for example build further upon the geographical work of Fincher and Shaw (2009, 2011) on degree mobile international students in the Australian context to explore how the spatial context in which students are situated enables or restrains contact possibilities with the local student population.

Seventh, scholars working in the field of education abroad who are mainly focused on Asian, Australian, European and North American contexts often used single case-studies within these contexts. Although the aim of this book has been to provide a truly global overview of what we know, most authors, for example, reported significant difficulties in finding and covering solid scientific studies in other contexts, such as Africa or South America. Future research could therefore also try to geographically diversify the focus to include these regions as well. After all, the efforts made by all authors in this book to incorporate insights from different world regions show that focusing on a wider variety of regions helps to better understand the general processes at play beyond geographical location.

In conclusion, the field of education abroad is developing at a fast pace in many different directions and in different fields. This is an evolution that we welcome, as it is a fascinating field, and many topics connected to education abroad are yet to be understood in-depth scientifically. In this concluding chapter, we indicated that the field could be significantly advanced by more theory-informed empirical studies that draw upon theoretical insights from different disciplines, comparative research designs, geographical diversification, attention to selectivity processes and the content of education abroad experiences, as well as the use of objective measurements and control/comparison groups. This way, we can truly get a better scientific insight into the dynamics, mechanisms and processes that underline education abroad.

## References

Fincher, R., and Shaw, K. (2009). "The unintended segregation of transnational students in central Melbourne." *Environment and Planning A*, 41 (8), 1884–1902.

Fincher, R., and Shaw, K. (2011). "Enacting separate social worlds: 'International' and 'local' students in public space in central Melbourne." *Geoforum*, 42 (5), 539–549.

Kratz, F., and Netz, N. (2018). "Which mechanisms explain monetary returns to international student mobility?" *Studies in Higher Education*, 43 (2), 375–400.

Kuhn, T. (2012). "Why educational exchange programmes miss their mark: Cross-border mobility, education and European identity." *Journal of Common Market Studies*, 50 (6), 994–1010.

Lombard, A. (2019). *International Students in Switzerland: Trajectories, Stay Rates, and Intentions for Post-Graduate Mobility.* Neuchâtel: University of Neuchâtel.

Lörz, M., Netz, N., and Quast, H. (2016). "Why do students from underprivileged families less often intend to study abroad?" *Higher Education*, 72 (2), 153–174.

Netz, N. (2015). "What deters students from studying abroad? Evidence from four European countries and its implications for higher education policy." *Higher Education Policy*, 28 (2), 151–174.

Netz, N., and Finger, C. (2016). "New horizontal inequalities in German higher education? Social selectivity of studying abroad between 1991 and 2012." *Sociology of Education*, 89 (2), 79–98.

Pisarevskaya, A., Levy, N., Scholten, P., and Jansen, J. (2019). "Mapping migration studies: An empirical analysis of the coming of age of a research field." *Migration Studies*. doi:10.1093/migration/mnz031

Salisbury, M. H., Umbach, P. D., Paulsen, M. B., and Pascarella, E. T. (2009). "Going global: Understanding the choice process of the intent to study abroad." *Research in Higher Education*, 50 (2), 119–143.

Van Mol, C. (2015). "Intra-Europese studentenmobiliteit: algemeen overzicht en tendensen," in C. Timmerman, R. Mahieu, F. Levrau, and D. Vanheule (eds.), *Intra-Europese migratie en mobiliteit. Andere tijden, nieuwe wegen?*Leuven: Leuven University Press, pp. 71–85.

Van Mol, C. (2018). "Becoming Europeans: the relationship between student exchanges in higher education, European citizenship and a sense of European identity." *Innovation: The European Journal of Social Science Research*, 31 (4), 449–463.

Van Mol, C. (2019). "Integrating international students in local (student) communities: A theory-to-practice perspective." *Journal of Comparative & International Higher Education*, 11 (4).

Waibel, S., Rüger, H., Ette, A., and Sauer, L. (2017). "Career consequences of transnational educational mobility: A systematic literature review." *Educational Research Review*, 20, 81–98.

# Index

Note: page references in bold indicate tables; 'n' indicates chapter notes.

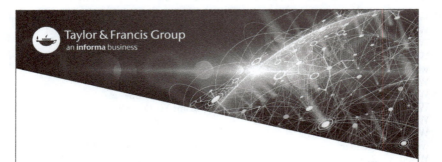